The Presbyterian Creed

A Confessional Tradition in America, 1729-1870

STUDIES IN CHRISTIAN HISTORY AND THOUGHT

A full listing of all titles in this series
appears at the close of this book

STUDIES IN CHRISTIAN HISTORY AND THOUGHT

The Presbyterian Creed

A Confessional Tradition in America, 1729-1870

S. Donald Fortson III

Foreword by David B. Calhoun

WIPF & STOCK · Eugene, Oregon

Wipf and Stock Publishers
199 W 8th Ave, Suite 3
Eugene, OR 97401

The Presbyterian Creed
A Confessional Tradition in America, 1729–1870
By Fortson, S. Donald, III
Copyright©2008 Paternoster
ISBN 13: 978-1-60608-480-9
Publication date 2/6/2009
Previously published by Paternoster, 2008

STUDIES IN CHRISTIAN HISTORY AND THOUGHT

Series Preface

This series complements the specialist series of *Studies in Evangelical History and Thought* and *Studies in Baptist History and Thought* for which Paternoster is becoming increasingly well known by offering works that cover the wider field of Christian history and thought. It encompasses accounts of Christian witness at various periods, studies of individual Christians and movements, and works which concern the relations of church and society through history, and the history of Christian thought.

The series includes monographs, revised dissertations and theses, and collections of papers by individuals and groups. As well as 'free standing' volumes, works on particular running themes are being commissioned; authors will be engaged for these from around the world and from a variety of Christian traditions.

A high academic standard combined with lively writing will commend the volumes in this series both to scholars and to a wider readership.

Series Editors

Alan P.F. Sell, Visiting Professor at Acadia University Divinity College, Nova Scotia, Canada

David Bebbington, Professor of History, University of Stirling, Stirling, Scotland, UK

Clyde Binfield, Professor Associate in History, University of Sheffield, UK

Gerald Bray, Anglican Professor of Divinity, Beeson Divinity School, Samford University, Birmingham, Alabama, USA

Grayson Carter, Associate Professor of Church History, Fuller Theological Seminary SW, Phoenix, Arizona, USA

To
S. Donald Fortson Jr.

Contents

Foreword

Donald Fortson's *The Presbyterian Creed* breaks new ground – not in source material and information exactly but certainly in interpretation and application. Fortson shows that the reunion movements of 1864 and 1869 were on the whole very positive achievements for American Presbyterianism. He claims that there has been a remarkable consensus on confessional subscription throughout American Presbyterian history. This disputes the often-held view that subscription to the Westminster Standards was a major deterrent to Presbyterian unity and a source of conflict and division from the Old Side/New Side division of 1741. A major rupture of the next century – the Old School/New School schism of 1837 – is usually seen as a repeat of the earlier division, with some special issues added. Modern Old School sympathizers generally fault the New School for its theological deviations and confessional compromises. Fortson gives a fresh and sympathetic portrayal of the New School. He argues that far from undermining confessional integrity New School leaders represented the true intent of the Adopting Act of 1729 and were loyal to the essential spirit of Presbyterianism in America. He acknowledges New School "faults" in tactics during the ten year struggle that led to the division, a charge that could, of course, be made equally about Old School "tactics." Fortson writes: "As the 1830s unfolded, trust eroded, charity dissipated, and the exercise of raw ecclesiastical power for party advantage created a chasm that was impassable."

In his major discussion – Old School/New School reunion – Fortson includes a helpful review of ten years of New School writings in *The Presbyterian Quarterly Review* (1852-62), an excellent survey of Charles Hodge's views on subscription (with a plausible explanation for what appears to be his shift from a strict to a more moderate position), and an important chapter on reunion in the South. Here is an ample and captivating presentation of the views and role of Southern Presbyterian leader Robert Lewis Dabney. Dabney urged the Southern Presbyterian Church (Old School) to unite with the Southern New School, while opposing strenuously any thought of union with the Northern Presbyterian Church. Dabney's stand on strict confessional integrity is well-known. His openness to union with the Southern New School counters effectively the argument that the New School was weak on subscription. Fortson appreciates the "moderate spirit" of the Southern Old School majority that welcomed the New Schoolers, while seeing it as a "clear affirmation of a broader Calvinism." Fortson rejects the commonly held view that the New School united with the Southern Old School Church on the latter's terms. There was a meeting of minds on the nature of subscription, he argues – an agreement that in "common Calvinism was room for diversity of opinion."

Fortson's history of 150 years of American Presbyterian history revolves around the important subscription issue, a matter that has been central to Presbyterian self-understanding. This book demonstrates that the American Presbyterian church (or churches) have held somewhat differing views on confessional subscription, but it also shows that the enduring view (through the reunions of the 19th century) has been a moderate rejection of extremes, a long lasting commitment to the genius of the Adopting Act of 1729. All of this is relevant to the modern Presbyterian experience, as Fortson clearly shows.

This book will interest Presbyterians and those who love history, the church, and theology. It gives an intriguing glimpse of intellectual activity and ecclesiastical politics during the tumultuous 19th century. And it shows how history can help shape and guide our thinking today.

David B. Calhoun
Professor of Church History
Covenant Theological Seminary
St. Louis, Missouri

Preface

The Reformed Tradition has affirmed the importance of creedal statements as essential tools for both catechetical instruction and protecting the church from doctrinal error. Teaching the church's creed has always been a primary calling of the Presbyterian ministry and public adoption of that creed, a sacred trust. Samuel Miller, Professor of Ecclesiastical History at Princeton Seminary (1813-1850), expressed it this way: "... subscribing a Church Creed, is not a mere formality; but a very solemn transaction, which means much and infers the most serious obligations. It is certainly a transaction which ought to be entered upon with much deep deliberation and humble prayer."[1] Historically, this has been serious business for Presbyterians and demanded the utmost integrity by ministers and the church.

The American Presbyterian creed up until the second half of the twentieth century has been the confessional tradition of the Westminster Assembly (1643-1648) which produced the Westminster Confession of Faith and Catechisms. This expansive theological framework, rooted in the heritage of the ancient church, the Protestant Reformation and the Puritan movement in England, has provided a cogent system of theology for generations of Presbyterians worldwide. Nevertheless, by the early twentieth century, American Presbyterians began distancing themselves from parts of the Westminster theological tradition. Additional chapters were added to the Westminster Confession in order to soften the perceived harshness of the Augustinian/Calvinist language of the original document.[2] Notwithstanding these additions, a substantial commitment to Westminster Calvinism endured among most American Presbyterians into the middle of the twentieth century when wholesale abandonment would begin, including a new confessional statement by 1967, modifications of the traditional ordination vow and a new Presbyterian *Book of Confessions*.[3]

---

[1] Samuel Miller, *The Utility and Importance of Creeds and Confessions: Addressed Particularly to Candidates for the Ministry* (Philadelphia: Presbyterian Board of Publication, 1839), 98.

[2] In 1903 two new chapters were added to the Westminster Confession of Faith by the Presbyterian Church in the United States of America (PCUSA), "Of the Holy Spirit" and "Of the Gospel of the Love of God and Missions;" the Presbyterian Church in the United States (PCUS) added those same two chapters to the Westminster Confession in 1942. Conservative Princeton Professor Benjamin Breckinridge Warfield offered some critique of the new chapters but he essentially viewed them as sound Calvinistic theology that addressed more fully the "ordinary Arminian assault" on Reformed doctrines. Benjamin B. Warfield, "The Confession of Faith as Revised in 1903" in *Selected Shorter Writings of Benjamin B. Warfield* (Nutley, New Jersey: Presbyterian and Reformed Publishing Company, 1973), 370-410.

[3] The Confession of 1967 was adopted by the United Presbyterian Church in the United States of America (UPCUSA) General Assembly along with a revision of the confessional subscription vow in 1967. For a brief history of that creed and its implications for the

Many factors contributed to the creeping desertion of traditional Calvinist orthodoxy among twentieth-century American Presbyterians. It is generally acknowledged that the first half of the twentieth century witnessed the beginnings of a major shift of theological commitments among the large bodies of Presbyterians in the United States.[4] Coinciding with this doctrinal shift has been the emergence of several small conservative Presbyterian groups that continue to affirm the Westminster tradition as their symbol of faith.[5] These evangelical Presbyterian groups viewed the departure from historic American Calvinism with disdain while the mainline churches heralded the transition as an inescapably necessary freedom from outmoded theological formulations.

Mainline Presbyterians believed their evolving estrangement from Westminster's theological system was faithful to the Presbyterian tradition of *ecclesia reformata semper reformanda*. Conservatives, on the other hand, understood themselves to be the faithful progeny of early American Presbyterianism. A catalyst for much of the scholarly debate on the nature of colonial Presbyterianism revolved around the publication of Leonard Trinterud's *The Forming of an American Tradition* in 1949 which was hailed by mainline scholars but decried by some conservatives as revisionist. Trinterud's interpretive framework for understanding the colonial era centers on his assertion that eighteenth-century American Presbyterianism consisted of two widely divergent streams – the strict first generation Scotch-Irish party and the much broader English, Welsh and New England group. Party conflict erupted in the subscription controversy which resulted in the 1729 compromise formula for subscribing the Westminster Confession and Catechisms.

Late twentieth-century discussions over confessional subscription among conservative Presbyterians have had to interact with Trinterud's research.[6] As conservatives seek to justify their departure from the mainline Presbyterian Church, and thoughtfully consider how to avoid the same slide into heterodoxy, much attention has been refocused on the 1729 Adopting Act and the Old School/New School schism and reunion.[7] Conservative writers have tended to downplay the

---

Presbyterian reunion of 1983, see Aurelia T. Fule, "The Book of Confessions and the Confession of 1967," *American Presbyterians* 66 (Winter 1988): 326-332.

[4] See Lefferts A. Loetscher, *The Broadening Church: A Study of Theological Issues in The Presbyterian Church Since 1869* (Philadelphia: University of Pennsylvania Press, 1957).

[5] The Presbyterian Church of America (1936) later known as the Orthodox Presbyterian Church, The Presbyterian Church in America (1973) and the Evangelical Presbyterian Church (1981) are the three main groups of conservative churches that departed from the PCUSA, the PCUS and the UPCUSA in the twentieth century.

[6] See David W. Hall, ed., *The Practice of Confessional Subscription* (Lanham, Maryland: University Press of America, 1995). Several essays in this work argue against Trinterud's interpretation. Note particularly the essay: "Re-examining the Re-examiners of the Adopting Act," by David Hall, 263-291,

[7] See e.g., Morton H. Smith, *How is the Gold Become Dim: The Decline of the Presbyterian Church, U.S., as Reflected in its Assembly Actions* (Jackson Mississippi: The

differences in the colonial era, preferring to view the genesis of loose subscription in the early nineteenth-century Old School/New School controversy. Much of this interpretive perspective is based on the *Constitutional History of the Presbyterian Church in the United States of America* published by Old School theologian Charles Hodge in 1840. Hodge's purpose in writing had been to demonstrate that the Old School was the rightful heir of historic Presbyterianism.[8]

New School historians did not agree with Hodge's thesis, arguing instead that their branch of Presbyterianism equally shared the Presbyterian legacy.[9] Much of the nineteenth-century debate on subscription revisited the 1729 Adopting Act and re-examined the Old Side/New Side schism and reunion to uncover the roots of their own strife. The nineteenth-century Old School/New School parties intensely debated the meaning of confessional subscription and that discord became one of the primary issues behind the great schism of 1837/38. The two branches of Presbyterianism were separated for three decades but reunited in the 1860s.

Twentieth-century historians have underscored the perpetual gulf between Old School/New School perspectives, despite the reunions.[10] These interpretations tend to underestimate the genuine theological meeting of the minds that emerged from the reunion negotiations. The reunion movements did bring together disparate parts

---

Steering Committee for a Continuing Presbyterian Church, Faithful to the Scriptures and the Reformed Faith, 1973), 37-40.

[8] Charles Hodge, *The Constitutional History of the Presbyterian Church in the United States of America, Part I* (Philadelphia: Presbyterian Board of Publication, 1851), preface, iii-vi.

[9] See William Hill, *A History of the Rise, Progress, Genius, and Character of American Presbyterianism: Together with a Review of the "Constitutional History of the Presbyterian Church in the United States of America,* by Chas. Hodge, D.D. Professor in the Theological Seminary at Princeton, N.J."* (Washington City: J. Gideon Jr., 1839); E.H. Gillett, *History of the Presbyterian Church in the United States of America,* Vols. *I, II* (Philadelphia: Presbyterian Publication Committee, 1864); Edward D. Morris, *The Presbyterian Church New School, 1837-1869: An Historical Review* (Columbus Ohio: The Chaplain Press, 1905).

[10] Edwin H. Rian described the 1869 reunion of the Old School / New School in these negative terms: "That union should never have taken place, for it brought together two parties who disagreed fundamentally as to doctrine. It was one of the tragic events in Presbyterian history." Edwin H. Rian, *The Presbyterian Conflict* (Grand Rapids, Michigan: Wm. B. Eerdmans Publishing Co., 1940; reprint, Philadelphia: The Committee for the Historian of the Orthodox Presbyterian Church, 1992), 7. Lefferts Loetscher similarly highlighted the doctrinal divide: "Once again in 1869, as in 1758, the Presbyterian Church was restoring unity not by resolving its differences, but by ignoring and absorbing them ... The result was, of course, that the theological base of the Church (especially of the former Old School branch of the Church) was broadened and the meaning of its subscription formula further relaxed." *The Broadening Church,* 8. Rian and Loetscher both traced the Presbyterian fundamentalist/modernist debates of the early twentieth century back to the reunion of 1869. Of course, this connection is impossible to ignore, however, it is an unfair judgment to impugn the reunion generation of evasion when the historical data suggests serious and open discussion produced concurrence on a number of doctrinal issues.

of the Presbyterian family and undoubtedly there were acute differences between the two parties. Notwithstanding these facts, the reunion agreements of 1864 and 1869 were on the whole very positive achievements for American Presbyterianism. The Old School and New School had frank theological debates in the reunion conferences where serious disagreements were openly debated. One laudatory result of the candid reunion discussions was the attainment of remarkable consensus on confessional subscription.

The Old School/New School reunions of 1864 and 1869 brought significant closure to the issue of confessional subscription for American Presbyterians. During the reunion discussions of the 1860s (North and South), the two parties came to understand one another more fully and the overwhelming majority of all four denominations[11] agreed that the old compromise position of the Adopting Act was still the best solution to the problem of subscription to the Westminster Standards. In the crucible of theological conflict, ecclesiastical schism and civil war, Presbyterians came to terms with acceptable boundaries of doctrinal latitude in the Presbyterian household. After these rigorous nineteenth-century reunion negotiations, one observes a general consensus on the meaning of confessional subscription which had eluded American Presbyterians prior to this time. There remained a few discordant voices, but for the majority of the church it was a settled issue. This book is the story of how Presbyterians reached that consensus.

Several presuppositions will inform this study of the Old School/New School period of American Presbyterianism. First, it is the author's conviction that the data supports the New School interpretation of the eighteenth-century context which rightfully found progenitors of their viewpoints in the earlier period. Trinterud's research supports this position. Some conservative writers have not dealt candidly with the sources that Trinterud has highlighted in his investigation. Part of the conservative resistance to Trinterud's conclusions is the obvious dependence of his work on the prior research of Charles Augustus Briggs who was known for his dislike of the Westminster Standards and advocacy of a new shorter creed for Presbyterians. The present writer believes Trinterud and Briggs before him fairly rehearse the historical data which is generally consistent with the analyses offered by the New School historians of previous generations.

A second presupposition of this study is that any examination of the subscription issue cannot be removed from the actual practice of confessional subscription in the church. It is reckless historiography to lift an issue out of its historical context and divorce it from the rest of the church's life during a particular period. As we look at the Old School/New School period, we will take an integrative approach that asks

---

[11] By 1861 there were four distinct Presbyterian bodies - The Presbyterian Church in the United States of America (1838-69, Old School), The Presbyterian Church in the United States of America (1838-69, New School), The United Synod of the South (1858-64, New School), and The Presbyterian Church in the Confederate States of America (1861-64, Old School).

how the subscription question fits into the entire fabric of the church's faith and practice during this era.[12]

A third presupposition is that careful examination of the nineteenth-century reunion discussions will help clarify the common ground of the reunion terms that were endorsed by both Old School and New School. The language of the public declarations was carefully chosen and the full meaning of those words is understood in the fine print of the negotiations behind the scenes. Too often, hasty conclusions are drawn from the public declarations alone without sufficient attention to the array of debate behind the final language that is selected. Examining the details of the negotiations gives one a much clearer picture of both the consensus and compromise inherent in discussions which navigate differences between groups.

Several factors motivated the author to write this book. First, is the widespread ignorance of this period among Christian laymen, seminary students and pastors. It is a forgotten era but has much light to shed on contemporary discussions of what is means to be Presbyterian and an Evangelical. Secondly, there is still significant misunderstanding about the nature of New School Presbyterianism and simplistic distortion of New School views on confessional subscription. The third motivating factor is a response to the truncated telling of the Presbyterian story which suggests that the Southern Old School Church was the last bastion of orthodoxy in the late nineteenth century. This book will humbly attempt to display the whole scope of Presbyterian perspectives on confessional subscription during the time frame of our study. It is my hope that the telling of this American Presbyterian story (1729 – 1870) will encourage the Church to pursue biblical faithfulness in the present generation.

---

[12] The study of "practice" has emerged in recent years as an analytical and interpretive method in religious history. For examples: *Practicing Theology: Beliefs and Practices in Christian Life*, Miroslav Volf and Dorothy C. Bass eds. (Grand Rapids: William B. Eerdmans, 2002) and *Practicing Protestants: Histories of Christian Life in America 1630-1965*, eds. Laurie F. Maffy-Kipp, Leigh E. Schmidt and Mark Valeri (Baltimore: John Hopkins Press, 2006).

CHAPTER 1

The Colonial Confession

Presbyterian immigrants from England, Scotland and Ireland began arriving on American shores by the late 1600s and affiliated with Dutch Reformed churches and Congregationalists in places where there were no Presbyterian clergy. As ministers became available, the earliest colonial Presbyterian churches were established in the Middle Colonies. By 1706, a small group of Presbyterian ministers meeting in Philadelphia organized themselves into the first presbytery in America. Under the leadership of Francis Makemie and others, the fledgling group of churches began to grow and by 1717 they had established three presbyteries that were associated as the "Synod."

Early American Presbyterian clergymen had been nurtured in the Calvinism of the Westminster Confession in Britain or New England and cherished a strong attachment to Reformed doctrine. Though personally committed to Calvinistic principles, some of the colonial Presbyterians were not so sure about the wisdom of Synod requiring ministerial subscription to man-made statements of faith. The Protestant principle of Scripture alone had seemed a sufficient guide for the infant American church. There were other Presbyterians, however, who believed that a key ingredient for strengthening the young ecclesiastical body would be official adoption of the Confession of Faith.

Presbyterians in America were keenly aware of the subscription controversies in the Old World and the inherent problems that had accompanied adopting the Westminster Confession and Catechisms. From the sheer scope of the documents, how could it be expected that a large body of ministers would concur in the vast detail of these confessional statements? And having experienced the oppressive imposition of creeds and formularies by Roman Catholic and Anglican bishops, did colonial Presbyterians really want to go down this path? Each of the mother Presbyterian bodies had grappled with these vexing problems and the array of controversies in the Old World were fresh in the American consciousness in the 1720s as they considered the issue of confessional subscription.

Subscription in the Old World

In 1690 the Scotch Parliament had ratified the Westminster Confession "as the public and avowed Confession of this Church, containing the sum and substance of the doctrine of the Reformed Churches." This Confession was to be subscribed by all probationers licensed to preach, all intrants into the ministry, and all ministers and elders. In 1693, the Parliament required subscription of all ministers, with this formula: "I do sincerely own and declare the above Confession of Faith, approven by former General Assemblies of this Church, and ratified by law in the year 1690, to be the Confession of my faith, and that I own the doctrine therein contained to be the true doctrine, which I will constantly adhere to."[1] By 1696, the Church of Scotland further declared that no minister may write or publically speak anything contrary to or inconsistent with the Confession.[2] The Scottish Kirk consistently

---

[1] Charles Augustus Briggs, *American Presbyterian* (New York: Charles Scribner's Sons, 1885), 200, 201. Briggs said: "... many Presbyteries accepted a modified subscription which originated between 1690 and 1694: 'I subscribe and will adhere to the Confession of Faith therein contained as founded on, and consonant to, the Holy Scriptures.' " He argued that this form of subscription was interpreting the 1690 Act of Parliament which referred to the "sum and substance of the doctrine of the Reformed Churches." Charles A. Briggs was an Old Testament professor at Union Seminary in New York (1876-1904) and champion of the higher-critical method which concerned conservative Presbyterians. Briggs clashed with the Princeton faculty over his views of Scripture and the Westminster Confession. He disliked the Presbyterian doctrinal standards and favored a new shorter creed that could open the door to broader church union. Suspended from the Presbyterian ministry in 1893, he eventually became Episcopalian. American Presbyterianism raised suspicion among conservatives, skeptical of Briggs's political agenda, nevertheless, it is a very useful study that fairly treats the primary sources.

[2] Leonard J. Trinterud, *The Forming of an American Tradition* (Philadelphia: The Westminster Press, 1949), 39. Trinterud's research is one of the most significant studies of American Presbyterianism in the last half century. Book reviews have praised Trinterud's research as groundbreaking for its insights into colonial Presbyterianism. Church historian Sidney Mead declared: "Hereafter, anyone who intends to say anything about colonial Presbyterianism will overlook this book only at the risk of having himself branded as ignorant." Sidney E. Mead, *Christian Century*, 67, Pt. 1 (1950): 430. Robert Hastings Nichols described *The Forming of an American Tradition* as "Our first thoroughgoing, surely grounded, fair-minded study of eighteenth-century Presbyterianism. As never before, we know what went on, and its meaning." Robert Hastings Nichols, *Interpretation*, 4 (1950):366. Notwithstanding these high marks, some conservatives have evaluated Trinterud's work in a very different light. Professor Paul Woolley of Westminster Seminary concluded that "... the book is not simply history, it is also propaganda.... Trinterud has not only not hit the bull's-eye; he is not even on target.... I find it difficult to resist the conviction that this book is a tract for the times. In any case it certainly will serve for one in the current campaign of the dominant authorities of the Church from whose Press it issues to depreciate the importance of creedal standards and doctrinal emphases." Paul Woolley, *Westminster Theological Journal*, XII (May 1950): 167, 169. David W. Hall charges Trinterud with "ideological biases" that produced "historiographical errors" in interpreting the Adopting Act. David W. Hall, "Re-examining the Re-examiners of the Adopting Act" in *The Practice of Confessional Subscription*, ed. David W. Hall (Lanham, Maryland: University Press of America, 1995), 274-288. Trinterud's re-evaluation has its own prejudice - the bias toward the New Side over against the Old Side "rationalists" is evident throughout, nonetheless, his research is a valuable contribution because of its expansive use of primary sources. Trinterud added significant material on the New England element in the Presbyterian Church, the influence of

favored strict subscription to the Confession of Faith with only minor reservations related to government and church/state relations.[3] Scottish Presbyterians that immigrated to America brought the tradition of strict confessional subscription with them.[4]

The 1690 Scottish Parliament's act of subscription could not be replicated in Ireland because the state church was Episcopal not Presbyterian. In Ireland, the Synod of Ulster in 1689 declared: "That young men licensed to preach be obliged to subscribe to our Confession of Faith in all the articles thereof, as the Confession of their faith."[5] Faced with dangerous Arian theology that had surfaced in Thomas Emlyn of the Dublin Presbytery, the General Synod tightened the subscription formula in 1705; this move created a reaction among some Presbyterians who formed the Belfast Society in opposition to subscription. This in turn produced renewed efforts to push for unconditional subscription in Ireland. In order to secure peace among the brethren, Robert Craighead[6] of Dublin, the moderator of Synod in 1720, proposed a conciliatory plan known as the Pacific Act.

The 1720 Irish Pacific Act was a compromise intended to harmonize the disparate parties. The Act begins by denying that there had been any attempt to "lay aside" the Confession and Catechisms, but on the contrary, "we do still adhere to the said Confession and Catechisms." The Irish Synod encouraged the study and use of the Confession "as being a good abridgment of the Christian doctrines contained in

---

the Great Awakening on Presbyterianism, the ethos of the Synod of New York, and the history leading up to the first General Assembly. While he contributed new detail to the Presbyterian story, yet, Trinterud's narrative of major events (i.e., formation of the Synod, the Adopting Act, reunion of Old Side/New Side) was not novelty but recited the interpretive framework of nineteenth-century New School historians; see e.g., E.H. Gillett, *History of the Presbyterian Church in the United States of America*, vols. I, II (Philadelphia: Presbyterian Publication Committee, 1864).

[3] J. Ligon Duncan, "Owning the Confession: Subscription in the Scottish Presbyterian Tradition," in *The Practice of Confessional Subscription*, ed. David W. Hall (Lanham, Maryland: University Press of America, 1995), 81.

[4] Some material in this chapter has appeared earlier in *Colonial Presbyterianism: Old Faith in a New Land* (Eugene, Oregon: Pickwick Publications, 2007), 63-85. Used by permission.

[5] Briggs, *American Presbyterianism*, 201.

[6] Luder Whitlock points out the important role played by Thomas Craighead, Robert's brother, in the American subscription controversy. Thomas was a member of the committee that drafted the American Adopting Act in 1729. Thomas was still in Ireland at the time of the Pacific Act and would have been strongly influenced by both his brother Robert and his own experience with the Irish controversy leading up to the Pacific Act of 1720. Robert's role in the American situation is another indicator of the important influence of the Pacific Act on the American version of confessional subscription. Luder G. Whitlock, Jr. "The Context for the Adopting Act" in *The Practice of Confessional Subscription*, ed. David W. Hall (Lanham, Maryland: University Press of America, 1995), 98,99.

the sacred Scriptures."[7] The 1705 Act of the General Synod is reiterated with this understanding of subscription:

> ... which is thus to be understood as now is practised by the Presbyteries, that if any person called upon to subscribe shall scruple any phrase or phrases in the Confession, he shall have leave to use his own expressions, which the Presbytery shall accept of, providing they judge such a person sound in the faith and that such expressions are consistent with the substance of the doctrine, and that such explications shall be inserted in the Presbytery books; and that this be a rule not only in relation to candidates licensed by ourselves, but all intrants into the ministry among us, tho' they have been licensed or ordained elsewhere.[8]

The Pacific Act did not satisfy either party in the Irish Church. Ministers declining to subscribe were excluded and organized themselves into the Presbytery of Antrim in 1726. Conservatives in the Synod of Ulster announced that they were no longer able to maintain ministerial communion with the non-subscribers and ejected them from the Synod in 1727.[9] The Irish rupture was crisp in the minds of American Presbyterians as they approached their own battle over subscription just

---

[7] Briggs suggested that the 1720 Irish Pacific Act (in contrast with the Scotch Act of 1690) emphasizes "Christian doctrines" rather than the distinctive "doctrine of the Reformed Churches"- the language used by the Scots. He added that the American Adopting Act favors the language of the Irish Articles. *American Presbyterianism*, 200. Briggs has imagined a distinction that does not exist. While it is true the 1729 Adopting Act speaks of "systems of Christian doctrine," this is obviously inclusive of the Calvinistic system of doctrine in the Confession. Early American Presbyterian history places it beyond doubt that Americans viewed themselves as a Reformed Church and their creed as more than an affirmation of basic Christian orthodoxy. There is no purpose of adopting the Westminster Standards if one removes the particular Reformed doctrines that constitute the Calvinistic system of the Confession. Scotch and Irish subscription as well as American subscription involved a commitment to historic Calvinism and not mere assent to a generic Christianity.

[8] Ibid., 216-219. Briggs argued that the 1720 Irish Pacific Act was foundational for the American Adopting Act of 1729 and demonstrates this by a careful comparison of the two documents. Trinterud furthermore said the Adopting Act "was modeled in great part after the Irish Pacific Articles of 1720." *Forming of an American Tradition*, 49. The American act is not a mirror image of the Pacific Act, nevertheless, the language of the Adopting Act shows obvious dependence on the Irish document.

[9] George Ellswood Ellis contrasts the Scottish and Irish subscription controversies in this way: "Both Scots and Irish enforced subscription inconsistently but for quite different reasons. The Scots had pressed subscription rigidly in order to prevent the Episcopalian clergy from entering but in dealing with their own ministers they were more lax and apprehensive of being too strict. The Irish discipline was still developing. They attempted to enforce subscription but when it came to punishing the recalcitrants they drew back and compromised. In their final action the Irish put the liberal element out. In contrast, the Scots forced out those who complained about laxness." George Ellswood Ellis, "Nation, Creed and Unity: The Significance of the Subscription Controversy for the Development of Colonial Presbyterianism," (Ph.D. diss., Temple University, 1983), 570.

two years after the Irish division. In many American minds, debate over subscription spelled trouble.

English Presbyterians also experienced dissension over subscription. Semi-Arianism[10] appeared in England through Thomas Emlyn's friend, James Pierce of Exeter and produced a great controversy in 1718-19. In the case of Pierce, three denominations in London (Presbyterian, Congregational, Baptist) were called upon to deliberate on the matter of Pierce and his followers. There were two groups that emerged – those advocating a strong creedal statement on the Trinity and those opposed to requiring subscription to creeds. Unable to secure a joint doctrinal statement on the Trinity, a group of conservative ministers withdrew from the inter-denominational discussions and held their own meeting in which they subscribed to the first of the Thirty-Nine Articles of the Church of England and questions five and six of the Westminster Shorter Catechism.[11]

Many Presbyterian and Congregational ministers in England had historically been opposed to creedal subscription, however, the semi-Arian crisis had made it a necessity according to conservatives. The London ministers now divided into three groups – the subscribers, non-subscribers and the neutrals.[12] The non-subscribing majority made this declaration:

> If after all, a publick hearing be insisted on, we think the Protestant principle, that the Bible is the only and the perfect rule of faith, obliges those who have the case before them, not to condemn any man upon the authority of human decisions, or because he consents not to human forms or phrases: But then only is he to be censured, as not holding the faith necessary to salvation, when it appears that he contradicts, or refuses to own, the plain and express declarations of Holy Scripture, in what is there made necessary to be believed, and in matters there solely revealed....[13]

By pushing for subscription as the answer to the semi-Arian problem, the subscribers alienated non-subscribers and neutrals, therefore, bringing division into the ranks of the London ministers. All three parties for the most part were orthodox on the Trinity, but could not agree on subscribing to a creed as the proper method of handling the issue. Many of the non-subscribers eventually conformed with the Church of England; a few ended up embracing Arianism. The situation in London would also influence American thinking on subscription. In the English case, it

---

[10] Mr. Pierce stated his view thus: "I am not of the opinion of Sabellius, Arius, Socinus, or Sherlock. I believe there is one God, and can be no more. I believe the Son and Holy Ghost to be divine persons, but subordinate to the Father; and the unity of God is, I think, to be resolved into the Father's being the fountain of the divinity of the Son and Spirit." Briggs, *American Presbyterianism*, 195.

[11] Ibid., 196; Trinterud, *Forming of an American Tradition*, 41.

[12] Of the Presbyterians, 50 were non-subscribers, 26 subscribers, and 9 neutrals. Briggs, *American Presbyterianism*, 197.

[13] Ibid., 197.

appeared that some of the unwillingness to subscribe had signified the harboring of heresy.[14]

American Subscription

Up until the year 1729, American Presbyterians as an ecclesiastical body had adopted no formal creed or constitution for church government and discipline. Controversy concerning proper order among the Presbyterians first arose in 1720 over a case of discipline when Robert Cross, a minister in New Castle Presbytery, was found guilty of fornication. The case came before Synod which censured Cross by removing him from the pulpit for four Sundays but allowed the restoration of his pastoral ministry if the people would have him. George Gillespie, a fellow minister in New Castle Presbytery, protested the Synod's gentle treatment of Cross. The Synod replied to Gillespie: "... if any Brother have any Overture to offer to be formed into an Act by the Synod for the better carrying on in the Matters of our Government and Discipline, yt he may bring it in against next Synod."[15] Jonathan Dickinson and five others protested against this reply of Synod; after much debate the protest was withdrawn and a compromise statement of four articles was adopted by the Synod. The four articles acknowledged the ecclesiastical right to acts of discipline "provided yt these Acts be not imposed upon such as conscientiously dissent from them."[16] These articles brought peace to the Synod for a season.

Jonathan Dickinson, as moderator, began the 1722 Synod meeting with a sermon based upon 2 Tim. 3:17. In the sermon Dickinson emphasized the theme of his protest – the church has no authority to make new laws or add to the Bible. "I challenge the world to produce any such *dedimus potestatem* from Christ, or the least lisp in the Bible, that countenances such a regal power."[17] Dickinson's conviction about the sole authority of the Scriptures included not only the making of ecclesiastical laws but also the binding of consciences to any creed of human composition. This view was not shared by a number of the Presbyterians and a showdown over the necessity of adopting a formal creed would soon follow.

---

[14] Trinterud said that the brief controversy in England "became for many the classical illustration of what opposition to constitutionally imposed creeds really meant. Those who rejected subscription were thereafter not infrequently considered secret heretics or hypocrites." *Forming of an American Tradition*, 41.

[15] *Minutes of the Synod*, 27 September 1721 as printed in Guy S. Klett, ed. *Minutes of the Presbyterian Church in America 1706-1788* (Philadelphia: Presbyterian Historical Society, 1976), 51. Subsequent citations of Synod minutes (including both the Synod of Philadelphia and Synod of New York) will come from Klett's critical edition of the original manuscript minutes. Spelling, capitalization and abbreviations from the original manuscripts are preserved.

[16] *Minutes of the Synod*, 27 September 1722, 57.

[17] Richard Webster, *A History of the Presbyterian Church in America From its Origin Until the Year 1760 with Biographical Sketches of its Early Ministers* (Philadelphia: Joseph M. Wilson, 1857), 100.

The origins of creedal subscription among American Presbyterians surfaced in the action of New Castle Presbytery, which in 1724 required candidates to subscribe the Confession in these words: "I do own the Westminster Confession as the Confession of my faith."[18] By 1727 John Thompson, of New Castle Presbytery, introduced an overture to Synod in favor of requiring confessional subscription. Thompson claimed it was not his intention to bring "any heat or contention" to the Synod, but he is concerned for the "vindication and defense of the truths we profess, and for preventing the ingress and spreading of error." The infant Presbyterian Church, which has not its own seminary of learning, is defenseless in an era "of so many pernicious and dangerous corruptions in doctrine."[19]

Thompson admits his own consternation that some of the Presbyterian brethren "have the edge of their zeal against the prevailing errors of the times very much blunted." These brothers exhibit "a kind of indifference and mistaken charity, whereby they think they ought to bear with others, though differing from them in opinion about points which are mysterious and sublime, but not practical nor fundamental, such as predestination." Thompson, on the other hand, is convinced that the Presbyterians should hold fast to the distinctives of Reformed doctrine. "Now although I would grant that the precise point of election and reprobation be neither fundamental nor immediately practical, yet take predestination completely, as it takes in the other disputed points between Calvinists and Arminians, such as universal grace, the non-perseverance of the saints, foreseen faith, and good works, &c., and I think it such an article in my creed, such a fundamental of my faith, that I know not what any other articles could be retained without it."[20]

For the reasons cited, Thompson recommends that Synod "publically and authoritatively adopt the Westminster Confession and Catechism, &c., for the public confession of our faith." Further, the overture asked Synod to "make an act to oblige every Presbytery within their bounds, to oblige every candidate for the ministry to subscribe or otherwise acknowledge, *coram presbyterio*, the said Confession of Faith, and to promise not to preach or teach contrary to it." In addition, it was proposed "that if any minister within our bounds shall take upon him to teach or preach any thing contrary to any of the said articles, unless, first, he propose the said point to the Presbytery or Synod, to be by them discussed, he shall be censured so and so."[21] There was initial resistance to the overture which was brought to Synod

---

[18] Quoted in Briggs, *American Presbyterianism*, 210.

[19] Charles Hodge, *The Constitutional History of the Presbyterian in the United States of America*, Part I, 1705-1741 (Philadelphia: Presbyterian Board of Publication, 1851), 137-139.

[20] Ibid., 140. Thompson was worried about the laxity of his brethren. He desired a strict Reformed Presbyterian Church wherein only true Calvinists find a home. Thompson believed mandating that ministers strictly subscribe the Westminster Confession would safeguard the purity of Calvinist teaching.

[21] Ibid., 140, 141. Thompson's overture acknowledged that there may be objections to some articles of the Confession and he proposed a method to deal with exceptions by having the presbytery or synod discuss the matter. This suggestion opened the door for the eventual compromise plan that would allow for scruples to be publically declared and discussed.

again by New Castle Presbytery in 1728; it was deferred to the next year when all members of the Synod could be present to debate this all important question.

The Thompson/New Castle overture was opposed by a number of presbyters, the most influential being Dickinson. The essence of Dickinson's objection was not disagreement with the Calvinistic theology of Westminster but his resistance to imposing any creed in principle. Dickinson, wrote to Thompson in April 1729, stating that he believed "a joint agreement in the same essential and necessary articles of Christianity, and the same methods of worship and discipline, are a sufficient bond of union.... we have already all the external bond of union that the Scriptures require of us." He further stated that requiring any "unscriptural terms of union or communion is a direct and natural means to procure rents and divisions in the church.... we all of us know that the subscription under debate has been scrupled by many godly, learned, and faithful ministers of Christ, that it has made horrible divisions and confusion in other churches...." The sole authority of Scripture will be undermined because "a subscription to any human composure as the test of our orthodoxy is to make it the standard of our faith, and thereby to give it the honour due only to the word of God."[22] Liberty of conscience was a vital principle for Dickinson and he pointed out that there is a "most glorious contradiction" in subscribing "God alone is Lord of the Conscience" (Chapter XX, Article 2 of the Westminster Confession) and then to "impose the rest" of the Confession which would be a denial of that very principle.[23]

Dickinson rejected Thompson's premise that subscription will protect the Presbyterian Church from corruption in doctrine. "Tho subscription may shut the door of the church communion against many serious and excellent servants of Christ who conscientiously scruple it; yet its never like to detect hypocrites, nor keep concealed hereticks out of the church." Dickinson is also concerned about the inordinate elevation of a human document. "Upon the whole then, tho' I have a higher opinion of the Assemblies Confession than of any other book of the kind extant in the world, yet I don't think it perfect. I know it to be the dictates of fallible men, and I know of no law either of religion or reason, that obliges me to subscribe it."[24] The magnitude and breadth of the Westminster Standards make it problematic for any minister. Was it realistic to expect all candidates to strictly embrace the entire Confession and Catechisms? Dickinson pondered, "If all qualified Candidates can well understand the whole of that large Confession, it's a just Matter of shame to me, who have be'n a Minister between twenty and thirty Years; and yet don't understand several Things in it.... I'm afraid therefore, that most of our Candidates must subscribe blindfold, or be kept out of the Ministry from invincible necessity."[25]

Instead of imposing subscription, Dickinson suggested that candidates be carefully examined, that strict discipline against immoral ministers be enforced, and

---

[22] Ibid., 144.

[23] Briggs, *American Presbyterianism*, 213.

[24] Ibid., 212, 213.

[25] Trinterud, *Forming of an American Tradition*, 47.

"that the ministers of the gospel be most diligent, faithful, and painful in the discharge of their awful trust."[26] While a number of Presbyterians sympathized with Dickinson's position, the climate of Synod was advantageous for moving ahead with Thompson's overture. Nevertheless, Dickinson's sensitivities set the tone for much of the discussion during the 1729 meeting of Synod which hammered out the subscription compromise. Many of Dickinson's concerns would be incorporated into the final 1729 subscription principles that accommodated the convictions of subscriptionists and non-subscriptionists alike.

In the period immediately leading up to 1729, the anxiety over Thompson's overture was very real. There emerged distinct parties on the subscription issue and the specter of schism hung over the Presbyterians. Jedediah Andrews, writing to a friend, describes the conflict and his own fears about the future:

We are now like to fall into a great difference about subscribing the Westminster Confession of Faith. An overture for it, drawn up by Mr. Thompson of Lewistown was offered to our Synod the year before last, but not then read in Synod. Means were then used to stave it off, and I was in hopes we should have heard no more of it. But last Synod it was brought again, recommended by all the Scotch and Irish members present and being read among us, a proposal was made, prosecuted and agreed to that it should be deferred till our next meeting for further consideration. The Proposal is, that all ministers and intrants shall sign it or else be disowned as members. Now what shall we do? They will certainly carry it by number. Our countrymen say, they are willing to joyn in a vote to make it the Confession of our church, but to agree to the making it the test of orthodoxy [27] and term of ministerial communion, they say they will not. I think all the Scots are on one side, and all the English and Welsh on the other, to a man.... This business lies very heavy upon my mind, and I desire we may be directed in it, that we may not bring scandal upon our profession. Tho' I have been sometime an instrument of keeping them together when they were like to fall a pieces, I have little hope of doing so now. If it were not for the scandal of division, I should not be much against it, for the different countrymen seem to be most delighted in one another and to do best when they are by themselves. My congregation being made up of diverse nations of different sentiments, this brings me under a greater difficulty. I am afraid of the event. However I'll endeavour to do as near as I can what I understand to be duty, and leave the issue to Providence.[28]

---

[26] Briggs, *American Presbyterianism*, 213.

[27] Luder Whitlock suggests that the hesitancy to use Westminster as a "test of orthodoxy" may be rooted in his concern for personal holiness as the chief criteria for ministry. "The Context of the Adopting Act," 98. The theme of clergy piety was a hotly disputed issue during the Old Side / New Side controversy.

[28] Hodge, *Constitutional History*, Vol. I, 142. Briggs stated: "This letter of Andrews is a faithful portraiture of the serious state of affairs in the youthful Presbyterian Church. There were two parties in sharp antagonism, but they both dreaded the evils and perils of separation, and were thus prepared for concessions and compromise." *American Presbyterianism*, 215. Andrews differentiated between adopting Westminster as the confession of the church but not making it a test of orthodoxy or ministerial communion.

Compromise of 1729

It was with great trepidation that the young Synod of Philadelphia convened in 1729. Diverse parties met in Philadelphia, each with strong principles of conscience on the questions at hand. There was dread for the scandal of division that would dishonor the name of Christ and the recent Irish schism over subscription made the potentiality of a split very real. Could the Americans maintain union? With schism as the alternative choice, both sides were willing to accommodate one another for the greater good of the church. Twenty members were present for the Synod meeting, seven were absent.[29] The affair of the Confession was remitted to a committee of eight (Andrews, Dickinson, Pierson, Thompson, Anderson, Craighead, Conn and John Budd)[30] to draft a recommendation for the Synod. The committee members represented the spectrum of opinion on the question, therefore, a unanimous proposal would have to satisfy all parties if unity was to be preserved.

In the morning session of September 19, the proposed overture on the confession was presented to the Synod. The overture would be unanimously adopted "after long debating upon it." The preamble of the Act clearly bore the imprimatur of Dickinson and exhibited that charitable spirit which acknowledged the valid concerns of both parties – freedom of conscience was essential, at the same time, a formal creed was necessary for the good of the church. The preamble explained:

> Altho' the Synod do not claim or pretend to any Authority of imposing our faith upon other men's Consciences, but do profess our just Dissatisfaction with and Abhorrence of such Impositions, and do utterly disclaim all Legislative Power and Authority in the Church, being willing to receive one another, as Christ has received us to the Glory of God, and admit to fellowship in sacred ordinances all such as we have Grounds to believe Christ will at last admit to the Kingdom of Heaven; yet we are undoubtedly

---

This was a significant distinction that would influence the 1729 Adopting Act which embraced both the adopting of the Confession as a whole by the Synod and the allowance of scruples over "non-essential articles" by individuals.

[29] Trinterud described the 1729 Synod: "Present at the meeting were three New Englanders, one Welshman, and fourteen Scotch-Irish. The actual strength of the two parties was thus about one to two in favor of the subscriptionists. The compromise was due to moderates within both parties." *Forming of an American Tradition*, 49.

[30] Briggs claimed the group was well-balanced with Thompson and Anderson representing the "strong subscriptionists," Dickinson and Pierson the "anti-subscriptionists" and the remaining four, Craighead, Andrews, Budd and Conn, holding a mediating position. *American Presbyterianism*, 216. This seems to be a fair characterization of the committee and helps explain why the compromise outcome reflected such a variety of influences and granted something to everyone. Thompson got his formal adoption of the Confession (Scottish confessional influence), Dickinson got his declaration of not imposing faith on other men's consciences (English non-subscribers influence) and Craighead got the scruples principle. (Irish Pacific Act influence).

obliged to take Care that the faith once delivered to the Saints be kept pure and uncorrupt among Us, and so handed down to our Posterity.[31]

As the members of Synod expressed their approbation of the Westminster Standards, they were also careful to make an important distinction between "all the essential and necessary articles," which each minister shall adopt, and liberty on articles "not essential and necessary." After the preamble, the Synod pronounced their unanimous consent that all ministers,

> ... shall declare their agreement in and approbation of the Confession of Faith with the larger and shorter Catechisms of the assembly of Divines at Westminster, as being in *all the essential and necessary Articles*, good Forms of sound words and systems of Christian Doctrine; and do also adopt the said Confession and Catechisms as the Confession of our Faith. And we do also agree, yt all the Presbyteries within our Bounds shall always take Care not to admit any Candidate of the Ministry into the Exercise of the sacred Function, but what declares his Agreement in opinion with *all the Essential and Necessary Articles* of said Confession, either by subscribing the said Confession of Faith and Catechisms, or by a verbal Declaration of their assent thereto, as such Minister or Candidate shall think best (italics mine).[32]

The Synod also endorsed a method whereby ministers could exercise liberty of conscience by stating scruples publicly before the brethren. These scruples, however, must "be only about articles not essential and necessary." The Synod or Presbytery shall make final judgment on these scruples and determine whether or not said scruples are about "essential and necessary articles of faith." The paragraph about exceptions states:

> And in Case any Minister of this Synod or any Candidate for the Ministry shall have any Scruple with respect to any Article or Articles of sd. Confession or Catechisms, he shall at the Time of his making sd. Declaration declare his Sentiments to the Presbytery or Synod, who shall notwithstanding admit him to ye Exercise of the Ministry within our Bounds and to Ministerial Communion if the Synod or Presbytery shall judge his scruple or mistake to be only about articles *not Essential and necessary* in Doctrine, Worship or Government. But if the Synod or Presbytery shall judge such Ministers or Candidates erronious in *Essential and necessary Articles of Faith*, the Synod or Presbytery shall declare them uncapable of Communion with them (italics mine).[33]

Anticipating that there would be differences of opinion over "extra-essential and not-necessary points of doctrine" the Synod included a statement of brotherly charity toward all, and denounced prejudice between ministers who differ. The Adopting Act[34] concluded with these words: "And the Synod do solemnly agree,

---

[31] *Minutes of the Synod*, 19 September 1729, 103.

[32] Ibid., 103, 104.

[33] Ibid., 104.

[34] While there is debate over whether the morning session (sometimes called the "Preliminary Act') or the afternoon session, or both, comprise the official "Adopting Act,"

that none of us will traduce or use any opprobrious Terms of those yt differ from us in these *extra-essential and not-necessary points of doctrine*, but treat them with the same friendship, kindness and brotherly Love, as if they had not differed from us in such Sentiments" (italics mine).[35]

The magnanimous spirit of the Adopting Act was embodied in Dickinson's phrase "essential and necessary," which phrase is repeated five times in the Synod's overture. The Synod adopted the Westminster Standards with the understanding that ministers are free to take exceptions to articles provided they are not about "essential" points of doctrine. The Synod or Presbytery determines what is essential or necessary not the candidate or minister. The "essentials" language of the Adopting Act was a compromise.[36] One party had desired subscription to all articles, another party was opposed to subscribing fallible human creeds; the 1729 compromise required that ministerial communion be based on receiving the "essential and necessary" doctrines of the Confession. The Synod adopted the Confession and Catechisms as the church's doctrinal standards, however, this was not understood to be a wooden acceptance of every article.

In the afternoon session, the Synod having previously adopted the foundational principles of subscription, proceeded to implement this Act among themselves. After reading the minutes of the morning session, which articulated the agreed upon meaning of subscription, each member of the Synod now had to personally adopt the Westminster Standards as the confession of his faith before the Synod brethren. In order to accomplish this end, each member was given the opportunity of "proposing all the Scruples yt any of them had to make against any Articles and

---

the Synod minutes indicate a continuity of the day's activity. There is a direct flow into the afternoon session after a break from the long session of the morning. After having defined the foundational principles of subscription in the morning, the afternoon session was an outworking of those principles among those present at the Synod meeting. Both the morning and afternoon sessions declare that the Synod adopts the Confession and Catechisms as "the confession of our faith" (morning), and "the confession of their faith" (afternoon). The two sessions are inseparable - the adoption of principles (morning) and the immediate implementation of those principles by members of the Synod (afternoon).

[35] *Minutes of the Synod*, 19 September 1729, 104.

[36] Trinterud made this observation: "The Adopting Act of 1729 was therefore a compromise. The first part was a preamble or general agreement as to what was to be understood by subscription. All legislative power in the Church was renounced; only administrative power was claimed. The need of a standard of doctrine and practice was admitted. A distinction was made between the essential and necessary articles of the standards, and those not essential and necessary." *Forming of an American Tradition*, 48. Charles Hodge also characterized the Synod's 1729 action as a "compromise" between disparate groups. Hodge stated: "It is very evident, indeed, that the act was a compromise. Both parties were desirous to avoid a schism; yet both were anxious that their own views should prevail. Their only expedient was to find some common ground on which they could stand." *Constitutional History*, I, 152. This is a significant admission by Hodge who generally argued for a conservative interpretation of 1729 and 1736. For further discussion of Hodge's viewpoint see *infra* chp. 8.

Expressions in the Confession of Faith and larger and shorter Catechisms." The afternoon minute states that after these opinions were presented, the Synod "unanimously agreed in the solution of those Scruples."[37]

After individual scruples were "unanimously agreed" to be acceptable, i.e., not about "essential and necessary" doctrines, the whole Synod "unanimously declare" exceptions to two sections of the Confession wherein every member had scruples about "some clauses."[38] Since these scruples were held in common by every member present, they were recorded in the minutes. These uniform exceptions having been noted, the Synod declared the "Confession and Catechisms to be the Confession of their faith."[39] The afternoon session thus completed the work that had begun in the morning. The Synod accomplished two purposes on September 19, 1729: principles for understanding the meaning of subscription were adopted; and Synodical members executed those principles among themselves in their adoption of the Westminster Standards individually and as an ecclesiastical body. Both individual and common scruples were voiced that day, yet, none of those scruples were judged to be about "essential and necessary articles." Having openly acknowledged every scruple before one another as the morning minute had directed, the Synod had now completed their work of adopting the Westminster Standards.

Practicing Confessional Subscription

The first Synod record of examining an individual minister according to the new 1729 directives came the next year. David Evans, who had withdrawn from the

---

[37] The unanimous "solution of those scruples" should not necessarily be interpreted as uniformity in the Synod about excepting only certain clauses in chapters 20 and 23 of the Confession. The afternoon minute states, "after proposing all the Scruples yt any of them had against any Articles and Expressions," which does not indicate how many or what kind of scruples were mentioned by all the individuals present. Limiting "scruples" to only the "unanimous" scruples of chapters 20 and 30 is not clear from the minutes. What is certain is that all of these scruples met the Synod's criteria of subscription, i.e., being scruples over "extra-essential and not-necessary points of doctrine" which principle had just been established that morning. The Presbyterian practice of asking candidates to state "scruples" after 1729 indicates an understanding that men might take exception to articles other than the two chapters originally noted in 1729; otherwise, to ask candidates for a statement of scruples would be meaningless.

[38] The Synod inscribed their universal scruple: "excepting only some Clauses in ye 20. And 23. Chapter, concerning which Clauses, the Synod do unanimously declare, yt they do not receive those Articles in any such sense as to suppose the civil Magistrate hath a controlling Power over synods with Respect to the Exercise of their ministerial Authority; or Power to persecute and for their Religion, or in any sense contrary to the Protestant succession of the Throne of Great Britain." *Minutes of the Synod*, 19 September 1729, 104.

[39] Publically stating scruples with the Confession and then formally adopting the Westminster Standards as the confession of one's faith were the two main elements of confessional subscription. Together they comprised the meaning and intent of ministerial subscription to the creed of the church.

Synod three years previously, desired to reunite with his brethren. The 1730 Synod minutes record: "And having proposed *all the Scruples he had to make about any articles* of the Confession and Catechism &c: to the Satisfaction of the Synod, and *declared his adopting the Westminster Confession of faith and Catechisms agreeable to the last years adopting Act*, he was unanimously received in as a Member again"[40] (italics mine). Identical to the Synod's actions of 1729, Evans proposes scruples "about any articles" none of which violated the "essentials" principle for it met "the satisfaction of the Synod." After the scruples were examined, then Evans adopted the Confession of Faith.

On the same day of Evans' examination, an overture was presented to the 1730 Synod requesting a clarification on the meaning of the Adopting Act:

> Whereas some Persons have been dissatisfied at the Manner of wording our last years Agreement about the Confession &c: supposing some Expressions not sufficiently obligatory upon Intrants; overture yt the Synod do now declare, that they understand those Clauses that respect the Admission of Intrants or Candidates in such a sense as to oblige them to receive and adopt the Confession and Catechisms at their Admission in the same Manner and as fully as the Members of the Synod did that were then present. Which overture was unanimously agree to by the Synod.[41]

It appears that questions had been raised about the "manner of wording" in the Adopting Act. Some persons had queried whether certain "expressions" or "clauses" in the Act had been misunderstood. The Synod responded by reiterating their expectation that all Intrants to the ministry must "receive and adopt the Confession

---

[40] *Minutes of the Synod*, 17 September 1730, 108. Evans articulated all his scruples and then adopted the Westminster Confession and Catechisms "agreeable to last years Adopting Act." These were two separate actions - he joined in the unanimous exceptions of 1729 (chps. 20 and 23), one would presume, by declaring his adoption of the Westminster Standards in the same manner as the original Synod of 1729, and just prior to this declaration, he "proposed all the scruples he had about any articles" as the Adopting Act required (italics mine).

[41] Some interpret this overture as advocating strict subscription to the whole confession, chapters 20 and 23 only being excepted. See Ellis, "Nation, Creed and Unity: The Significance of the Subscription Controversy for the Development of Colonial Presbyterianism," 710; *Paradigms in Polity*, ed. David W. Hall and Joseph H. Hall (Grand Rapids: Wm. B. Eerdmans Publishing Co., 1994),350, 351; George W. Knight, III, "Subscription to the Westminster Confession of Faith and Catechisms," *Presbyterion* (Spring-Fall 1984): 24,25; Morton H. Smith, *The Case for Full Subscription to the Westminster Standards in the Presbyterian Church in America* (Greenville, SC, 1992), 27,28. The 1730 statement may mean that only the universal exceptions of the 1729 afternoon minute are sanctioned by the Synod, on the other hand, the overture may simply be intended as a general restatement of 1729 and not have those specific exceptions in mind. One thing is indisputable, the 1730 overture with which Synod agreed, must be understood as consistent with the immediately preceding minute describing Evans's examination by the Synod. Evans stated his scruples according to the directives of the 1729 morning minute and Synod accepted Evans because his scruples were within the "essential and necessary" boundaries.

and Catechisms at their Admission in the same Manner and as fully as the Members of the Synod did that were present" – referring back to the 1729 Adopting Act of the previous year.[42]

The mediating stance of the Adopting Act satisfied the immediate needs of the church, however, there were rumblings among conservatives jealous for a stricter form of subscription and fearful that they had given away too much. The Synod statement of 1730 addressed some initial concerns about the potential latitude latent in the Adopting Act itself. A catalyst for the strengthening of the conservative perspective was the first heresy trial in American Presbyterianism – the trial of Samuel Hemphill of Philadelphia. Hemphill was received by the Synod in 1734 from the Presbytery of Straban in Ireland where he had been ordained. Hemphill had subscribed the Confession according to the formula used in Ireland and he was recommended to the Synod with "satisfactory Certificates from the same Presbry of his Qualifications for and Ordination to the sacred Ministry." Synod minutes record simply that he was "admitted a member of this Synod."[43]

Hemphill served as an assistant to Jedidiah Andrews at the (First) Presbyterian Church in Philadelphia and quickly drew attention in the city as a fine preacher. It was soon discovered, however, that Hemphill had plagiarized a sermon from a Dr. Clarke, known openly to be an Arian, along with stealing several other sermons. A commission investigated the situation and charges were brought against Hemphill for Arminianism and Socinianism. The charges were sustained unanimously and Hemphill was suspended from ministerial office in 1735. The case sheds significant light on the emerging tension over understanding subscription at this point in the Synod's history. Dickinson, responding to Benjamin Franklin's criticism of the Synod's disciplinary action against Hemphill, offered this explanation: "We allow of no Confession of Faith as a test of orthodoxy for others, but only as a declaration of our own sentiments; nor may this be imposed upon the members of our own society, nor their assent required to anything as a condition of their communion with us, but what we esteem *essentially necessary*" (italics mine). Appended to the reply to Franklin was a copy of the Adopting Act, morning minute.[44]

Dickinson[45] also wrote a formal defense of the Synod's action in 1735 entitled *A Vindication of Reverend Commission* responding to a second pamphlet by Franklin on the Hemphill matter. According to Dickinson, Hemphill had brought this trouble on himself. At his admission into the Synod, Hemphill was "called upon to propose

---

[42] *Minutes of the Synod*, 17 September 1730, 108.

[43] *Minutes of the Synod*, 21 September 1734, 121

[44] *Remarks upon a Pamphlet entitled a Letter* was Dickinson's first response to Franklin's criticism of the Commission of Synod; quoted in Briggs, *American Presbyterianism*, 232. Note the use of "essentially necessary" alluding to the Adopting Act (morning minute).

[45] William S. Barker points out that both Ebenezer Pemberton, the moderator of Synod, and Robert Cross probably had a hand in *A Vindication of the Reverend Commission*. See William S. Barker, "The Samuel Hemphill Heresy Case (1735) and the Historic Method of Subscribing to the Westminster Standards," in *The Practice of Confessional Subscription* ed. David W. Hall (Lanham, Maryland: University Press of America, 1995), 161, 162.

his Objections, if he had any; but he replied, he had none to make." He assented to the Confession *in toto* without exception as he had done previously in Ireland. This was dishonest. Hemphill "should have particularly offered his objections, and submitted it to the judgment of the Synod, whether the articles objected against were essential and necessary or not." Dickinson added: "Nor is it any excuse that the Synod have not defined how many fundamental articles there are in the Confession, since they have reserved to themselves the liberty to judge upon each occasion what are, and what are not, fundamental."[46] The basic principles of the Adopting Act are recounted by Dickinson as the pattern that should have been followed and would have prevented this embarrassment over Hemphill.[47]

The 1735 Synod, distraught over this egregious breech of integrity and the dangers of heresy,[48] sent an overture to the Synod of Ulster stipulating that in the future every minister coming to America would be expected to have a "firm Attachment to sd. Confession, &c., in opposition to the new Upstart Doctrines and Schemes, particularly such as we condemn'd in Mr. H-ll's Sermons." The Synod also pronounced that each minister or probationer must "subscribe or adopt the westminstr. Confessn. of Faith & Catechisms before sd. Pry *in Manner and Form as they have done*" (italics mine).[49] Pointing back to their own action in 1729, the Synod's letter informs the Irish that ministerial trials in America will require that "scruples" be publically stated and the Synod will judge if the essentials criteria be met or not.

Another indicator of the concern over heterodoxy and the subscription standard of 1729, are minutes from the 1735 meeting of Synod which inquire if those admitted to presbyteries since the last meeting of Synod "have adopted ye Westminster Confession of faith & Catechisms &c: according to ye adopting Act of the Synod...." The answer is affirmative and then the minutes state: "Mrs. Isaac

---

[46] Ibid. Barker comments on the *Vindication*: "Here we have again the preliminary part of the Adopting Act from the morning of September 19, 1729 with two very significant aspects included. First, five years after the Confession was adopted, with exceptions acknowledged only with regard to clauses in the 20th and 23rd chapters concerning the civil magistrate, the procedure was followed of asking Hemphill whether he had any exceptions to declare, not just to these portions of the Confession. Second, it is stated that the Synod has not defined which articles are fundamental but has reserved that judgment to itself."

[47] The Hemphill situation was a case study in the prudence of the 1729 Adopting Act which mandated careful scrutiny of candidates and ministers. Rather than a flippant acceptance of the Westminster Standards as a whole, individuals should be pressed to declare where they take exceptions; and in most cases there will be some exceptions given the human fallibility of both the subscriber and the Westminster Divines.

[48] The Synod was very concerned about false doctrine. The letter denounces "...the great & almost universal Deluge of pernicious Errrs. [Errors] & damnable Doctrines yt so boldly threaten to overthrow the Christian world...when so many Wolves in Sheeps Cloathing are invading the Flocks of Xt. Every where in the world...." *Minutes of the Synod*, 22 September 1735, 131.

[49] Ibid., 132.

Chalker[50] and Hugh Carlisle not having seen the adopting Act, have now had the same read to them and now concur in their assent to the Terms of the Adopting Act." Synod minutes of 1735 also record: "Ordered yt each Presbry have the *whole*[51] adopting Act inserted in their Presbry Book" (italics mine). There was apparently apprehension that every presbytery was not utilizing the Adopting Act in its examination of ministers and in at least these two cases it was true. Chalker had been ordained by East-Jersey and Carlisle admitted to New Castle in the last year, yet, neither one knew the contents of the Adopting Act.[52] Requiring that the Adopting Act be inserted into each Presbytery Book was one way to remedy the problem.

Synod of 1736

Concern over subscription in the wake of the Hemphill trial, the seeming neglect in a few presbyteries, and suspicions of doctrinal latitude raised the stakes for interpreting the Adopting Act. While the Adopting Act had conferred a degree of freedom for individual scruples as well as presbytery's right of judgment on "essentials," the situation was now more serious, since the Adopting Act had apparently failed to protect the church in the Hemphill case.[53] The Adopting Act problem was a principal consideration of the Synod at its annual meeting in 1736. After the perfunctory taking of attendance and the reading of last year's minutes, the Synod heard a report from Dunagall Presbytery: "The Presbry of Dunagall report yt Mr. Alexdr Creaghead was last winter ordained to ye work of the Ministry, and at yt Time did adopt the Westminster Confession of Faith &c. And also both he and Mr.

---

[50] Chalker had come under criticism from one of his flock "as being averse from conforming to ye ordr of ye Synod in Respect of our adopting the westminstr. Confession." The ministers appointed to investigate the accusations, reported to the Synod that the charges were "groundless." On the other hand, the commission also noted that "Pry was too hasty in their Proceeding to Mr. Chalker's ordination in so short a Time after the Presentation of his Call and Tryals, and cannot approve of its being performed at such a Distance from the People where he was to officiate." *Minutes of the Synod*, 23 September 1735, 134.

[51] By "whole" Adopting Act, one should probably understand both the morning and afternoon sessions of September 19, 1729. Which half had been neglected? Dickinson certainly kept the principle of "essentials" (the morning) before the church in his writings during this period. Perhaps some of the conservatives had been emphasizing only the afternoon session. It is difficult to determine the answer with certainty; however, given the reemphasis on the afternoon minute during the 1736 meeting of Synod, it is most likely that the morning session alone had been circulating throughout the church as "The Adopting Act"- at least in some corners. The Synod of New York, ten years later, when it recorded the Adopting Act in its original 1745 minutes, still listed only the text of the 1729 morning session as the "Adopting Act." See Appendix, *Minutes of the Synod of New York*, 1745, 322.

[52] *Minutes of the Synod*, 18 September 1735, 127, 128.

[53] Dickinson argued that the failure in the Hemphill case was the neglect of the Adopting Act principles, i.e., mandatory stating of scruples. If Hemphill had been honest enough to state his exceptions plainly, the crisis could have been averted.

Jno. Paul lately from Ireland having now heard the several Resolutions and Acts of ye Synod in Relation to ye adopting sd. Confession &c. did before the Synod declare their Agreement thereunto."[54]

An overture was presented to the 1736 Synod from the people of Paxton and Derry which raised questions about the meaning of the Adopting Act. A Synod response was drawn up by a committee which stated in part:

> That the Synod do declare, yt inasmuch as we understand yt many Persons of our Perswasion both more lately and formerly have been offended with some Expression or distinction in the first or preliminary act of our Synod, contained in the printed Paper, relating to our receiving or adopting the westminster Confession & Catechisms &c: That in order to remove said offence and all Jealousies yt have arisen or may arise in any of our People's minds on occasion of sd. Distinctions and Expressions, the Synod doth declare, yt the Synod have adopted and still do adhere to the westminstr. Confession Catechism and Directory without the least variation or alteration, and without any Regard to sd. Distinctions. And we do further declare yt this was our meaning and true Intent in our first adopting of sd, Confession, as may particularly appear by our adopting act which is as followeth.[55]

Immediately following the above statement is the text of the 1729 afternoon minute only.[56] There is a significant shift of emphasis by highlighting the afternoon minute to the exclusion of the agreed upon principles of the morning session. It is interesting to note that Dickinson and what would become most of the New Side party were absent from the meeting of Synod that year. The overture was unanimously approved by the 20 members present but 21 members were absent in

---

[54] *Minutes of the Synod*, 16 September 1736, 137.

[55] *Minutes of the Synod*, 17 September 1736, 141.

[56] Some argue that the 1736 explanation of the Adopting Act should be the definitive commentary on the Synod's original intent. See David W. Hall, *Paradigms in Polity*, 353, 354 and George W. Knight, III, "Subscription to the Westminster Confession of Faith and Catechisms," 24-28. This interpretation follows Charles Hodge's Constitutional History which underscored the consistent confessional strictness of the framers of the Adopting Act. Hall emphasizes that the "official acts" of the Synod should take preeminence in interpreting original intent. Knight points out that there is no record of objection to the 1736 statement in the Synod minutes. These are impressive arguments; nonetheless, it is bewildering to think that the act of 1736 could be consistent with the Adopting Act principles of 1729. Since the morning minute of 1729 had so plainly declared the Synod's own unanimous definition of confessional subscription, the apparent jettisoning of those principles in 1736 begs significant historical questions. It is interesting to observe that Hall's rehearsal of the "official acts" of Synod up until 1758 are predominately from the Old Side (Synod of Philadelphia) minutes, whereas, Trinterud's account highlights New Side (Synod of New York) sources. Nineteenth-century Presbyterian historians attempted to explain 1736 within these same two paradigms. The historiographical puzzle and variety of interpretations, underscores the fact that eighteenth-century sources offer competing pictures of colonial Presbyterianism.

1736.[57] One would surmise that the 1736 "clarification" would not have been approved by Dickinson and his colleagues had they been present. The 1736 Synod asserted its adherence to the Confession and Catechisms "without any Regard to sd. Distinctions" in the "first or preliminary act." This was a brazen discountenancing of the morning minute which had been the heart and soul of the compromise.[58] This new exclusive interpretation may well have served the purposes of the conservative party but it was not reflective of the whole Synod's point of view.[59] The original compromise of the 1729 Adopting Act was beginning to disintegrate by 1736 and the seeds of schism were being planted.[60] Each party would begin emphasizing either the morning or afternoon minute as "the Adopting Act," whereas, the original framers had included both parts as the one act of Synod. After the Old Side/New Side division of 1741, it was the New Side custom to refer to the morning session alone as the Adopting Act in reaction to the 1736 reinterpretation. When the Synod

---

[57] According to Briggs, only 3 of the 20 members who voted for the 1736 overture would end up in the New Side camp - William Tennent Sr, William Tennent Jr., and Richard Treat. Of the 21 absent from Synod in 1736, only 2 would join the Old Side - George Gillespie and Hugh Conn. It appears that a conservative majority in 1736 passed a conservative interpretation of 1729. *American Presbyterianism*, 237, n.

[58] Trinterud called the conservative reinterpretation a "ruse." He said: "In this manner adoption of unqualified subscription was proved. The only permissible scruples were those concerning the civil magistrate. This was, however, a breach of faith. Any impartial reading of the minutes must reveal that the morning's session was devoted to reaching a basis for the agreement that followed in the afternoon." *Forming of an American Tradition*, 49. Trinterud in essence is correct, although he is overly severe in his condemnation of the 1736 statement. One can appreciate the strict subscriptionist's over-reaction to the trial of Hemphill and their sincere conviction that the morning minute could potentially undermine the authority of the Confession. What made the 1736 declaration divisive is that these earnest convictions were not shared by the entire Synod (notably those absent), many of whom did not believe strict subscription was the cure. The history of the 1741 schism conclusively confirms that the New Side resented the revision of 1736; see discussion of the schism *infra* chp. 2.

[59] Briggs commented on the interpretation of 1736: "This act does not antagonize the Adopting Act, but it points in the direction of strict subscription. It was doubtless so designed, and has been generally so interpreted. It was, however, so phrased that liberal subscriptionists, whose scruples as to certain sections had been allowed, could hardly oppose it without giving occasion to the suspicion that they had other scruples which they had not made known." *American Presbyterianism*, 236. This is an interesting hypothesis given the sensitive atmosphere that the Hemphill trial had created and seems a plausible explanation for why there was not more immediate resistance.

[60] Albert E. Freundt referred to the "uneasy peace" of the 1729 Adopting Act. He stated: "The emphasis upon 'essential' articles, as well as its allowance for mental reservations, marked a victory for Dickinson's party. However, this victory was not to last. The Great Awakening divided Presbyterians over the issue of revivalism and drove the wedge deeper yet between subscriptionists and antisubscriptionists." Albert E. Freundt, "Jonathan Dickinson," in *Dictionary of the Presbyterian and Reformed Tradition in America*, ed. D.G. Hart and Mark Noll (Downers Grove, Illinois: InterVarsity Press, 1999), 81, 82.

of New York was established in 1745, it was ordered that the "Adopting Act" be recorded in their first set of minutes – only the *morning minute* of 1729 appears.[61]

---

[61] The text of the "Adopting Act" was the first item inscribed in the Appendix of the Minutes of the Synod of New York. Only the morning minute of 1729 was recorded there with this introduction: "A Copy of the adopting Act, taken out of the Synod Book of Philadelphia made in the Year 1729, referred unto in Page 2d. Of this Book." An Appendix, Minutes of the Synod of New York, 1745, 322. This is incontrovertible evidence that the Synod of New York understood by "Adopting Act" the morning minute of 1729; it also helps explain why the "essentials" concept (so prominent in the morning minute) was fundamental to New York's understanding of ministerial communion in the reunion discussions with the Synod of Philadelphia (1749-1758).

CHAPTER 2

Schism and Subscription

Alongside the growing suspicion over subscription, was an ancillary concern that certain candidates for the ministry were receiving inadequate theological training. The context for the controversy was the dearth of Presbyterian ministers in the Middle Colonies which had no theological schools like New England. In order to address this problem, William Tennent Sr., a Presbyterian pastor in Neshaminy, Pennsylvania, began his own academy for ministerial studies, which detractors called "the Log College." By 1736 two presbyteries had raised concerns about the inadequacy of Log College instruction; the Synod responded in 1738 by establishing an examining committee to test privately educated candidates in "Philosophy and Divinity and the Languages."[1] The "examining act" passed by a large majority, however, it was opposed by the newly established New Brunswick Presbytery who believed the examination rule was usurping legislative power contrary to Presbyterian practice. A defiant New Brunswick Presbytery licensed a Log College graduate, John Rowland, just three months after Synod's new rule had been adopted. Rowland had been rejected by New Castle Presbytery in 1736 which made his licensure even more appalling.[2]

As early as 1734 Gilbert Tennent (William's son) began raising questions about spiritual declension in Presbyterian congregations and presented an overture to Synod asking that "they particularly enquire into the Conversations, Conduct & Behaviour of such as offer themselves to the Ministry, and that they diligently examine all Candidates for the Ministry in their Experiences of a work of

---

[1] *Minutes of the Synod*, 29 May 1738 in Guy S. Klett, ed. *Minutes of the Presbyterian Church in America 1706-1788* (Philadelphia: Presbyterian Historical Society, 1976), 156, 157. William Tennent, Sr. had a good reputation as instructor in biblical languages; however, there were questions about his expertise in philosophy and theology. Apparently, the Old Side felt that Log College training was inadequate in both liberal arts and theology. See Milton J. Coalter, *Gilbert Tennent, Son of Thunder* (New York: Greenwood Press, 1986), 49, 50.

[2] Ibid., 48-51. There was hot debate over the examination issue at the 1739 Synod meeting between Log College advocates and the traditionalists. The examination requirement passed by a "Great majority." *Minutes of the Synod*, 26 May 1739, 162. Elizabeth Nybakken argues that the examination act is what ultimately caused the schism of 1741. She states: "It was to save the examination act and a learned clergy that the Old Side introduced its protest in 1741." Elizabeth I. Nybakken, "Irish Influences on Colonial Presbyterianism" in *The Journal of American History*, 68, 4 (March, 1982): 822.

sanctifying Grace in their Hearts; and yt they admit none to the sacred Trust yt are not in the Eye of Charity serious Christians."[3] Tennent and his Log College colleagues believed that "experimental divinity" was the fundamental qualification for ministerial office and not learning alone; graceless ministers could not help sinners examine their souls. New Side understanding of conversion and piety would be an ongoing point of contention among Presbyterians.[4]

The Great Awakening

When George Whitefield came to Philadelphia in 1739, he aligned himself with the work of the Tennents. Through this partnership, the New Side Presbyterians played a significant role in the Great Awakening of the 1740s. Gilbert Tennent became one of the leading revival preachers in the Middle Colonies.[5] As a revivalist, Tennent advocated "preaching of the terrors" in order to awaken secure sinners to their plight before a Holy God. The Holy Spirit used this kind of preaching to convict lost souls, and clergymen who did not preach the terrors were hindering God's work. Tennent felt this so strongly that he publicly declared that some of the Presbyterian ministers resisting the revival were themselves unconverted.[6] The Old Side ministers objected to this emotional method of preaching and bitterly resented Tennent's judgmentalism. Itinerate preaching, which sometimes meant invading the pulpits of established ministers, aggravated the strain as revivalists encouraged church members to separate themselves from unconverted ministers.[7]

In May of 1740 Gilbert Tennent and Samuel Blair exacerbated an already tense-filled meeting of Synod when they publicly read a list of complaints against their fellow ministers. Blair charged his colleagues with preaching works righteousness and ignoring the doctrine of the new birth. Tennent added that ministers were leaving sinners in deadly security and he rebuked his brethren for attacking revivals. He also accused the Synod of "Great stiffness in Opinion, generally in smaller

---

[3] *Minutes of the Synod*, 24 September 1734, 122, 123.

[4] Coalter, *Gilbert Tennent*, 38-40.

[5] Whitefield was very impressed with Gilbert Tennent's preaching and at Whitefield's request, Tennent followed him in a preaching tour through New England in 1740-41 that was very successful.

[6] Ibid., 42-46. Gilbert Tennent's infamous sermon, "The Danger of an Unconverted Ministry," was preached at Nottingham, Pennsylvania in March of 1740 and infuriated many of his fellow Presbyterian ministers.

[7] Several attempts were made to deal with the itinerate problem. The first instance of conflict came in 1737 when Gilbert Tennent preached to a congregation in Maidenhead, New Jersey without first getting the approval of Philadelphia Presbytery. A proposal to establish rules for itinerate preaching came before the Synod in 1738 and met with stiff resistance. Finally a compromise "itineracy act" was approved which provided detailed stipulations regulating this controversial issue. The revivalists were not ultimately satisfied with this solution and did not always honor the Synod's regulations. See *Minutes of the Synod*, 25 May 1738, 153, 154.

Matters where good Men may differ." The Old Side brethren in turn considered the revivalists as fanatics who had compromised Presbyterianism.[8]

Four months after the synod meeting had adjourned, several members of New Castle Presbytery presented a list of defects in George Whitefield's theology. Samuel Blair, who was present, attempted to answer the accusations but the presbytery authorized the printing of the accusations anyway. Whitefield's Calvinism was questioned on several points and he was particularly criticized for ecumenical cooperation.[9] There were several doctrinal issues that had surfaced between conservatives and the "enthusiasts." Revivalists emphasized the importance of discerning genuine conversion; traditionalists countered that it was impossible to read men's hearts infallibly. The New Side preachers also taught that genuine conversion produced assurance of one's salvation; the Old Side did not believe that all Christians attained full assurance. The theological differences, compounded by itinerate divisive preaching, was becoming more than the Old Side could endure.[10]

Old Side Protest

The censorious spirit of the revivalists had become intolerable. By 1741 the situation reached a crisis when a conservative protest, announcing that continued ecclesiastical union with the New Brunswick ministers had become impossible, was presented to Synod. The protesters declared that the New Side "have at present no right to sit and vote as Members of this Synod," because of their "unwearied, unscriptural, antipresbyterial, uncharitable divisive Practices."[11] After listing all of their grievances against the revival preachers, the protest concluded:

> For these and many other Reasons we protest, before the Eternal God, his Holy Angels, and you Rev. Brethren, and before all here present, That these Brethren have no Right to be acknowledged as Members of this Judicatory of Christ, whose Principle and Practices are so diametrically opposite to our *Doctrine* and Principles of Government

---

[8] Ibid., 69, 70, 72, 80, 81. In December of 1740, David Alexander and Alexander Craighead had charges filed against them in Donegal Presbytery for intruding into the parishes of Francis Alison and John Thompson. When Craighead was asked to answer the charges, he accused his prosecutors of whoredom, drunkenness, Sabbath breaking, and lying. Donegal Presbytery suspended the young Craighead. At their next meeting Donegal Presbytery declared that participation in revival meetings would result in barring members from the communion table.

[9] *The Querists, Or An Extract of Sundry Passages taken out of Mr. Whitefield's printed Sermons, Journal and Letters: Together With Some Scruples propos'd in proper Queries raised on each Remark. By some Church-Members of the Presbyterian Persuasion* (Philadelphia, 1740); the work is credited to David Evans of New Castle Presbytery. Several other published works under the title *Querists* further attacked both George Whitefield and Gilbert Tennent.

[10] Ibid., 68.

[11] "A Protestation presented to the Synod June 1. 1741" in *Minutes of the Synod*, 31 May 1743, 188.

and order, which ye great King of the Church hath laid down in his word.... Again, Is not ye Continuance of Union with our protesting Brethren very absurd, when it is so notorious that both their *Doctrine* and Practice are so directly *contrary to the adopting Act*, whereby both They and we have adopted the Confession of Faith, Catechisms and Directory composed by the Westminster Assembly?... In sum a continued Union, in our Judgment is most absurd and inconsistent, when it is so notorious, yt our *Doctrine* and Principles of Church Government, in many Points are not only diverse but directly opposite: For how can two walk together, except they be agreed (italics mine)?[12]

The protest demanded that the 1736 interpretation of subscription be enforced.

(1) We protest that it is the indispensable Duty of this Synod, to maintain and stand by the Principles of Doctrine, Worship and Government of the Church of Christ, as the same are summed up in the Confession of Faith, Catechisms and Directory composed by the Westminster Assembly, as being agreeable to the word of God, and which this Synod have owned, acknowledged and adopted; as may appear by our Synodical Records of the years 1729, 1729[sic], 1736, which we desire to be read publickly.

(2) We protest yt no Person, Minister or Elder should be allowed to sit and vote in this Synod, who hath not received, adopted, or subscribed the said Confessions, Catechisms and Directory, as our Presbyteries respectively do, according to our *last Explication of the adopting Act* (italics mine).[13]

---

[12] Ibid., 189, 190. Note the Old Side protester's assertion that the revivalists had forsaken the doctrines of the Confession. Contrary to those who suggest there were no substantive theological differences but merely differences over practice, the Old Side protesters claimed the New Side were propagating theological views "directly contrary to the adopting Act." The protesters objected to these alleged revivalist doctrines: "Their industriously persuading People to believe yt the Call of God whereby he calls Men to the Ministry, does not consist in their being regularly ordained and set apart to yt work according to the Institution and Rules of the word; but in some invisible Motions and workings of the Spirit ... That the Gospel preached in Truth by unconverted Ministers, can be of no saving Benefit to Souls; ... Their Preaching the Terrors of the Law in such a Manner and Dialect as has no Precedent in the word of God ... Their or some of Them preaching and maintaining, yt all true Converts are as certain of their gracious State, as a Person can be of what he knows by his outward Senses; and are able to give a Narrative of the Time and Manner of their Conversion ... and that a gracious Person can judge of anothers gracious state, otherwise than by his Profession and Life. That people are under no sacred Tye or Relation to their own Pastors lawfully called, but may leave them when they please, and ought to go where they think they get most Good."

[13] Ibid., 187. This was an explicit attempt to make the strict subscription declaration of 1736 the final arbiter. Briggs said: "The differences between the Synods are distinctly drawn...The Synod of Philadelphia insisted upon strict verbal subscription 'according to their last explication of the Adopting Act' in 1736; the Synod of New York agreed that the Westminster symbols 'be the public confession of their faith in such manner as was agreed unto by the Synod of Philadelphia in the year 1729,' and thus maintained liberal and substantial subscription." Charles Augustus Briggs, *American Presbyterianism* (New York:

A majority signed the Protest thereby proclaiming themselves to be the true synod. The meeting was thrown into confusion as the revivalist party attempted to get the floor but was rebuffed by the moderator. Having been unilaterally condemned and prohibited from defending themselves against the Protest's accusations, the New Brunswick men withdrew as the meeting adjourned.[14] The next day the excluded group organized themselves into the "Conjunct Presbyteries of New Brunswick and Londonderry." The brethren from the Presbytery of New York, who were absent from the synodical meeting of 1741, would eventually join with the revivalists to establish the Synod of New York.

The New Side concluded that they had been illegally ejected from the Synod without due process. The Protesters, contrariwise, believed they had justly purged the church of ministers deviating from the Confession and Presbyterian polity. The Old Side now denominated themselves the "The Synod of Philadelphia," the previously united body being known only as "the synod." The schism would last for 17 years, the breach being mended only after awakening fires had abated and tempers cooled with the passing of time. The mediators of the reunion would be the New York Presbyterians whose moderate approach to the Great Awakening would win the day.

Synod of New York

From the very beginning of the 1741 schism, the first pleas for reunion were initiated by the Presbytery of New York. Up until his death in 1747, Jonathan Dickinson was the leader of the mediating movement which abhorred the division. Dickinson and his New York brethren believed that the scandal of schism had to be removed from the Presbyterian Church as soon as possible. They found the unlawful excision of the New Brunswick revivalists unacceptable and were unwilling to participate in such ecclesiastical despotism. The New Yorkers pursued healing the fracture through several overtures presented to the Synod of Philadelphia for consideration. Unable to bring about the desired reconciliation, Dickinson and his

---

Charles Scribner's Sons, 1885), 271, 272. Briggs was essentially correct that there were two distinct positions, however, he goes too far in his description of the New York view as "liberal and substantial subscription." New York did not hold some vague "substance" of doctrine position, rather they took the statements of the Confession with utmost seriousness, albeit, allowing for exceptions to "non-essential" doctrines.

[14] Differences over subscription were indeed a significant ingredient in the division. Trinterud indicated that Samuel Blair's *Vindication of the Brethren*, written a few months after the 1741 schism, "specifically attacked the Act of 1736." Trinterud commented: "The Conjunct Presbyteries stood, however, where Dickinson had stood in 1722 and 1729. They were as orthodox doctrinally and as Presbyterian ecclesiastically as the Adopting Act of 1729 required. But they did not recognize the legality or validity of the acts of 1732 and 1736, and the Scotch-Irish knew it. For that matter, neither did the Dickinson group ever acknowledge these acts as binding." Leonard J. Trinterud, *The Forming of an American Tradition* (Philadelphia: The Westminster Press, 1949), 111.

associates would eventually establish a separate Synod of New York and unite themselves with the expelled New Brunswick Presbytery.

In 1742 Dickinson and nine other ministers from New York Presbytery presented a formal protest to the Synod, repudiating the actions of the previous year, "excluding the Presbytery of New-Brunswick and their Adherents from the Communion of the Synod by a Protest without giving them a previous Trial, as an illegal and unpresidented Procedure; contrary to the Rules of the Gospel and subversive of our excellent Constitution." The protesters expressed their dismay with the pamphlets circulating among the churches which criticize "the work of divine Power and Grace which has been carrying on in so wonderful a Manner in many of our Congregations." It is the duty of all ministers to encourage this "glorious work."[15] The Synod did not respond positively and was unwilling to acknowledge any wrongdoing in excluding the censorious New Side men.

The next year, the Presbytery of New York presented a compromise overture to the Synod recommending some potential solutions to the conflict. The overture pleaded for all former differences to be laid aside, for removal of the Protest of 1741, and for allowing the New Brunswick brethren to retake their seats in the Synod. In order to alleviate some of the former tensions, several moderating practical solutions to the divisive issues of itinerant preaching, education of candidates, and differences in doctrine and conduct were proposed. In the event that this "Plan of Accom[m]odation" was not acceptable to the Synod of Philadelphia, the overture requested that a separate Synod, the "Synod of New York," be established, allowing ministers to choose their Synod. After discussion, the Synod of Philadelphia voted unanimously in the negative on the overture. To this, Dickinson replied: "I look upon the New Brunswick Presbytery and those other Brethren yt adhere to them, and are therefore shut out of the Synod on yt Account, to be truly members of this Synod as myself or any others whatsoever, and have a just Claim to sit and act with us. I cannot therefore at present see my way clear to sit and act as tho' we were the Synod of Philada. While the New Brunswick Presbytery and other Members with them are kept out of the Synod in the Manner they now are."[16]

The Synod of Philadelphia forwarded a proposal of "Agreement and Union" to the conjunct meeting of the New Brunswick and New Castle Presbyteries, outlining seven grievances that must be corrected if these brethren are to take their seats again in the Synod. William Tennent, Jr., answering for the Conjunct presbyteries, replied to the Synod that there was no path for proceeding "until their illegal Protest be withdrawn, yt so they and we may both stand upon an equal foot in the regular Trial of the Difference between us. That their Paper contains sundry Misrepresentations

---

[15] "A Protest," May 29, 1742 in *Minutes of the Synod*, 177,178.
[16] "Overture from the Presbytery of New York," May 15, 1743 in *Minutes of the Synod*, 30 May 1743, 181-183.

and unreasonable Demands; and yt we have several Charges against them to be satisfied in before we could come into a settled Union with them."[17]

In 1745, the Synod of Philadelphia presented their plan of accommodation to New York Presbytery which was promptly rejected. The New York men requested that the Synod concur in their request to establish a second Synod not to act in opposition but to act in concert and "maintain Love and brotherly Kindness with each other." Although the Synod judged that there is "no just Ground to withdraw from us," nevertheless, given the friendly manner of the request, they agreed "to maintain charitable and Christian affections toward them."[18] A separate Synod of New York was thus organized in September of 1745 with Dickinson as the moderator. The new Synod contained the presbyteries of New York, New Brunswick and New Castle.

The first act of the New York Synod was the adoption of certain articles which would serve as "the Plan & Foundation of their Synodical Union." The first article dealt with the Westminster Standards: "They agree that the Westminster Confession of Faith, with the larger & shorter Catechisms be the publick Confession of their Faith in such Manner as was agreed unto by the Synod of Philadelphia in the Year 1729 & to be Inserted in the latter End of this Book.[19] And they declare their Approbation of the Directory of the Assembly of Divines at Westminster as the general Plan of Worship & Discipline." The language and spirit of 1729 is self evident in the explicit endorsement of the original Adopting Act. The Synod of New York clearly interpreted confessional subscription in the light of the 1729 compromise rather than the 1736 interpretation given by the Synod.[20]

The new Synod adopted other agreements to avert falling into the same divisive situations that had plagued the old Synod. Charges against a minister must follow procedures "according to the Rules of the Gospel & the known Methods of their Discipline." If an insurmountable difference of conscience surfaces in the Synod, a dissenter from Synod actions "promises peaceably to withdraw from the Body, without endeavoring to raise any Dispute or Contention upon the debated Point or any unjust Alienation of Affection from them." And the Synod promised to maintain a correspondence with the Synod of Philadelphia "...in Order to avoid all divisive Methods among their Ministers and Congregations & to strengthen the Discipline of Christ in the Churches in these Parts...."[21]

---

[17] Ibid., 183-185.

[18] *Minutes of the Synod of Philadelphia*, 25 May 1745, 204-207.

[19] The Appendix to the *Minutes of the Synod of New York* records the 1729 morning minute only as "the adopting Act." See supra chp. 1, n. 51, 61.

[20] *Minutes of the Synod of New York* (1745-1758), 263. Nichols observed that New York Synod's 1745 adoption of the Westminster Standards "meant that the subscribers were not bound to verbal assent." Robert Hasting Nichols, *Presbyterians in New York State* (Philadelphia: The Westminster Press, 1963), 44.

[21] *Minutes of the Synod of New York*, 19 September 1745, 263, 264.

"That Paragraph About Essentials"

By 1749 Dickinson was dead and a more temperate Gilbert Tennent began to take over as the New Side mediator. That year a new proposal on union was initiated by the Synod of New York. Having observed "a Spirit of Moderation increasing between many of the Members of both Synods," the New York Synod boldly approached Philadelphia with peaceable terms to resolve the impasse. New York recommended that the two synods unite on consent to the Confession "according to the Plan formerly agreed to by the Synod of Philadelphia in ye Year 1729."[22] The proposed articles further stipulated that all should desist publicly accusing brothers of immorality or errors in doctrine unless these charges are formally presented according to the rules of Discipline. To avoid future division, the proposal also made provisions for a brother peaceably to withdraw if his conscience dictated such action.

3. That every Member promise, that after any Question has been determined by the Major Vote, he will actively concur or passively submit to the Judgment of the Body: But if his Conscience permit him to do neither of these that then he shall be obliged peaceably to withdraw from our Synodical Communion without any Attempt to make a Schism or Division among us: Yet this is not intended to extend to any Cases but those which the Synod Judges *essential* in Matters of Doctrine or Discipline (italics mine).[23]

In October of 1749, a Commission of both Synods met at Trenton to discuss the plan for union. The New York representatives demanded that the 1741 Protest, which had excluded the New Brunswick men, be declared null and void. The debate on this point was heated and no prospect of resolution emerged, thereupon, the two groups agreed that more detailed proposals for accommodation and interchange be prepared by each Synod. It was further agreed that the three central issues each side must address were: the Protest, Presbytery boundaries and "That Paragraph about Essentials."[24] The delegates from the Synod of New York had made certain concessions including: approving synodical examinations for candidates or requiring a college diploma or certificate (only Gilbert Tennent objected), agreeing

---

[22] *Minutes of Synod of Philadelphia*, 4 September 1751, 229. The original proposal included in the 1749 New York Synod Minutes reads: "2. That every Member assent unto & Adopt the Confession of Faith & Directory according to the Plan formerly agreed to by the Synod of Philada. In the Years_____." *Minutes of Synod of New York*, 18 May 1749, 270. The year is missing in the original New York minutes while the Philadelphia record of the document, which is included in the 1751 Philadelphia minutes, has the date - "1729." *Minutes of the Synod of Philadelphia*, 4 September 1751, 229. There seems no reason to doubt that the Philadelphia version is a genuine reproduction of the original. By emphasizing 1729, the Synod of New York is specifically rejecting the revisionist interpretation of 1736.

[23] *Minutes of Synod of New York*, 18 May 1749, 270. The Philadelphia Synod minutes are identical except that they add "Worship" to doctrine and discipline at the end of the sentence. *Minutes of Synod of Philadelphia*, 4 September 1751, 229.

[24] *Minutes of the Synod of New York*, 16 May 1750, 271, 272.

that there should be no intrusions into churches or presbyteries without permission, and acknowledging that good men may have different opinions and should therefore have the liberty "to lay their Grievances before ye Synod in a peaceable Manner."[25]

A committee appointed to draft a more extended proposal for union, presented to the 1750 Synod of New York a plan with eight articles which was adopted. The first two articles reiterated the two key propositions of the previous year, i.e., reaffirming the 1729 Adopting Act[26] and insisting that the paragraph about essentials be accepted. Other articles dealt with how to handle accusations against ministers, college requirements for ministerial candidates ("except in Cases extraordinary"), itinerant preaching, presbytery boundaries and revoking the 1741 Protest. Article eight addressed the Awakening: "Forasmuch as this Synod doth believe (as they have before declared) that a glorious Work of God's Spirit was carried on in the late religious Appearances; (tho we doubt not but there were several Follies & Extravagancies of People, & Artifices of Satan intermixed therewith). It would be pleasing & desirable to us, & what we hope for, that Both Synods may come so far to agree in their Sentiments about it, as to give their Joynt Testimony thereto."[27]

The Synod of Philadelphia responded to the New York proposal pointing out where there were agreements and where differences still existed. On the question of understanding the Adopting Act, the synod agreed "yt Every Member give his assent to ye Westmstr. Confession of faith & Directory According to ye Plan Agreed on in our Synod."[28] The Philadelphia Synod, however, added: "... no Acts be made but Concerning Matters yt appear to ye Body plain duty or Concerning opinion yt. We believe relate to ye Great truths Of Religion & that all publick & fundamental aggreements of this Synod Stand Safe." The paragraph on essentials

---

[25] *Minutes of the Synod of Philadelphia*, 1751, 229.

[26] Article One: "That every Member assent unto and receive the Westminster Confession of Faith and Catechisms as the Confession of his Faith according to the Plan formerly mentioned & proposed [1749 proposal which specifically mentions 1729] and also agree to the Directory as the general Plan of Worship and Discipline." *Minutes of Synod of New York*, 28 September 1750, 274.

[27] Ibid., 274, 275.

[28] It is not absolutely clear whether this "plan agreed on in our synod" was an acknowledgment of the original 1729 compromise or a veiled reference to the 1736 interpretation of the Adopting Act. The Synod of New York seems to have received this reply as agreement with their specific proposal concerning 1729. The Synod of Philadelphia put this statement in the "areas of agreement" category. Further negotiations make no further reference to 1729, therefore, it seems fair to assume the New York position was accepted. The focus of debate became the "paragraph about essentials" rather than 1729 vs. 1736. As Hodge pointed out the essentials paragraph in these negotiations had to do with exclusion from ministerial communion rather than inclusion. Charles Hodge, *Constitutional History of the Presbyterian Church of America*, Part II (Philadelphia: Presbyterian Board of Publications, 1851), 273. For New York, it was a matter of principle (based on the agreement of 1729) that no man could be put out of the Presbyterian ministry unless his exceptions to the Confession were over "essential" doctrines.

was rejected with this counter-proposal to New York on how dissent should be handled:

> yt Every Member Engage yt after any Question has been determind by a major vote, he will Actively Concur or passively Submit to ye Judgment of ye Body or if his Conscience permit him to Comply wt neither of these, he Shall be Oblidged to withdraw peaceably, allways reserving him a Liberty to Sue for a review & to Lay his Grievances Before ye Body in a Christian Manner.[29]

New York answered that they disagree with the Philadelphia position. The essentials paragraph must remain. New York countered in point one of the reply: "Tho the Synod should make no Acts but concerning Matters of plain Duty or Opinions relating to the great Truths of Religion, Yet as every thing that appears plain Duty & Truth unto the Body, may appear at the same Time not to be *essential*; so we Judge that no Member or Members should be obliged to withdraw from our Communion upon his or their not being able Actively to concur or passively Submit unless the Matter be judged *essential in Doctrine or Discipline* (italics mine)."[30]

The "paragraph about essentials" was a sensitive issue to the Old Side. The Synod of Philadelphia did not believe such an idea was necessary and they answered back to the New York Synod: "...we Apprehend that such an Alteration as Stated by you, has a bad Aspect & opens a Door for an unjustifiable Latitude both in Principles & practices." On the other hand, the Philadelphia Synod invoked the "essentials" paragraph back against the New York Synod when it requested a joint statement, declaring "the late religious Appearances" to be a "glorious Work of God's Spirit." This demand is unfair. Philadelphia protested:

> How is this Consistent with your former professed Sentiments that no Difference in Judgment in Cases of plain Sin & Duty & Opinions relating to the Great Truths of Religion is a sufficient reason why the differing Member should be oblidg'd to withdraw, unless the Sd: Plain Duty or truth be Judged by the body Essential, in Doctrine or Discipline & We think it Strange you Would insist on this or even Mention it as a Proposal for union Seeing your Delegates before us Conceded that both great & good men had differed from them on that Head....[31]

The 1753 meeting of the Synod of New York replied back to Philadelphia's concerns in a letter adopted by the synod. New York asserted that the essentials paragraph was a non-negotiable point of principle for them.

---

[29] *Minutes of the Synod of Philadelphia*, 6 September 1751, 230, 231.

[30] *Minutes of the Synod of New York*, 27 September 1751, 278.

[31] *Minutes of the Synod of Philadelphia*, 29 May 1752, 235. There was blatant inconsistency in the Philadelphia invocation of the essentials paragraph to complain against what they considered an unjust New York demand for concurrent testimony on the Awakening and then to turn around and condemn the essentials paragraph as latitudinarian. Apparently, the Synod of Philadelphia wanted to reserve to itself the right to dissent but was unwilling to offer that same privilege to the Synod of New York.

... there is no Inconsistency between our present Proposal, & our declared Sentiments, that Difference in Judgment Should not oblige a dissenting Member to withdraw from our Communion, unless the Matter were Judged by the Body, to be essential in Doctrine or Discipline. And this we must own is an important Article with us, which we cannot any way dispense with. And it appears to us to be Strictly Christian & Scriptural, as well as presbyterian. Other wise we must make every thing, that appears plain Duty to us, a *Term of Communion*; which we apprehend the Scripture prohibits. And it appears plain to us, that there may be many Opinions relating to the great Truths of Religion, that are not great themselves, nor of Sufficient Importance to be made *Terms of Communion*. Nor can these Sentiments 'open a Door to an unjustifiable Latitude in Principles & Practice,' any more than the apostolick Prohibition of receiving those that are week[sic] to doubtful Disputations. What is plain sin & plain Duty in ones Account, is not so in another's. And the Synod has still in their Power to Judge what is essential & what is not.[32] In order to prevent an unjustifiable Latitude we must not make *Terms of Communion*, which Christ has not made,[33] & we are convinced, that he hath not made every truth & every Duty a Term (italics mine).[34]

Distinguishing essential and non-essential doctrines was a commonplace in the Synod of New York and her presbyteries. One gets a glimpse of this practice from the pen of Samuel Davies in 1754. Davies and Gilbert Tennent had been commissioned by the Synod of New York for a journey to Britain in order to solicit funds for the College of New Jersey. In his travels throughout England and Scotland, Davies was turned off by the overly strict Calvinism he observed among some ministers. He records in his diary: "In the evening visited Mr. Winter, a Congregational minister; but his dry orthodoxy, and severe reflections upon those that deviated from rigid Calvinism, were disagreeable to me."[35] When asked about how American Presbyterians practiced confessional subscription, Davies offered

---

[32] This was a power granted to the presbyteries and synod by the Adopting Act of 1729. See *Minutes of the Synod*, 19 September 1729, 104.

[33] It was not implied here that Presbyterian ministers should be expected to affirm the essential doctrines of Christianity only. In fact, the Synod of New York explicitly stated that it expected ministerial candidates to be Calvinists. Poor students at the College of New Jersey, in order to qualify for the donated funds to assist their education, must "be of promising Genius's *Calvenistic Principles* & in the Judgment of Charity, experimentally acquainted with a Work of Saving Grace & to have a distinguished Zeal for the Glory of God & Salvation of Men (italics mine)." *Minutes of the Synod of New York*, 3 October 1755, 298. A similar expression is recorded in the minutes of 1757 which describes "Support of Such pious Youths as are of Calvenistic Principles & are unable to Support themselves at the College of New Jersey." *Minutes of the Synod of New York*, 18 May 1757, 314.

[34] *Minutes of the Synod of New York*, 5 October 1753, 287. For the New York men, "terms of communion" for ministers in the Presbyterian Church may only include "essential and necessary" doctrines. Allowing for freedom on non-essentials in faith and practice was a foundational principle for the Synod and it refused to alter that position. This liberty was agreed upon in the compromise of 1729.

[35] Samuel Davies' dairy quoted in William Henry Foote, *Sketches of Virginia*, First Series (1850; reprint, Richmond: John Knox Press, 1966), 246.

this explanation: "I replied that we allowed the candidate to mention his objections against any article in the Confession, and the judicature judge whether the articles objected against were essential to Christianity; and if they judged they were not, they would admit the candidate, notwithstanding his objections."[36]

In May of 1755, the Synod of Philadelphia's next communication back to the Synod of New York did not specifically address the essentials paragraph.[37] The New York men responded in disappointment that the Philadelphia Synod had not "descended to particulars" which would have enabled them to discern if some satisfaction could be expected in meeting their demands for a broader understanding of ministerial communion (i.e., paragraph concerning essentials).[38] New York reminded Philadelphia that their understanding of appropriate terms of ministerial communion had been repeated in each of the reunion proposals for 1749, 1750 and 1751. And these principles "we esteem always Scriptural & rational Terms." According to Christ's command, it was a necessary duty to forgive one another's injuries and offenses, notwithstanding, New York's insistence "on certain Preliminaries" was "necessary to preserve & promote the publick Interests of Religion amongst us...." Since the Protestation of 1741 appeared to be the "principal Obstruction to the Union of both Synods," New York was willing to retract the demand that the protest be declared null and void. If Philadelphia is willing to acknowledge that the protest was not a synodical act but merely the action of certain members of the synod, New York will agree to proceed with reunion discussions on the basis of the terms it has proposed in previous years – 1749, 1750, 1751.[39]

Philadelphia satisfied the New York Synod that the protest of 1741 was never adopted as a term of ministerial communion. The letter from the Synod of Philadelphia stated: "we declare, & do assure you, that we neither adopted nor do adopt sd. Protestation, as a Term of ministerial Communion."[40] It should be recalled that it was article two of the original Protest of 1741 that had issued the demand for full subscription (according to the 1736 interpretation) to every doctrine of the Confession without distinguishing essential from non-essential doctrines. The 1741 Protest document had stated:

2. We protest yt no Person, Minister or Elder should be allowed to sit and vote in this Synod, who hath not received, adopted, or subscribed the said Confessions, Catechisms and Directory, as our Presbyteries respectively do, *according to our last Explication of the adopting Act*; or who either accused or convicted, or may be convicted before this

---

[36] Ibid., 257. Trinterud observed that these passages from Davies's diary "provide an excellent unposed picture of a typical New Side Presbyterian." *Forming of an American Tradition*, 127

[37] See *Minutes of the Synod of Philadelphia*, 31 May 1755, 246.

[38] Richard Webster, *A History of the Presbyterian Church in America From its Origin Until the Year 1760 with Biographical Sketches of its Early Ministers* (Philadelphia: Joseph M. Wilson, 1857), 236.

[39] *Minutes of Synod of New York*, 7 October 1755, 302 - 304.

[40] *Minutes of Synod of Philadelphia*, 28 May 1756, 252.

Synod, or any of our Presbyteries, of holding or maintaining any Doctrine, or who act and persist in any Practice contrary to any of these Doctrines or Rules contained in said Directory (italics mine).[41]

This Philadelphia pledge that the protest was never adopted as a term of ministerial communion seems to have been read by New York as a disavowal of the 1736 revision. The "paragraph about essentials," which was so critical from the New York perspective, is not mentioned again after this admission by Philadelphia that "the protest" was not understood by them as a term of ministerial communion. New York was apparently satisfied that adherence to the original 1729 Adopting Act was now safeguarded.[42] The letter from the Synod of Philadelphia, after clarifying its position on the 1741 protest document, added this statement: "We only Adopt & design to adhere to our Standards, as we formerly agreed when united, in one Body. We adopt no other."[43] The former agreement would seemingly point to the 1729 Adopting Act since there had not been agreement on the revision of 1736.

The letter from Philadelphia announced opposition to New York's suggestion of dialogue between the protesters and those protested against for "it may inflame Men's Spirits that are now cool, & revive the ungrateful Remembrance of many Things, that are better buried in Oblivion." This was fifteen years ago and all these things need to be "for ever buried." The letter concluded with a proposal for committees of both synods to meet and "adjust Matters previous to an Union." Philadelphia's correspondence ignored the specific issues raised by New York, but, a strong reunion spirit now motivated both groups to proceed anyway. The Philadelphia letter expressed the urgency: "If ever Union & Peace was necessary, it is so now in our present melancholly Circumstances."[44]

---

[41] "Letter from Synod of Philadelphia to the Synod of New York," Appendix, *Minutes of the Synod of New York*, 1756, 331, 332.

[42] Having the Synod of Philadelphia officially declare that the protest of 1741 was not a "term of ministerial communion" was a major concession because it was that protest that had highlighted the interpretation of 1736. One explanation for New York's willingness to back off the "paragraph about essentials" debate could be that Philadelphia's disowning of the 1741 protest put them back on the 1729 basis which included the all important essential / non-essential distinctions for ministerial communion.

[43] *Minutes of Synod of Philadelphia*, 28 May 1756, 252. It would appear from this statement that Philadelphia was endorsing the Synod of New York's position on the 1729 Adopting Act. The statement spoke of a "formerly agreed" position which would necessarily exclude the controversial explication of 1736. The Synod of Philadelphia added, "We adopt no other," which would seem to indicate the exclusion of the 1736 interpretation. On the other hand, if the "formerly agreed" position referred to the 1736 statement (in the mind of Philadelphia), then it certainly was not a common agreement but in fact one of the grounds of debate. It may be purposefully vague, leaving itself open to either interpretation. Whichever was the case, New York was sufficiently appeased with this statement from Philadelphia and reunion discussions moved forward.

[44] An Appendix, *Minutes of the Synod of New York*, 1756, 331, 332.

The 1756 Synod of New York agreed to the mutual conference recommended by Philadelphia, however, New York again protested that "... the Synod of Philada. have not given a Satisfactory Answer to the Particulars contained in Our Letter, which were judged necessary to be settled previous to an Union...."[45] In that same meeting of Synod, the New Yorkers reiterated their commitment to the original Adopting Act of 1729 during a controversy with a Presbyterian congregation in New York. The congregation had written an "arrogant, presumptuous" letter to the Synod of New York and one of the questions concerned requiring the Westminster Confession as a "Test of Orthodoxy." The Synod answered that "all who are licensed to preach the Gospel; or become Members of any Presbytery in our Bounds, Shall receive the Same, as the Confession of their Faith, according to our constituting Act, which we see no Reason to repeal."[46] The 1745 "constituting Act" of the new Synod of New York had specifically cited the 1729 Adopting Act (morning session) in the minutes and that is reaffirmed here. This is entirely consistent with New York's unrelenting insistence that reaffirming the 1729 principles of subscription must be foundational to the reunion platform.

Reunion in 1758

Representatives of the two synods met at Trenton in 1757 to begin drawing up a formal Plan of Union. There was cordial agreement on many matters; each side declared its body ready to proceed with union. Another meeting was set for Philadelphia in 1758 where both synods would convene at the same time. After all the "Alterations and Amendments" had been presented by commissions from both sides, the Plan was finally approved by each synod. The two synods met together on May 29, 1758 and formal union was consummated. Gilbert Tennent was selected as the moderator of the new "Synod of New York and Philadelphia."

The Plan of Union followed the pattern of the earlier proposals from the Synod of New York with the key elements of the plan reflecting New Side concerns about piety, the revival and subscription. The reunited Presbyterian Church designated itself the "Synod of New York and Philadelphia," the order of the names reflecting New Side predominance. The Synod of New York was now three times the size of the Old Side Synod of Philadelphia, with 73 of the 96 ministers being New Side men. The 1758 plan did exhibit some compromise with Old Side perspectives, nonetheless, all the New York principles remained intact. As one historian has

---

[45] *Minutes of the Synod of New York*, 2 October 1756, 311. The phrase "not given a Satisfactory Answer to the Particulars" may still have included the "paragraph about essentials," but this is not certain.

[46] *Minutes of the Synod of New York*, 1 October 1756, 311. The "constituting act" may refer back to the 1729 Adopting Act, however, since the context of the question was the specific requirements of the Synod of New York, the "constituting act" most likely referred to New York's particular constitution of 1745.

noted, "the reunited colonial church bore in large part the character thus derived from the Synod of New York."[47]

The irenic spirit of accommodation was evident in a sermon by the Old Side's Francis Alison which was delivered before both groups. Alison proclaimed:

> We must maintain *union in essentials, forbearance is lesser matters, and charity in all things....* In promoting and preserving peace and unity among Christians, we are carefully to follow the commands and example of Christ and his apostles; and not the expedients of our own devising...We should remember, that no two men are all agreed in all points; and that where they are agreed, they generally differ in their ways of explaining and defending them.... In a church like ours in America, collected from different churches of Europe, who have followed different modes and ways of obeying the 'great and general command of the gospel,' there is a peculiar call for charity and forbearance (italics mine).[48]

Article one of the Plan of Union affirmed the doctrinal standards with these words:

> Both Synods having always approv'd and receiv'd the Westminster Confession of Faith, Larger and Shorter Catechisms, as an orthodox & *excellent System of Christian Doctrine*, founded on the word of God; w[e] do Still receive the Same, as the Confession of our Faith ... Strickly enjoining it on all our members, and Probationers for the Ministry, that they preach & teach according to the Form of Sound Words in Said Confession & Catechisms, and av[oid] and oppose all Errors contrary thereto (italics mine).[49]

Here is a thorough commitment to the Westminster Standards that the New Side could endorse, notwithstanding, their firm commitment to the essential/non-essential distinctions in the Adopting Act. Though no specific reference is made to 1729, the New Side understanding of subscription was the implicit position behind the 1758 compromise. The phrase "excellent system of Christian Doctrine" clearly points back to the language of the 1729 (morning session) which spoke of the Confession "as being in all the essential and necessary Articles, good Forms of sound words, and systems of Christian Doctrine."[50]

---

[47] Robert Hastings Nichols, ed. *Presbyterianism in New York State* (Philadelphia: Westminster Press, 1963), 60,61.

[48] Trinterud, *Forming of an American Tradition*, 148.

[49] *Minutes of the Synod of New York and Philadelphia*, 29 May 1758, 340.

[50] *Minutes of the Synod*, 19 September 1729, 103. Trinterud observed: "No reference was made to the controversial 'essential-non-essential' phrases of the 1729 Adopting Act. Neither was any repetition made of the unqualified demands of the Act of 1736. The section on the adoption of the Westminster symbols was definitely a compromise statement. Alison's sermon revealed very well the mood of the majority of the Old Side. They had known since the schism of 1741 that the abandonment of the Act of 1736 would be a part of the price of reunion.... The 'systematic' form of subscription embodied in the Act of 1729 was, therefore, restored in spite of avoidance of all reference to the past controversies." *The Forming of an American Tradition*, 148,149. While technically Trinterud was correct that the exact

The "paragraph about essentials" was incorporated into the Plan of Union albeit in a slightly modified form. Article two stated: "That when any Matter is determined by a Major Vote, every Mem[ber] Shall either actively concur with, or passively Submit to Such Deter[min]ation; or, if his Conscience permit him to do neither, he Shall, [after] Sufficient Liberty modestly to reason and remonstrate, peaceab[ly with]draw from our Communion, without attempting to make any Sc[hism:] provided always, that this Shall be understood to extend only to [Such] Determinations, as the Body Shall Judge *indispensable in Doct[rine]* or Presbyterian Gover[n]ment"[51] (italics mine). The word "essential" is dropped and the word "indispensable" is substituted, but the principle is unchanged. The entire paragraph is almost verbatim what the Synod of New York had proposed as a term of reunion as far back as 1749.

Articles three through eight address respectively: (III.) the right to protest and the right to a fair trial; (IV.) denial of the 1741 protest as a synodical act; (V.) appropriate restraint in accusations against brethren and brotherly courtesy when preaching in another's pulpit; (VI.) ordination requires sufficient learning, competent satisfaction as to "experimental Acquaintance with [Re]ligion," and acceptance of the Westminster Standards and Presbyterian plan of government; (VII.) presbytery and congregational alignments shall continue unless mutual edification requires otherwise; (VIII.) a balanced appraisal of the "late religious Appearances" as both the "gracious Work of God" and pointing out where there had been "dangerous Delusion" associated with the Awakening.[52]

The Plan of Union concluded with an exhortation to orthopraxis as well as orthodoxy, a primary concern of the New Side. The reunited Synod proclaimed: "... we unanimously declar[e] [our] Serious and fixed Resolution, by divine Aid, to take

---

phraseology about "essentials-non-essentials" from 1729 is not incorporated into the reunion articles, the substance of that principle was included in article two which made a distinction between doctrines that were "indispensable" and those that were not.

[51] *Minutes of Synod of New York and Philadelphia*, 29 May 1758, 341. Compare *Minutes of the Synod of New York*, 18 May 1749, 270. Charles A. Briggs underscores the importance of the phrase "indispensable in doctrine." Briggs observed: "We see in the phrase 'indispensable in doctrine and Presbyterian government' only a synonym of the 'essential and necessary articles,' and 'agreeable in substance to the Word of God' of the Adopting Act of 1729.... The system of Christian doctrine contained in the Westminster Standards was adopted, and this embraced only that which was 'indispensable in doctrine or Presbyterian government,' that which was 'essential and necessary' to the Westminster system." *American Presbyterianism*, 319, 320.

[52] *Minutes of Synod of New York and Philadelphia*, 29 May 1758, 341-343. The eighth article, which was by far the longest section, included an extended exposition on "the Nature of a Work of Grace." The joint declaration carefully defined a Calvinistic understanding of grace that was "effected only by the powerful Operations of the Divine Spirit." The statement also emphasized the fruit of true conversion, "when they hate and bewail their Sins of Heart and Life; delight in the Laws of God, without Exception; reverently and diligently attend his Ordinances; become humble & Self-deny'd; and make it the Business of their Lives to please & glorify God, and do Good to their fellow Men."

heed to ourselves, that our hearts be upright, our Discourse edifying, and our Lives exemplary for Purity and Godliness – to take heed to our Doctrine, that it be not only orthodox, but evangelical & Spiritual, tending to awaken the Secure to a Suitable concern for their Salvation, and to instruct and encourage Sincere Christians." The synod further pronounced its opposition to a "Contentious Disposition" and its dedication to overlook former differences. "The Synod Agree, that all Differ[en]ces and Disputes are laid aside and buried; and that no future Enquiry, or Vote Shall be proposed in this Synod concerning these things; but if any Member Seek a Synodical Enquiry, or Declaration about any of the Matters of our past Differences, it Shall be deem'd a censurable Breach of this Agreement; and be refus'd and he be rebuk'd accordingly."[53] The breach was healed and all agreed to forgive and forget past grievances. The united body had reaffirmed its attachment to the original interpretation of 1729 and this perspective would continue to inform the majority practice of the Presbyterian Church for the remainder of the eighteenth century.

Samuel Davies officiating at the ordination service of two men just six weeks after reunion, asked the subscription question in this manner: "Do you receive the Westminster Confession of Faith as the Confession of *your faith*; that is, do you believe it contains an excellent summary of the pure doctrines of Christianity as taught in the Scriptures?... And do you propose to explain the Scriptures according to the *substance* of it?"[54] Davies speaks of the "substance" of the Confession, i.e., the central or "essential" doctrines which make up the doctrinal system of Westminster. This is consistent with Davies' explanation of American subscription to the British in 1754 wherein he described how the ministerial candidate is allowed "to mention his objections to any articles in the Confession" and he would then be admitted to the presbytery, notwithstanding these objections, as long as the presbytery did not judge them "essential" to Christianity.[55] Davies, who had been moderator of the Synod of New York in 1758, envisioned no change whatsoever in his understanding of the practice of confessional subscription.

The Subscription Formula

Reunion did not produce perfect clarity on the subscription issue. A misunderstanding of the Adopting Act surfaced again in the heresy trial of Samuel Harker who would eventually be deposed from office in 1763. Harker protested his expulsion and appealed to 1729 in order to justify his own position. John Blair, writing to defend the action of the Synod, reiterated the original intent of adopting the theological system of Westminster:

---

[53] Ibid., 343. The commitment to avoid all public strife over former grounds of difference would certainly include the opposing interpretations of the Adopting Act. This declaration helps explain the dissipation of subscription controversy for the remainder of the eighteenth century. Both parties had agreed not to raise the contentious issue in synod meetings.

[54] Davies quoted in Trinterud, *Forming of an American Tradition*, 149.

[55] See Davies *supra* n.35, 36.

He (Mr. Harker) would have it believed to be a violation of an Act of Synod, A.D. 1729, which he calls *one of the great Articles of their Union* and which he thought *sufficiently secured the right of private judgement*, wherein it is provided that *a minister or candidate shall be admitted notwithstanding scruples respecting article or articles the Synod or Presbytery shall judge* not essential or necessary in DOCTRINE, WORSHIP,` AND GOVERNMENT. But in order to improve this to his purpose, he takes the words *essential or necessary* in a sense in which it is plain from the Act itself the Synod never intended they should be taken. He would have them to signify what is essential to 'Communion with Jesus Christ,' or the Being of Grace in the heart, and accordingly supposes that no error can be essential which is not of such malignity as to exclude the advocate or maintainer of it from communion with Jesus Christ. But the Synod say essential in *Doctrine, Worship and Government* – i.e., essential to the system of doctrine contained in our *Westminster Confession of Faith* considered as a system, and to the mode of worship and plan of government contained in our Directory.... That, therefore, is an essential error in the Synod's sense, which is of such malignity as to subvert or greatly injure the system of doctrine and mode of worship and government contained in the Westminster Confession of Faith and Directory.[56]

Opposition to Harker was unanimous. Formerly Old Side as well as New Side men agreed that Harker's view was an unacceptable interpretation of the Adopting Act. Harker's appeal to the morning minute of 1729, though he misunderstood it, is evidence of the prevailing use of the Adopting Act (morning minute) among Presbyterians in the 1760s. Harker is not criticized by Blair for appealing to the "essentials" principle of the Adopting Act, rather he is condemned for distorting its original intent. While Blair and his Old Side colleagues may have had different opinions about the role of the morning minute, they were agreed that Harker's perspective was a serious distortion of the Presbyterian commitment to Westminster Calvinism.

Twenty years later, Presbyterians encountered the subscription issue again in their ecclesiastical union discussions with the Low Dutch Reformed Synod of New York and New Jersey and the Associate Reformed Synod in 1785. The Presbyterian committee members described their doctrinal commitment in this manner:

The Synod of New York & Philadelphia adopt, according to the known & established meaning of the Terms, the Westminster confession of Faith as the confession of their faith; save that every candidate for the gospel Ministry is permitted to except against so much of the twenty third Chapter as give authority to the Civil Magistrate in matters of Religion. The Presbyterian Church in America considers the Church of Christ as a spiritual Society intirely distinct from the Civil Government; & having a right to

---

[56] John Blair, *The Synod of New York and Philadelphia Vindicated* (Philadelphia, 1765), 10,11 quoted in Briggs, *American Presbyterianism*, 321,322. Blair denied that "essentials" referred to fundamentals of the gospel only which was Harker's position. Blair, answering for the synod, declared that "essentials" was referring to the fundamentals of the system of doctrine contained in the Westminster Standards, i.e., essentials of Calvinism. Charles Hodge acknowledged that John Blair's equating of "essentials" with the "system of doctrine" was a valid interpretation of 1729. *Constitutional History*, I, 170; II, 273. See *infra* chp. 8.

regulate their own ecclesiastical policy independently on [of] the Interposition of the Magistrate.[57]

The Synod's statement was obviously a reference back to the afternoon minute of 1729 and rehearses those places in the Confession where the reunited Synod took unanimous exceptions. At the time of this statement, American Presbyterians were in the middle of their own internal discussions about permanently amending the Westminster Standards to exclude these objectionable portions which were incongruent with church/state separation in America.[58]

Presbyterians still used the "essentials" language during this period. The early draft of the new Presbyterian Plan of Government in 1786 had stated: "Teachers [, this Church believes, should] be sound in the faith, and hold the essential doctrines of the gospel; they also believe that there are truths of less moment and forms as to practice or omission of which men of the best characters and principles may differ, and in all these they think it the duty ... [to exercise] forbearance, and neither to judge rashly nor refuse such communion as may shew that they look upon all such as brethren who in the judgment of charity love our Lord Jesus Christ in sincereity, and that they believe in the unity of the catholic church." The final draft of 1788 modified portions of this paragraph stating that teachers should be "sound in the faith," but, excluded the phrase about holding the "essentials of the gospel."[59] Perhaps the Synod had become more conservative; nevertheless, there were still Presbyterians who preferred to use the "essentials" terminology that had been in common use in the Presbyterian Church since 1729.

The great venture to reorganize the American Presbyterian Church into a delegated General Assembly with a formal constitution began in 1785. After

---

[57] *Minutes of the Synod of New York and Philadelphia*, 19 May 1786, 604. The subscription statement reported to the union convention mentions the universal scruple to which the Synod had taken a constitutional exception as far back as 1729. The committee was speaking for the Synod as a whole and reiterated its common objection to portions of chapter 23. (The original minute of 1729 had objected to sections in both chapters 20 and 23.) There was silence on the essentials principle of the Adopting Act; perhaps there were strategic reasons for not interjecting this into negotiations with other ecclesiastical bodies.

[58] The citation of the 1729 afternoon minute only may be evidence of continued strife over subscription. The statement could be interpreted as the strict subscription position. When the report was read to the 1786 Synod of New York and Philadelphia it was "approved & adopted." This was almost 30 years after the reunion and perhaps the number of conservatives had increased as Trinterud argued. *Forming of an American Tradition*, 279-306. Of course, in inter-church discussions, the Synod could only be expected to list their "official" scruples (i.e., church/state issues) and would not attempt to interpret the "essential and necessary" doctrines. Even if one understood this as strict subscription, conceivably the broader Presbyterians may not have viewed this as a critical issue to debate in the Synod meeting, since their long-standing perspective on subscription (1729 morning minute) was secure in their own presbyteries.

[59] *Draught of the Plan of Government*, 1786 quoted in Trinterud, *Forming of an American Tradition*, 297.

prolonged debate and amendment to draft proposals brought before the Synod, Presbyterians finally adopted a *Plan of Government and Discipline*, a revised *Westminster Directory for Public Worship* and an amended *Westminster Confession of Faith* in 1788. The altered paragraphs in the Confession included: chapter 20 (fourth paragraph), chapter 23 (third paragraph) and chapter 31(first paragraph) – each amendment underscoring the freedom of the church from state interference.

The changes to the Confession, and a slight amendment of the Larger Catechism (Q. 109), were all discussed in detail and finally approved as part of the Constitution of the Church. Any future alterations or amendments would require that two-thirds of the presbyteries and the General Assembly approve such changes.[60] The inherent fallibility of the Form of Government and Discipline and the Confession was imbedded in the constitutional recognition that, in contrast to Holy Scripture, these documents may be altered. The Introduction to the Plan of Government declared: "God alone is Lord of the conscience, and hath left it free from the doctrines and commandments of men; which are in anything contrary to his word, or beside it in matters of faith or worship.... The Bible is the only rule that is infallible in matters of faith and practice. It is the only authoritative constitution, and no church may make rules binding upon men's consciences."[61]

The new constitutional ordination/subscription vow for ministers asked this question: "Do you sincerely receive and adopt the confession of faith of this church, as containing the system of doctrine taught in the holy scriptures?"[62] The phrase "system of doctrine" pointed back to the original morning minute of 1729, as well as the reunion language of 1758, and firmly grounded the new Constitution in the historic Adopting Act. The 1788 ordination question did not resolve the subscription controversy but was rather a compromise formula upon which future generations would place a variety of interpretations. And each of the competing perspectives would claim to be the genuine heir of the 1729 heritage.

The nineteenth-century debates over subscription had deep roots in the earlier century of American Presbyterianism. Conservatives would continue to argue that the old Synod of Philadelphia was correct in interpreting 1729 in terms of the afternoon minute and the strict reinterpretation of 1736. Receiving and adopting the "system" of the Confession meant embracing the whole confession without exception since the originally scrupled chapters had been amended in 1788. A larger group of Presbyterians, recalling the original intent of the morning minute, believed the "system" referred to the Confession's Calvinistic doctrines; this body advocated the distinction between doctrines "essential" to the system and those that were not. The spirit of Dickinson and the old Synod of New York would be alive and well in the nineteenth century.

---

[60] *Minutes of the Synod of New York and Philadelphia*, 28 May 1788, 636.

[61] Trinterud, *Forming of an American Tradition*, 297, 298. The preface to the Plan of Government listed eight principles upon which the Presbyterian ecclesiology would be established. These citations are from points I and VII.

[62] *The Constitution of the Presbyterian Church in the United States of America* (Philadelphia: Thomas Bradford, 1792), 158.

And there was a third small party which held that "system of doctrine" referred to the fundamental doctrines shared in common with all Christian churches. This minority expression drew inspiration from the 1729 language "systems of *Christian* doctrine." Some of the early pre-1729 discussions about subscription had advocated this opinion; however, it ultimately had been rejected in the compromise of 1729. Nonetheless, this explication still had its eighteenth-century advocates in such men as Hemphill and Harker. Even in the nineteenth century, a few voices would continue to herald a loose view of subscription which favored mere assent to catholic Christianity as the "substance" of Westminster doctrines.

The issue of subscription had not been laid to rest in neither the 1758 reunion nor the establishment of the General Assembly in 1789. The Westminster Confession and Catechisms were unanimously adopted as constitutional documents of the Presbyterian Church, but, there was no consensus on the degree of confessional attachment required for ministerial communion. The early history of nineteenth-century Presbyterianism clearly demonstrates that strongly held differences over subscription in the eighteenth-century maintained momentum into the next generations. So potent were these diverse convictions that they would be one of the primary factors creating another Presbyterian schism in the nineteenth century.

CHAPTER 3

New Divinity and Revivalism

The early decades of the nineteenth century were a time of expanding organization for American Presbyterians. As the nation moved westward, Presbyterians had great opportunities for gospel proclamation and the establishment of new churches in the frontier regions. Responding to the urgent need for more clergy, the Presbyterian Church devoted substantial energy to the training and sending of ministers to these new mission fields. Seminaries and mission agencies were organized as the denomination rallied to meet these challenges. One of the consequences of this fresh burst of organizational vigor was nascent contention between those Presbyterians who preferred distinctly denominational efforts and those in favor of ecumenical cooperation in mission.

The early nineteenth century would witness a new wave of religious revivals in various parts of the country. As had happened in the previous century, the excesses associated with revivals produced consternation among Presbyterians more accustomed to orderly religious exercises. The revivals of the nineteenth century tended to be more Arminian than the eighteenth-century New England awakenings. The new revivals with their Arminian-like theology (sometimes labeled "Pelagian" by opponents) ushered Presbyterians into an intense period of theological controversy. The kernel of the debate was the struggle to define the essential Calvinism of the Presbyterian creed. As some churchmen stretched the boundaries of acceptable Calvinism, an Old School party would stridently resist these innovations as departures from orthodoxy. Opposing the conservative party, was a New School party which practiced a broader Calvinism and allowed more latitude in expressing the Reformed Tradition.

Jonathan Edwards and New England Theology

The emergence of a distinctive New School party within Presbyterianism must be traced to the fountainhead – the theology of Jonathan Edwards. Edwards shines as the great Reformed theologian of colonial America; none other was as prolific a writer nor possessed his theological acumen. A Congregationalist by association, his theology was Calvinistic[1] and he stood in the English Puritan Tradition that had

---

[1] Congregationalists in New England adopted a modified version of the Westminster Confession of Faith in 1680 and 1708. This modified version did not include any substantive changes in the Reformed theology of Westminster. See Williston Walker, *A History of the*

made New England its home in America. The influence of Edwards in nineteenth-century America would primarily come through the Congregational Churches of New England which had an increasingly close relationship with the Presbyterian Church.

In order to understand the distinctive doctrines that would become associated with New School Presbyterianism, one must look at the innovative contributions of Jonathan Edwards to the American Reformed Tradition. During his lifetime, Edwards combated Unitarian, Pelagian and Arminian theology that had begun undermining the Puritan theology of New England. Edwards would become the great stalwart of Reformed orthodoxy for his generation. In this polemic context, Edwards began to revise some of the traditional ways in which Calvinists had typically expressed the faith. Two of Edwards's theological treatises illustrate the nature of the modifications he utilized in explaining Reformed doctrine: *Original Sin Defended* and *Freedom of the Will.*

In his work *Original Sin*, Edwards, responding to John Taylor's *The Scripture Doctrine of Original Sin,*[2] gave this definition: "By Original Sin, as the phrase has been most commonly used by divines, is meant the innate, sinful depravity of the heart. But yet, when the doctrine of Original Sin is spoken of, it is vulgarly understood in that latitude, as to include not only the depravity of nature, but the imputation of Adam's first sin; or in other words, the liableness or exposedness of Adam's posterity, in the divine judgment, to partake of the punishment of that Sin."[3] Every person comes into the world in a state of sinful depravity before God. Edwards' explanation for this depravity of heart is the sin of Adam and the participation of all human beings in that first sin. All men lost the "superior divine principles" and were left with the "common natural principles" which led to total corruption of the heart.[4]

All people were included in Adam's sin due to a "constituted oneness" of Adam with the rest of the human race. Thus, all sinned in Adam and "come into the world mere *flesh*, and entirely under the government of natural and inferior principles; and

---

Congregational Churches in the United States (New York: The Christian Literature Company, 1894): 188-190, 206-209.

[2] See Conrad Wright, *The Beginnings of Unitarianism in America* (Boston: Starr King Press, 1955); Perry Miller, Jonathan Edwards (New York: Meridian Books, Inc., 1959).

[3] Jonathan Edwards, *The Works of President Edwards* (New York: Leavitt and Allen, 1843), II. 309. For this discussion of New England influence in Presbyterianism the writer is indebted to the work of Earl Pope. Pope said: "New England had abandoned the doctrine of imputation of sin by the opening of the nineteenth century, but all the Calvinists maintained that in one form or another man's nature was polluted prior to the actual commission of sin. The situation was considerably different in the Presbyterian Church, however, where controversy centered on both elements within the doctrine of original sin." Earl A. Pope, "New England Calvinism and the Disruption of the Presbyterian Church" (Ph.D. diss., Brown University, 1962), 26.

[4] Ibid., 476.

so become wholly corrupt, as Adam did."[5] This "constituted union of the branches with the root" brought forth moral depravity, however, the "corrupt disposition in their hearts, is not to be looked upon as sin belonging to them, *distinct* from their participation of Adam's first sin."[6] For Edwards, the evil heart was not a result of the imputation of Adam's sin, rather "the evil disposition is *first*, and the charge of guilt *consequent.*" He continues, "the sin of the apostasy is not theirs, merely because God *imputes* it to them; but it is *truly* and *properly* theirs, and on that ground, God imputes it to them."[7]

Edwards's articulation of Adam's union with humanity and his idea of imputation as a consequence of an evil disposition were both departures from the Federal Theology of Westminster. The Westminster Divines had understood Adam's relation to posterity as that of a representative head and they described the depraved heart as a result of God's imputing Adam's sin to all men.[8] New England theologians would eventually abandon the imputation of sin concept altogether and it appeared that the groundwork had been laid by Edwards. Presbyterians would have to deal with the repercussions of Edwards's revisions throughout the nineteenth-century debates.[9]

Another area of Edwards's thought that would have a lasting impact on Presbyterianism is the issue of the human will. Edwards made a clear distinction between natural and moral ability in order to explain personal moral responsibility. In *Freedom of the Will*, which was written by Edwards to answer Arminian objections, Edwards says that while man has all the natural faculties (ability) to do God's will, yet he lacks the moral ability to do so because of his innate depravity.

---

[5] Ibid., II, 478.

[6] Ibid., 482.

[7] Ibid., 482-83, 493. Edwards was here articulating the mediate view of imputation, i.e., the imputation of Adam's first sin to all humanity is mediated through the inheritance from Adam of a corrupt nature. This view was adopted by a number of New England theologians and became identified with New School Presbyterians as a distinctive of their party. For example, New School theologian Henry B. Smith wrote against immediate imputation, i.e., the guilt of Adam's sin is immediately imputed to his posterity who therefore becomes corrupt in nature. Henry B. Smith, *System of Christian Theology* (New York: A.C. Armstrong, 1884), 304-308. Edwards was interpreted by both Old and New School theologians as teaching mediate imputation, however, Benjamin Breckinridge Warfield and John Murray denied that Edwards held this view. See John Murray, *The Imputation of Adam's Sin* (Philipsburg, New Jersey: Presbyterian and Reformed Publishing Co., 1959), 52-64.

[8] See *Westminster Confession of Faith*, "On the Covenant of Works."

[9] Lyman Atwater, "Jonathan Edwards and the Successive Forms of Divinity" *The Biblical Repertory and Princeton Review* XXX (October, 1858): 586-620; Archibald Alexander, "An Inquiry into That Inability Under Which the Sinner Labours, and Whether It Furnishes Any Excuse for His Neglect of Duty," *The Biblical Repertory and Theological Review* III (July, 1831): 360-83; Charles Hodge, "Review of an Article in the June Number of The Christian Spectator, entitled, 'Inquiries Respecting the Doctrine of Imputation,'" *The Biblical Repertory and Princeton Review* II (October, 1830): 425-72.

This moral inability consists "in the want of inclination; or the strength of a contrary inclination; or the want of sufficient motives in view, to induce and excite the act of the will, or the strength of apparent motives to the contrary."[10] Man's will is at liberty to do whatsoever he wants, however, the human will does not determine itself but rather is determined by antecedent causes. Edwards's arguments were intended to answer the Arminian critique of Calvinism. Edward states:

> The things which have been said, obviate some of the chief objections of Arminians against the Calvinistic doctrine of the total depravity and corruption of man's nature, whereby his heart is wholly under the power of sin, and he is utterly unable, without the interpositing of sovereign grace, savingly to love God, believe in Christ, or do anything that is truly good and acceptable in God's sight.[11]

Jonathan Edwards offers an able defense of Calvinism; his distinction between moral inability and natural ability would be a common place in New School theology of the nineteenth century. While Edwards's understanding of the will rang true with New School Presbyterians, some of the later New Haven theologians, influenced by Arminian ideas, found his position insufficient for safeguarding human freedom; on the other hand, some of the Old School Presbyterians rejected Edwards's view as granting too much. No one in America could do serious theological work without interaction with Edwards, especially those churchmen within the Reformed Tradition. Old School historians would point back to Edwards as the father of New School "heresies."[12]

Edwardsean theology was transmitted to the next generation of New England Congregationalists through a number of sources, including Samuel Hopkins[13] and Timothy Dwight.[14] Dwight, the grandson of Edwards, would become the President

---

[10] Jonathan Edwards, *The Works of Edwards*, Vol. I, Freedom of the Will, ed. Paul Ramsey (New Haven: Yale University Press, 1957), 159.

[11] Ibid., 432.

[12] Samuel J. Baird, *History of the New School* (Philadelphia: Claxton, Remsen, and Haffelfinger, 1868), 167-70.

[13] Samuel Hopkins (1721-1803) was a Congregationalist pastor, revival preacher and theologian. Hopkins was personally tutored by Jonathan Edwards and became one of his closest friends. Hopkins developed Edwards's pro-Awakening theology into a modified American Calvinism known as Hopkinsianism. Hopkins believed that sin manifested itself in humanity through self love. Utilizing Edwards's idea of virtue as "benevolence to being in general," Hopkins taught that the essence of Christian virtue is selflessness or what he called "disinterested benevolence." This theology provided a basis for social reform, particularly abolition. For the development of Hopkinsian theology see J.A. Conforti, *Samuel Hopkins and the New Divinity Movement* (Grand Rapids: Christian University Press, 1981).

[14] Timothy Dwight (1752-1817), a Congregationalist pastor and educator, graduated from Yale College and was tutored by his uncle, Jonathan Edwards Jr., a New Divinity man. During Dwight's tenure as President of Yale, students experienced some of the earliest waves of revival in the Second Great Awakening. While often identified with Hopkinsianism, Dwight questioned some of the doctrine and practices of New Divinity. His attempts to

of Yale in 1795 and influenced many students including Lyman Beecher and Nathaniel Taylor. New School men would later cite Dwight's theological system as representative of their views.[15] Samuel Hopkins, a Congregationalist pastor in Massachusetts, studied under Edwards and imbibed Edwardsean theology, along with his own modifications. A number of New England trained Presbyterian clergy were influenced by Hopkinsian theology which was viewed with suspicion by traditional Calvinists.

Much of the Presbyterian debate on Hopkinsian thought centered upon the imputation of Adam's sin and the natural/moral ability distinction.[16] Hopkins affirmed human unity with Adam by divine constitution but he argued that the moral corruption of the race comes through actual sin. The first moral acts of the individual define participation in the sin of Adam. He declared: "It is not properly distinguished into original and actual sin, because it is all really actual sin, and there is, strictly speaking, no other sin but actual sin. As soon as sin exists in a child of Adam, though an infant, it consists in motion or inclination, of the same nature and kind with sin in adult persons."[17] Hopkins reiterated Edwards' concept of natural ability that is not erased as a result of Adam's sin. "The constituted consequence and effect of the sin of Adam, as it respects his posterity, is their total moral depravity or sinfulness, and not the removal or debasing of their natural powers of mind in the least degree...." Yet, there is in fallen man a moral inability that hinders him from the exercise of holiness. When that moral corruption of heart is removed by grace, the proper exercise of one's natural powers is possible.[18]

Timothy Dwight in Edwardsean fashion spoke of the corruption of human nature which is evident in the depraved moral conduct of all men. Concerning the imputation of sin, which he believed in principle, Dwight was not convinced that any explanations were fully satisfying. He declared, "I shall not add to these difficulties by any imperfect explanations of my own." All sinned in Adam, however, the human race is not guilty of his transgression. "The personal act of any agent is, in its very nature, the act of that agent solely; and incapable of being transferred, or participated. The guilt is inherent in the action; and is attributable,

---

protect Connecticut Congregationalists from disestablishment by Jeffersonian Baptists earned him the title, the "Pope of Federalism."

[15] 'Old and New School Theology," *The Presbyterian Quarterly Review* IX (January, 1860): 368.

[16] Elwyn A. Smith explains that no real debate existed among Presbyterians over original sin during the era of Jonathan Dickinson who simply reiterated the traditional categories. The creativity of Jonathan Edwards "furnished the mind of Hopkins;... It was in that form that the 'Edwardean' divinity was evaluated and debated by American Presbyterians." Elwyn A. Smith, "The Doctrine of Imputation and the Presbyterian Schism of 1837-1838," *Journal of the Presbyterian Historical Society* 38 (September 1960): 139.

[17] Samuel Hopkins, *The Works of Samuel Hopkins with a Memoir of His Life and Character*, ed. Edward A. Parks (Boston: Doctrinal Tract and Book Society, 1854), 224.

[18] Ibid., 229.

therefore, to the Agent only."[19] Dwight emphasized the personal responsibility of the individual for his own actions. He asserted:

> Man is the actor of his own sin. His sin is, therefore, wholly his own; chargeable only to himself; chosen by him unnecessarily, while possessed of a power to choose otherwise; avoidable by him; and of course guilty, and righteously punishable. Exactly the same natural power is in this case possessed by him, while a sinner, which is afterwards possessed by him, when a saint; which Adam possessed before he fell; and which the holy angels now possess in the Heavens. This power is also, in my view, perfect freedom; a power of agency, as absolute as can be possessed by an Intelligent creature.[20]

In addition to the modifications by Hopkins and Dwight on imputation and human ability, a few New England theologians also began to revise traditional Calvinist views of the atonement. Joseph Bellamy (1719-1790) and Jonathan Edwards the Younger (1745-1801) were key contributors to the emerging departure from limited atonement. A general atonement for mankind was understood to be grounded in a moral government theory of the atonement. Rather than a vicarious death of Christ as payment of a debt, the cross was a demonstration of the moral government of God over his creation. Through this public display of His justice and hatred for sin, God mercifully forgives all those who repent of their sin. This was a significant departure from the doctrine of substitutionary atonement as understood by the Protestant Reformers and the Reformed Tradition. All these doctrinal innovations would cause concern in the Presbyterian Church.

1801 Plan of Union

The influence of New England theology in the Presbyterian Church was attributable to several historical factors. Congregationalist and Presbyterian relationships had deep roots – both shared a common Reformed heritage and both churches had committed themselves theologically to the Westminster Standards. Cordial ecclesiastical relations and mutual respect had existed between the two groups from the early years of the American colonies. By 1801 this friendly correspondence was consummated in a formal Plan of Union between the General Association of Connecticut and the Presbyterian Church. The Plan's ultimate intent was to encourage the evangelistic efforts of both churches. The American frontier beckoned; the needs were great and the two churches were constrained to labor together in gospel witness rather than compete.

In order to facilitate the joint westward mission, certain ecclesiastical agreements were adopted in the 1801 Plan of Union. Missionaries to the new settlements were instructed to seek "mutual forbearance and a spirit of accommodation" among

---

[19] Timothy Dwight, *Theology: Explained and Defended, In a Series of Sermons*, 10th ed. (New Haven: T. Dwight and Son, 1839), 478-480.

[20] Ibid., 414.

members of both churches. Congregational churches could call a Presbyterian minister and keep their Congregational polity. If there were problems between the minister and the congregation, issues would be referred either to the Presbytery or to a council comprised of equal numbers of Presbyterians and Congregationalists. Presbyterian churches could call a Congregational pastor; Presbyterian polity would be in force in this situation. In the event of difficulties, problems would either be referred to the Congregational Association of the minister or to a council of equal number of Congregationalists and Presbyterians. If a congregation was made up of both Presbyterians and Congregationalists, a standing committee would be chosen to provide supervision of the flock. In the case of appeal, a Presbyterian could appeal to Presbytery and a Congregationalist to members of the church or a council. Members of a standing committee in such a church could vote in Presbytery as a ruling elder in the Presbyterian Church.[21]

The Plan of Union was unanimously adopted by the Presbyterian General Assembly in 1801. At this period, a genuine ecumenical spirit prevailed in the Presbyterian Church. There had been some concern with the modifications of the Edwardseans, nonetheless, Presbyterians were overwhelmingly supportive of this magnanimous gesture of Christian goodwill. While the underlying motives of this charitable venture were compelling, the arrangement had the potential for great division in the Presbyterian body.[22] Chief among the controversial issues would be the right of Congregational "committee men" to vote in Presbyteries. Men who did not sincerely adopt the Westminster Confession of Faith were now allowed an equal voice in the deliberations of the Presbyterian Church. As the numbers grew so did the tensions. The new polity provisions would eventually invoke the wrath of Old School Presbyterians, many of whom, believed the Plan of Union had seriously compromised the church's allegiance to the Presbyterian form of government.

In addition to the irritating polity question, there was grave concern about the influence of the theology coming out of New England. Many Presbyterian ministers received their theological training in New England, therefore, Congregational

---

[21] *Minutes of the General Assembly of the Presbyterian Church in the United States of America 1789-1837* (Philadelphia) 1801, 224,225. Suggested authors of the 1801 Plan include Jonathan Edwards the Younger who had joined the Presbyterian Church; Pope, "New England Calvinism," 40, n. 13. Ashbel Green has also been suggested; Frederick Kuhns, "New Light on the Plan of Union," *Journal of the Presbyterian Historical Society* XXVI (1948): 19-43.

[22] Samuel Miller reflecting on the action of 1801, notes both the good and evil of the Plan. He stated: "In looking back on the origin and object of the 'Plan of Union,' (this 25th of November, 1847) I cannot take the retrospect without sorrow and shame. Never, I suppose, did a large body of ministers act from purer motives, or with more entire fraternal harmony, than did the members of the General Assembly, in adopting this measure. The avowed and the sincere object of it was to avoid discord, and to promote and establish peace. But it was a most unfortunate measure. It led eventually to an amount of abuse and to conflicts by no means anticipated by either Presbyterians or Congregationalists." Samuel Miller, Jr., *Life of Samuel Miller* (Philadelphia: Claxton, Remsen and Haffelfinger, 1869), 140.

novelties began to creep into the Presbyterian household. The Old School party in the early decades of the nineteenth century would become identified as that group of Presbyterians that viewed New England Theology as undermining the distinctive doctrines of the Reformed heritage. Many Old School partisans viewed the association with Congregationalism as the root of doctrinal dispute in the Presbyterian Church. Old School journals would wage theological warfare against what they viewed as perversions emanating from Congregationalism.

The New School, on the other hand, would be more tolerant of the New England Theology. There were serious reservations about the extremism of a few New England men, nevertheless, New School Presbyterians gladly joined hands with their Congregational brethren. Plan of Union congregations, that joined the Presbyterian Church, identified themselves with the New School party and generally embraced the broader vision of New England Calvinism. The 1801 Plan fostered a spirit of liberality and interdenominational cooperation that was cherished by New School Presbyterians.

New Divinity and Subscription

Old School reaction to the "New Divinity"[23] coming out of New England was increasingly harsh. Presbyterians had great respect for Jonathan Edwards, at the same time, they recognized that Edwards's theological progeny had produced a diluted form of Calvinism in New England.[24] Debate among Presbyterians centered on the degree to which New England doctrines had deviated from the Westminster Standards. New England Congregationalists had adopted the Westminster Confession of Faith, however, they practiced a loose form of subscription. The New England men emphasized essential elements of the faith rather than the full Calvinistic system of doctrine. As New England ideas began to permeate the Presbyterian body, attention again was focused on what it meant for Presbyterians to receive and adopt the "system of doctrine" in the Confession of Faith.

One of the early incidents that highlighted the growing antagonism within American Presbyterianism was the publication in 1811 of *A Contrast Between Calvinism and Hopkinsianism* by Ezra Stiles Ely,[25] a former Hopkinsian. Ely

---

[23] 'New Divinity" was a term used for the Edwardsean party within Congregationalism. It became identified with Edwards's students, Joseph Bellamy, Jonathan Edwards Jr. and Samuel Hopkins. The New Divinity men stressed piety, supported revivalism and restated Calvinism in the Edwardsean theological framework. The terms "Consistent Calvinism" and "Hopkinsianism" were also used to describe this group of theologians.

[24] See Atwater, "Jonathan Edwards and the Successive Forms of New Divinity."

[25] Ely Stiles Ely (1786-1861) was a Presbyterian pastor in Philadelphia, 1814-1835; he served as the Stated Clerk of the Presbyterian Church, 1825-1836 and was Moderator of the General Assembly in 1828. Ely was for a time the editor of the *Philadelphian* which became a New School paper and he defended Albert Barnes in his first trial. He is also notorious for his infamous letter to President Andrew Jackson which led to the resignation of his entire cabinet.

asserted that Hopkinsianism was a dangerous threat to the doctrinal purity of the Presbyterian Church and he singularly pointed to the doctrines of original sin, human ability and atonement. In the book, he compared Hopkinsian theology to both Arminianism and Pelagianism. At the conclusion of his attack on Hopkinsian thought, Ely addressed the issue of subscription to the Standards:

> When an individual is admitted in the Presbyterian Church he either professes or tacitly consents sincerely to 'receive and adopt the confession of faith of this Church, as containing the system of doctrine taught in the Holy Scripture.' It has been proved in the preceding pages, that the system of Hopkinsianism is repugnant to this confession of faith. This conclusion therefore, irresistibly follows, that no person, who is fully convinced of the truth of this system, or who is not a Calvinist in sentiment, can conscientiously unite himself to the Presbyterian Church, by assent to its confession of faith.[26]

A reply to Ely was published a few years later by Samuel Whelpley[27] in a book entitled, *The Triangle*. Whelpley defended New England Calvinism and attacked what he called the "triangular theology" of Ely – the points of the triangle being the imputation of Adam's sin, human inability, and limited atonement. Whelpley caricatured traditional Calvinism: "The whole of their doctrine, then amounts to this, that a man is, in the first place, condemned, incapacitated, and eternally reprobated for the sin of Adam; in the next place, that he is condemned over again, for not doing that which he is totally in all respects, unable to do; and, in the third place, that he is condemned, and doubly and trebly condemned, for not believing in a Saviour, who never died for him, and with whom he has no more to do than a fallen angel."[28] In his rejection of the theological triangle, Whelpley declared the Westminster Confession to be the work of "fallible men" and it should not be laid beside the sacred book as the final word. "It was never in the dreams of its authors to set it up as the sovereign arbiter of conscience; or that any deviations from any points therein contained were to be stigmatized as deviation from the eternal standard of truth, or subject those who deviated to censure and excommunication."[29]

Hopkinsianism continued to trouble some parts of the church and these publications helped keep the conflict alive. Another incident in 1816 would involve two key figures in later Presbyterian controversies. Samuel Hanson Cox was refused a commission by the Young Men's Missionary Society of New York because of his

---

[26] Ezra Stiles Ely, *A Contrast Between Calvinism and Hopkinsianism* (New York: S. Whiting and Co., 1811), 278. It is interesting to note that Ely is contrasting two systems of doctrine and seems to imply that subscription is to the essential Calvinism of the Confession.

[27] Samuel Whelpley (1766-1817) was a retired Baptist minister who lived with his son Philip, the pastor of First Presbyterian Church in New York.

[28] Samuel Whelpley, *The Triangle* (New York: O. Halsted, 1832), 16; quoted in Pope, "New England Calvinism," 57.

[29] Ibid., 58.

Hopkinsian views. He was defended by Gardiner Spring,[30] the chairman of the society's board of directors. Cox would later be a prominent leader in the New School and a target of attack from Princeton Seminary.

In 1817, the Hopkinsian question came before the Presbyterian General Assembly. The Synod of Philadelphia had adopted a pastoral letter, written by Ely, in which "Hopkinsian heresies" were condemned. The letter declared: "May the time never come in which our ecclesiastical courts shall determine that Hopkinsianism and the doctrines of our Confession of Faith are the same thing." Responding to the Synod's condemnation, a General Assembly committee, chaired by Samuel Miller of Princeton Seminary, presented a resolution which stated: "While they commend the zeal of the Synod in endeavoring to promote a strict conformity to our public standards, a conformity which cannot but be viewed as of vital importance to the purity and prosperity of the church, the Assembly regret that zeal on this subject should be manifested in such a manner as to be offensive to other denominations, and especially to introduce a spirit of jealousy and suspicion against ministers in good standing which is calculated to disturb the peace and harmony of our ecclesiastical judicatories." The resolution was adopted by the majority but some strongly objected to the Assembly's unwillingness to concur in the denunciation of Hopkinsianism. The protesters believed the preaching of these doctrines would place one "in violation of ordination vows."[31] Intense discord over what constituted faithfulness to the Confession would become the nucleus of the nineteenth-century subscription debate within the Presbyterian Church.[32]

A new controversy erupted in 1818 which highlighted the growing tensions over subscription to the Confession of Faith. The Synod of New York and New Jersey in 1816 had appointed a committee, chaired by Samuel Miller, to start an African School for the training of candidates for the ministry. In 1818 the Synod of Philadelphia was brought into African School discussions in order to enlist their support. The Philadelphia Synod insisted that the teachers in the new school should make the same pledge as the Professors at Princeton Seminary. The original 1812 plan for Princeton Seminary had included this formula of subscription:

Every person elected to a professorship in this Seminary, shall, on being inaugurated, solemnly subscribe the Confession of Faith, Catechisms, and Form of Government of

---

[30] Gardiner Spring (1785-1873) was a moderate Hopkinsian. He served as pastor of the Brick Church (First Presbyterian) in New York City for 63 years. Spring was respected by strict Old School men such as Ashbel Green, who nominated him for Moderator in 1831. A moderate Old School man, he defended Albert Barnes and opposed the schism of 1837. Spring would play a crucial role in the Old School schism in 1861 as well as the Old School / New School reunion in 1869-70.

[31] The ordination vows included this question: "Do you sincerely receive and adopt the confession of faith of this church, as containing the system of doctrine taught in the Holy Scripture." *The Constitution of the Presbyterian Church in the United States of America* (Philadelphia: Thomas Bradford, 1792), 158.

[32] *Minutes of the General Assembly*, 1817, 653-656.

the Presbyterian Church, agreeably to the following formula; viz.- 'In the presence of God and of the Directors of this Seminary, I do solemnly, and *ex animo* adopt, receive, and subscribe the Confession of Faith, and Catechisms of the Presbyterian Church in the United States of America, as the confession of my faith; or as a summary and just exhibition of that system of doctrine and religious belief which is contained in Holy Scripture, and therein revealed by God to man for his salvation; and I do solemnly, *ex animo* profess to receive the Form of Government of said Church, as agreeable to the inspired oracles. And I do solemnly promise and engage, not to inculcate, teach, or insinuate any thing which shall appear to me to contradict or contravene, either directly or impliedly, any thing taught in the said Confession of Faith or Catechisms; nor to oppose any of the fundamental principles of Presbyterian Church government, while I shall continue a Professor in the Seminary.'[33]

The Synod of Philadelphia's recommendation was "warmly opposed" by Drs. Gardiner Spring, Edward Griffin[34] and others. Professor Samuel Miller says that the Princeton formula "had been, from the first, as too stringent in their estimation, distasteful to those called Hokinsians in the Presbyterian Church." Finally the Philadelphia proposal was rejected and the Princeton formula did not become the standard for the African School.[35]

Reacting to the Synod of Philadelphia's strict view of subscription, Dr. Griffin wrote an anonymous pamphlet, *An Appeal to the Presbyterian Church on the Subject of the New Test.* Griffin criticized the Princeton formula and expressed a "substance of doctrine" view of subscription to "the great doctrines of our standards, and not extended to all the *minima* of human expression." For Griffin, the Princeton statement, "sanctifies every word and letter, as though they had come in that precise shape from the mouth of God." He asserted that the Princeton formula was a "new principle in the Presbyterian Church." Many ministers in the Presbyterian Church could not sign such a statement without violating their consciences.[36]

A response to Griffin came from the pen of Jacob Janeway[37] who was moderator of the General Assembly in 1818. Janeway asserted, "if every man in answering the constitutional question in regard to the Confession, is at liberty to frame what

---

[33] *Life of Samuel Miller*, I, 356, 357.

[34] Edward Dorr Griffin (1770-1837) was a Congregationalist pastor who served several churches including the Second Presbyterian Church in Newark, New Jersey and the Park Street Congregational Church in Boston. He was also a professor at Andover and served as the President of Williams College in his final years. Griffin was one of the founders of the American Bible Society and the United Foreign Missionary Society.

[35] *Life of Samuel Miller*, II, 24, 25.

[36] Edward Griffin, *An Appeal to the Presbyterian Church on the Subject of the New Test.* (n.p., 1819), 7,20,26; quoted in Pope, "New England Calvinism," 62-64.

[37] Jacob Janeway (1774-1858) had been co-pastor with Ashbel Green at Second Presbyterian Church in Philadelphia for 13 years. In the 1830s he served briefly as pastor of the First Dutch Reformed Church in New Brunswick, New Jersey but reunited with the Presbyterian Church.

exceptions to its doctrines he pleases, it is not even a test of his present faith. Such an engagement would not be worth receiving." Receiving and adopting the Confession was assent "not merely to its great doctrines" but a declaration that it contains the "system of doctrine taught in the Holy Scriptures." There must be agreement among Presbyterians beyond the fundamental doctrines in order to safeguard the peace and purity of the church.[38]

Janeway impugned the notion that personal judgment could determine what constituted that system. "We maintain that in receiving and adopting the Confession of Faith we do more than assent to it as a system. This was much too indefinite a commitment. If only mere assent is made to the great doctrines of the Bible, provision is made for exceptions to doctrines embraced in the Confession; and who is to determine what may be included in receiving it as a system? If every candidate is to be guided by his own judgment, the man whose conscience is the most elastic will blot out the greatest number." The Bible is the "supreme and infallible rule" for purity of doctrine, however, the Presbyterian Church, has a "subordinate rule" which is "her interpretation of that word." He added: "That standard contains, in her estimation the truth of the gospel, and exhibits them in all their purity."[39]

The Princeton pledge was a necessary addition for seminary professors, "that the fountain destined to send its refreshing streams to every part of our Church should be kept pure and uncontaminated." Ministerial ordination vows alone were "insufficient to preserve a faithful adherence to the standards of our Church, and that doctrines at variance with them had been preached by some ministers in our communion." Janeway seemed to imply that the ministerial vow and the pledge of the professors were in essence the same. If a Princeton professor changes his views, he has agreed to be silent "just as every minister in our connexion is bound not to propagate any opinions that militate against the Confession."[40]

---

[38] Jacob Janeway, *The Appeal Not Sustained or an Answer to a Pamphlet Entitled 'An Appeal to the Presbyterian Church on the Subject of the New Test.'* (n.p., 1820),5,13,14; quoted in Pope, "New England Calvinism," 64-66.

[39] Pope, "New England Calvinism," 66, 67.

[40] Ibid., 67, 69. Samuel Miller indicated that he understood the Princeton pledge to be an expectation beyond that required of ministers. He stated, "theological professors, in addition to what is required of them as ministers, that they should teach nothing in the least inconsistent with the Confession or Catechisms, or opposed to the essential principles of Presbyterian government. This gradation of requirement is obviously agreeable to the gradation of function, responsibility, and influence for which it provides." *Life of Samuel Miller*, I, 357. Pope says the Princeton formula became the standard for the conservative Old School party. "What the New School frequently appeared to do was to interpret the Confession in the light of the laymen's confession with an emphasis on the doctrines essential to salvation. The ultra conservatives appeared to make their interpretation in the light of the Princeton formula, which precluded any challenge of the Confession whatsoever." Pope, "New England Calvinism," 70. Pope's characterization of the two parties may be valid for a minority wing of each group; however, within each party there was a much larger moderate group that rejected both of these extreme positions.

Janeway asserted that Griffin's understanding of subscription has never been the view of the Presbyterian Church. This new view is not "indigenous to the soil and climate of our Church." The seeds of this debate were the recent doctrinal innovations that had now infiltrated the Presbyterian Church. He lists the theological issues at stake: "We deny that ministers in our connexion dared till lately to deny the representative character both of Adam and Christ; to deny the imputation of the guilt of Adam's first sin, and of the righteousness of Christ; to assert and maintain that the holy God is the author of sin, and to propagate the doctrine of an indefinite atonement, which represents Christ as suffering, not for the sins of his elect, who were given to him by his Father to be redeemed, but merely for sin in general, and to make an exhibition of its evil."[41] These doctrines would continue to be the heart of theological debate leading up to the Old School/New School schism. Juxtaposed to these specific theological issues was always the question of subscription to the doctrinal standards of the Church.

Revivals in the South

While most of the Old School's attention was centered on aberrations coming out of New England, the South had to deal with its own versions of modified Calvinism. The frontier revivals in Kentucky at the turn of the century brought schism in the Presbyterian household. The camp meetings at Cane Ridge under Presbyterian minister Barton W. Stone had exhibited immoderate physical manifestations in the eyes of many and two parties developed among the Presbyterians in this area – a New Light, pro-revival party and a party opposed to revivalist excesses. Accompanying opposition to revivalist methods came objections to the doctrines of the revival preachers. The New Light revivalists intentionally avoided any references to election in their preaching. In 1803 the Synod of Kentucky became involved when the Presbytery of Washington refused to reexamine two of her ministers (Richard McNemar, John Thompson) who had been accused of Arminianism. As the synod met, five of the revival preachers protested the review of Washington Presbytery's proceedings and announced that they were withdrawing from synod to form the Springfield Presbytery.[42]

A war of words ensued in print and pulpit, each party vehemently defending its own position. New Lights declared that the doctrines of the Confession of Faith were a hindrance to revival and religion of the heart. The revivalists preached only the doctrines of the Bible and a free offer of the gospel to all men. Reception of the gospel was not dependent on the prior work of regeneration by the Spirit.[43] The new

---

[41] Ibid., 64, 69.

[42] Ernest Trice Thompson, *Presbyterians in the South*, vol. I, 1607- 1861 (Richmond, Virginia: John Knox Press, 1963), 155-61.

[43] Thompson commented: "Thus was launched an open and uncompromising attack on the Standards of the Presbyterian Church ... it was one of many signs which indicate that the theological climate of America was shifting from the high Calvinism of the colonial period to Arminianism...." *Presbyterians in the South*, I, 162.

Presbytery of Springfield stated: "We know that God is sovereign, but do not believe that he mocks men's misery by offering relief which the poor wretch cannot possibly receive."[44] The departed ministers rejected the use of creeds which had divided the church into parties. Springfield Presbytery was dissolved in less than a year as the New Lights renounced denominationalism and began referring to themselves only as "Christians." Under the leadership of Barton Stone the Christian Church was founded and by the 1830s Stone joined with Alexander Campbell and the Disciples of Christ. Eventually, a number of the New Light ministers recanted their errors and returned to the Presbyterian Church.[45]

With the success of the Kentucky revivals came petitions for more ministers to carry on the work; this led several Presbyteries to waive ministerial education requirements. In Transylvania and Cumberland Presbyteries a number of young men were licensed as catechists, exhorters and even ordained to the Presbyterian ministry without meeting the traditional educational standards; in several cases these licentiates had not been required to adopt the Westminster Confession. Protests were lodged against these irregular licensures and ordinations. A number of the revivalists with irregular credentials had objected to the idea of "fatalism" in the doctrine of predestination, therefore, suspicions of Arminianism began to surface.[46]

The Synod of Kentucky got involved again by investigating these irregular practices and charges were brought against three ministers for denying the doctrine of election. Two men were suspended from the ministry and Cumberland Presbytery was dissolved in 1806; the ministers transferred to Transylvania Presbytery. The 1807 General Assembly considered a protest against the synod's action and asked the Synod of Kentucky to review its proceedings. The review took place and the General Assembly in 1809 confirmed that the synod had indeed acted properly. Several ministers from the dissolved Cumberland Presbytery organized themselves into an independent Presbytery of Cumberland which eventually became the Cumberland Presbyterian Church organized as a General Assembly by 1829.[47]

In addition to these Kentucky frontier schisms, the South also had to wrestle with Hopkinsianism. While the New Divinity had not infiltrated the South as it had other parts of the Presbyterian Church, nevertheless, some influences were evident. The first inroads of Hopkinsian ideas into the South can be traced back to Hezekiah Balch[48] of Tennessee. Balch was charged with teaching doctrines contrary to the Confession and his ministry caused such friction that eventually a new presbytery of

---

[44] Presbytery of Springfield, *An Apology for Renouncing the Jurisdiction of the Synod of Kentucky, to which is added a Compendious View of the Gospel, and a few remarks on the Confession of Faith* (Lexington, Kentucky, 1804), 112; quoted in *Thompson, Presbyterians in the South*, I, 160, 161.

[45] Ibid., 162-64.

[46] Ibid., 144-148.

[47] Ibid., 148-152.

[48] Dr. Hezekiah Balch (1741-1810), raised in Mecklenburg County, N.C., was a College of New Jersey graduate and Presbyterian pastor of Mount Bethel Church in East Tennessee. He founded Greenville College in 1794 where he served as President.

Union was formed in 1797. The next year Balch's case came before the General Assembly which found him guilty though he was later restored to fellowship. Another Hopkinsian pioneer pastor, Isaac Anderson, would also have significant influence in Eastern Tennessee through Southern and Western Theological Seminary (later Maryville College) near Knoxville. Anderson, unable to secure Presbyterian pastors from the North, decided to begin training ministers for the frontier mission in 1819. At least 100 ministers studied under Anderson.[49]

The Synod of Virginia likewise encountered Hopkinsian ministers. In 1820 Robert Glenn of Union Presbytery was refused admission to Abingdon Presbytery because he was a Hopkinsian. On appeal to the Synod of Virginia, the synod replied that the presbytery had not acted properly in censuring Glenn. Nevertheless, the synod stated: "it would be very desirable that those who have attached themselves to what are called the doctrines of the new school should avoid as much as possible those novel forms of expression which are calculated to alarm the minds & weaken the confidence of their fellow professors." The synod asserted that it is highly important "that judicatories should unite prudence, lenity & a wise forbearance with Christian firmness in maintaining the truth ...we would recommend the old maxim, in essentials let us have unity, in things not essential, lenity, & in all things charity."[50]

In South Carolina, a discipline case against a Presbyterian minister would give birth to a new denomination in the South. William C. Davis of First Presbytery was charged with teaching that faith precedes regeneration. The Synod of South Carolina directed the presbytery to examine Davis; the presbytery condemned some of Davis' doctrines but declared that allowable latitude of expression would permit Davis to continue his ministry. In 1808 Davis published *The Gospel Plan* which was condemned by the 1810 Presbyterian General Assembly. First Presbytery, being unwilling to discipline Davis, was dissolved by the Synod of South Carolina. Davis and his fellow presbyters were assigned to Concord Presbytery where Davis was summoned to trial. Davis resigned, but, his new presbytery deposed him anyway. Davis withdrew and along with several other congregations established the Independent Presbyterian Church in 1813.[51]

Outside of these challenges from revival preachers, Presbyterians in the South had been somewhat untouched by the theological controversies in the North. Revivalism had deep roots in the South and Southern preachers did not hesitate to ameliorate the rough edges of rigid Calvinism in their preaching of the Gospel. Some took this liberty to extremes and jettisoned moderate Calvinism for blatant Arminian schemes. Presbyterians in the South disciplined these ministers for radical

---

[49] E.T. Thompson, *Presbyterians in the South*, I, 353-355. Thompson stated: "Tennessee was the only Southern state in which the 'new divinity' secured a firm footing. Some of Balch's teaching, however, may have borne fruit in the New Light revival in northern Kentucky." This was also Baird's opinion. *History of the New School*, 133.

[50] *Ms. Minutes, Synod of Virginia*, 301-303; quoted in *Thompson, Presbyterians in the South*, I, 354, 355.

[51] Thompson, *Presbyterians in the South*, I, 358-360.

departures from the Reformed Tradition. With the expulsions of New Lights, Cumberlands and Independents, Presbyterians in the South exhibited a more harmonious ecclesiastical arrangement than their Northern brethren who were experiencing a widening theological chasm.[52]

Finney and New Revivalism

The revival fires of early and mid-eighteenth-century New England, which had played a significant role in the evolving Edwardsean Theology, were reignited in late eighteenth century/early nineteenth century New England under the preaching of Timothy Dwight, the president of Yale. Under Dwight's leadership, many Yale students were converted to Christ and a number of them became leaders in the Second Great Awakening. One of Dwight's "awakened" pupils was Lyman Beecher,[53] who would become a key leader in both the New England revivals as well as the Old School/New School controversy in the Presbyterian Church. Beecher, a Congregationalist for many years, took a joint call to the Second Presbyterian Church of Cincinnati and the new Lane Presbyterian Seminary in 1832. During his tenure as president of Lane, the Cincinnati Presbytery tried Beecher on charges of departing from the Westminster Confession in 1835. Beecher was exonerated but remained the subject of Old School complaint throughout his years in the Presbyterian Church.

The premier evangelist of the Second Great Awakening was Charles G. Finney.[54] Finney was pursuing the study of law when he had a dramatic conversion experience and sensed God's call to become an evangelist in 1821. After being tutored by a Presbyterian mentor, the Rev. George Gale, he was ordained as a Presbyterian minister in July of 1824.[55] Commissioned as a missionary to upstate

---

[52] Ibid., 361; Thompson stated: "...in the opening decade of the 19th century pastors, and particularly evangelists, were seeking to soften the rigidities of the Calvinistic system in the South, along with the weightier theologians and their disciples in New England and adjoining areas. It would also appear that the 'new divinity' found no solid foothold in the South except in eastern Tennessee, where first Greenville and later Maryville College became training centers for a modified Calvinism."

[53] Lyman Beecher (1775-1863) was first licensed as a Congregationalist minister but served both Congregational and Presbyterian churches during his ministry. Beecher was a revival preacher, social reformer and staunch opponent of Unitarianism in New England. In 1832 he became President and Professor of Theology at the Presbyterian Seminary in Cincinnati, Lane Theological Seminary.

[54] Charles Grandison Finney (1792-1875), known as the "Father of Modern Revivalism," began his revivalist career in upstate New York. Finney led revival meetings throughout the northeast, including the large urban areas of New York, Philadelphia and Boston as well as several revival tours in England. Ordained as a Presbyterian, he left the Presbyterian Church and became President and Professor of Theology at Oberlin Collegiate Institute (Oberlin College).

[55] Finney's attachment to the Westminster Standards was minimal. While certainly he must have been asked the standard questions about the Confession and Catechisms of the

New York by the Female Missionary Society of the Western District, he began his infamous preaching career in the 1824 revivals in Jefferson and St. Lawrence Counties.[56] Finney's preaching immediately yielded a harvest of souls in a number of small villages as well as the towns of Troy, Utica, Rome (Oneida County) and Auburn. These "Western Revivals" were the scenes of Finney's experiments with new methods of revivalism which would attract so much protest from conservatives. The so-called "new measures" of Finney included his preaching style and innovations such as the "anxious seat," protracted meetings, particular prayer, the "prayer of faith" and allowing women to pray and exhort in public meetings.[57] Before Finney's work in New York, earlier revivals had taken place within the churches with parish pastors. Finney's itinerant ministry inaugurated a new approach to revival ministry in upstate New York.[58]

One of the early critics of Finney's methodology was Lyman Beecher. Beecher, along with fellow Yale revivalist Asahel Nettleton,[59] were opposed to the excesses reported from Finney's revival meetings. Presbyterians in New York likewise raised concerns about the new methods but were restrained by the apparent success of

---

Presbyterian Church when examined by the St. Lawrence Presbytery, Finney admitted: "I had never examined it with any attention, and I think I had never read it through." Charles E. Hambrick-Stowe, *Charles Finney and the Spirit of American Evangelicalism* (Grand Rapids: Wm.B. Eerdmans, 1996), 26. Charles Hodge critiqued Finney's theology in "Review of Finney's Lectures on Systematic Theology," *Biblical Repertory and Princeton Review* XIX (April 1847): 237-77.

[56] Finney found this area "burned over" by enthusiastic Methodist preachers and he believed nothing less than animated preaching would reach these people. See Cross, *The Burned-over District: the Social and Intellectual History of Enthusiastic Religion in Western New York*, 1800-1850 (Ithaca, New York: Cornell University Press, 1950).

[57] The "anxious seat" was a pew at the front for seekers to come forward, sit and pray. Particular prayer was the practice of praying for potential converts by name. The "prayer of faith" was the idea that if all agreed in prayer the requests would be granted. Another target of attack was the hasty admission of these new converts into church membership. A later Presbyterian objection to Finney was his emphasis on perfectionism or "entire sanctification." This theme developed during Finney's years at Oberlin College after he had left the Presbyterian Church. Presbyterians of both schools condemned perfectionist teaching as contrary to the Scriptures. Two New York evangelists were removed from the Presbyterian ministry by Oneida Presbytery in 1833/35 in part for teaching perfectionism; Robert Hastings Nichols, *Presbyterianism in New York*, ed. James Hastings Nichols, (Philadelphia: Westminster Press, 1963), 102,103.

[58] Ibid., 99-101. Nichols asserted that 1825 was the beginning of a new epoch in the history of revivalism. Earlier "revivalist Calvinism" had been marked by careful doctrinal preaching and orderliness; with the genesis of the Finney revivals, a new type of revivalism was introduced to Congregationalism and Presbyterianism.

[59] Asahel Nettleton (1783-1844) was a conservative Congregational itinerant evangelist in New England and New York. He and Bennet Tyler established the Theological Institute of Connecticut (later, Hartford Seminary) in 1833 as a bulwark against "new measures" and the New Haven theology increasingly associated with revivalism.

Finney's ministry. Nathan Beman, a New School pastor in Troy, recommended that a meeting be called for the purpose of discussing differences among the revival preachers. The consultation of eighteen evangelists took place at New Lebanon, New York in the summer of 1827. Consensus emerged from the conference and Finney, the new leader of the movement, began suppressing some of his more excessive behaviors in the coming years.[60]

Beecher, while initially holding serious reservations about Finney, was moderately supportive of Finney as a result of the New Lebanon meeting. Nettleton, however, continued to denounce Finney's new approach to revivals. Beecher wrote to Nettleton in 1829: "There is such an amount of truth and power in the preaching of Mr. Finney, and so great an amount of good hopefully done, that if he can be so far restrained as that he shall do more good than evil, then it would be dangerous to oppose him, lest at length we might be found to fight against God; for though some revivals may be so badly managed as to be worse than none, there may, to a certain extent, be great imperfections in them and yet they be, on the whole, blessings to the Church."[61] New School Presbyterians, while continuing to raise objections to extreme revivalist measures, shared the moderate viewpoint of Beecher and looked for the good that emerged from the apparent large numbers of conversions.[62]

Old School Presbyterians, on the other hand, believed the revivalist new measures should be resisted and severely censured Finney. The association of bad theology with Finney-like revivals was a given in many Old School minds. Of primary concern was the perceived implication in some revivalist preaching that the sinner was the active agent of his own salvation. The emotional appeal to turn to Christ was viewed by Old School skeptics as denying the necessity of the

---

[60] Nichols said there was a stalemate at the conference as New Yorkers were unwilling to acknowledge the authority of New England ministers; *Presbyterianism in New York*, 101.

[61] Letter of Lyman Beecher to Asahel Nettleton, May 28, 1828 in Lyman Beecher, *Autobiography, Correspondence, etc.,of Lyman Beecher*, ed. Charles Beecher (New York, 1865), II, 106; quoted in George Marsden, *The Evangelical Mind and the New School Presbyterian Experience* (New Haven: Yale University Press, 1970), 77,78.

[62] At the 1837 Auburn Convention, the New School made a strong denunciation of errors associated with revivals: "Resolved, That while we bear in mind that with the excitement of extensive revivals indiscretions are sometime intermingled - and that in the attempt to avoid a ruinous practical Antinomianism, human obligation is sometimes urged in a manner that favors Arminian errors – yet, we are bound to declare, that such errors and irregularities have never been sanctioned by these synods or presbyteries - that the prejudice has in a great degree arisen from censorious and exaggerated statements, and from the conduct of persons not in connexion with the Presbyterian Church – that all such departure from the sound doctrine or order of the Presbyterian Church we solemnly disapprove, and when known, deem it our duty to correct by every constitutional method." "The Auburn Declaration" in Maurice Armstrong, Lefferts Loetscher, Charles Anderson, *The Presbyterian Enterprise* (Philadelphia: Westminster Press, 1956):167. The text cited above was the first resolution in the doctrinal section, indicating New School awareness that differences over revivals had been central to doctrinal strife.

regenerating work of the Spirit. Moderate Old School Princetonian Samuel Miller expressed this concern:

> I feel constrained to add, that when this highly exciting system of calling to 'anxious seats,' – calling out into the aisles to be 'prayed for,' &c., is connected, as, to my certain knowledge, it often has been, with erroneous doctrines; – for example, with the declaration, that nothing is easier than conversion; – that the power of the Holy Spirit is not necessary to enable impenitent sinners to repent and believe; – that if they only resolve to be for God – resolve to be Christians – that itself is regeneration – the work is already done: – I say, where the system of 'anxious seat,' &c., is connected with such doctrinal statements as these, it appears to me adapted to destroy souls by wholesale! I will not say that such revivals are never connected with sound conversions; but I will be bold to repeat, that the religion which they are fitted to cherish, is altogether a different one from that of the Gospel. It is, I sincerely believe, a system of soul-destroying deception![63]

Presbyterian support for revivalism was strongest among the New School ranks. The heart of the debate was evangelistic methodology; how would Presbyterians present the gospel to the spiritually destitute of America? Theological controversies were a subsidiary concern of the overarching concern for lost souls. False conversions were rampant in these revivals as far as some of the Old School men were concerned.[64] Many Old Schoolers were convinced that revivalist errors were dangerous and produced easy conversions which were contrived and would fade with time. New School advocates, on the contrary, believed that a great harvest of souls was at hand and to oppose this was resisting God's work of revival. This was a personal, deeply felt issue as the souls of men were at stake and few held dispassionate opinions.[65] Some New School men were convinced that Finney's revival meetings in western New York were the cause of the Presbyterian split. Lyman Beecher, reminiscing about the Old School/New School schism in later years, is reported to have said: "The Oneida revivals did it."[66]

---

[63] Samuel Miller, *Letters to Presbyterians on the Present Crisis in the Presbyterian Church in the United States* (Philadelphia: Anthony Finley, 1833), 165, March 1833. It should be noted that Miller was sincerely supportive of "genuine" revivals: "Long may the Presbyterian Church be favored with genuine revivals of religion, of greater and greater power, in all her borders; and long may she be blessed with ministers and members who love them; who pray for them without ceasing; and who habitually and faithfully use those means for promoting them, which the Scriptures warrant, and which the great Head of the Church is wont to own and bless!" *Letters to Presbyterians*, 151.

[64] Baird described an Old School perspective on Finney-styled revivals: "Unconverted persons, who were of a susceptible disposition and tender conscience, have been wrought up to an intense state of excitement.... Others, more self-confident, have accepted the terms of salvation, presented to them; by electing Jesus as King, and determining, henceforward to be on his side, they have 'made themselves new hearts.' Thus, the impenitent are deceived. The Church is filled with false professors." *History of the New School*, 233,234.

[65] Marsden, *The Evangelical Mind*, 75-82.

[66] *The Memoirs of Charles G. Finney*, eds. Garth M. Rosell and Richard A.G. Dupuis (Grand Rapids: Zondervan, 1989), 145, n. 11.

CHAPTER 4

Missions, Education and Taylorism

Concurrent with revival interests, was the Presbyterian desire to obey the Great Commission. Presbyterians in America had been committed to the work of missions from the beginning. In 1722 the first group of itinerant missionaries was appointed for ministry with dissenting families in Virginia. Mission work among the Indians also began in the eighteenth century. Presbyterian congregations supported these missions through annual collections in all the churches. Records of church courts indicate that often the chief business of their deliberations was the spread of the gospel. Unfortunately, efforts to coordinate Presbyterian efforts for this grand missionary enterprise would also sow seeds of discord in the church.

Early in the nineteenth century, as the American frontier extended westward, Presbyterians continued to answer the missions call. In 1802 a standing Committee on Missions was appointed by the General Assembly to process information for the Assembly. Eventually their powers increased and by 1816 the name was changed to the Board of Domestic Missions. Alongside these denominational efforts was a parallel Presbyterian participation in multi-denominational mission societies. These parallel structures caused friction in the Presbyterian family as each zealously appealed to Presbyterian laymen for resources.

Debate over Missions

At the 1816 General Assembly a United Foreign Missionary Society was proposed which would include members from the Dutch Reformed, Associate Reformed and the Presbyterian Church. The new organization was to be supported by the patronage of the three denominations. The United Foreign Missionary Society (UFMS) was formally organized in 1817 and began its successful labors. By 1826 the United Society, under the conviction that undue competition was hindering contributions, approached the Congregationalist society, the American Board of Commissioners for Foreign Missions (ABCFM),[1] about uniting the two groups. The ABCFM accepted the terms of union which were then recommended for adoption to

---

[1] The American Board of Commissioners for Foreign Missions grew out of the famous 1806 haystack prayer meeting of students from Williams College in Massachusetts. After making their pact to serve overseas, the students were instrumental in getting Massachusetts Congregationalists to organize the ABCFM in 1810. A number of Reformed denominations used the board as their own foreign missions agency.

the 1826 General Assembly. The Assembly consented to this amalgamation but not without some dissent and questions about the implications of this new arrangement. Union with the ABCFM raised suspicions with a few conservative Presbyterians fearful of liberal New England influences and concerned about moving foreign missions outside the direct oversight of the Church.[2]

Domestic mission was also an arena of anxiety for those Presbyterians who favored denominational boards. By 1826 a number of the voluntary societies were united under the newly constituted American Home Missionary Society (AHMS). The AHMS was organized in New York by representatives from Presbyterian, Dutch Reformed and Congregational churches.[3] During this same period, the General Assembly in 1828 reorganized its own Board of Missions in order to bolster its efficiency. Again, competition arose between those who favored the Presbyterian Board and others who supported the AHMS. The Home Missionary Society had proposed that the Board of Missions become an auxiliary of the AHMS, claiming that two separate organizations could not harmoniously occupy the same field without working in concert. The Presbyterian Board resisted this overture as did the 1829 General Assembly; nevertheless, the Assembly gave its blessing to support of AHMS. The Assembly resolution struck a moderate tone: "While the Assembly would affectionately solicit the co-operation of the churches with their own Board of Mission; yet as many of our churches have already united their efforts with the A.H. M. Society, and the A.B.C.F. Missions, therefore, Resolved, as the sense of the Assembly, that the churches should be left entirely to their own unbiased and deliberate choice of the medium through which their charities shall flow to bless the perishing."[4]

The Assembly's compromise policy of 1829 did not resolve the antagonism. Part of the conservative wing of the Old School believed the AHMS was subverting Presbyterian missions.[5] Dr. Absalom Peters, the Secretary of the AHMS, was relentless in his pursuit of merging the two groups. Peters made further attempts to bring the Board and the Society together in the Western Presbyteries and was met by conservative resistance. The 1831 Assembly (with a New School majority) offered another compromise and instructed several Western Synods and their presbyteries to correspond with the AHMS and "devise a plan for carrying on

---

[2] See Samuel J. Baird, *History of the New School* (Philadelphia: Claxton, Rensen & Haffelfinger, 1868), 297-309. Baird said the union, "stripped the Presbyterian Church, of every mission ... and transferred their control to a body over which the Church of God has not the slightest official authority."*History of New School*, 308.

[3] The AHMS had broad support in the Presbyterian Church, including Old School men such as Alexander and Miller of Princeton; H. Woods, *The Presbyterian Controversy, with Early Sketches of Presbyterianism* (Louisville: N.H. White, 1843), 48, 49.

[4] *Minutes of the General Assembly of the Presbyterian Church in the United States of America 1789-1837* (Philadelphia) 1829, 374.

[5] Baird claimed that AHMS Secretary Dr. Absalom Peters and the Executive Board of AHMS had determined to "destroy the Board" by soliciting support for the Society in the West and South. *History of the New School*, 321.

missions in the West."[6] In order to carry out this directive, the Western Convention was held in November 1831 in Cincinnati with representatives from 20 Western Presbyteries. There was such a wide variety of views on a possible solution that no consensus plan of action emerged. The Convention's recommendation, therefore, was to change nothing but continue the Board's work as it presently stood. New School men protested the Western Convention's inaction as subverting the will of the General Assembly.

Conservatives in the West censured the AHMS for its attempts to control the Board of Mission and exert its influence in the Presbyterian Church. Dr. Joshua Wilson[7] of Cincinnati Presbytery denounced the AHMS in a pamphlet, "Four Propositions sustained against the claims of the A.H.M. Society." Wilson asserted, "they profess to be Presbyterians for the purpose of subverting the doctrines, and overthrowing the Presbyterian church." Dr. Peters replied: "If any have suspected us of ulterior views unfriendly to the Presbyterian church, will not our steady attachment to its best interests, and our zealous efforts to build up its desolations, in a little while convince all candid men, who are willing to come to the light, that their suspicions are unjust and cruel?"[8]

Old School conservatives, fearful of New School ecclesiastical domination, organized a resistance movement in 1831 with committees in every Synod. A "Central Committee" in Philadelphia orchestrated the strategy to retake control of the General Assembly. A "Circular," published by the Central Committee in the *Calvinistic Magazine*, declared: "The Voluntary Associations that seek to engross the patronage of our church, and have already engrossed a large part of it, have taken the start of us, in the all-important concerns of education and of missions. They now labor to get the whole of these into their own hands; well knowing that if this be effected, they will infallibly, in a very short time, govern the church."[9]

Old School stalwart Ashbel Green in July 1831 published a series of articles on "The present state of the Presbyterian Church" in the *Christian Advocate*. Green decried the theological diversity he observed in the Assembly of 1831 and warned that unless "there is a general waking up of the Old School Presbyterians, to a sense of their danger and their duty, their influence in the General Assembly will forever afterward be subordinate, and under control."[10] The "principle cause" of animosity was the battle over missionary operations. Green states: "But the peculiar ardor of excitement now prevalent, is principally attributable to a special cause, which ought to be more distinctly marked. It is not the case of Mr. Barnes. That case was indeed made an adjunct, and an auxiliary of the principle cause; but the cause itself, the

---

[6] *Minutes of General Assembly*, 1831, 189.

[7] Joshua L. Wilson, pastor of First Presbyterian Church of Cincinnati had originally supported the AHMS but he had come to believe that this support was harmful to the Presbyterian Church.

[8] Wilson and Peters quoted in Woods, *The Presbyterian Controversy*, 50, 51.

[9] Ibid., 53.

[10] Ashbel Green, "The Present State of the Presbyterian Church," *Christian Advocate* IX (July 1831): 362-66; quoted in Woods, *The Presbyterian Controversy*, 53.

baneful apple of discord which has been thrown into the midst of us, is the inflexible purpose and untiring effort of the Corresponding Secretary and General Agent of the A.H.M. Society, to amalgamate the Board of Mission of the General Assembly with that Society."[11]

Dr. Beman answered Green's essays on the "present crisis" in the *Philadelphian.* Beman agreed with Green that the Barnes case was not ultimate. He pointed out that Old School as well as New School men sustained Mr. Barnes. The differences in doctrinal views evident at the 1831 Assembly "did not produce any uniform or settled arrangement of parties." He continued, "the majority and the minority in the last Assembly, were not formed on the principle of doctrinal distinction, but on the principle of ecclesiastical order." Rather than using the labels "New School" and "Old School," more appropriate terms would be "High Church" and "Low Church." Beman asserted: "The great controversy now carried on in the Presbyterian Church principally relates to questions of ecclesiastical order; and among these the mode of conducting missions appears to be considered the most important by the High Church party."[12]

Tensions continued, with advocates of the Assembly's Board supporting the distinctive denominational mission and other Presbyterians actively participating in voluntary mission societies. Ecclesiastical maneuvering by both groups exacerbated the already sensitive situation. Extreme advocates from each side accused the other of manipulating the church in order to further its own theological bias. Differences over the mode of mission operations was not always strictly along Old School/New School party lines, nevertheless, the most vocal advocates tended to fall into the two camps. Outspoken Old School men proclaimed themselves the "orthodox" and the "true friends of the Presbyterian Church," while New School sympathizers decried the exclusive policy of the "High Church" party. The advocates of strict

---

[11] Ibid., 54. Charges against Albert Barnes were twice brought before the General Assembly in the 1830s; see *infra* chps. 5,6.

[12] Ibid., 55-57. New School opinion after the schism continued to assert that ecclesiastical control not doctrine was the determining factor in the division. Woods stated: "It appears from the documents of 1831, that the Old School party endeavored to secure the control of the church, the funds, Missionary operation, &c., by creating an alarm about doctrines." The 1852 New School authorized *History of the Division of the Presbyterian Church* declared: "The spirit of intolerance, which manifested itself respecting doctrine, was more strikingly exhibited in efforts to control the benevolent operations of the church ... hostility to Voluntary Societies, and a desire to rule the Church, were the chief causes of the acts of the Assembly of 1837, which rent the Church asunder...." *History of the Division of the Presbyterian Church in the United States of America by a Committee of the Synod of New York and New Jersey* (New York: M.W. Dodd, 1952), 92,139. See Earl R. McCormac, "Missions and the Presbyterian Schism of 1837," *Church History* 32 (March 1963): 32-45. E.T. Thompson, citing Professor Elywn Smith, said, "... there are reasons for believing that this development of rival institutionalism was the actual root of the schism..." Ernest Trice Thompson, *Presbyterians in the South* vol. I (Richmond: John Knox Press, 1963), 352.

Presbyterian polity feared the dilution of Calvinism through these organizational entanglements outside the direct authority of the General Assembly.

Educating Presbyterian Ministers

Animosity also surfaced among Presbyterians over the proper mode of educating ministers. In the early decades of the nineteenth century, Presbyterians began to plant their own seminaries in order to meet the needs of a growing nation. Presbyterian students had more educational options, yet the increase of theological schools tended to evoke suspicion from the conservative party. Old School men were apprehensive about the doctrinal instruction received by New School candidates for the ministry. Conservative Old Schoolers were annoyed that New School seminaries were often not controlled by the General Assembly but had either independent boards or reported to regional judicatories where New School men were predominant.[13] Subscription to the doctrinal standards was always mandatory for Presbyterian professors but there were variations in the forms of subscription used by the theological seminaries.

In the eighteenth century the Presbyterian Church had depended on New England Schools, Scottish universities or the College of New Jersey where such stalwarts as Jonathan Edwards, Samuel Davies and John Witherspoon had served as presidents. There was also the academy of William Tennent in Neshaminy, Pennsylvania, the infamous "Log College." Many Presbyterian clergy of the eighteenth century were tutored privately by experienced pastors to prepare them for ordination. As the nineteenth century began, it was increasingly clear that Presbyterians must have additional theological schools. Archibald Alexander, addressing the 1808 General Assembly, declared: "We shall not have a regular and sufficient supply of well-qualified ministers of the Gospel until every Presbytery, or at least every Synod, shall have under its direction a seminary...." Alexander's plan for regional seminaries, while originally rebuffed, was eventually vindicated as the only practical solution. By 1812 Old School Princeton Seminary would be established and the proliferation of Presbyterian seminaries in America would begin.[14]

In New England, Andover Theological Seminary had exhibited significant influence in the Presbyterian Church and numbers of New School clergy studied at Andover due in part to the 1801 Plan of Union. Andover's original purpose was to oppose Unitarianism and to this end Old Calvinists and Hopkinsians within Congregationalism joined forces in establishing Andover in 1808. There were

---

[13] Baird, *History of the New School*, 283-296.

[14] Samuel Miller Jr., *Life of Samuel Miller*, Vol. I (Philadlphia: Claxton, Remsen and Haffelfinger, 1869), 201, 315. Dr. R.C. Reed noted that one of the advantages of the 1801 Plan of Union was its contribution "in no small degree" to the founding of most of the Presbyterian Seminaries during this period. R.C. Reed, *History of the Presbyterian Churches of the World* (Philadelphia, 1905), 255; quoted in William Childs Robinson, *Columbia Theological Seminary and the Southern Presbyterian Church, 1831-1931* (Decatur, GA, 1931), 19.

conservative professors at Andover such as Professor of Theology, Dr. Leonard Woods,[15] respected by Old School men as a Calvinist opponent of Nathaniel Taylor. But other Andover faculty, such as Wood's successor Moses Stuart, held broader Calvinist views and was closely scrutinized by orthodox Presbyterians.[16]

Faculty at Andover subscribed an elaborate creed, drawn up by its founders, as well as the Westminster Shorter Catechism. A renewal of this subscription was required every five years. There was certain latitude in the founder's interpretation of Calvinism but it was a generally conservative creed. Professor Moses Stuart was opposed to the imposition of extended creeds upon the clergy and favored rather a creed that affirmed the essentials of Christianity only. Stuart criticized the inconsistency of Presbyterian subscription in 1836 because they "adopt a creed which explicitly avows that the Scriptures of the Old and New Testament are the SUFFICIENT and ONLY rule of faith and practice, and yet advance, as a condition of Christian fellowship, a belief in some merely human doctrine or mode of expression."[17]

The 1811 Presbyterian General Assembly decided to focus its energy on the establishment of one Presbyterian seminary. Ashbel Green designed a plan for the new seminary which was adopted by the General Assembly. Green was elected as the first president in 1812 and served in that position until his death in 1848. The Princeton plan was carefully orchestrated to safeguard the seminary from doctrinal aberrations. Princeton professors were to take a strict subscriptionist pledge to the Westminster Standards. The Princeton pledge included this vow: "... I do solemnly promise and engage, not to inculcate, teach, or insinuate anything which shall appear to me to contradict or contravene, either directly or impliedly, anything taught in said Confession of Faith or Catechism;...."[18] Full subscription to the

---

[15] Leonard Woods (1774-1854) was a Congregational pastor and seminary professor who led New England Calvinists against Unitarianism and the inroads of Taylorism into Congregationalism. He was a mediator between the Old Calvinists and Hopkinsians in New England as they jointly established Andover Seminary. The Princeton professors had great respect for Dr. Woods and viewed him as an ally against Taylorism. He was heavily involved in the voluntary societies, being a founder of the American Board for Foreign Missions (1810), American Tract Society (1814), Educational Society (1815), and the American Temperance Society (1826).

[16] Elwyn A. Smith, *The Presbyterian Ministry in American Culture: A Study in Changing Concepts, 1700-1900* (Philadelphia: Westminster Press, 1962), 107-111. See Leonard Wood, *The History of Andover Theological Seminary* (Boston: James Osgood and Company, 1885).

[17] Moses Stuart, "Have the Sacred Writers Any Where Asserted that the Sin or Righteousness of One is Imputed to Another," *The Biblical Repository and Quarterly Observer*, First Series, Vol. VII, No. 22 (April 1836): 327; quoted in George M. Marsden, "The New School Presbyterian Mind: A Study of Theology in Mid-Nineteenth Century America" Ph.D. diss., Yale University, 1966, 101.

[18] *Life of Samuel Miller*, I, 357. For the early history of Princeton Seminary see: William S. Selden, *Princeton Theological Seminary: A Narrative History, 1812-1992* (Princeton: Princeton University Press, 1992; David B. Calhoun, *Princeton Seminary*, Vol.1, Faith and Learning, 1812-1868 (Edinburgh: The Banner of Truth Trust, 1994).

Confession was required of the faculty at Princeton but this would not be the explicit requirement of professors at all the Presbyterian seminaries.

Another Presbyterian Seminary was started in Auburn, New York in 1820 by the Synod of Geneva. Western New York desperately needed ministers and Princeton was too inaccessible for students. Auburn professors promised "to receive and adopt the Confession of Faith and the Catechisms ... as containing the System of Doctrines taught in the Holy Scriptures,"[19] which was essentially the same vow taken by Presbyterian ministers. Dr. James Richards,[20] Professor of Theology at Auburn and among the most respected New School theologians, opposed both New Haven and Finney.[21] The Old School seldom had any criticism of Richards, however, this was not the case with some of his later Auburn colleagues such as Samuel Hanson Cox who became Professor of Sacred Rhetoric and Pastoral Theology in 1835. By 1837 Auburn had graduated over 200 students and ultra conservatives worried about Auburn's influence in the church.[22]

Dr. Richards defended New School orthodoxy claiming that Presbyterian ministers in Western New York were committed to Calvinism. Richards described the understanding of subscription in the Synod of Geneva:

As to corruption in doctrine, I know of none which is deep and fundamental among the ministers and churches which stand connected with our Synod. The ministers have all solemnly professed to receive the Confession of Faith, and the Catechism of our church, as containing that system of doctrine which is taught in the Holy Scriptures. At the same time, I do not suppose that they consider this as amounting to a declaration that they receive every proposition included in this extended confession, but such things only as are vital to the system, and which distinguish it from Arminianism, Pelagianism and Semipelagianism. They believe in the doctrine of total depravity by nature – Regeneration by the Sovereign and efficacious influence of the Holy Spirit, – Justification by the righteousness of Christ, as the only true and meritorious cause – the perseverance of the saints, and the interminable punishment of the wicked. They have

---

[19] John Quincy Adams, *A History of Auburn Theological Seminary, 1818-1918* (Auburn New York: Auburn Seminary Press, 1918), 82.

[20] James Richards (1767-1843) studied under Timothy Dwight and was considered a Hopkinsian by Old School conservatives; see Baird, *History of New School*, 240. He was elected moderator of the Presbyterian General Assembly in 1808 and served as a director of Princeton Theological Seminary 1812-1819. Richards was Professor of Christian Theology at Auburn from 1823 until his death.

[21] George Marsden says that Richards, while considering New Haven theology "dubious and dangerous," was willing to tolerate their views "as long as they did not explicitly subvert the fundamentals of the faith." George Marsden, "The New School Presbyterian Mind,"102,103.

[22] Ibid., 106.

no scruple about the doctrine of particular and personal election, but maintain it firmly as a doctrine of the Bible which ought to have a place in the instruction of the pulpit.[23]

During the turbulent years of the 1830s, New School Presbyterians launched two more seminaries. The first was Lane Seminary in Cincinnati, Ohio followed three years later by the formation of Union Seminary in New York. Lane was started with the resources of two Baptist businessmen. Lyman Beecher, the Congregational revivalist and champion of orthodoxy in New England, was appointed the first president in 1832. Conservative clergyman Joshua Wilson, who had originally endorsed Beecher's call to Lane, turned on Beecher and by 1835 Wilson became the prosecutor of Beecher's trial in Cincinnati Presbytery.[24] The theology of Lane was the moderate Edwardsean approach of Beecher who fairly represented the ethos of the seminary. After the schism, Lane would provide strategic institutional support for the New School as a denomination. One of Beecher's colleagues at Lane, Dr. Baxter Dickinson, would be the primary author of the New School's 1837 Auburn Declaration.[25]

In 1836, on the eve of the Presbyterian Schism, Union Seminary in New York was established. Union was started by a group of four Princeton graduates with New School convictions, but, there was also some Old School support for the new

---

[23] Letter of Dr. Richards to Rev. J.C. Stiles, November 13, 1838 in Samuel H. Gridley, *James Richards, Lectures on Mental Philosophy and Theology, with a Sketch of His Life* (New York: M.W. Dodd, 1846), 53.

[24] For a summary of conservative Old School objections to Beecher's theology see Joseph Harvey, *An Examination of the Pelagian and Arminian Theory of Moral Agency As Recently Advocated by Dr. Beecher in His 'Views of Theology'* (New York: Ezra Collier, 1837).

[25] See John Vant Stephens, *The Story of the Founding of Lane*, rev. ed. (Cincinnati, 1940); Edward Morris, a professor at Lane, 1867-1897, described the progressive nature of New School Calvinism which was inculcated by his predecessors at Lane – Beecher, Allen and Nelson. Morris offered a New School perspective on the progression and diversity of Calvinism: "To suppose that a system of truth, having in it so many elements, and holding these in an organic unity so elaborate, should have sprung forth at once as a consummate flower into its final and perfected shape – a system from which nothing could ever be eliminated, and to which the study of future time could add nothing – is to fancy what never has existed, and what, from the nature of the case, never can exist. Calvinism was a thousand years older than Calvin; it had its real genesis in the exigencies of that ancient Pelagian conflict which rent the Christian Church during the fourth and fifth centuries. What Calvin did was to revive and recast, to define and expand, and to formulate afresh what Augustine had already taught ... the Confession and Catechisms of Westminster were not the expression of one unvarying, unanimous form of theological thought – a type of Calvinism in which all were perfectly agreed, as to both substance and expression; but rather were the final outcome of strenuous and prolonged debates, assuming at last the form of a mediatory compromise between recognized extremes.... And is it not one of the glories of that memorable Council that its members, however widely they differed in particulars, were still able to discern the broad, underlying Calvinism which led them together, and made them essentially one?" Edward D. Morris, *Thirty Years in Lane and Other Lane Papers*, n.p., 1897, 96-99.

seminary. One of the founders was Absalom Peters, an outspoken proponent of voluntary societies and a primary defender of Albert Barnes in the 1836 trial. The stated objective of Union Seminary was "to provide a Theological Seminary in the midst of the greatest and most growing community in America around which all men of moderate views and feelings, who desire to live free from party strife, and to stand aloof from all extremes of doctrinal speculation, practical radicalism and ecclesiastical domination, may cordially and affectionately rally."[26]

Union was organized as a seminary for moderate men dedicated to the cooperative catholic spirit of the benevolent societies. Union was also distinctly Presbyterian. Professors at the seminary made this pledge:

I believe the Scriptures of the Old and New Testament to be the word of God, the only infallible rule of faith and practice; and I do now, in the presence of God and the Directors of this Seminary, solemnly and sincerely receive the Westminster Confession of Faith as containing the system of doctrine taught in the Holy Scriptures. I do also, in like manner, approve of the Presbyterian Form of Government; and I do solemnly promise that I will not teach or inculcate anything which shall appear to me to be subversive of said system of doctrines or of the principles of said Form of Government so long as I shall continue to be a Professor in the Seminary.[27]

Union faculty committed themselves to Westminster orthodoxy, but, in the light of recent New School activities in the mid-1830s, Union's establishment in 1836 was viewed as a threat by both ultra conservatives and Princeton.

The South was also in dire need of theological schools and planted several new seminaries in the southern and western regions. Union Seminary in Prince Edward County Virginia grew out of the theological instruction of Hampden-Sydney College. By 1824 Union Seminary was organized after the Princeton model with the leadership of John Holt Rice who became the first professor. Union was jointly under the oversight of the Synods of Virginia and North Carolina as well as the General Assembly. Union Seminary professors were moderate men who lived in the bonds of charitable toleration until the Presbyterian schism. The seminary declared

---

[26] George Lewis Prentiss, *The Union Theological Seminary in the City of New York: Historical and Biographical Sketches of Its First Fifty Years* (New York, 1889), 8; quoted in Smith, *The Presbyterian Ministry in American Culture*, 169; George Marsden, *The Evangelical Mind and the New School Presbyterian Experience* (New Haven: Yale University Press, 1970), 109-114. See also Robert T. Handy, *A History of Union Theological Seminary in New York* (New York: Columbia University Press, 1987). Handy comments on this paragraph: "Here the New School stamp was clearly evident as the founders protested what they regarded as the over-rigid subscription to the Westminster Confession on the part of the Old." Robert T. Handy, "Union Theological Seminary in New York and American Presbyterianism, 1836-1904," *American Presbyterians* (Summer, 1988):117.

[27] Prentiss, *Fifty Years of Union Seminary*, 43,44; quoted in Robert T. Handy, "Union Theological Seminary in New York and American Presbyterianism, 1836-1904," *American Presbyterians* (Summer, 1988): 116.

itself for the Old School at the time of the separation and two professors opposed to the schism had to resign.[28]

Kentucky Presbyterians started ministerial training for the western regions when the charter of Centre College was revised to include theological instruction and the first professor was appointed in 1828. Danville Seminary (later, Louisville Seminary) was officially established in 1853 by the Old School Assembly and would eventually become part of the Northern Old School Church in 1861. In western Pennsylvania, the 1827 General Assembly authorized Western Seminary (later, Pittsburgh Seminary) and elected the first board of directors who were all Old School men. The new seminary in Allegheny Pennsylvania "reproduced the Plan of Princeton and the Presbyterianism of Ashbel Green."[29]

The Synod of Tennessee established the Southern and Western Seminary in 1819, after Isaac Anderson's failed attempt to entice Princeton graduates to the west. At least 100 divinity graduates of Southern and Western would serve in the Presbyterian Church. The Tennessee seminary had a New School orientation due to the Hopkinsian convictions of Isaac Anderson, the founder. Anderson has been described as "a Calvinist, who held the doctrines of Edwards, Dwight and Spring with some of the peculiarities of the Hopkins' system." In 1842 the seminary took the name – Maryville College, and came under the full control of the New School Synod by 1845.[30]

In South Carolina a seminary was organized at Columbia with classes beginning in 1831. The Theological Seminary of South Carolina and Georgia (later, Columbia Theological Seminary) was responsible to the Synod of South Carolina and Georgia and afterward the Synods of Florida and Alabama added their support. The seminary had the same arrangement with the General Assembly as Union in Virginia – direct oversight by the synod(s) with the Assembly's right to intervene if necessary. The seminary at Columbia was influenced by the curriculum at Andover and Princeton. Two of the first professors, George Howe and Aaron W. Leland, were New Englanders who avoided "the agitating questions of party" believing they had something "more important to do," i.e., the instruction of theological students. For this neutrality they were accused of unsoundness in the ecclesiastical heats of 1836 which the Synod promptly denied. In 1838 the Synod of South Carolina and Georgia decided to favor the Old School position which in turn placed the seminary in the Old School camp.[31]

---

[28] William Henry Foote, *Sketches of Virginia*, Second Series (Philadelphia: J.B. Lippincott & Co., 1855), 541-42. The Synod of North Carolina passed a resolution supporting the action of the 1837 General Assembly, declaring that the views of the seminary professors should "harmonize with those of this Synod." This action brought pressure on the Board of Directors who forced the issue with the faculty at Union. Two professors (Goodrich and Taylor) declared it their duty to oppose the action of the General Assembly disowning the four synods. The Synod of Virginia adopted no such resolution concerning the seminary.

[29] Elwyn Smith, *The Presbyterian Ministry in American Culture*, 163.

[30] E.T. Thompson, *Presbyterians in the South*, I, 355.

[31] Robinson, *Columbia Theological Seminary*, 36.

An adjunct to Old School/New School competition over seminaries, was debate over the recruitment and provision for young ministers entering these schools. Raising funds for seminary students became another battleground between those who supported voluntary societies and advocates of denominational administration of benevolences. The American Education Society was established in 1815 in order to raise funds for seminary students and many Presbyterians had channeled their finances in that direction. By 1818, members of the Synod of Philadelphia consulted on the possibility of erecting their own Presbyterian Education Society. The Philadelphia Board wanted their society under the direct oversight of the General Assembly. At about the same time, a similar plan was pursued in New York where a group of Presbyterians started The Education Society of the Presbyterian Church in the United States of America. An overture came from the New York Society proposing that they join hands with the Philadelphia Board to consolidate efforts for the church. This merger never occurred and one of the apparent issues was doctrinal differences.[32]

At the General Assembly of 1819, a denominational Board of Education was formally organized. The Philadelphia Board had wished to see both Philadelphia and New York become subsidiaries of the new General Assembly Board but this was not to transpire. Old School men were frustrated with the independent New York Society, believing that the ultimate goal of the New Yorkers was to get young men into New England Seminaries. A spirit of jealousy and competition heightened tensions as the needed resources were being diverted from the General Assembly Board to either the New York Society or the American Education Society. Dispute over theological education continued up through the time of the Presbyterian schism.

Taylorism

Old School Presbyterians had compiled a host of ecclesiastical grievances against the New School by the end of the 1820s. People with deeply held convictions on both sides collided regularly in presbyteries, synods and the General Assembly. Nevertheless, the great divide from the conservatives' viewpoint was the perceived doctrinal error permeating the church. Old School conservatives openly attacked evidence of compromise with doctrinal standards while New School men were inclined to allow greater latitude of theological expression. The Hopkinsian

---

[32] Baird, *History of the New School*, 283-289. Baird said that Professors Alexander and Miller of Princeton attended the organizational meeting of the New York society. He commented: "But they found the prevalent feelings so hostile to the authority of the General Assembly, to the doctrines of the standards, in their strict acceptation, and to the plan of Princeton Seminary, that they withdrew, and returned home." *History of the New School*, 286. Undoubtedly, there were some underlying doctrinal differences, however, Baird, known for his extreme overstatement of New School positions, was exaggerating New School sentiments when he described it as "hostile" to the General Assembly and Presbyterian doctrine.

controversy had not yielded a uniform response in the Presbyterian Church. Old School conservatives had resisted Hopkinsianism, however, many Old School moderates joined with the New School in tolerating Hopkinsian theology as an acceptable articulation of Calvinism. Notwithstanding majority detente with Hopkinsianism, the early 1820s generated further revision of New England theology coming out of Yale College. New Haven Theology would head in a radical direction which moved far beyond the boundaries of acceptable Calvinism. New Haven innovations incited the indignation of both moderate and conservative Old School men as well as some New Schoolers and conservative Edwardseans.

A distinctive New Haven Theology was primarily identified with the work of Nathaniel Taylor (1786-1858) who became the Dwight Professor of Didactic Theology at Yale in 1822. Taylor and his Yale colleagues claimed that their revisionist theology was genuinely Calvinist. Taylorism, however, moved beyond the adjustments of Hopkinsianism to a serious diluting of traditional Calvinist orthodoxy. Charges of Arminianism, Pelagianism and even Unitarianism would be brought against the Taylorites.

Taylor had been heavily influenced by Scottish Common Sense Philosophy[33] which exalted the use of reason as a critical component of the theological task. Reason is the "umpire" of truth and it should be considered an infallible guide that the Word of God will never contradict. Reason and revelation will always be in harmony. Common sense is defined as "the competent, unperverted reason of the human mind, whose decisions in the interpretations of the Scriptures, are to be relied on as infallible. Man must know some things beyond the possibility of mistake, or there is an end to all knowledge and all faith." It was this elevation of reason that would lead Taylor to modify the doctrines of original sin, human inability and regeneration.[34]

---

[33] Common Sense Philosophy (Scottish Realism, Empiricism) was an eighteenth-century philosophical school originating with Thomas Reid's (1710-1796) work which opposed both David Hume's (1711-1776) skepticism and the idealism of George Berkeley (1685-1753). Reid argued that human beings gain accurate knowledge of the world through the use of their senses. In addition to this empirical knowledge, there is an innate "moral sense" common to man which enables him to have intuitive knowledge of foundational principles of morality. This philosophy had a considerable impact in American Protestantism up until the War Between the States. Presbyterian clergyman, John Witherspoon, was instrumental in introducing Common Sense Philosophy to America through his influence as President of the College of New Jersey. See Sydney Ahlstrom, "Scottish Philosophy and American Theology," *Church History* XXIV (September, 1955): 257-72.

[34] Nathaniel W. Taylor, *Essays, Lectures, Etc. Upon Select Topics in Revealed Theology*, (New York: Clark, Austin, and Smith, 1859): 221-223. See also two articles by Taylor: "Application of the Principles of Common Sense to Certain Disputed Doctrines," *The Quarterly Christian Spectator* III (September, 1831): 453-76; "On the Authority of Reason in Theology," *The Quarterly Christian Spectator* XI (March, 1837): 151-61. For an overview of Taylor's theology see Douglas A. Sweeney, *Nathaniel William Taylor, New Haven Theology and the Legacy of Jonathan Edwards* (New York: Oxford University Press, 2002).

Concerning original sin, Taylor denied that all humanity had acted in the sin of Adam and was therefore guilty of his sin. If this were true, "I must renounce the reason which my Maker has given to me." Further, Taylor believed that the depravity of the human heart was the result of one's own choices. Taylor declared: "Not a human being does or can become thus sinful or depraved but by his own choice. God does not compel him to sin by the nature which he gives him. Nor is his sin, although a consequence of Adam's sin, in such a sense its consequence, as not to be a free voluntary action of his own. He sins freely, voluntarily."[35] Since the free choice of each person is behind his own moral depravity, the free agency of man is not lost as a result of the fall.[36] Further, the Edwardsean distinction between natural ability and moral inability does not fit within Taylor's system because the genesis of moral inability is the voluntary act of a free moral agent.[37]

Instead of innate depravity, Taylor posits that within every person there exists a constitutional principle of self-love which is the instinctive desire for happiness. In the initial exercise of man's free moral agency, the self-love principle is directed towards the world rather than love for God. Regeneration, according to Taylor, is not the creation of a new disposition in man but rather the voluntary change of the governing principle of one's life. This change of heart involves a new love for God in the place of seeking happiness in the world. Man has the power to make this change but will never do so without the gracious work of the Holy Spirit. In order to safeguard man's genuine freedom, Taylor believed it was necessary to speak of the power of contrary choice, nevertheless, he acknowledged man's dependence on grace.[38] Taylor stated, "I suppose a necessity of grace, not to constitute men moral agents, or able to obey God, but to influence those to obey God who can, but from willfulness in sin never will obey him without grace."[39]

---

[35] Nathaniel W. Taylor, *Concio ad Clerum, A sermon delivered in the chapel of Yale College September 10, 1828* (New Haven: Hezekiah Howe, 1828) 6, 28, 29. Taylor attributed the doctrine of imputation to the distorted thinking of St. Augustine who "foisted this error upon the Church by his ignorance of Greek and his undue attachment to his pre-Christian philosophy;" Nathaniel Taylor, *Essays, Lectures, Etc., Upon Select Topics in Revealed Theology* (New York: Clark, Austin, Smith, 1859), 171; quoted in Earl A. Pope, "New England Calvinism and the Disruption of the Presbyterian Church" Ph.D. diss., Brown University, 1962, 95.

[36] Pope described Taylor's view: "Taylor had an early encounter with the Arminians of his day, who claimed that man's 'free agency was lost by the fall of Adam, and that man is now a free agent only by supernatural grace through Jesus Christ.' This Taylor vigorously denied, claiming that man was a free moral agent independent of supernatural aid. He maintained that man's nature was basically uncorrupted and that there was no need of 'supernatural grace' to make man a responsible creature." "New England Calvinism," 77.

[37] Ibid., 93, 94. Pope pointed out, "the crucial authority of Taylor in his whole argument was common sense."

[38] Ibid., 104-121.

[39] Nathaniel W. Taylor, *Lectures on the Moral Government of God*, vol. II, (New York: Clark, Austin, Smith), 132. Taylor believed that the explanations of inability by Augustinians, Calvinists, Arminians and Edwardseans all fell short of supporting the moral

Here was significant theological movement away from Edwardsean theology. While Taylor claimed to be an orthodox Calvinist and frequently invoked the name of Edwards, there was grave concern in New England that Taylor was coming dangerously close to Pelagianism. Leonard Woods, a professor at Andover, stated his concern in a letter to Taylor: "How would you expect us to feel, when a brother who has professed to be decidedly orthodox, and has our entire confidence, and is placed at the Head of one of our theological schools, makes an attack upon several of the articles of our faith, and employs language on the subject of moral agency, free will, depravity, divine influence, etc., which is so like the language of Arminians and Pelagians, that it would require some labor to discover the difference?"[40] Taylorism brought theological turbulence to the Congregationalists of New England where many Old Calvinists found Taylor's theology woefully insufficient.

In 1834 a Yale trustee[41] brought charges against Taylor for teaching doctrines that were out of accord with the Saybrook Confession of Faith.[42] There had historically been periods of both loose and strict subscription required of faculty at Yale. When Taylor was appointed professor at Yale in 1822, he had signed the confession with the "substance of doctrine" understanding of subscription. This had been the received conception of faculty subscription since the presidencies of Ezra Stiles and Timothy Dwight in the late eighteenth century. The Corporation of Yale cleared Taylor of these charges and tried to assure the public of Yale's orthodoxy.

The Yale professors defended themselves against the charges of heterodoxy by arguing for a distinction between the primary and secondary doctrines of the confession. The secondary doctrines were explanations of the primary ones which attempted to place them into a harmonious system of doctrine. The New Haven professors asserted that a number of these secondary explanatory doctrines had been

---

responsibility of man. Unless man has the power to obey "it is absolutely inconceivable that he should obey, for the act of obedience is his own, done in the use or exercise of his own power to obey." *Moral Government*, 133.

[40] Leonard Woods, *Letters to Rev. Nathaniel W. Taylor* (Andover: Mark Newman, 1830), 98; quoted in Pope, "New England Calvinism," 99. For a detailed account of the debates over Taylorism within Congregationalism see Zebulon Crocker, *The Catastrophe of the Presbyterian Church in 1837, Including a Full View of the Recent Theological Controversies in New England* (New Haven: B. & W. Noyes, 1838), 113-297.

[41] Daniel Dow, a member of the Corporation, would leave Yale and help found the East Windsor Institute as a reaction to New Haven Theology. He wrote a book contesting the orthodoxy of Yale – *New Haven Theology and Taylorism Alias Neology In Its Own Language* (Thompson: George Roberts, 1834).

[42] The Saybrook Confession of Faith (1708) was a Congregationalist creed that incorporated the substance of the Westminster Confession of Faith. See Williston Walker, *The Creeds and Platforms of Congregationalism* (New York: Charles Scribner's Sons, 1893), 517.

discarded and better modes of expressing the primary doctrines had been adopted.[43] Presbyterians reacted strongly to Taylor whose innovations were often the catalyst for fierce theological warfare. For most Presbyterians, Taylorism could not be squared with an honest embrace of Westminster Calvinism.

Reaction to New Haven

The Princeton professors had raised cautionary voices about Hopkinsian doctrines, but had still considered it within the boundaries of honest subscription to the Confession of Faith. Taylorism, on the other hand, would so push the boundaries of acceptable doctrinal latitude that moderates as well as conservatives heralded a genuine departure from essential Calvinism. In 1830-31 the *Biblical Repertory* would publish seven articles protesting the errors of Taylorism.[44]

By the early decades of the nineteenth century, the Presbyterian Church had a significant number of ministers who had received their training in the New England seminaries. Since many of these men no doubt had embraced the theological tenets of their professors, traditional Calvinists were gravely concerned about the influx of New England theology into Presbyterianism. Archibald Alexander of Princeton Seminary, through the pages of *The Christian Advocate*, began to raise concern over the doctrines coming out of New England. In 1824 he wrote an essay critiquing a sermon preached at Andover on the atonement. An anonymous letter to the editor (probably Ashbel Green), responded to Alexander's review and pointed out that there were two parties within the Presbyterian Church which he denominated the Old School and the New School.[45] This appears to be one of the earliest references which used these designations for the two nascent Presbyterian parties.

As irritation with New England and especially New Haven continued to mount, the theological faculty at Princeton, who viewed themselves as the faithful upholders of historic Calvinism, began to offer rebuttals to this impeachment of traditional Reformed theology. In this new situation, the Princeton professors would find themselves aligned with the Old School conservatives of Philadelphia in opposing New Haven innovations. Taylorism in particular could not be reconciled with the Westminster Confession of Faith from the Princeton perspective. Hodge

---

[43] Earl A. Pope, *New England Calvinism and the Disruption of the Presbyterian Church* (New York: Garland, 1987), 81-84. The *New York Observer*, September 6, 1834 printed a statement from the Yale Theology professors explaining their views.

[44] Most of these articles have been reprinted in a recent volume, *Princeton Versus The New Divinity* (Edinburgh: Banner of Truth Trust, 2001).

[45] Archibald Alexander, "Review of 'Nature of the Atonement'" *The Christian Advocate*, II (February 1824) and (March 1824); Zeta, "Letter to the Editor" *The Christian Advocate*, II (May, 1824) and (July, 1824). Baird suggests that Zeta was Samuel H. Cox. *History of the New School*, xxi.

asserted that Taylorism was much worse than Arminianism; there is "four-fold more truth and aliment for piety in Arminianism than in these new doctrines."[46]

Archibald Alexander weighed in on Taylorite views in an 1831 article which addressed Taylor's understanding of the power of contrary choice. Alexander utilized the Edwardsean distinction between natural ability and moral inability to counter Taylorism. Edwards's conception of moral inability was set in opposition to Taylor's notion that men could change their own hearts, albeit with God's aid. Alexander favored the old Edwardsean position, however, he was deeply concerned that this distinction was being abandoned by some of the younger ministers. Alexander exclaimed, "These new preachers, in their addresses to the impenitent sinner, say nothing about natural and moral inability. They preach that man is in possession of every ability requisite for the discharge of his duty. That it is as easy for him to repent, to exercise faith, and to love God, as to speak, or eat, or walk, or perform any other act. And men are earnestly and passionately exhorted, to come up at once to the performance of their duty."[47]

Alexander and Hodge generally viewed the New School as orthodox on regeneration and inability. Where the New School and Princeton would collide was over the doctrine of the imputation of Adam's sin. Taylorites had jettisoned this doctrine. Alexander initiated the conflict over imputation through an article he wrote on the history of Pelagianism. Here, Alexander named the kernel of Pelagius's error to be a denial of original sin. Alexander argued that Augustine had definitively answered Pelagius and demonstrated that Adam's sin was indeed imputed to his posterity and a corrupt nature passed on to them. This was the historic position of the Christian Church. Alexander's essay seemed to imply that some contemporary theologians were advocating Pelagian-like ideas which were in fact very old ideas. Alexander stated: "It is attended with many advantages to bring into view ancient heresies: for often what modern innovators consider a new discovery, and wish to pass off as a scheme suited to remove all difficulties, is found upon examination to be nothing else than some ancient heresy clothed in a new dress."[48] The New Haven

---

[46] Charles Hodge, "A Brief History and Vindication of the Doctrines Received and Established in the Churches of New England," *The Biblical Repertory and Princeton Review*, XI (July, 1839): 396.

[47] Archibald Alexander, "An Inquiry Into That Inability Under Which the Sinner Labours, and Whether It Furnishes Any Excuse For His Neglect of Duty," *The Biblical Repertory* III (July, 1831): 370, 371. Pope pointed out that both Alexander and Hodge were still convinced that the main body of the New School was sound in doctrine. "Both Hodge and Alexander made every effort in their respective analyses of Taylorism to indicate their faith in the substantial orthodoxy of the New School. Hodge was convinced that the New School held to the orthodox position on regeneration, and Alexander claimed that in the final analysis the moral inability of which the New School spoke was the same as that maintained by the Old School." Pope, "New England Calvinism," 148, 149.

[48] Archibald Alexander, "The Early History of Pelagianism," *The Biblical Repertory and Theological Review* II (January 1830): 92, 104, 112, 113.

press promptly reacted with several journal articles responding to Alexander's accusations.[49]

Responding to New Haven's defense, Hodge stated that Alexander had called no man a Pelagian. Hodge pointed out the essential tenets necessary to avoid a Pelagian system. "So long, however, as these brethren hold to a moral certainty that all men will sin the moment they become moral agents; that the first sin leads to entire moral depravity; and that an immediate influence of the Spirit is necessary in conversion, they differ from that system in these important points." Hodge expressed his concern over where New Haven thought may be leading because "history informs us, that when men have taken the first step, they or their followers soon have taken the second."[50]

What was at stake for Hodge were the potential ramifications of denying imputation. Hodge stated: "The Spectator thinks this is a mere dispute about words. We think very differently. A principle is involved in the decision of this question, which affects very deeply our views, not only of the nature of our relation to Adam, and of original sin, but also of the doctrines of the atonement and justification; the most vital doctrines of the Christian system." The imputation of Adam's sin was considered an essential doctrine because of its inseparable connection to the imputation of Christ's righteousness to the human race. "As we have been condemned for a sin which is not our own, so are we justified by righteousness which is not our own ... the disobedience of one is the ground of our being treated as sinners; and the obedience of the other is the ground of our being treated righteous."[51]

Placed in the context of soteriology, outright dismissal of original sin ultimately could point to a denial of the gospel. This was of utmost seriousness and not simply a matter of diversity among Reformed thinkers. Taylorism appeared to echo Pelagian-like ideas that struck at the root of Augustinian theology. At the very least it was a severe Arminian position clearly outside the boundaries of Westminster Calvinism. The strict Old School men had a valid point: How could a true Taylorite publicly profess to adopt the Confession of Faith and simultaneously deny doctrines fundamental to that Confession? Many Presbyterians, in both Old and New School, were certain that Taylor and his disciples had crossed the line of acceptable Presbyterian orthodoxy; but, the extent to which Taylorism had made consequential

---

[49] Protestant and Editors, "Inquiries Respecting the Doctrine of Imputation," *Quarterly Christian Spectator* II (June 1830). Hodge said that "Protestant" was Moses Stuart, professor at Andover; Archibald Alexander Hodge, *Life of Charles Hodge* (New York: Charles Scribner's Sons, 1880), 267.

[50] Charles Hodge, "Review of an Article in the June Number of The Christian Spectator Entitled 'Inquiries Respecting the Doctrine of Imputation,'" *The Biblical Repertory and Theological Review* II (October, 1830): 429.

[51] Ibid., 464-468. For a survey and critique of Hodge's views on imputation see George P. Hutchinson, *The Problem of Original Sin in American Presbyterian Theology* (Presbyterian and Reformed Publishing Company, 1972), 28-35.

inroads into the Presbyterian Church was always a matter of debate.[52] Parts of the New School, however, were willing to tolerate conservative interpretations of Taylorism.[53]

Old School Discord Over Subscription

At the same time that Princeton moderates were joining hands with Old School conservatives to condemn Taylorism, a rift developed over the degree of strictness required in subscribing the doctrinal standards. Princeton maintained that most of the New School were orthodox and believed a certain degree of toleration was an ecclesiastical necessity. The ultra conservatives disagreed. The conservative Philadelphia paper, *The Presbyterian,* asserted that the Confession of Faith "must be subscribed fully."[54] The Princeton professors, on the other hand, held a more inclusive perspective on adopting the Confession. Princeton sought middle ground which did not condemn all those who identified with the New School but directed its attack against the extremism of Taylor and his disciples. Archibald Alexander wrote in 1834 that the Princeton faculty was "not disposed to consider every man a heretic who differs in some few points from us."[55]

Professor Charles Hodge formally addressed the subscription issue in a review of a published sermon preached by Samuel Cox at the 1829 opening session of the Synod of New York. Cox's sermon had emphasized the role of man in regeneration and attacked the idea of human inability. Hodge responded in the pages of the *Biblical Repertory* that Cox had unfairly characterized the doctrines of Calvinism. In his defense of genuine Calvinism, Hodge cited a number of theologians including Edwards, Bellamy and Dwight. Arguing from Jonathan Edwards's exposition of regeneration in *Religious Affections*, Hodge summarized the debate: "All the Old Calvinists, and the great majority, we hope and believe, of the new school also, hold that the result of the Holy Spirit's operation on the soul, is a holy principle of disposition; Dr. Cox says, if we understand him, that the result is a holy act. This is

---

[52] Hodge believed that the New Haven party in the Presbyterian Church was "inconsiderate as to numbers." Charles Hodge, "General Assembly of 1836," *Princeton Review*, VIII (July 1836): 458. Conservatives in the 1837 "Testimony and Memorial" declared that they had "conclusive proof" that errors were "widely disseminated" in the Presbyterian Church. "Testimony and Memorial" in Isaac Brown, *A Historical Vindication of the Abrogation of the Plan of Union by the Presbyterian Church in the United States of America* (Philadelphia: William S. and Alfred Martien, 1855), 217.

[53] Marsden, "The New School Mind," 92.

[54] *The Presbyterian*, April 23, 1836.

[55] James A. Alexander, *Life of Archibald Alexander* (1854; reprint, Harrisonburg, Virginia: Sprinkle Publications, 1991), 474. Pope commented: "Princeton persisted in the conviction that Taylorism, which Princeton interpreted in its most liberal sense, was the real source of error within the Church against which both the Old School and the New School ought to unite their forces." "New England Calvinism," 304.

the whole ground of debate, and to lookers on it may appear too narrow to be worth disputing about."[56]

Cox's rebuttal included a criticism of Hodge's citation of theologians as authorities rather than Scripture as the "only rule." Cox retorted, "Owen, Charnock, Bates, Edwards, Bellamy, Dwight! When the sun is up, these stars of the first magnitude are no longer discernible. What do I care primarily and practically, in investigation of the revealed doctrines of God, for them? For you? For the standards of the church themselves? Or even for the General Assembly?"[57]

In Hodge's 1831 rejoinder to Cox, he addressed the meaning of "system of doctrines" in the ministerial subscription vow. Hodge advocated avoiding two extremes: "On the one hand, there are some, who seem inclined to give the phrase in question, such a latitude that any one, who holds the great fundamental doctrines of the Gospel, as they are recognized by all evangelical denominations, might adopt it, while on the other, some are disposed to interpret it so strictly as to make it not only involve the adoption of all the doctrines contained in the Confession, but to preclude all diversity in the manner on conceiving and explaining them."[58]

Opposing both of these inordinate views of subscription, Hodge argued that the term "system of doctrine" specifically referred to the distinctive Calvinistic system of doctrine in the Confession. Hodge explained the meaning of the subscription pledge: "In professing to adopt the Confession of Faith as containing the system of doctrines taught in the sacred Scriptures, a man professes to believe the whole series of doctrines constituting that system, in opposition to every other. That is, he professes to believe the whole series of doctrines which go to make up the Calvinistic system, in opposition to the Socinian, Pelagian, Semi-Pelagian, Arminian, or any other opposite and inconsistent view of Christianity." Hodge listed the essential doctrines of the Calvinistic system,[59] and asserted that anyone who "believes all these doctrines, does, according to the correct interpretation of

---

[56] Charles Hodge, "Review of 'Regeneration,'" *Biblical Repertory and Theological Review* II (April, 1830): 255, 266.

[57] Samuel Cox, "Reply of Dr. Cox," *The Biblical Repertory and Theological Review* III (October, 1831): 490.

[58] Charles Hodge, "Remarks on Dr. Cox's Communication," *The Biblical Repertory and Theological Review* III (October, 1831): 520-521. Pope stated: "Princeton attempted to resolve the tensions between Old Calvinism and New England Calvinism with a more relaxed interpretation of subscription, a corollary of which was a more tolerant attitude toward the New School doctrinal position." Pope, "New England Calvinism," 304.

[59] Hodge's list of essential doctrines: "These doctrines are clearly expressed; such as the doctrine of the trinity, the incarnation and supreme deity of Christ, the fall and original sin, atonement, justification by faith, unconditional personal election, effectual calling, perseverance of the saints, eternal punishment of the wicked, &c.&c.&c." Hodge added: "With respect to each of these several points, there are, and safely may be, various modes of statement and explanation consistent with their sincere reception." Hodge, "Remarks on Dr. Cox's Communication," 522.

language, hold the 'system of doctrines' contained in the Confession of Faith."[60] On the other hand, Hodge clearly rejected a latitudinarian *pro forma* subscription as "morally wrong." If a Presbyterian minister rejects one of the "constituent elements" of the Calvinistic system (original sin or election, for example) "it would effectually destroy the very intent of a creed." Hodge stated: "For if the principle be once admitted that one of the doctrines of the system may be rejected, there is an end to all meaning in the profession to adopt."[61]

Hodge was convinced that his articulation of creedal subscription was the commonly held understanding of the Presbyterian Church. He declared:

> If the question, what do these words, 'system of doctrines' as they occur in the ordination service mean? were submitted to a thousand impartial men – nine hundred and ninety-nine would no doubt answer, they mean the Calvinistic system distinctly as exhibited in our standards; and consequently that no man, who denied original sin, efficacious grace, personal election, decrees, or perseverance of the saints, or any other of its characteristic parts, could, with a good conscience profess to receive it.... These are the principles, which if we mistake not, the great mass of Presbyterians are ready to adopt. They are ready to say that no man can consistently be a minister in our Church, who rejects any one of the constituent doctrines of the Calvinistic system contained in the Confession of Faith; while, from necessity and from principle, they are willing to allow any diversity of view and explanation not destructive of their nature, that is, not amounting to their rejection.[62]

Hodge and his Princeton colleagues' position on the ordination vow did not sit well with the ultra conservative wing of the Old School party. It sounded much too close to the more liberal New School viewpoint. Hodge appeared to grant the New School distinction between primary and explanatory doctrines in the Confession, implying, one could subscribe the Confession without having to adhere to every article as long as the primary doctrines of Calvinism were maintained. Old School strict subscriptionists contrariwise believed there was an inseparable connection between the primary and explanatory doctrines of the Confession; the rejection of explanatory doctrines undermined the primary ones.[63] The conservatives insisted that the Westminster Standards "must be subscribed fully or its reputation is lost."[64] Indifference to the doctrines of the Confession was the great sin of the church as far as *The Presbyterian* was concerned.[65]

As the 1830s began, Princeton had been well aware that disagreement over subscription was a crucial problem separating the church into Old School/New School parties as well as fracturing the Old School itself. Concerning subscription, Hodge observed in 1831: "In the present agitated state of our Church, we are

---

[60] Ibid.
[61] Ibid., 524.
[62] Ibid.
[63] *The Presbyterian*, April 2, 1835, 53.
[64] *The Presbyterian*, April 23, 1836, 62.
[65] *The Presbyterian*, January 6, 1838, 2.

persuaded that this, of all others, is the subject of the most practical importance. If it could be once clearly ascertained and agreed upon, where the line was to be drawn, there would be an end to a great part of the contention and anxiety which now unhappily exists."[66] The Princeton "peace men," as the conservatives pejoratively dubbed them, believed that if a general consensus on subscription could be achieved, it would alleviate some of the pressure building in the Presbyterian Church. There were a multitude of issues alienating Presbyterians from one another, yet, one's view of subscription was foundational for approaching the other contentious problems. The subscription question pointed directly to the doctrinal divide in the Presbyterian household.

The controversies within Presbyterianism in the early decades of the nineteenth century indicate that doctrinal diversity was the primary culprit of Presbyterian factions. Hopkinsian innovations had been challenged by conservatives who claimed that New Divinity men had transgressed the doctrinal boundaries of the Confession of Faith. Old School/New School strife over revivals was often a doctrinal concern about the theology promoted by the new revivalist preachers who appeared to be departing from Calvinism. Doctrinal differences also lay behind the ecclesiastical fragmentation over missions and education. In addition to ardent convictions about Presbyterian polity, the substance of conservative suspicion about voluntary societies was the perceived absence of Reformed theological commitments in those societies, which therefore, made them subversive of Presbyterianism.

Taylorism was the target of Presbyterian denunciation from many directions. While Princeton did not believe that Hopkinsians, moderate New England Calvinists nor the New School as a whole were outside the confines of fair confessional subscription, unorthodox New Haven theology was another case entirely. Attempts to square Taylorism with Westminster Calvinism were futile as far as both Princeton and the ultras were concerned. As Princeton continued to attack the doctrines of New Haven, it further inspired the ultra conservatives to cleanse the church of heresy.[67] The ultras, however, did not distinguish between the moderate Calvinism of the New School majority and the more radical versions of Taylorism. For Old School conservatives, doctrinal purity in the church could only be safeguarded by full subscription to the Westminster Confession and Catechisms. This position was completely unacceptable to New School Presbyterians who viewed this as a new test of orthodoxy.

Theological sparring would continue in pulpit and print as the 1830s began. In the first half of this decade the battle intensified as the controversies moved into heated battles in the General Assembly meetings. The "heresy" trial of a prominent New School pastor at the 1831 General Assembly aroused the entire church to the seriousness of the doctrinal dilemma. Party dissension was now out in the open and witnessed by the church collectively. Presbyterian tempers would be ignited by this public display of animosity and as strain approached the breaking point by the mid-1830s, everyone was forced to side with one party or the other.

---

[66] Hodge, "Remarks on Dr. Cox's Communication," 525.

[67] *The Presbyterian*, April 16, 1835, 61.

CHAPTER 5

A House Divided

Old School conservatives intensified their efforts to rid the church of the New School party in the tumultuous 1830s. Princeton continued to play the middleman as long as possible, but eventually, the Presbyterian seminary professors would be forced to side with one of the parties. Southern Presbyterians who had remained neutral on the Northern doctrinal strife up until the 1830s would also have to make a decision. Issues would surface in the General Assemblies that aroused latent Old School/New School sentiments within the previously peaceful Southern ranks. As the rhetoric proliferated and passions were aroused, schism appeared to be inevitable. Doctrinal dispute had moved beyond the realm of charitable disagreement to dividing lines that could not be crossed. Within a few short years of the tempestuous 1831 Assembly, the impending Presbyterian division had reached the point of no return. It was only a question of when and how the schism would occur.

First Trial of Albert Barnes

A turning point in Old School/New School rivalry occurred at the Assembly of 1831. On appeal, the case of Albert Barnes came before the General Assembly where party loyalties were now fully displayed before the whole church. For conservatives, Barnes symbolized the diluted New School theology that was undermining the church and they were determined to purge it from the Presbyterian household. With battle lines emerging, many presbyters still longed for union and compromise.

Old School worries about Albert Barnes began to crystallize in 1830 when Barnes was called as pastor of First Presbyterian Church in Philadelphia within the ultra conservative Presbytery of Philadelphia. The focal point of negative reaction to Barnes's call was a sermon he had preached the previous year in Morristown, New Jersey and published under the title, "The Way of Salvation."[1] Barnes's sermon was

---

[1] Earl A. Pope pointed out that based upon this sermon, historians have "commonly identified Barnes with Taylorism." He argued that there is no justification for this evaluation; instead, Barnes is more fairly characterized as a representative of "moderate New England Calvinism ... which was probably shared by the majority of the New School." Earl A. Pope, "New England Calvinism and the Disruption of the Presbyterian Church" (Ph.D. diss., Brown University, 1962), 198, 199. One month before the 1831 Assembly, New Haven had come out in support of Barnes in the pages of the *Quarterly Christian Spectator*. New Haven

intended as an exposition of the gospel plan for laymen; it also included some explanatory footnotes in the published version. Old School conservative, Ashbel Green, and others resisted Barnes's call to First Presbyterian and pointed to what they considered the theological inadequacy of this sermon. One of the underlying factors which made the Barnes case extremely sensitive was the strategic importance of First Presbyterian since the General Assembly annually convened in this church which was considered "the mother of us all."[2]

The first published criticism of "The Way of Salvation" was by William Engles in *The Philadelphian*.[3] Engles's review of the sermon included a challenge to Barnes's commitment to the Westminster Standards; he believed the sermon was "neither Calvinistic nor Presbyterian." A pro-Barnes response was printed in the next issue of *The Philadelphian* and the war in print began. In addition to the question of whether or not Barnes fairly expressed the teachings of the Confession, the series of debating articles also clashed over the right of presbyteries to examine

---

identified its own views with those of Barnes and this seemed to seal Barnes' connection with Taylorism, in the minds of some Presbyterians. Ashbel Green was incensed that New Haven, "a miserable compound of Pelagianism and Arminianism" was meddling in Presbyterian affairs and charged them with a calculated attempt to favor the New School party. "Review of Review," *The Christian Advocate* (December, 1831): 652; quoted in Pope, "New England Calvinism," 225, 231.

[2] Samuel Miller, Jr., *Life of Samuel Miller*, vol. II (Philadelphia: Claxton, Remsen and Haffelfinger, 1869), 154. Barnes wrote his former professor, Dr. Miller, asking for his advice on accepting the call to First Presbyterian. Miller gave this advice to Barnes: "Now, if your convictions of truth and duty will allow you, in case you go to Philadelphia, to unite in helping forward the cause of the Presbyterian Church, *in tolerable accordance with the public standards*; if you can see your way clear to fall in with brethren there in harmonious and affectionate co-operation (*I do not mean in petty peculiarities*, but) in the great interests and efforts of our church, as such; then I think you may be eminently useful in Philadelphia, and ought to go thither"(italics mine). When Ashbel Green wrote Miller expressing concerns about *The Way of Salvation*, Miller replied: "With my present views, if I were a member of Presbytery, and if a call for Mr. Barnes were laid before that body, I should utterly oppose a motion to refuse to allow it to be prosecuted." 151.

[3] William Engles, see "Review: The Way of Salvation," *The Philadelphian*, April 9, 1830; "Review Defended," *The Philadelphian*, April 23, 1830; "Rejoinder," *The Philadelphian*, May 14, 1830; cited by Pope, "New England Calvinism," 206-209. William Engles (1797-1867) was pastor of the Seventh Presbyterian Church in Philadelphia. He was a leader in the ultra-conservative party of the Old School and became editor of *The Presbyterian* in 1833. Through the pages of *The Presbyterian*, Engles was a leading spokesman of the censorious conservative minority. Engles and George Junkin, the opposition leader against Barnes in 1835, both came into the Presbyterian Church from the Associate Reformed Church through the 1822 union of the two denominations. The New School considered Engles and Junkin a trouble-making "foreign element" in the Presbyterian Church with their *ipsissima verba* interpretation of subscription. See "The Spirit of American Presbyterianism," *The Presbyterian Quarterly Review* III (June 1854): 152.

a transferring minister already in good ecclesiastical standing.[4] The Barnes controversy was a case study in Old School/New School differences in both theology and polity.[5]

The majority of Philadelphia Presbytery concurred in prosecuting the call of Rev. Barnes as pastor of First Presbyterian (21 in favor and 12 opposed). The conservative minority, nevertheless, insisted that they had a right to examine Barnes when he later presented his credentials to the presbytery; they were overruled by a vote of 20 to 18. Ezra Stiles Ely, the old enemy of Hopkinsianism, presented a paper to the presbytery describing Barnes' theological convictions which Ely declared were orthodox. Barnes was finally received but not without complaint from conservatives.[6]

A protest to Barnes' reception into Philadelphia Presbytery was entered before the Synod of Philadelphia. The conservative protest asserted that the views expressed in *The Way of Salvation* were "opposed to the doctrinal standards of the Presbyterian Church."[7] Barnes defended himself before the Synod in 1830 and offered explanations of his views. On the imputation of Adam's sin, Barnes affirmed that "men are the subjects of a hereditary depravity." Yet, he sided with the Old Calvinists of New England and "ninety-nine of a hundred of all ministers of the Presbyterian Church" in rejecting the notion that Adam's sin is "properly ours." Barnes argued that he had never denied the doctrine of original sin but he had merely objected to certain explanations of how Adam's sin is transmitted to the human race. Barnes declared that "to express doubt about the way of explaining a fact, is not to deny that fact."[8]

Barnes also addressed concerns about his articulation of the atonement which some had charged as denying its vicarious nature. Barnes countered: "Christ died in

---

[4] The Presbyterian Form of Government was revised in 1821. The Presbytery of Baltimore at that time had requested an amendment to Chapter 10, Article 12; the proposed amendment had stated: "Every Presbytery shall judge of the qualifications of its own members." The overture was denied. Some had interpreted this as a denial of the right of presbyteries to examine ministers who were already in good standing in presbyteries. H. Woods, *The Presbyterian Controversy* (Louisville: N.H. White, 1843), 64.

[5] For the pro-Barnes arguments see essays in *The Philadelphian* by James P. Wilson, "Hasty Review to the Reviewer of 'The Way of Salvation,' " April 16, 1830; "A Reply to the Review Defended," April 30, 1830; and "An Answer to 'Rejoinder,'" May 14, 1830; see Pope, "New England Calvinism," 210. Wilson was the pastor of First Presbyterian immediately preceding Barnes.

[6] Ibid., 212, 213.

[7] W.L. M'Calla, *A Correct Narrative of the Proceedings of the Presbytery of Philadelphia Relative to the Reception and Installation of Mr. Albert Barnes* (Philadelphia: Russell and Martien, 1830), 10.

[8] Albert Barnes, *The Way of Salvation: A Sermon Delivered at Morristown, New Jersey, February 8, 1829 Together With Mr. Barnes's Defense of the Sermon, read Before the Synod of Philadelphia, at Lancaster, October 29, 1830; and His "Defense" before the Second Presbytery of Philadelphia, in Reply to the Charge of the Rev. George Junkin* (New York: Leavitt, Lord, and Company, 7th ed., 1836), 59-61.

the place of sinners." On human ability he declared that all men are "wholly inclined to evil, and opposed to good; and that this native propensity was so strong as never to be overcome but by the influence of the Holy Spirit." Having offered these doctrinal explanations, Barnes believed that he had not violated the teaching of the Confession.[9]

In his defense, Barnes rebuffed those who charged him with dishonoring the Confession. From his perspective, the Old School conservatives were giving preeminence to Creeds over the Bible. According to Barnes, his accusers implied that a Presbyterian minister "is to ask himself primarily not what is the fair grammatical construction of the text, but what doctrines does the Confession require him, on pain of violating ordination vows, to draw out of the sacred Scriptures." Barnes retorts that while the Confession is a solid interpretation of Scripture, yet, he will "investigate the Scriptures, without reference to any theological system.... This course is adopted because in this way only can I express my views of the Bible, as supreme and authentive over all creeds and councils of men.... This was indubitably the path in which the apostles and reformers trod."[10]

The Synod of Philadelphia, upon hearing Barnes' explanations and not being fully satisfied, referred the case back to the Presbytery of Philadelphia which remained severely divided over Barnes. Old School conservatives continued their assault on *The Way of Salvation* but would not formally put Barnes on trial. Unable to reach consensus, the whole affair was appealed to the General Assembly of 1831. Old School moderates in the Assembly believed that conservatives had pushed too far in their condemnation of Barnes. The case was handed to a committee chaired by Dr. Miller of Princeton. The following recommendation was adopted by the Assembly (158 in favor, 33 opposed):

1. Resolved, that the General Assembly, while it appreciates the conscientious zeal for the purity of the church, by which the Presbytery of Philadelphia is believed to have been actuated, in its proceedings in the case of Mr. Barnes; and while it judges that the sermon, by Mr. Barnes, entitled 'The Way of Salvation,' contains a number or unguarded and objectionable passages; yet is of the opinion, that, especially after the explanations which were given by him of those passages, the Presbytery ought to have suffered the whole to pass without further notice.

2. Resolved, That in the judgment of this Assembly, the Presbytery of Philadelphia ought to suspend all further proceedings in the case of Mr. Barnes.[11]

Old School ultras like Engles were infuriated by the 1831 General Assembly actions: "To refuse to testify against existing error is tantamount to a protection of it. By this proceeding the Assembly has virtually declared that heresy may find an

---

[9] Ibid., 73, 77.

[10] Ibid., 83-85.

[11] *Minutes of the General Assembly of the Presbyterian Church in the United States of America 1789-1837* (Philadelphia 1831), 329.

undisturbed asylum in the Presbyterian Church."[12] Ashbel Green, convinced that the Presbyterian Church was facing a serious crisis, began printing a series of articles on "The Present State of the Presbyterian Church" shortly after the Assembly of 1831 concluded. Unless the Old School soon wakes up to New School schemes aimed at controlling the Assembly, her influence will be forever lost. Green believed a conspiracy was underway to subvert the integrity of the Presbyterian Church. The New School are latitudinarian in doctrine and tolerate error. Green expressed appreciation for the Old Calvinism of New England but this new Presbyterian theological polarization he attributed to the influence of New Haven which is "no Calvinism at all, but a miserable compound of Pelagianism and Arminianism."[13]

According to Green, the two parties in the church hold very different understandings of subscription to the doctrinal standards. The Old School conservatives and moderates "put the same construction on our Confession of Faith, catechisms, and Form of Government, that was put on these Formularies when the Constitution of our Church was adopted, and for several years afterwards." For Green strict subscription was the only position acceptable in the Presbyterian Church. He stated: "We regard as a most unworthy and criminal equivocation, the plea, that our standards may be adopted as containing 'the system of doctrines taught in the Holy Scriptures,' while yet an objection is taken to several doctrines, regarded as highly important, and even fundamental, in those standards."[14]

A serious rift over polity also emerged out of the Barnes trial. In order to avert future tensions, the 1831 Assembly made a controversial decision concerning the partition of the Presbytery of Philadelphia. This action further alienated the conservatives and would be a factious issue at successive Assemblies up to the schism. The 1831 Assembly decided: "Resolved, That it will be expedient, as soon as the regular steps can be taken, to divide the Presbytery in such a way, as will be best calculated to promote the peace of the ministers and churches belonging to the Presbytery."[15] The Synod of Philadelphia was instructed to implement the presbytery realignment but refused to do so. A complaint was then registered against the Synod for failure to carry out General Assembly directives. After lengthy discussion in the 1832 Assembly, the Second Presbytery of Philadelphia

---

[12] *The Presbyterian*, June 19, 1834.

[13] Ashbel Green, "Review of Review" *The Christian Advocate*, IX (December, 1831): 652; see also the July issue of the *Advocate* for that year. Cited in Pope, "New England Calvinism," 231, 232.

[14] Green, "Review of Review," *The Christian Advocate* X (March, 1832): 129; quoted in Pope, "New England Calvinism," 233. Green asserted that conservatives and moderates within the Old School shared the same views of subscription. Charles Hodge offered a different interpretation of the facts when he advocated a middle position between the conservative Old School men and extreme New School views. See Charles Hodge, "Remarks on Dr. Cox's Communication," *Biblical Repertory and Theological Review* III (1831): 514-543.

[15] Ibid.

was created; it was comprised of Barnes and 13 other ministers and 14 churches. This "elective affinity" plan though overwhelmingly adopted, met with hot conservative Old School resistance that claimed authorization of two presbyteries covering the same region was unconstitutional. New School advocates and Old School moderates, on the other hand, supported the realignment as essential to secure ecclesiastical peace.

In the fall of 1832, the Synod of Philadelphia refused to recognize delegates from the newly formed Second Presbytery and again the General Assembly had to reiterate its position in 1833. After further defiance, the 1834 Assembly finally erected a new Synod of Delaware and transferred Second Presbytery under its jurisdiction. However, by 1835 the Synod of Delaware was dissolved by an Old School majority Assembly and Second Presbytery was again placed within the bounds of the Philadelphia Synod. The Synod of Philadelphia promptly dissolved Second Presbytery at its next meeting. At the 1836 Assembly a New School majority renamed Second Presbytery as "Third Presbytery" and assigned geographical limits to allay criticism about the constitutionality of elective affinity. This compromise was short-lived, however, as the 1837 Old School majority in the Assembly "swept this Presbytery from existence!"[16]

"Letters to Presbyterians"

As ecclesiastical anxieties continued to mount from year to year in the Assembly, Princeton tried to play a mediating role. Professor Samuel Miller in 1833 attempted to pacify the smoldering situation through a series of sixteen "Letters to Presbyterians"[17] that were published in *The Presbyterian*. Miller's letters addressed the scope of issues dividing Presbyterians – voluntary associations and ecclesiastical boards, revivals, requirements for ministerial candidates, Presbyterian government and adherence to doctrinal standards. The letters were widely circulated and eventually published in book form.

In several letters, Miller addressed the tension over subscription to the Confession of Faith.[18] Doctrinal diversity exists in the church and the "rigor which some appear to consider as necessary" must be rejected. If ecclesiastical discipline is

---

[16] Henry Woods, *The History of the Presbyterian Controversy with Early Sketches of Presbyterianism* (Louisville: N.H. White, 1843), 64-67. The New School pointed out that elective affinity was not new but had been utilized in the 1821 union with the Associate Reformed Church which allowed Reformed presbyteries to either choose amalgamation with existing Presbyterian presbyteries or "retain their separate organization." This provision permitted two separate presbyteries to cover the same geographical boundaries. See *Minutes of General Assembly*, 1821, 14.

[17] Samuel Miller, *Letters to Presbyterians in the Present Crisis in the Presbyterian Church in the United States* (Philadelphia: Anthony Finley, 1833). Originally, the essays appeared as "Letters to Presbyterians on the Present Crisis in the Presbyterian Church in the United States" in *The Presbyterian* (January - May, 1833).

[18] Letters VI-VIII were titled "Adherence to our Doctrinal Standards."

applied "for not expounding every doctrine contained in the Confession of Faith in the same precise manner," the Presbyterian Church will be kept in a state of conflict. On the other hand, some Presbyterians appear reticent to censure any form of doctrinal error; this position also divides the church. Miller advocated a "course between these ruinous extremes" that is held together by a "spirit of mutual affection and accommodation."[19]

The "great practical question" was how assent to the Confession of Faith was understood. Miller protested against any notion that subscription precludes variety of opinion. He declared: "To expect such perfect uniformity, among two thousand ministers of the gospel, is a chimera. It never was or can be realized. And to attempt to enforce such a principle, would be worse than useless." Miller argued that sincere Calvinists have always had minor differences. He pointed to the Westminster Divines, members of the Synod of Dordt and the old 1729 Synod of Philadelphia as historical examples of diverse viewpoints. The question was the allowable limits of this diversity.[20]

The key for Miller was the phrase "system of doctrine" in the ordination formula. The clear meaning to any intelligent person is that "the manifest design of the Confession of Faith of the Presbyterian Church is to maintain what is commonly called the Calvinistic system." This system is set in opposition to Arian, Pelagian, Socinian and Arminian systems of doctrine. There are distinguishing features of the Calvinistic system[21] and there are particular errors "which it was the special design of the Confession to exclude." As long as one adopts these Calvinistic doctrines of the Confession and does not embrace any of these errors, "we judge that they may all adopt it without any breach of good faith." Miller stated: "While, therefore, some diversity, in explanations adopted of an extended series of doctrines, must be expected among the teachers in every church, and has been ever found to exist; there cannot, it appears to me, be a plainer dictate of common sense, and common honesty, than that a Pelagian, a Semi-Pelagian, or Arminian – to say nothing of

---

[19] Miller, *Letters to Presbyterians*, 91, 92.

[20] Ibid., 92.

[21] Miller offered his summary of essential Calvinism: "But we cannot resist the conclusion, as fair and honorable men, that unless a candidate for admission does really believe in the doctrine of the Trinity; the incarnation and true Deity of Jesus Christ; the personality and Deity of Jesus Christ; the personality and Deity of the Holy Spirit; the fall and entire native depravity of man in virtue of a connection with Adam, the progenitor of our race; the vicarious atoning sacrifice of the righteousness of Christ, set to our account, and made ours by faith; sovereign and unconditional personal election to eternal life; regeneration and sanctification by the power of the Holy Spirit; the eternal punishment of the impenitently wicked, etc., etc.; unless he sincerely believes all these, and the essentially allied doctrines which have ever been considered as the distinguishing features of the Calvinistic system, and believes them in substance, as they are laid down in the Confession, our verdict is that he cannot honestly subscribe it." *Letters to Presbyterians*, 94.

more radical errorists – cannot possibly, with a good conscience, subscribe the Confession of Faith of the Presbyterian Church."[22]

Miller pointed to the doctrine of the vicarious atonement to illustrate the distinction between the essential nature of a doctrine and its explanation. What is indispensable is the "strictly vicarious" nature of the atonement. Miller added: "As long as any one holds the true scriptural nature of the atonement, he may be allowed some latitude in his mode of explaining its extent, without being considered, in reference to this article, as recreant from the standard which he has subscribed. And so of other leading doctrines."[23]

Personal honesty and sincerity of heart must adorn one's adherence to doctrinal standards. Some Presbyterian ministers apparently have justified their equivocation by adopting the Confession with "a mental reservation, implying that they received it only so far as they considered it as agreeing with the Scriptures." This was a "subterfuge" which would allow a minister to subscribe any confession. Miller stated: "The only object of subscribing a creed is to ascertain whether the subscriber believes a certain set of doctrines: or, in other words, whether he believes them to be taught in the Bible. But is it not evident that he who subscribes, with the mental reservation before us, entirely defeats this object.... It would be unspeakably better, in my opinion, to abandon at once all church creeds, than to continue their use upon a principle so utterly subversive of all fairness and sincerity."[24]

Another subterfuge that evades honest subscription has been the attempt to distinguish theological facts and the "philosophical solution of those facts." Miller said:

> ... it is supposed by some, that those who agree in what are called Calvinistic facts may conscientiously subscribe our Confession of Faith, though all their philosophical explanations of those facts be thoroughly Pelagian or Arminian ... beware of those who talk of Calvinistic facts explained by Pelagian, or Semi-pelagian philosophy. It is an utter and ruinous delusion. The Pelagian philosophy never fails to transform all the facts which it perverts and tortures into Pelagian facts, with this dangerous circumstance attending them, that they are really Pelagian under a deceptive name and false colors. Let Pelagian philosophy prevail in the Church for a few years, and he is an

---

[22] Ibid., 96, 97. Miller referenced the Cumberland schism as an example of Presbyterian opposition to Arminianism. He stated: "... the whole history of the Cumberland Presbyterians, in the West, bears witness that our venerable Fathers, thirty years ago, when there was no special jealousy or prejudice excited in reference to this subject, thought the adoption of Arminian opinions altogether inconsistent with an honorable subscription to our Confession, and considered it as their duty to cast out of the Church a large body of otherwise respectable ministers and members who, though they decisively preferred and still retain Presbyterian order, yet could not subscribe a Calvinistic confession."

[23] Ibid., 95.

[24] Ibid., 99, 100.

infatuated man who flatters himself that Pelagian doctrines will not soon be the reigning creed.[25]

In Miller's discussion of subscription, he was chiefly concerned about the inroads of Pelagian-like ideas into the Presbyterian Church.[26] This kind of theology subverted the integrity of a Calvinistic system of doctrine. Many charges of heterodoxy have been leveled against ministers of the Presbyterian Church and "if any of these doctrines are held and taught by any of the ministers connected with the Presbyterian Church, it is deeply to be deplored...." Miller did not list specific names nor did he offer an evaluation of the truthfulness of the accusations. He enumerated the erroneous doctrines to which objections have been raised and asserted that Pelagian and Semi-Pelagian sentiments are here "in all their unquestionable and revolting features.[27]

Miller confessed that Old School misstatement had sometimes been the occasion for New School avoidance of the "Old Orthodoxy." He admitted: "They have heard,

---

[25] Ibid., 102, 103.

[26] Ibid., 123. Miller believed the Pelagian errors were real. "I can confidently say, that I have heard preachers of my own denomination, with my own ears, deliver sentiments (and have seen, in print, tenets which others, of the same class, publicly avowed), which constrained me - and not me only, but some of the wisest and most moderate ministers in the Presbyterian Church - to say 'that we had rather, much rather, sit habitually under the ministry of a pious Methodist brother, with all his avowed Arminianism, than under that of the Presbyterian brethren alluded to.' "

[27] Ibid., 109,110. Miller enumerated the alleged errors: "... that we have no more to do with the first sin of Adam, than with that of any other parent; that he was not constituted the covenant head of his posterity, but was merely their natural progenitor; that there is no such thing as original sin; that infants come into the world as perfectly free from corruption of nature as Adam was when he was created; that to speak of innate corrupt inclinations and propensities is an absurdity; that by human depravity is meant nothing more than the universal fact that all the posterity of Adam, though born entirely free from moral defilement, will always begin to sin when they begin to exercise moral agency; that the doctrine of imputed sin, or imputed righteousness, is nonsense; that the human will determines itself; that the impenitent sinner is, by nature, in full possession of all the powers necessary to a full compliance with all the commands of God; that he is in possession of plenary ability to repent and believe, without the aid of the Holy Spirit; that if he labored under any kind of inability, natural or moral, which he could not remove himself, he would be fully excusable for not complying with God's will; that man is active in his own regeneration - in other words, that his regeneration is his own act; that it is impossible for God, by a direct influence on the mind, to control its perceptions and practical choices, without destroying its moral agency; that, consequently, Omnipotence cannot exert such an influence on men as shall make it certain that they will choose and act in a particular manner, without making them mere machines; that we have no evidence that God could have prevented the existence of sin, or that he could now prevent any that exists, without interfering with the moral agency of man; that he would, no doubt, be glad to do it, but is not able; that he elected men to eternal life, on a foresight of what their character would be; and that his sovereignty is confined to the revelation of truth, and exhibition of it to the mind."

perhaps, some who professed to be advocates of 'Calvinism,' represent some of the features of that system, and especially the subject of human inability, in a manner rather adapted to diminish a sense of responsibility, and lull to sleep, than rouse and alarm the impenitent sinner. They have thence hastily concluded, that the fault was in the system itself, and not in the preacher.... This, I have no doubt, is a real statement of facts; and that we have, of course, to thank the occasional mistakes of 'Old School' preaching for some of the most serious departures of 'New School' champions from the simplicity of Bible truth." New School men should not confuse the truthfulness of the Calvinistic system with the "mode of presenting truth."[28]

Miller did not buy the argument that the differences are "only in words." This diversion is as old as Arianism which declared only a diversity of terms until they came into power and thence revealed their hand in opposing the orthodox. This has been the means of escaping ecclesiastical discipline throughout church history. Having said this, Miller was still inclined to be as charitable as possible. He believed that some of the brethren "have completely succeeded in persuading themselves that the doctrines specified are truly, for substance, those which are found in our public formularies. Yet it is impossible for me to doubt that these brethren are laboring under an entire mistake; that they are really, without being aware of it, teaching dangerous errors."[29]

There is an integrity gap with ministers who play mental games with the formula of subscription. It is blatantly dishonest to affirm a creed that one in fact denies. The Calvinistic theology of the Confession of Faith has an historically defined meaning and only an honest embracing of this creed is worthy of honorable men. Miller warned: "Allowing men to subscribe to a confession which they obviously do not believe ... may have the appearance of great 'liberality,' and may seem to promise a most enviable harmony among brethren of different opinion. But the appearance is delusive. The hope is a miserable dream. It requires no spirit of prophecy to foresee that whenever our ecclesiastical judicatories begin deliberately to admit of subscription to our public standards on any such principle, they are paving the way for trouble and dangers of the most ruinous kind."[30]

New School and Old School bear responsibility for the party strife that has occurred. The Old School should not be "over rigorous in their demands; that they should not be perpetually and vexatiously occupied in the work of 'heresy hunting.'" The New School for her part must not "persist in the public, habitual use of a theological language which impartial judges consider Pelagian in its obvious import." New School Presbyterians should cease to "license and ordain men who give too much reason to fear that they do not, *ex amino*, receive the doctrines and order of our Church." Likewise, the New School should be careful not to "always sustain and acquit lax theology, to whatever extreme it may go" when questions come in the higher judicatories. Miller cited several examples of ministerial

---

[28] Ibid., 116.

[29] Ibid., 122.

[30] Ibid., 104.

candidates being turned down by Old School presbyteries and the candidate immediately going to a New School presbytery where "he was promptly licensed, notwithstanding the refusal of the sister judicatory, and with a distinct knowledge of that refusal." This practice is "adapted to destroy mutual confidence among judicatories" among brethren that are one body in the Lord. If these current New School practices persist, "it requires no spirit of prophecy to foresee, that growing alienation, strife, and eventual rupture must be the consequence."[31]

Protests Against the General Assembly

The strict Old School party, outraged by the toleration of error and fearing the increase of New School political power in the Assembly, began publishing dissent papers. These protests were an attempt to herald specific ecclesiastical/theological concerns and to recruit Old School moderates against erring New School individuals and presbyteries. The first of these protest documents came before the 1834 Assembly and was known as the "Western Memorial." The paper originated in Cincinnati Presbytery and had also been adopted by the Presbytery of Philadelphia. The Western Memorial denounced: the 1801 Plan of Union, voluntary associations operating in the Presbyterian Church, elective affinity presbyteries, the practice of ordaining men *sine titulo* and laxity in subscribing the Confession. The conservatives listed numerous doctrinal innovations on imputation, ability and the atonement "which are held and taught within the Presbyterian Church, which the General Assembly are constitutionally competent to suppress." Albert Barnes, Lyman Beecher, George Duffield and Nathaniel S. S. Beman were implicated by name as primary sources of New School errors. The memorial called the church to censor these doctrinal aberrations and faithfully deal with the cases that were referred to the General Assembly.[32]

The Western Memorial asked the Assembly to address several questions "concerning which conflicting sentiment exist, creating difficulties, perplexities, and tendencies to division." One of the questions dealt with subscription:

> Whether in receiving and adopting the Confession of Faith and Catechisms, the candidate for licensure, ordination, or admission from a foreign body, is at liberty to receive and adopt them according to his own private construction of their meaning, while that construction may be unusual as well as different from the most obvious sense – or while he adopts them as containing the system of doctrine taught in the Holy Scriptures generally, he is at liberty to reject as many particular propositions as he pleases to consider contrary to the said 'system,' without stating what those propositions are, to the Presbytery, at or before the time of his being licensed, ordained, or admitted: or, whether every such person is not bound to receive and adopt the said

---

[31] Ibid., 126.

[32] Samuel J. Baird, *A Collection of the Acts, Deliverances, and Testimonies of the Supreme Judicatory of the Presbyterian Church from its Origin in America to the Present Time* (Philadelphia: Presbyterian Board of Publication, 1856), 659-668.

formularies, according to the obvious known and established meaning of the terms, as the confession of his faith; and if any proposition appear to him objectionable, to state freely and candidly his scruples, leaving it for the Presbytery to decide upon the propriety of licensing, ordaining, or admitting him as his objections may be judged consistent with soundness in the faith, or otherwise.[33]

The 1834 Assembly did not concur with the judgment of the Western Memorial, and reprimanded its advocates for publicly defaming ministers without trial. A protest was entered against the Assembly's rejection of the Western Memorial and another resolution condemning specific errors in doctrine was brought to the floor. The resolution was indefinitely postponed and a second protest was entered against this action; the second protest was excluded from the minutes by a vote of 56 to 42.[34] The General Assembly responded further by reaffirming allegiance to the Confession of Faith: "Resolved, That this Assembly cherish an unabated attachment to the system of doctrines contained in the standards of their faith, and would guard with vigilance against any departure from it; and they enjoin the careful study of it upon all the members of the Presbyterian Church, and their firm support by all scriptural and constitutional methods."[35] Defeated in their efforts to acquire Assembly support, conservatives appointed a committee of nine to revise the Western Memorial and write a new statement, the "Act and Testimony." Since the General Assembly would not satisfactorily address false doctrine, conservatives would now appeal to the entire church against the Assembly.

Robert J. Breckinridge, the chairman of the committee, desiring to have Princeton support, consulted with Charles Hodge. Though reluctant to participate, Hodge gave significant input to the revised document, believing that if errors were to be condemned, the protest at least needed to be accurate. The resulting Act and Testimony focused more on the errors of Taylorism rather than the broader

---

[33] Ibid., 668. According to Pope, the Western Memorial was based upon the presupposition of "strict subscription," but, the question related to subscription clearly implied that exceptions ("scruples") may be taken. The controversial point had to do with Presbyteries deciding what were allowable scruples and not the individual. Certain latitude was indicated but only within limits determined by a presbytery. Pope, "New England Calvinism," 306. The Assembly replied to the subscription question: "That, in receiving and adopting the formularies of our Church, every person ought to be supposed, without evidence to the contrary, to receive and adopt them according to the obvious, known and established meaning of the terms, as the Confession of his Faith; and that if objections be made, the Presbytery, unless he withdraw such objections, should not license, ordain, or admit him." *Minutes of the General Assembly*, 1834, 441. It is interesting that the Assembly response appeared stronger than the memorialist's question implied and yet this answer was from what was considered a New School majority Assembly! A conservative protest dealt with numerous items in the Assembly's reply to the Western Memorial but not one word was said about the subscription question which seems to indicate that the Assembly statement of subscription must have been satisfactory.

[34] *Minutes of the General Assembly*, 1834, 446-449.

[35] Ibid., 441.

condemnation of the Western Memorial. The Act and Testimony, nonetheless, denounced the 1834 General Assembly for its refusal to condemn the errors delineated in the Western Memorial. The paper was distributed throughout the church and was eventually endorsed by 374 ministers, 1,789 elders, 14 licentiates, 5 synods and 30 presbyteries.[36]

The doctrinal section of the Act and Testimony addressed subscription and a noticeable shift had occurred. While the Western Memorial had inferred a strict adherence to the Confession, the Act and Testimony pointed to the denial of essential Calvinism as the cardinal error. The Act and Testimony declared:

> 1. We do bear our solemn testimony against the right claimed by many, of interpreting the doctrines of our standards in a sense different from the general sense of the Church for years past, whilst they still continue in our communion: on the contrary, we aver, that they who adopt our standards, are bound by candour and the simplest integrity, to hold them in their obvious, accepted sense.

> 2. We testify against the unchristian subterfuge to which some have recourse, when they avow a general adherence to our standards as a system, while they deny doctrines essential to the system, or hold doctrines at complete variance with the system.

> 3. We testify against the reprehensible conduct of those in our communion, who hold, and preach, and publish Arminian and Pelagian heresies, professing at the same time to embrace our creed, and pretending that these errors do consist therewith.[37]

The final published version of the Act and Testimony had three sections: doctrine, discipline and recommendations to the church. Reaction to the Act and Testimony at Princeton was not what Breckinridge had planned. Hodge came out against the Act and Testimony in the *Biblical Repertory* stating that he believed only a small minority of the church would support it. Rather than a legitimate testimony against error, "the signing of the Testimony as a test of orthodoxy" was being proposed; this will bring division to the Presbyterian Church. The Act and Testimony asserted that doctrinal errors "are held and taught by many persons in our church." Hodge disagreed, countering, "We have not the least idea, that one-tenth of the ministers of the Presbyterian Church would deliberately countenance and sustain the errors specified." Under the section of recommendations, the Testimony called for a pre-Assembly Old School convention to be held in 1835. This idea Hodge

---

[36] Baird, *Collection*, 675; Pope, "New England Calvinism," 269, 270; Pope said of Hodge's imprint on the Act and Testimony: "It is clear that Princeton was attempting to ease the pressure on the basically orthodox majority of the New School and to direct the fury of the ultra conservatives against Taylorism. It is illuminating to note some of the basic doctrinal changes which emerged. Princeton always was appalled by the theological immaturity of the ultra conservatives. In the revision of the errors Hodge attempted to strike at fundamental error instead of emphasizing a literal conformity to Westminster."

[37] Baird, *Collection*, 674.

characterized as a "revolutionary proceeding" which calls on the church to circumvent its constitution.[38]

According to Hodge, there were not sufficient grounds for dividing the Presbyterian Church; schism implicitly undergirded the conservative position. Hodge stated:

> So long as the standards of any church remain unaltered, its members profess the same faith which they avowed when they joined it. I do not profess to hold or to teach what A.B. or C. may be known to believe, but I profess to believe the confession of faith of the church to which I belong. It matters not, therefore, so far as this point is concerned how corrupt a portion, or even the majority, of the church may be, provided I am not called upon to profess their errors. Instead of my mere ecclesiastical connexion with them being a countenancing of their errors, it may give me the best opportunity of constantly testifying against them.[39]

Hodge's article appeared to have given some Old School advocates more resolve to oppose a Presbyterian schism. Princeton's reaction to the Testimony angered the ultra party who were determined to purify the church. Hodge acknowledged that his article opposing the Act and Testimony had given "prodigious offence to the Philadelphia men." The "Philadelphia men" were dividing the Old School and "driving matters to an extremity." The Synod of Philadelphia pronounced a lack of confidence in Princeton and proposed transferring its patronage to Pittsburgh or to start a new seminary.[40] Conservatives observed with dismay that all the New School papers were praising Princeton for its disapproval of the Act and Testimony.[41]

Breckinridge's rebuttal to Hodge and Princeton charged that Alexander, Miller and Hodge "have done us harm in the present contest," he then added, "there is reason to fear, that Princeton will not lead the church in this crisis."[42] Breckinridge accused Princeton with retreating from her former stands against error in the church. He boldly declared: "The whole plan of the Princeton party, or *middle party* stands now fully revealed. They will not only war against this Act and Testimony, *ad*

---

[38] Charles Hodge, "Act and Testimony," *Biblical Repertory and Theological Review* VI (October, 1834): 506, 509, 510, 517. Hodge also expressed his opinion on the Western Memorial, stating that he was not surprised the Assembly rejected this list of errors. He commented: "Instead of wondering that a majority of the Assembly did not vote for them, we wonder that any considerable number of voices was raised in their favour, so various are the errors they embrace, and so different in degree; some of them serious heresies, and others (at least as we understood the resolutions) ... held and tolerated ... in our church since its very first organization." As an example of tolerated doctrinal difference, Hodge asked: "Is it to be expected that, at this time of the day, the Assembly would condemn all who do not hold to the doctrine of a limited atonement?"

[39] Ibid., 520.

[40] "Dr. Hodge to his Brother" (Nov. 21, 1834) in Archibald Alexander Hodge, *Life of Charles Hodge* (New York: Charles Scribner's Sons, 1880), 305, 306.

[41] *The Presbyterian*, January 29, 1835, 18.

[42] *The Presbyterian*, December 4, 1834, 193.

internecionem; but they will (as many always said) *do nothing*, ... The moderates are against the Pelagians, and still more against action, and most of all apparently against us. We have no longer any reason to expect forbearance from Princeton, than from New Haven" (italics his).[43] Engles, recognizing that moderates or "peace men" held the keys to resolving the Presbyterian controversy, took a more charitable approach toward Princeton. He offered Princeton a challenge: "With fraternal feelings for our brethren who disagree with us in measures, although uniting with us in doctrine, we would affectionately recommend, that instead of expending their force against the Act and Testimony, to the grief of its friends and the triumph of the enemies of truth; they could devise and propose some plan upon which they could unite with their brethren in cleansing the sanctuary."[44]

Archibald Alexander admitted that Princeton found itself in the middle, yet, he defended Princeton's stance: "Our opinions and feelings did not entirely coincide with EITHER CLASS of the ultra partisans who have, for several years past, divided and agitated our church." Could Princeton stand by silently and "see our beloved church torn in pieces by honest, but misguided friends, on the one hand, and a really small hostile junto on the other, without lifting a hand or voice to stay the catastrophe?" Princeton opposed the Act and Testimony because she was "persuaded that nine-tenths of our ministry are in great measure free from the unsound opinions in question. We believe, moreover, that the errors to which reference is here made, are declining rather than gaining ground." Alexander urged Presbyterians to stop fighting each other instead they should "have but one matter of strife – namely, who shall love the Master most, and who shall serve him with the greatest zeal."[45]

With nothing resolved between the ultras and Princeton, the pre-Assembly Old School meeting summoned by the signers of the Act and Testimony, convened at Pittsburgh in May of 1835. The convention composed a Memorial to the 1835 General Assembly which reiterated the concerns raised in the Western Memorial and the Act and Testimony. Samuel Miller became chairman of the Assembly committee responsible to answer the memorialists. The committee recommendations addressed the multiple questions that had agitated the church for a number of years. The preamble of the report moved quickly to the heart of the matter and addressed both the commitment of Presbyterians to her Confession as well as acknowledging that a diversity of views had always been present in Presbyterianism. Miller's committee explained:

> The committee, indeed, by no means expect, and do not suppose the Assembly would think of enforcing, that perfect agreement of views in every minute particular, which, in a body so extended as the Presbyterian, Church, has perhaps never been realized. But that an entire and cordial agreement in all the radical principles of that system of

---

[43] Robert J. Breckinridge, "A Plain Statement," *The Presbyterian*, April 16, 1835, 61.

[44] *The Presbyterian*, January 22, 1835, 15.

[45] Archibald Alexander, "The Present State and Prospects of the Presbyterian Church," *Biblical Repertory and Theological Review* VII (January, 1835): 58, 61, 64, 72.

truth and order which is taught in the Holy Scriptures, which is embodied in the Confession of Faith and Form of Government, and which every Minister and Elder of the Presbyterian Church has solemnly subscribed and promised to maintain, may not only be reasonably expected, but must be as far as possible secured, if we would maintain 'the unity of the Spirit , in the bonds of peace' and love – it is presumed this General Assembly will be unanimous in pronouncing.[46]

In addition to the moderate statement on subscription, the 1835 Assembly concurred with some of the issues raised in the Memorial and rejected others. The Old School dominated Assembly declared that Presbyteries have the right to examine transferring ministers and the elective affinity principle was jettisoned. The General Assembly agreed to pursue negotiations with the Association of Connecticut in order to annul the 1801 Plan of Union; however, all churches previously formed on the plan maintain full standing in the church. Voluntary associations were affirmed but it was the first duty of Presbyterians to support their denomination's boards. On the doctrinal statements in the Memorial, the Assembly declared that these errors were indeed incompatible with the Confession, but, the Assembly was unwilling to make any judgment on the degree to which these errors had pervaded the church.[47]

Engles was elated that Miller and Princeton had joined hands with the ultra conservatives in supporting some of the memorialists' issues.[48] Charles Hodge was also pleased with the general outcome of the 1835 General Assembly and hoped that the "safe middle ground has at length been found, on which the friends of truth and order (according to the common interpretations of our standards) can stand side by side."[49] Presbyterian harmony, which had seemed more hopeful after the 1835 Assembly, proved to be illusory. A spirit of moderation had prevailed in the Old School controlled 1835 Assembly but a New School majority the next year would exhibit a rigid resistance to charitable compromise.

---

[46] *Minutes of the General Assembly*, 1835, 485. Miller was sensitive to the personal attacks made against him by New School men in Virginia and Northern Synods accusing him of being a "convert to high church doctrines." His rejoinder reminded critics of his "Letters to Presbyterians" with which his actions at the 1835 Assembly were consistent. See letter to Rev. John McElhenny of Lewisburgh, Virginia, April 15, 1837 in *Life of Samuel Miller*, II, 229-236.

[47] *Minutes of the General Assembly*, 1835, 484-488. "Resolved, That while this General Assembly has no means of ascertaining to what extent the doctrinal errors alleged in the memorial to exist in our church do really prevail, it cannot hesitate to express the painful conviction that the allegation is by no means unfounded; and at the same time to condemn all such opinions, as not distinguishable from Pelagian or Arminian errors; and to declare their judgment that the holding of the opinions referred to is wholly incompatible with an honest adoption of our Confession of Faith."

[48] *The Presbyterian*, June 25, 1835, 103.

[49] Charles Hodge, "The General Assembly of 1835," *The Biblical Repertory and Theological Review* VII (July, 1835): 480.

Southern Awakening

The South viewed all this Northern theological rankling of the 1830s with chagrin. John Holt Rice, the first professor of Union Seminary in Virginia was dismayed at the spirit of controversy he observed in a trip North. He wrote to a friend in 1830: "My last journey made me sick at heart. Both in New York and Philadelphia I was in continual pain and mortification.... The church is not purified by controversy, but by love. By knowing Christ crucified we know enough to kindle up holy love. I have therefore brought my mind to the conclusion that the thing most needed at this present time is a revival of religion among churches, and especially a larger increase of holiness among ministers."[50] Rice felt so strongly about the need for charity that, writing from what would be his death bed, he had dictated a memorial to the 1831 Assembly pleading for compromise on the foreign missions question. Rice declared that he would never do anything "to injure the wisest and best missionary society in the world, – the American Board. But can no ingenuity devise a scheme of a Presbyterian Branch, – coordinate, – sufficiently connected with the Assembly to satisfy scrupulous Presbyterians, yet in union with the original Board?"[51]

The South generally maintained a charitable spirit toward the New England brethren and wished to avoid the contention brewing among Northern antagonists. There was harmony in the Southern ranks who had managed to stay above the fray over New England Theology in the period leading up to the 1830s. While the Northern men sparred over doctrine, many moderates in the Southern portion of the church discountenanced this distracting dissension. Dr. George Baxter, Rice's successor at Union Seminary, believed the troubles at the North were essentially differences in terminology. Baxter said:

> A minister may disturb the peace of his church, by appearing to deviate from its creed, when he does not do so in reality. He may do this by the substitution of new terms, to give an air of novelty to his speculations. How often has the peace of the Church been disturbed for years, congregations distracted, and almost ruined, and mutual confidence between pastors and people destroyed, by things which when brought to the test of dispassionate explanation, have been pronounced on all hands as unworthy of a moment's contention. I sincerely believe that much of the uneasiness which pervades our church at the present moment, has arisen from this cause. Much of new divinity

---

[50] William Henry Foote, *Sketches of Virginia*, Second Series (Philadelphia: J.B. Lippincott & Co., 1855), 496.

[51] E.H. Gillett, *History of the Presbyterian Church in the United States of America*, vol. II (Philadelphia: Presbyterian Publication Committee, 1864), 453, 454. Dr. Rice's advice went unheeded. Gillett commented on the aftermath of the 1831 Assembly: "The fraternal spirit which allowed free voluntary contributions on both sides was fast disappearing. Compromise was no longer possible. Dr. Rice, who might have acted as a mediator in the strife, had already passed from the scene."

would become old divinity, if the terms of our Confession, or similar terms, were used to express, what on fair explanation, appear to be the real sentiments of the authors.[52]

As much as the South wished to exclude themselves from the Presbyterian debates, it was becoming impossible. The circulation of Presbyterian papers, pamphlets and periodicals filled the church with the reality of the tensions. Political committees established by both parties lobbied their cause and Southerners could not escape the dilemma of having to choose sides. The period of compromise was past; an ecclesiastical showdown was becoming eminent as the decade of the 1830s progressed. The Southern men were being drawn into the "vortex of contention." William Henry Foote, a Virginia pastor, described Southern sentiments after the Assembly of 1831: "And now, in less than a year, there is evidence that leading men were beginning to feel that the neutrality of the South was at an end. On what ground should the South meet the coming tempest, that was moving down from the North? Should it be that of more, or less, strictness of creed? Should she cast her influence with either of the distinctly formed parties at the North, or should she

---

[52] Foote, *Sketches of Virginia*, Second Series, 457,458. At Baxter's inauguration as professor in September of 1831, Dr. William Hill, pastor of the Presbyterian Church in Winchester Virginia presented a charge to the new professor and expressed his own fears that the South was being drawn into Northern disputes. Hill observed: "It has so happened heretofore that our Southern churches have been distinguished of their unanimity of sentiment, and for their uniform moderation in disputed doctrines, and in their conduct toward their brethren at large. While our brethren at the North have been split into parties, and agitated by angry controversies, we have happily preserved the unity of the Spirit in the bonds of peace.... While many of our Northern brethren have acquired either an extravagant rage for innovation, or an indiscreet zeal for orthodoxy, have been classed as belonging either to the New School or to the Old School, and have become zealous partizans of course, we have stood aloof, and wondered and grieved at their indiscretion.... Great danger has arisen in former times, and is likely to arise again, to the peace and prosperity of the Church from angry and unnecessary disputes about orthodoxy.... It is not to be supposed, however, that the orthodox are, or ever have been, entirely unanimous in their opinion on the subject of religion. In matters comparatively unessential, and in their modes of stating and explaining and establishing essential truths, there has always been a diversity of opinion.... I would by no means speak disparagingly of creeds and confession, for I readily admit their lawfulness and utility. Religious liberty includes the right to have creeds, if men please, as well as to have none, if they please. But scriptural, and venerable, and useful as creeds have been and are, their efficiency falls infinitely below the exigencies of the Church of Christ. They do not produce holiness of themselves, nor do they ensure it; nor can they preserve themselves from innovation in times of declension. And of all stupidity, orthodox stupidity is the most dreadful. It ought to be remembered that ice palaces have been built of orthodox as well as heterodox materials. And when the creed, which is but the handmaid of religion, is regarded with more zeal than religion itself, then the reign of high church and creed idolatry has begun." 459, 460.

endeavor to repress extremes, and call the church back to its primitive charity and belief? The first alternative she dreaded; of the last, she almost despaired."[53]

An indicator of diversity on the doctrinal question is seen in the reaction of Southern Synods to the conservative Act and Testimony of 1834. Only two Synods in the South, Kentucky and South Carolina/Georgia, adopted the Act and Testimony. At the Old School pre-Assembly convention of 1835 only a few Southern presbyteries were present and no representatives attended from either North Carolina or Virginia. The *Princeton Review* had accosted the Act and Testimony and this appeared to carry great weight in the South.[54] Many in the South were still not convinced.

A voice for moderation in the South was Amasa Converse, the editor of the *Southern Religious Telegraph* in Richmond. Converse believed the opposers of the New School were seeking impossibility if they wanted "all the ministry adopt not only the same system of doctrine, but the same philosophical views of doctrine." Converse declared that he belonged to the "old fashioned Virginia School of Presbyterians" that had existed long before the Old School and New School had appeared in the Presbyterian Church. The *Southern Religious Telegraph* was endorsed by the Synods of North Carolina and Virginia as well as several influential Southern leaders; nonetheless, Converse came under scrutiny for his neutrality.[55]

---

[53] Ibid., 459. Foote, a contemporary who lived through this tense period, observed that while there was significant Southern unity, there was also diversity in the degree of attachment to the Confession. Foote stated: "The men that had given tone to the Southern Church were eminent for their adherence to the doctrines of the Confession of Faith, and equally so for their fervent charity among themselves. They had neither been fond of innovation, or ready to make a man an offender for a word.... On the subject of creeds and confessions, all were united in maintaining their necessity as bonds of union; and an honest exposition to the public on these bonds, drawn out in precise well-arranged words. Some thought a very careful attention to the formulas not only appropriate, but necessary. Others thought there might be too great stress laid on uniformity, and too much reliance on the virtue of creeds, and were alarmed lest on these subjects there should arise a controversy to distract the Southern church."461, 462.

[54] Baird asserted that the sources behind information flowing into the South were the culprit behind Southern neutrality. Princeton Seminary, especially Dr. Alexander of Virginia, was very influential in the Southern States and the "religious press of the South was under the control of the Moderate party." Baird stated: "The idea was assiduously disseminated among them, that the whole trouble arose out of an unholy lust for power, among a few persons connected with the Boards in Philadelphia and its vicinity."Samuel J. Baird, *History of the New School* (Philadelphia: Claxton, Rensen & Haffelfinger, 1868), 404, 405.

[55] Ernest TriceThompson, *Presbyterians in the South*, vol. I (Richmond: John Knox Press, 1963), 380-381. Elwyn Smith claimed: "The South could not feel that anything critical was at stake between Old and New School parties." He added that Converse and Benjamin Gildersleeve, editor of the *Charleston Observer* ("the two leading editorial voices of the southern church") "repudiated the doctrinal-disciplinary schism itself and urged the need to be ready for a southern secession." Elwyn A. Smith, "The Role of the South in the Presbyterian Schism of 1837-38," *Church History* 29 (1960): 48.

A significant factor in the sudden Southern awakening to Northern ecclesiastical strife was the radical abolition movement. In 1835 the volatile subject of slavery was brought to the floor of the Assembly which elicited a predictable Southern reaction. The Presbyterian Church in 1818 had adopted a very strong anti-slavery statement which both condemned slavery yet acknowledged the particular difficulties of the South with her inherited situation. This moderate policy had kept the slavery topic at bay in Assembly deliberations until 1835 when an overture from Ohio reintroduced the subject. The incendiary nature of the overture, calling on the church to remove the evils of slavery, ignited Southern passions against the New School.[56] Advocates of immediate abolition, very visible at the 1835 General Assembly, vexed Southerners accustomed to Presbyterian toleration of slaveholding. For the first time since 1818 the General Assembly commissioned a full study of the slavery question. Samuel Miller was selected as the chair of the Committee on Slavery which would report back to the 1836 Assembly.

Nothing provoked theological tempers like debate over the prudence of abolition. The revival movements under Finney and his disciples had initiated a renewal of anti-slavery agitation in the North. The abolitionist cause became increasingly identified with the New School since radical abolitionist rhetoric was strongest in regions where the New School predominated. The Princeton professors as well as the conservative Philadelphia party were agreed in their opposition to allowing abolitionist agitation to harass the Presbyterian Church. Southern synods reiterated their position that the General Assembly had no constitutional authority to legislate on slavery. Several of the presbyteries and synods threatened to withdraw from the Assembly if the subject were introduced.[57] When the 1836 Assembly would gather,

---

[56] Bruce Staiger argued that the slavery question was the decisive issue that brought the South into the Old School/New School controversy. He said the "South, embracing both New and Old School tendencies, was not yet sufficiently excited about the doctrinal quarrel to take a stand with either School." Bruce Staiger, "Abolition and the Presbyterian Schism of 1837-38," *Mississippi Valley Historical Review* XXXVI (December 1949): 395. William Warren Sweet, before Staiger, stated that "the most important and far-reaching of the schisms in the American churches over slavery, which began nearly a century ago, are still with us. Therefore any study of the peculiar factors which have determined the course of American church history must of necessity give a prominent place to slavery." Quoted in Elwyn Smith, "The Role of South in the Schism of 1837-38," 44. See Sweet's study of Presbyterianism: *Religion on the American Frontier*, vol. II: *The Presbyterians* 1783-1840 (New York: Harper & Brothers Publishers, 1936).

[57] Staiger made a compelling case for slavery being the deciding factor in the schism of 1837. He argued that both Old School and New School courted the South in 1836, making concessions in order to secure Southern votes which would decide the contest. Staiger pointed out that in 1836, "the South, voting according to its theological inclinations, divided its vote upon the doctrinal issue, and the New School received a large minority of southern votes." Bruce Staiger, "Abolition and the Presbyterian Schism," 401. It is noteworthy that the South had been hesitant to become embroiled in Northern theological discussions, yet, clearly she took sides when the threat of abolition tyranny became evident. Several Southern Synods even threatened to withdraw from the Presbyterian Church over abolition. At the very

41 delegates from slave-holding states were present and held a caucus. Some feared they were about to be "unchurched," but remained firm in their resolve to resist abolitionist oppression.[58]

---

least, objective appraisal of the historical materials requires an admission that slavery was one critical factor in the Presbyterian schism. Elwyn Smith suggested that the disappearance of the slavery controversy after emancipation is one reason for "the obscuring of sectional interests as a factor in the division" by historians. While discussions continued on the other divisive issues, the slavery question had disappeared. Elwyn Smith, "The Role of the South in the Presbyterian Schism," 45.

[58] Elwyn Smith, "The Role of the South in the Presbyterian Schism," 48.

CHAPTER 6

The Great Schism

While tempers were flaring over abolition, Albert Barnes emerged again in 1835 as the target of conservative Old School attacks. The catalyst for this second assault on Barnes was the publication of his Romans commentary early that year. Barnes's *Notes on Romans* was intended as a layman's resource – for "Sunday-School teachers; for Bible classes; and for the higher classes in Sabbath-schools." Old School opposition soon began in the periodicals and papers. William Engles, a former Barnes adversary in 1831, reentered the contest and declared Barnes's new book "unsound and dangerous." Engles placed the *Notes on Romans* alongside *The Way of Salvation* as "both alike in conflict with the doctrines of Presbyterianism."[1]

Charles Hodge, joined the fray over *Notes on Romans* in an April 1835 review in the *Biblical Repertory* which was reprinted in the May and June issues of *The Presbyterian*. Hodge was in a solid position to evaluate Barnes's work since he was in the process of writing his own commentary on Romans. In his review of the *Notes*, Hodge, while agreeing with the conservative criticisms on numerous points, did not believe Barnes was a dangerous heretic attempting to introduce Arminian doctrines into the church. There were erroneous statements in the *Notes*, on the other hand, Hodge observed that there were also orthodox Calvinistic statements "in perfect accordance with the system of doctrines which he has professed to believe."[2] Hodge's astute and balanced appraisal of the *Notes* as a whole did not assuage conservative's determination to proceed with prosecuting Barnes.[3]

Second Barnes Trial

The opposition leader in this new wave of theological controversy was Dr. George Junkin,[4] president of Lafayette College in Pennsylvania. Junkin sent Barnes a

---

[1] William Engles, "Barnes on Romans," *The Presbyterian*, February 25, 1835, 35.

[2] Charles Hodge, "Barnes on the Epistle to the Romans," *Biblical Repertory* VII (April, 1835): 238, 239; Charles Hodge, "Review of Barnes on Romans," *The Presbyterian*, May 21, 1835, 81,82; May 28, 1835, 85; June 4, 1835, 92.

[3] Earl Pope asserted that Hodge's review of Barnes on Romans was "the justification for the compromise decision which Samuel Miller attempted to bring about in the General Assembly of 1836." Earl A. Pope, "New England Calvinism and the Disruption of the Presbyterian Church," Ph.D. diss., Brown University, 1962, 325.

[4] George Junkin (1790-1868) became President of Lafayette College in 1832. He also served briefly as president of Miami University in Ohio and then as president of Washington

personal letter in March of 1835 accusing him of falling "into serious error" and declaring his intent to press charges against Barnes in the church judicatories. Barnes responded by letter that he did not fear a trial, had made no claim to infallible views and would be willing "to retract them if I am convinced of their error."[5] Charges were brought before the Second Presbytery of Philadelphia in April 1835. The indictment included a listing of doctrines that Junkin claimed were "contrary to the Standards of the Presbyterian Church" and a list of doctrines "taught in the Standards of the Church" which Junkin alleged had been denied by Barnes.[6] The formal trial of Barnes began in July of 1835.

Barnes recognized that Junkin's complaint was directed towards alleged infractions of the Westminster Standards; he clarified that his intention in interpreting Romans was to express the truth of the Bible and not to defend the Westminster Confession.[7] In his defense against Junkin, Barnes first addressed the question of subscription to the doctrinal standards before he responded to specific charges. In each charge, there was an indictment of violating the Confession of Faith, therefore, accusing Barnes of breaking his ordination vows. Barnes explained his views on subscribing the Confession:

> Of the Confession of Faith of the Westminster Assembly, I may be allowed to say, that when I expressed my assent to it as a 'system of doctrines,' I did it cordially, and that I have never had occasion to regret the act. I then regarded it as I do now, and ever have done, as the best summary of the doctrines of the Bible which I have seen, and as expressing my views of the true scheme of Christian theology in a manner far better than any other articles of faith which I have ever examined. The *system of truth* contained there, as distinguished from all other systems – the Socinian, the Pelagian, the Arian, the Arminian, &c., has appeared to me to be the true system; and without hesitation, or fluctuation, I have received it. I have not forgotten, however, that nearly

---

College in Virginia from 1848 until the outbreak of the war when he returned North. One of his daughters married Confederate General Stonewall Jackson. Junkin was a leader among the ultra conservatives and a strident advocate for ecclesiastical division as the only solution to Presbyterian problems.

[5] George Junkin, *The Vindication, Containing a History of the Trial of the Rev. Albert Barnes by the Second Presbytery, and by the Synod of Pennsylvania* (Philadelphia: William S. Martien, 1836), iv, v.

[6] For a list of the ten doctrinal points brought against Barnes see Samuel J. Baird, *A Collection of the Acts, Deliverances, and Testimonies of the Supreme Judicatory of the Presbyterian Church from its Origin in America to the Present Time* (Philadelphia: Presbyterian Board of Publication, 1856), 684. The doctrines included: imputation, ability, atonement, regeneration, and justification. Five of the ten points relate to the doctrine of original sin.

[7] Albert Barnes, *The Way of Salvation: A Sermon Delivered at Morristown, New Jersey, February 8, 1829 Together With Mr. Barnes's Defense of the Sermon, read Before the Synod of Philadelphia, at Lancaster, October 29, 1830; and His "Defense" before the Second Presbytery of Philadelphia, in Reply to the Charge of the Rev. George Junkin* (New York: Leavitt, Lord, and Company, 1836), 108.

two hundred years have elapsed since it was formed; that language often varies in meaning; and that views of philosophy, which insensibly insinuate themselves into theology, seldom continue the same for two hundred years. I have thought that there was, perhaps, somewhat too much harshness, and severity of language, in the general cast of that Confession; and that a few expressions do not convey, without much labored exposition, the meaning of sacred Scriptures. To a few of those expressions, small in number, and not affecting the *system* as a system, I have always taken the exceptions which others have been allowed to do. My views have not been disguised, neither before, at the time, nor since my licensure and ordination (italics his).[8]

Barnes insists that the phrase "system of doctrine" in the ordination vow denotes the "arrangement of doctrines" as distinguished from other systems (i.e., Socinian, Arian, Pelagian, Arminian) and "not to express our unqualified assent to every feature, and every particular, in the system." He added, "If this was not the meaning, the term 'system' would never have been inserted." The "system of doctrine" is embraced if one adheres to the "substantial or essential nature of those doctrines, but who may, in some unimportant points, differ as to the modes of explanation." There is difference between facts and explanations of facts; presbyteries are to determine whether or not the "essential facts in the case have been adhered to, or departed from." Barnes illustrates his point with the Fall of Adam:

> In the same way, men may agree, that it was by the sin of one man – that his sin secured their fall and ruin – that in virtue of the connection with him, all come into the world subject to sin, and wo[e], and death; and that all this is in accordance with a divine arrangement – and yet one may suppose that this is to be explained on the theory, that all were one in Adam, and that there was a personal identity between them and him: another, that he acted as their representative; and that thus, though personally blameless, his sin is charged on them: and a third, that neither of these theories explain, but rather embarrass the subject; and that it is wise to be contented with the simple facts as they are presented in the Scriptures, and in the world. Now while the facts in the case which are essential to the 'system of doctrine' are held, who shall assume that his explanation is the only one possible, and that the others are to be deemed heretical?[9]

Barnes raises the practical issue of the sheer size of both the Confession and the Presbyterian Church. In such an extended statement of faith, it is impossible "to secure perfect uniformity in every minute article of doctrine." One is sadly mistaken if he thinks "a quarter of a million minds in one generation could be made to think just alike ... and that this process can be kept up to meet the advancing millions of coming generations who shall adopt the Confession ..." Given these differences of opinion, "it is for the church to declare, in a constitutional manner, what shall be

---

[8] Ibid., 111, 112.
[9] Ibid., 120-122.

regarded as a departure from the essential doctrines of the Confession, and shall deserve deposition or excommunication."[10]

Barnes argued that Presbyterians in America had never contemplated such "exact uniformity of opinion." He contrasted the subscription vow of the Scottish Church, assenting to the "whole doctrine contained in the Confession," with the American Presbyterian ordination vow which gave assent to the "system of doctrine" contained in the Confession. Furthermore, the unique American form of subscription was evidenced in the "difference in the ordinary assent of licentiates and ordained ministers to the Confession, and the subscription required by the professors in our theological seminaries." Barnes commented on the seminary faculty pledge: "This great particularity and exactness would not have been required, if it had been supposed that this point had been sufficiently secured by the fact of their having adopted the Confession, as containing 'the system of doctrine,' at their ordination. The fact that this office is so strongly and minutely guarded, shows that greater latitude and liberty are contemplated among the ordinary ministers of the gospel, and members of the churches."[11]

The Adopting Act of 1729 sealed the argument for Barnes. The "proviso" adopted in the synodical act allowed a minister to state his scruples whereupon the synod or presbytery would make a judgment on whether the scruple was a denial of doctrines "essential or necessary." This proviso has "never been withdrawn or repealed" and it has been the practice of the church for over a century. Barnes emphatically stated: "It is the inalienable privilege and right of each and every Presbytery to judge in this matter; and this right is secured, no less by the constitution of the church, than by the word of God." The adoption of the proviso indicated clearly that difference of opinion on some points existed among ministers in 1729. The original act of 1729 served as the basis of union in 1758.[12]

Barnes pointed back to the Assembly action of 1831, which exonerated him, as contemporary evidence that Presbyterians continue to practice the "large and catholic spirit" of their founders. The Assembly's action of 1831 indicated "their inclination to allow the usual latitude of interpretation." The 1801 Plan of Union, which until recently was cordially received in the Presbyterian Church, was another indicator of the liberal and catholic spirit within the church. Presbyterians have historically been willing to cooperate with others "in all great plans of Christian benevolence." Assembly actions over the last few years confirming this catholic spirit "have been perfectly satisfactory to those in the church who have desired a liberal construction of the constitution, and unsatisfactory, in a high degree, to the other party. Barnes queried: "It remains to be seen, whether now, and in this Presbytery, the spirit which has so long and happily characterized the Presbyterian Church, is to be arrested ..."[13]

---

[10] Ibid., 122, 123.
[11] Ibid., 122-124.
[12] Ibid., 124-127.
[13] Ibid., 126-128.

To conclude his remarks on subscription, Barnes read several lengthy passages from the *Biblical Repertory* to Second Presbytery. Barnes quoted from an article in which Professor Hodge described the meaning of "system of doctrine" in the ordination vow. Like Hodge, Barnes believed that adopting the system of doctrine meant "a man professes to believe the whole series of doctrines which go to make up the Calvinistic system, in opposition to the Socinian, Pelagian, Semi-Pelagian, Arminian, or any other opposite and inconsistent view of Christianity." This mode of subscription excluded strict uniformity of views and left the right of judgment to the presbyteries. Barnes asserted: "My views of this whole subject cannot be better expressed than in the words of the *Biblical Repertory*...."[14]

Junkin, disagreeing with both Barnes and Hodge, argued for strict subscription as the historic position of the church. Junkin was opposed to Barnes's "considerable latitude of interpretation" which allowed for a "general" adoption of the Confession. Junkin protested: "*What are the standards of the church?* If you may reject one doctrine, as non-essential, may not I reject another? May not the next brother, reject a third? – and the next a fourth? And what will be left? ... Why, sir, is it not as clear as sunshine, that there *is* nor *can* be *any* standard of doctrine at this rate. Each man claims the privilege of judging for himself what is essential to the system ..."(italics his).[15]

Barnes had pointed back to the 1729 Adopting Act to support his assertion that exceptions to the Confession are allowed. Junkin countered that the "Proviso" to the Adopting Act was not part of the constitution of the church and has been "superseded by subsequent legislation." For Junkin, the key documents come from 1788 when the Form of Government and Discipline along with the "altered" Westminster Confession are officially adopted by the Presbyterian Church. He declares, "... this adopting act of 1729 has no more to do with the constitution of our church, than the adopting act of the church of Scotland has. The whole constitution has been revised since and formally ratified and adopted." Junkin argued that the conservative nature of 1788 Presbyterians was evidenced in their moderator Doctor John Witherspoon of the "rigidly orthodox party in Scotland." Witherspoon had battled "moderate men" in Scotland over latitude in doctrine and his leadership in America insured that the Presbyterian Church was "zealous for the doctrines of grace and the articles of religion in all their strictness."[16]

---

[14] Ibid., 129-132. Barnes quoted from: Charles Hodge, "Remarks on Dr. Cox's Communication," *Biblical Repertory* III (1831): 521-523.

[15] George Junkin, *The Vindication*, 22.

[16] Ibid., 25, 26. Junkin added: "But as to the 'Proviso' of 1729, I have a word more. Even supposing it binding now, (which is absurd,) there are three things required in regard to its 'scruples' of objection against the Confession of Faith. The first is, that they are *scruples*, and in order to admit a minister into the church, they must be *scruples* - merely the 288th part of a pound of truth, '*not essential or necessary*.' Secondly, the synod or presbytery; not the man who brings them, is to weigh them; they 'shall judge his scruples.' Thirdly, he, who has them, shall not conceal them, but shall offer them to the weigher, *before* he is or shall be 'admitted to the exercise of the ministry' " (italics his). Junkin then proceeded to apply these

In Junkin's written account of the second Barnes trial, he attached an appendix, "New Schoolism in the Seventeenth, compared with New-Schoolism in the Nineteenth Century." Junkin juxtaposed the position of the seventeenth-century Remonstrants with those of New School Presbyterians and argued for their substantial equivalence. Junkin said of the New School, "Are they not, in opposing Calvinism, reviving and propagating the heresy of Pelagius?" The Arminian and New School systems are identical; "false doctrines" must be condemned "as they were condemned by the Synod of Dordt." Barnes's position was very dangerous according to Junkin. He summarized his comparison of the two systems with this assertion: "... subscription to a creed which is not sincere and true, is a dereliction from correct principle, and may lead to farther deviations. Let us avoid all evil and all appearance of evil."[17]

Junkin advocated strict subscription which safeguarded full Calvinism. He believed that there were no distinctions possible between the primary doctrines of the Confession and the explanatory doctrines. He rejected the notion that one might affirm the substance of a doctrine but reject particular explanatory doctrines in the standards. Consistency demanded that Barnes adopt fully every part of the Confession. A particular example of Junkin's position was his disavowal of the New School distinction between natural ability and moral inability. Junkin chastised Barnes: "Let him either admit man's total depravity in understanding, will, and affections, and thus become a consistent Calvinist; or let him go over entirely and maintain moral ability and become a consistent Arminian."[18]

Junkin further charged Barnes with teaching: "That unregenerate men are able to keep the commandments, and convert themselves to God." Barnes is surprised by this unjustified accusation since his *Notes on Romans* "have expressed no opinion on the subject charged on me.... It is not a little remarkable that grave and formal accusations should be brought against a minister of the gospel, on a subject on which he expressly declines giving any opinion in the book under consideration." This charge demonstrated Dr. Junkin's design that Barnes be "held up to odium for holding certain opinions." Barnes confessed his perplexity at "the loose, and hasty, and undigested manner in which these charges have been brought against my ministerial character." The expression "men are able to convert themselves to God" had never been used by Barnes in writing or oral expression and there was no evidence to prove this assertion. Barnes admitted that there has been "popular rumor" about some ministers preaching this but he has never heard anyone declare

---

criteria to the Barnes case, claiming that it failed in each category - Barnes's errors are "fundamental;" he did not declare his scruples with the Confession to New Brunswick Presbytery, therefore, the presbytery was unable to weigh these scruples. Note: Junkin rejected the Adopting Act as authoritative, nevertheless, he clearly understood its original intent.

[17] Ibid., 151, 159.
[18] Ibid., 50.

such a thing. If such unfounded charges are allowed against a minister, "what man is safe from wholly unfounded and gratuitous accusations?"[19]

Barnes's defense of his own orthodoxy did not satisfy Junkin; but, the majority of Second Presbytery was ultimately convinced that Barnes had not transgressed his commitment to Westminster Calvinism. After a prolonged trial, Second Presbytery finally acquitted Barnes and adopted a paper responding in detail to each of the ten charges brought by Junkin. At the conclusion of the judgment, the presbytery stated: "... the evidence submitted on the part of the prosecution, in respect to the charges of erroneous doctrine, was that of inferences drawn from Mr. Barnes's language, which in the judgment of the presbytery, were not legitimate, but which, even if they were, ought not, and cannot, agreeably to the decision of the General Assembly of 1824, be used to convict of heresy or dangerous error, affecting the foundation of a sinner's hope, or the Christian's title to eternal life." The Presbytery dismissed the charges expressing their appreciation for the "Christian spirit manifested by the prosecutor" and their hope that "the result of all will be to promote the peace of the Church, and further the Gospel of Christ."[20]

Junkin rejected the decision of the presbytery and appealed to the Synod of Philadelphia. The Synod trial in October of 1835 was complicated by the refusal of Second Presbytery to hand over their records of the Barnes trial. Barnes appeared before the Synod and offered to read a statement he claimed would satisfy the Synod of his orthodoxy, but, he was unwilling to submit to trial without the official records of the presbytery in hand. After prolonged discussion, the Synod decided to proceed with the trial anyway. Presentations and debate lasted for a week. After hearing all sides, the Synod voted to reverse the decision of Second Presbytery, condemned Barnes's errors and suspended him from the ministry until "he shall retract the errors hereby condemned, and give satisfactory evidence of repentance." The final vote on the censure of Barnes was 116 ayes and 31 nays.[21]

After the judgment from Synod was announced, Barnes wrote to Samuel Miller asking for his counsel. Miller had questions about the legality of the Synod's decision and he advised Barnes not to cease his ministerial functions. Miller also confronted Barnes with the part he had played in this controversy: "Have you been as guarded in stating, and as frank in explaining your views, as the exigencies of your situation evidently demanded? Or has a proud and independent feeling perverted you from giving that satisfaction to your brethren, which the state of their minds earnestly called for? ... If you will allow me to use that paternal freedom which you have invited, and which my own feelings prompt me to indulge, I will say, that I have thought you were at fault in these respects."[22] Barnes did not heed Miller's advice and removed himself from active pastoral responsibilities. The

[19] Barnes, *The Way of Salvation and His Defense*, 148-152.

[20] Baird, *Collection*, "Minutes of the Second Presbytery," 686-687.

[21] Ibid., "Decision of the Synod of Philadelphia on the Appeal," 690.

[22] Letter of Miller to Barnes, Nov.11, 1835 in Samuel Miller, Jr., *Life of Samuel Miller* (Philadelphia: Claxton, Remsen and Haffelfinger, 1869), II, 279.

Synod's action was unjust according to Barnes who now appealed the case to the 1836 General Assembly.

Conservatives viewed the Barnes case as a showdown between the two parties in the Presbyterian Church. William Engles declared: "The crisis has arrived; and the General Assembly must decide whether the doctrines of the new divinity are any longer to be tolerated within the Presbyterian Church. Do they agree with its standards – can they consist with those standards – are they to be countenanced in those who have professedly adopted those standards?" Engles believed this was to be a watershed case – either the Synod's sentence is sustained and several New School Synods might secede or if the Synod's decision is reversed, part of the Old School may abandon the Church. The time for compromise was over. Engles prophesied, "The next Assembly is not to decide the fate of an individual, but the fate of the Presbyterian Church."[23]

Old School conservatives exhorted Presbyterians to uphold "strict views of subscription" as the only method to avoid "wild error" and to "preserve the peaceful existence of the church." *The Presbyterian* announced: "The Presbyterian Confession must be subscribed fully or its reputation is lost." For one to "receive and adopt" the Confession of Faith meant adopting the Confession "without any exceptions, as entirely coinciding with my views." New School views violate the constitution of the church which is clear in its intent. "The rule as it now stands is as explicit as language can make it, and as it provides for no exceptions, it must be by usurpation of authority and by a breach of faith that any presbytery admits of such exceptions... subscription to the formularies must be without exceptions and without mental reservations." Those who have exceptions to the Confession have two choices – "either to subscribe dishonestly or to be separate."[24]

New School men argued that there had never been a formal repeal of the "excepting clause" in the Adopting Act, therefore, it was still in force.[25] *The Presbyterian* countered that the Adopting Act was not part of the constitution and strict subscription had always been the practice of the Presbyterian Church. The only place where the *Presbyterian* editor admitted that exceptions had been allowed in Presbyterian history was the 1817 Pastoral Letter from the General Assembly.[26] The editor of the *Pittsburgh Christian Herald* threatened that if a New School dominated Assembly recognized the Adopting Act "as part of the standards of the church" he would retire alone or with other brethren. In some minds, the Adopting Act was becoming directly associated with the impending second trial of Barnes before the Assembly. The *Herald* editor declared: "Should the suspension of Mr.

---

[23] *The Presbyterian*, Dec. 3, 1835, 195.

[24] *The Presbyterian*, April 23, 1836, 62.

[25] Ibid. This position was held by Dr. Luther Halsey, Professor of Theology at Western Theological Seminary. Professor Halsey later served on the faculties of both Auburn and Union (New York) Seminaries.

[26] Ibid.

Barnes be reversed by the next General Assembly, under the proviso of the act of 1729, I think I can foresee a division of our Church at no very distant day...."[27]

New School Presbyterians also viewed the upcoming Assembly review of the Barnes trial as a test case for the confessional boundaries of the Presbyterian Church. Some of the New School men were clearly irritated by the censorious spirit exhibited by those attacking Barnes and considered it as an assault upon themselves. Absalom Peters commented on the Barnes suspension:

> When I heard the sentence, I regarded it as a blow struck at one-half of the Presbyterian Church. The doctrines held by Brother Barnes, he has proved to be substantially in accordance with the Confession of Faith. I shall not vote to restore him on the ground of toleration, he has a right to be a minister in our connexion. If any one is to be tolerated, it is the Prosecutor, who says, that 'man has in no sense ability to love God.' Yes, Sir, the time has come when the question is, whether such men are to be tolerated in the Presbyterian Church.[28]

General Assembly of 1836

There were a number of potentially explosive issues that would come before the Assembly of 1836 – slavery, missions and the Albert Barnes situation. Convictions on these subjects ran deep and mostly along party lines. The case of Albert Barnes was the immediate crisis of the Assembly and consumed 9 days as Junkin presented the charges and Barnes gave his defense. At one point it seemed that reconciliation might be possible since Barnes had explained himself satisfactorily. Junkin offered to drop the charges if Barnes would put his "concessions" in writing, but, Barnes replied that he had made no such "retractions."[29] This settlement was not to be and the appeal of Barnes was put to a vote. The vote to sustain the appeal of Barnes was 134 in favor, 96 opposed, and 6 abstentions. The next day a resolution from the Synod of Philadelphia asked to reverse the suspension of Barnes; it passed by a vote of 145-78, with 11 abstaining.[30]

At the conclusion of the vote reversing the suspension, Samuel Miller presented a compromise resolution which not only affirmed removing Barnes's suspension but also reiterated concern about the views published in *Notes on Romans*. Miller's resolution asserted that Barnes "has published opinions materially at variance with

---

[27] *Pittsburgh Christian Herald* quoted in *The Presbyterian*, May 7, 1836, 70.·

[28] "A Moderate Man to Moderate Men," *The Presbyterian*, July 2, 1836, 102. Old School men did not appreciate Peters's threat. See Charles Hodge, "The General Assembly of 1836," *The Biblical Repertory and Theological Review* VIII (July 1836): 459, 460.

[29] Baird commented: "Had Mr. Barnes been willing to put upon record the acknowledgments which he had made, on the floor, the case would there have ended, and the peace and unity of the Church might possibly have been preserved." Samuel J. Baird, *A History of the New School* (Philadelphia: Claxton, Rensen & Haffelfinger, 1868), 481.

[30] *Minutes of the General Assembly of the Presbyterian Church in the United States of America 1789-1837* (Philadelphia) 1836, 268-270.

the Confession of Faith of the Presbyterian Church, and with the word of God; ... the Assembly considers the work, even in its present amended form, as containing representation which cannot be reconciled with the letter or spirit of our public standards; and would solemnly admonish Mr. Barnes again to review this work; to modify still further the statements which have grieved his brethren." The New School men were in no mood to compromise and wanted Barnes fully exonerated from any stigma of error.[31] The resolution was rejected 122 to 109 with 3 abstentions.[32]

Two protests were issued against the Assembly's rejection of Miller's resolution. The first protest, signed by 101 members of the Assembly, charged the Assembly with violating the Constitution of the Church: "... we believe the constitutional standards of the Church, in their plain and obvious meaning, and in the sense in which they have always been received, are the rule of judgment by which all doctrinal controversies are to be decided.... Yet, in the above decision, there was, as we believe, a departure from our constitutional rule, a refusal to bear testimony against errors, with an implied approbation of them, and a constructive denial that Ministers of the gospel in the Presbyterian Church are under solemn obligations to conform in their doctrinal sentiments to our Confession of Faith and Catechisms." The number of signatures attached to this protest indicated both the growing indignation and swelling ranks of Old School who believed the time had come to excise New School errors.[33]

The second protest attempted to strike a conciliatory tone by offering an explanation for ambivalence in the Barnes case. Barnes's trial had been complex because some of Junkin's charges were "partly sustained" and other charges "were not fully, if at all sustained." The signers of the protest were opposed to both the "irregular proceedings" of the Synod's trial of Barnes as well as the Assembly's "overlooking erroneous doctrinal sentiments." They had desired to procure a "modified decision" but their efforts "were defeated by the positions occupied by different and opposite portions of the Assembly." The protest concluded with an expression of "painful apprehensions that these things will lead to extended and increased dissension, and endanger the disruption of the holy bonds which hold us together as one Church."[34] The 16 signers of this protest were here expressing the

---

[31] Ibid., 270.

[32] Ibid.,, 270, 271. It is noteworthy that the Synod of Philadelphia with 27 potential votes was excluded from the voting. Only 7 of the presbyters from the Synod of Philadelphia were New School men, therefore, the vote on Miller's resolution could have resulted in an even division of the Assembly! Conservatives later analyzed the vote and observed that the New School Synods of Utica, Geneva, Genesee and Western Reserve cast 63 votes against Miller's resolution with only 2 votes in favor. *The Presbyterian* declared that Barnes was indebted for his acquittal to Congregationalists. The Southern vote (including Kentucky and Missouri) on Miller's resolution was 43 in favor and 23 opposed. See "The Test Vote," *The Presbyterian*, July 9, 1836, 106 for the count from each Synod.

[33] *Minutes of the General Assembly*, 1836, 284, 285.

[34] Ibid., 285, 286.

same sentiments as the Church's 1831 compromise decision (authored by Miller) in the first Barnes trial but it was now 1836 and reconciliation between the combatants was wishful thinking. Most of the Assembly commissioners in 1836 had no alternative but to choose either the Old School or New School agenda since compromise was rejected. Samuel Miller had signed both protests. The influence of the moderate Princeton men was rapidly waning and they too would ultimately have to align with one party or be excluded altogether.

The Assembly answered these protests with a point by point justification of the Barnes acquittal by demonstrating that for each of the charges, the Assembly's decision had been confirmed "by a careful analysis of the real meaning of Mr. Barnes under each charge, as ascertained by the language of his book: and the revisions, disclaimers, explanations, and declarations which he has made." Further, the New School majority Assembly declared:

> So far is the Assembly from countenancing the errors alleged in the charges of Dr. Junkin, that they do cordially and *ex animo* adopt the Confession of our Church, on the points of doctrine in question, according to the obvious and most prevalent interpretation; and do regard it as a whole, as the best epitome of the doctrines of the Bible ever formed. And this Assembly disavows any desire, and would deprecate any attempt to change the phraseology of our standards, and would disapprove of any language of light estimation applied to them; believing that no denomination can prosper whose members permit themselves to speak slightly of its formularies of doctrine; and are ready to unite with their brethren, in contending earnestly for the faith of our standards.[35]

Undoubtedly this was a genuine expression of the New School point of view on the Westminster Confession. It was sincerely offered to answer Old School accusations that Assembly actions had forsaken the doctrinal standards of the Church. In the light of New School rejection of Miller's compromise, the statement of commitment to the Confession appeared incredulous to Old School conservatives.[36] It did underscore the wide gulf between the strict subscriptionist

---

[35] Ibid., 1836, 287-289. Baird suggested that this New School avowal of dedication to Confessional orthodoxy only hastened the march toward schism. "Whatever its meaning, - so earnest a protestation of orthodoxy, coming from such a quarter, and in such circumstances, - entirely failed to conciliate the confidence, or quiet the alarms of the minority. They read this declaration, in immediate connection with the incredible assertion that Mr. Barnes' contradictions were in perfect harmony with the doctrines of the standards.... it was impossible for them to believe that the history of a quarter of a century of controversy and rebuke, in defense of the doctrines of the gospel, was all an unreal figment of the imagination, a troubled dream. Nothing in the whole history so shocked the conscience of the Church, or so prepared it for the action of 1837, as did this attempt to cover the doctrinal derelictions of Mr. Barnes and the party." *History of the New School*, 487, 488.

[36] "Profession and Practice," in *The Presbyterian*, July 2, 1836, 102. The writer decried the New School profession of sincerely receiving the Confession, all the while they "sneer at its doctrines, and by a public act uphold an opposite system."

wing of the Old School and the broader New School perspective on confessional subscription. Alongside the doctrinal chasm in the 1836 Assembly, the missions question again brought the two parties into direct ecclesiastical conflict and with similar results – the Assembly split evenly and almost entirely along party lines.

The context of the 1836 confrontation was the transfer of the Western Foreign Missionary Society from the Synod of Pittsburgh to the direct supervision of the General Assembly. A committee had been appointed by the 1835 Assembly to negotiate this transfer and report back the following year. The proposed terms of the transfer stipulated that the Assembly "will never hereafter alienate or transfer to any other judicatory or Board whatever, the direct supervision and management of the said missions, or those which may hereafter be established by the Board of the General Assembly." The terms also included a constitution for the establishment of an Assembly Board of Foreign Missions. After much discussion, the report was referred to a committee for its review and recommendation back to the Assembly. The majority of the committee concluded that it was proper for the 1836 Assembly to proceed with these terms since it had agreed in principle to the transfer and the establishment of an Assembly mission board at the 1835 Assembly. A minority report opposed the formation of a separate Assembly board with this resolution: "Whereas, the American Board of Commissioners for Foreign Missions has been connected with the Presbyterian Church from the year of its incorporation, by the very elements of its existence; – and, whereas, at the present time, the majority of the whole of that Board are Presbyterians; and whereas it is undesirable, in conducting the work of foreign missions, that there should be any collision at home or abroad; therefore, Resolved, That it is inexpedient that the Assembly should organize a separate foreign missionary institution."[37]

Intense argument ensued with Dr. Peters claiming the Presbyterian Church was bound to the American Board because of their past history of cooperation. New School men pointed to the Presbyterian influence in the American Board as well as appealing to the catholicity of this organization versus the sectarian organization of an Assembly mission board. Old School men, on the other hand, believed it was the "right and duty" of the Church to have its own board and to fulfill her commitment

---

[37] Baird, *History of the New School*, 489-491. For an elaborate discussion of New School views on the American Board see Absalom Peters, *A Plea for Voluntary Societies By a Member of the Assembly* (New York: John S. Taylor, 1837). Gillett explained New School resentment due to feelings that the establishment of a denominational board was being "stealthily thrust upon the Church." Sentiment in the church had changed because of the success of the Assembly's Board of Domestic Missions which had proven its ability to raise funds and garner support in the church. Nevertheless, the New School majority approved the minority report which "was a grievance not less sore and sad than that of imputed theological errors." Gillett said there can be "little doubt that the exasperation produced by the rejection of the proposed transfer contributed not a little to the final result of division." E.H. Gillett, *History of the Presbyterian Church in the United States of America*, vol. II (Philadelphia: Presbyterian Publication Committee, 1864), 494.

to the Synod of Pittsburgh. The question was finally called and the Assembly sided with the minority report by a vote of 110 to 106.[38]

Samuel Miller again attempted to be a peacemaker and entered a protest against this action of the Assembly which was signed by 82 commissioners. The Old School protest asked for simple fairness from the Assembly. The New School has a Board that meets all their "wants and wishes ... but they refused to make such a decision as would accord to us a similar and equal privilege." The protest argued practically that a denominational Mission Board would "call forth the zealous cooperation of those in every part of the Church who wish for a general Presbyterian Board." It was the strong conviction of many Old School men that the Church "in her ecclesiastical capacity" is bound to obey Christ's command "to send the glorious gospel as far as may be in her power, to every creature." The protest also accused the Assembly of breach of contract with the Synod of Pittsburgh by not carrying into effect the decisions of the 1835 Assembly.[39]

The protest was answered by Peters and two others appointed to the task. The majority answer appealed to the universal mission call "not to the Presbyterian Church in her distinctive ecclesiastical capacity, but to the whole Church, to the collective body of Christ's disciples, of every name." It is imperative that Presbyterians unite with other denominations to spread the gospel rather than establish their own missions which will perpetuate divisions among Christians. The New School men countered that the Old School were free to pursue missions according to the dictates of their conscience but it is unreasonable for them to expect the Assembly to form "an organization, the principles of which we do not approve." The answer argued that giving to missions had greatly increased in America through "more expanded organizations." The New School also voiced their displeasure at what they perceived as the "unusual and unwarranted" authority given to the 1835 Assembly committee charged with confirming the transfer of the Western Foreign Mission Society to the General Assembly.[40] There was no palm branch in this reply to Old School consternation; the New School would not be moved from its resolve to protect the interests of the American Board.

---

[38] Ibid, 496. One thing that had prejudiced the New School men was a pamphlet circulated in the church by Dr. Anderson a secretary of the American Board before the 1836 Assembly.

[39] *Minutes of the General Assembly*, 1836, 280, 281.

[40] Ibid., 291-293. New School men were offended that the 1835 Assembly had taken action on the missions question on the last day of the Assembly when half of the members were already gone. They were further put off by the proposed terms of agreement between the Assembly committee and the Synod of Pittsburgh which stated: "... it being expressly understood that the said Assembly will never hereafter alienate or transfer to any other judicatory or board whatever, the direct supervision and management of the said missions, or those which may hereafter be established by the Board of the General Assembly."

In addition to the Barnes case and the missions controversy, the 1836 Assembly had to face the volatile question of slavery.[41] When the issue came to the Assembly floor, Dr. Miller's committee made a brief majority report which declined any action on the subject of slavery. A minority report included resolutions opposing slavery; the report was long and elicited earnest discussion. After several failed motions, Dr. Hoge of Virginia moved that the subject be indefinitely postponed; this passed 154 to 87. Protests to the postponement followed, the signers of which were all New School.[42] And there was also a protest against the disorderly conduct of abolitionists; this protest had more signatures from the Synod of New York than it did from the Southern delegates. The Old School, while differing on how to handle doctrinal disputes, was uniformly set against abolition agitation in the Assembly.

Some Southerners were not satisfied with postponement and walked out as they had been instructed. Most of the South was encouraged and convinced her interests aligned with the Old School.[43] An eyewitness review of the 1836 Assembly in the *Southern Religious Telegraph* noted, "And now it becomes a grave and serious question, whether the Southern section of our Church will any more, or again, expose its representatives to the scoffs and taunts, and jeers and misrepresentations, and excommunications and maledictions of the abolitionists, both male and female." The editor commented: "If the South cannot look for peace and rest in the Assembly, on the slavery question, is it not time for all the Southern Presbyteries to refuse unanimously to send representatives to that body?"[44]

In the Old School meeting that followed the adjournment of the 1836 Assembly, it appears that an arrangement was procured with the South; in exchange for her support in the separation, the Old School would keep the slavery question out of

---

[41] Archibald Alexander highlighted slavery along with the Assembly's refusal to both censure Barnes and ratify the Foreign Missions plan as the 1836 Assembly issues that had made division inevitable. See James W. Alexander, *Life of Archibald Alexander* (1854, reprint ed. Harrisonburg: Sprinkle Publications, 1991), 518.

[42] *Minutes of the General Assembly*, 1836, 272-273, 286-287, 293-294. Gillet observed: "Although the strong anti-slavery feeling of the Northern members was not limited to either party, it was most deeply shared by those who were classed as hostile to a rigid ecclesiastical system and in favor of voluntary boards. This was enough to unite the South - however divided or tolerant in sentiment upon other points - in opposition. From that direction the demand was loud for division, especially after the discussions in the Assembly of 1836." *History of the Presbyterian Church*, II, 524.

[43] Elwyn A. Smith, "The Role of the South in the Presbyterian Schism of 1837-38" *Church History* 29 (March 1960): 49.

[44] *Southern Religious Telegraph*, June 24, 1836 quoted in William Henry Foote, *Sketches of Virginia*, Second Series (Philadelphia: J.B. Lippincott & Co., 1855), 505,506. Archibald Alexander, writing shortly after the 1836 Assembly, noted the impending crisis over slavery: "The subject of slavery has been so imprudently managed, that a spirit of hostility between the northern and southern States has been excited, which in my opinion will not cease until a rupture shall take place, which will mark the end of our national prosperity. But the advance of our Church to a crisis had been more rapid and alarming than that of the nation." Letter to Rev. Samuel Hutchings, June 30, 1836 in *Life of Archibald Alexander*, 518.

Assembly deliberations.[45] Some denied that any such agreement ever existed.[46] There is no doubt, however, about abolitionism becoming associated in the Southern mind with New Schoolism.[47] New School "heresies" were viewed as the culprit for abolitionist frenzy. All four of the Synods to be purged from the church in 1837 (Western Reserve, Utica, Genessee, Geneva) had made pronouncements in favor of abolitionism.[48] After the meeting of the Old School post-Assembly conference, John Witherspoon of South Carolina remarked to a friend: "The die is cast: the Church is to be divided."[49]

Sudden Southern conversion to the Old School cause is exhibited in the adjustments of the Synod of Virginia.[50] This Synod had not supported the Act and Testimony, had not sent delegates to the Old School convention of 1835, and its delegates had voted in the 1835 Assembly on the New School side of issues. However, in 1836 the previously neutral Synod of Virginia unanimously issued the "Act of the Virginia Synod" which decried the evils present in the church. The document rehearsed the issues of doctrine and voluntary societies, but the major part of the paper addressed abolition. Baxter and William S. Plumer,[51] the authors,

---

[45] Gillett opined: "The South held in its hands the casting vote. To secure this, it was clearly understood that the slavery question was no longer to be allowed to disturb the Assembly. Although the members from the South should ever after be in the minority, they had already shaped the policy of the Church. To them the triumph of the memorialists was due. Their sympathies on the subject of slavery had not a little to do in ranging them with the party of the majority." *History of the Presbyterian Church*, II, 527. Foote made the same point: "... the parties agitating the Assembly were so equally divided in numbers, talent, wealth and intelligence that the southern vote, hitherto pledged on neither side, would give the decisive majority in the Assembly." *Sketches of Virginia*, Second Series, 513.

[46] Baird decried the attempts made to "stigmatize the majority" of the 1837 Assembly by the pretense of a "corrupt alliance with the South, in the interest of slavery.... As to any private understanding or compact, there is not a trace of evidence to sustain it." *History of the New School*, 534, 535.

[47] There were also well-known Old School opponents of slavery - R.J. Breckinridge of Kentucky, Thomas D. Baird, editor of the Pittsburgh Christian Herald, John W. Nevin, a Pittsburgh theology professor and Joshua L. Wilson of Cincinnati.

[48] Bruce Staiger, "Abolition and the Presbyterian Schism of 1837-38" *Mississippi Valley Historical Review* XXXVI (December 1949): 407. Staiger commented on the 1837 Assembly: "Although northern Old School leaders were ever to insist that slavery had not affected the decisions of the Assembly, it was significant that the South had voted with an unusual orthodoxy to cast fifty-one of its sixty-one votes in favor of every important Old School measure." 411.

[49] Gillett, *History of the Presbyterian Church*, II, 496.

[50] Foote also pointed to the reversal in the Synod of North Carolina. *Sketches of Virginia*, Second Series, 504; Staiger, "Abolition and the Presbyterian Schism," 406.

[51] Plumer founded the Richmond-based *Watchman of the South* in 1837. He opposed Converse's neutral approach, arguing that the conservative Old School party favored the South. Smith stated: "But Plumer was dramatically successful in his opposition to Converse. One by one, the Southern judicatories voted support for the acts of the 1837 Assembly and affiliated with the continuing Old School body, and within a year Converse transferred his

declared: "One thing which presses with particular force on the Presbyterian Church in the South is the spirit of abolition. This spirit, we believe, is entirely contrary to the word of God."[52] Abolition doctrine is attacked as well as raising the constitutional issue – when the General Assembly was founded, it was agreed that slaveholding is no bar to Christian communion. While the threat of "geographical separation" is mentioned, it is acknowledged that the likelihood of this necessity is not so great as it has been, but, "be the danger small or great, a vigilance corresponding to the exigencies of the times is our manifest duty." [53]

Charles Hodge had endeared himself to the Southern conscience in an April 1836 article in the *Biblical Repertory*. In a review of William Ellery Channing's attack on slavery, Hodge argued that the Bible does not condemn slavery, therefore, "slaveholding is not necessarily sinful." He also castigated the abolition movement for declaring slaveholding a crime. Hodge concluded, "The great duty of the South is not emancipation, but improvement."[54] The Presbytery of New Brunswick, where the Princeton professors held membership, in the same month adopted a resolution declaring that the church has no right to interfere with the civil relation between master and slave.[55]

---

press and paper to Philadelphia." Smith, "The Role of the South in the Presbyterian Schism," 49.

[52] Foote, *Sketches of Virginia*, Second Series, 507. The Synod cited St. Paul's directives concerning slaves in 1 Tim. 6:1-5 and added: "Certainly the modern abolitionist teaches otherwise than Paul taught, and if he cannot be convinced of his error, the only Scriptural remedy is to withdraw from such."

[53] Ibid., 507. The Synod of South Carolina also contemplated secession from the North. Gillett observed: "As a general thing the Southern churches gave their preference to Ecclesiastic Boards, and in the case of Mr. Barnes a respectable minority might be regarded as in sympathy with him. But on the subject of slavery there was but one sentiment. The project was subsequently agitated, especially in the South Carolina Synod of forming an independent Southern General Assembly and withdrawing altogether from connection with the North." *History of the Presbyterian Church*, II, 526.

[54] Charles Hodge, "Slavery. By William E. Channing. Boston: James Monroe & Co., 1835." *Biblical Repertory and Theological Review* VII (April 1836): 268-305. Smith stated: "Scarcely anything could have better fostered trust than this authoritative expression from 'The Seminary of the Presbyterian Church.' That Hodge was perhaps the most conservative man there did not count; already he was becoming the Catechist of the Church and the South sensed significance in his utterance." "Role of the South in the Presbyterian Schism," 55. For a survey of Hodge's views on slavery see Allen Guelzo, "Charles Hodge's Antislvery Moment" in *Charles Hodge Revisited: A Critical Appraisal of His Live and Work* eds. John W. Stewart and James H. Moorhead (Grand Rapids: William B. Eerdmans Publishing Company, 2002).

[55] "Resolved as the sense of this Presbytery, that the relation of Master and slave is a civil and not an Ecclesiastical relation, and with this relation the church has no right to interfere, further, than to inculcate and enforce the mutual interest existing between Master and slave, according to the example of Christ and his apostles." Adopted by Presbytery of New Brunswick, April 27, 1836 quoted in *The Presbyterian*, May 7, 1836, 70.

Reaction to the Assembly

An Old School post-Assembly meeting appointed a committee of correspondence to consult with the "orthodox brethren" in the church about what should be done in the present crisis. A circular letter with a series of questions was sent to Old School sympathizers within a few weeks of the Assembly's adjournment. One of the questions dealt with the Old School perception of New School subscription: "It was repeatedly avowed, by ministers in the last General Assembly, that they received the Confession of Faith of our Church, only 'for substance of doctrine,' – 'as a system,' or, 'as containing the Calvinistic system, in opposition to the Arminian,' etc. Hence we know not how much of our standards they adopt, and how much they reject. Is this, in your opinion, the true intent and meaning of receiving and adopting the Confession of Faith?" Other questions asked for lists of errors observed in the church, advice on whether the church should be divided and how to go about this. The final question, stating that most of the evils in the church had come "in consequence of our connection with Congregational churches," asked readers whether "it would not be better for us, as a Church, to have no other connection with Congregationalists."[56]

With information gleaned from the questionnaires, the committee issued a 41-page pamphlet, "An Address to the Ministers, elders, and members of the Presbyterian Church." Here the Old School conservatives impugned New School integrity, charging them with a "lack of honesty in the reception of our Standards." New School professions of orthodoxy are not to be taken seriously. The conservatives chided: "We must be excused if we express our fears that it is only a miserable attempt to deceive the Church, and the world, as to the real sentiments of those who, though in our Church, have no sympathies with us as Presbyterians." The letter accented the Barnes case, the rejection of Miller's proposal on Barnes' book, and the missionary question as evidence of the incompatibility of the two disparate groups. The political might of the New School was frightening; they are a powerful party and have demonstrated the will to use that power to control the church.[57] The "Address" drew this conclusion: "Fathers, Brethren, Fellow-Christians, whatever else is dark, this is clear, – We cannot continue in the same body. We are not agreed, and it is vain to attempt to walk together. That those whom we regard as the authors of our present distractions will retrace their steps, is not to be expected; and that those who have hitherto rallied around the standards of our Church, will continue to do so, is both to be expected and desired. In some way or other, therefore, these men must be separated from us."[58]

For ultra Old School men, the Assembly's acquittal of Barnes sealed the argument for a formal division of the church. Attempts at ecclesiastical discipline

---

[56] Baird, *History of the New School*, 507. Baird claimed the contents of this circular letter proved that the division of 1837 "was occupied almost wholly, with the doctrinal errors which prevailed."

[57] Pope, "New England Calvinism," 354-356.

[58] Baird, *Collection*, 508, 509.

had failed and now separation was the only option left for purifying the Church of New School "heresies." New School unwillingness to give any sort of rebuke to Barnes emboldened the strict Old School men to press their case for separation. Some of the Old School moderates now began abandoning their neutral position and aligning themselves in solidarity with Old School conservatives.[59] William Engles, writing in *The Presbyterian* immediately after the 1836 Assembly adjourned, observed that it was churches in Plan of Union areas that had cast the decisive votes exonerating Barnes. Engles stated: "Let the Church know it – Congregationalists have acquitted Mr. Barnes – Presbyterians condemned him.... This vote was obtained from the interior of New York and the Western Reserve, where they are almost without an exception, Congregationalists in principle, and many of whom have not even for substance of doctrine subscribed the Confession of Faith."[60]

Engles believed that the 1836 Assembly had given a now unified Old School party the resolve to pursue what had been previously unthinkable – a complete separation of two incompatible parties. Engles asserted: "The friends of orthodoxy have been organized; they form a solid phalanx; there are but few, if any neutrals, and the errorists are now known without disguise. When the controversy commenced, the orthodox contemplated no such extensive reform as they now demand; it is not now the condemnation of an erroneous book or of an erroneous man which will satisfy them, but the entire separation of that portion of the Church which has denied the faith."[61] The time was at hand and momentum was on their side.

Despite the moral victory of the ultra party, Princeton was unwilling to concede ecclesiastical separation as a foregone conclusion. In Hodge's review of the 1836 Assembly he expressed his dismay at New School unwillingness to compromise. The New School men should have been willing to make a distinction between Barnes and his book which would have made it possible "for the friends of truth to unite." As it now stood the New School had given "the implied sanction of the Assembly to doctrines which Mr. Barnes disclaimed, and which they themselves

---

[59] Pope observed: "In its eagerness to exonerate Barnes from fundamental error and to place New England Calvinism on the same basis as Old Calvinism within the Church, however, the New School had unwittingly played right into the hands of the ultra conservatives, thus heightening the fears of the Old School and giving the ultra conservatives a golden opportunity to prove to their skeptical Old School brethren the real intentions of the New School. Reversing the suspension alone seriously antagonized the ultra conservatives; full absolution made the breach within the Church irreparable.... The vindication of Barnes laid bare the deep tensions within Presbyterianism and plunged the Church into its most serious crisis of the nineteenth century." "New England Calvinism," 345, 346.

[60] "State of the Church," *The Presbyterian*, June 18, 1836, 94.

[61] *The Presbyterian*, July 2, 1836, 102. Engles condemned and slandered the New School party, declaring that the two parties "receive not the same Gospel; they adopt not the same moral code.... Truth on the one side, error on the other; honesty on one side, artifice on the other...." The problem, according to Engles, has been "an excess of charity" which has "delayed the decisive action in expelling the intruders." *The Presbyterian*, June 18, 1836, 94.

have, as a body hitherto professed to abhor." Hodge acknowledged the historic orthodoxy of the New School majority who were "Edwardean (or Hopkinsian as it is popularly but incorrectly called)." The New School has been "more violent in their opposition, and more severe in their denunciations of New Haven men and New Haven doctrines than any other men in the church;" but, New School refusal to testify against the errors in Barnes's book was a serious mistake.[62] Hodge stated:

> His book furnished no sufficient data to decide what his real opinions are. It is a complicated web of contradiction. And on the principle that every man has a right to explain himself, there can be no objection to allowing Mr. Barnes to pass for perfectly orthodox, if he chooses to endorse only the orthodox portion of his work....
>
> But when we are told the book itself does not contain censurable propositions, that even its language is not to be found fault with – a language which has led so large a portion of its readers to the conclusion that its author teaches the very doctrines he disclaimed – we cannot wonder at the feeling of surprise and indignation which has been excited.[63]

Hodge gave a charitable appraisal of New School faithfulness to the Westminster Standards in the Assembly's *Answer to the Protests*. It cannot be that the New School brethren are "disingenuous in all this." He added: "That men acting in their highest character, as members of the supreme court of the church to which they belong, in a solemn official document placed on permanent record, are guilty of such duplicity is too monstrous to be believed.... Our faith in the orthodoxy of the great body of the Presbyterian denomination, much as we disapprove of the acts of the majority of the late Assembly, remains unshaken." Hodge was opposed to schism and he believed there were not sufficient grounds at the present time to justify such action. "We cannot see, therefore, how any set of men can with a good conscience, desire to effect the division of the church until they are called upon to profess what they do not believe, or required to do what they cannot approve. This, as far as we can see, is the only principle which can bear the test; which will acquit us in the sight of God and man, for tearing asunder that portion of the church of Christ committed to our care."[64]

Notwithstanding these objections, the Princeton professors discerned that the signs were pointing to an unavoidable schism. Archibald Alexander conceded that perhaps a split would ultimately further the work of the church if a peaceful partition could be procured. On June 30, 1836, Alexander wrote to a friend:

> In my opinion, before another year the Presbyterian Church will be divided into two, and perhaps more sections. And if it could be effected amicably, I believe it would in present circumstances be a public blessing. The body is at present too large, too widely

---

[62] Charles Hodge, "General Assembly of 1836," *Biblical Repertory and Theological Review* VIII (July 1836): 457, 458.

[63] Ibid., 460, 461.

[64] Ibid., 461, 475.

extended, and too heterogeneous to be under one ecclesiastical regimen. Much of the strength of the two parties is now expended in disputation and mutual conflict. Separated, each would form a body sufficiently large, and might proceed in the works of piety and benevolence without collision or mutual interference. But there are many obstacles in the way of a peaceable separation.... And perhaps the greatest difficulty will be, that between the two contending parties there is a large neutral body which will be at a loss which way to go.[65]

Samuel Miller shared Alexander's sentiment but still held out hope that separation could be averted. Writing to Dr. David Elliott in December of 1836, Miller expressed his opposition to Old School talk of breaking away and declaring themselves the "True Presbyterian Church."

1. I am perfectly prepared to say, that, if we must go on as we have done for the last five or six years – in a state of perpetual strife and conflict – we had better separate, and the sooner the better. But 2. I am persuaded that by prudence, fidelity, patience and firmness, we may avoid a separation. I have no doubt that by a calm, steady, wise course, we may constrain the ultra New School men to withdraw from our own ranks, and leave us in a state of comparative purity and peace.... Might we not more successfully promote and extend the truth, by remaining in the body, and endeavoring, by faithful and persevering striving against error, to extend the influence of sound opinions? ... I am perfectly persuaded, that only a small fraction of the Old School brethren would consent to a division, or actually take a part in it.[66]

Differences were still extant in the Old School ranks and the ultra conservatives were determined to draw Princeton fully into their camp. To this end a meeting was arranged between five of the conservative men and the Princeton professors. The meeting took place in Dr. Hodge's office in the fall of 1836.[67] Both sides respectfully presented their views but there was little consensus on the appropriate actions required by the present crisis. Ultra plans to act with or without Princeton had been set in motion; funds had already been raised to start a new Old School seminary if Princeton did not align itself with the reforming policy of the conservatives. This plan never materialized.[68]

While the ultras were defeated in their immediate goal of solidarity with Princeton, the professors would begin modifying their positions as the division unfolded. By April of 1837 Miller admitted that "the general cause of the Old School brethren, in this contest, is the cause of God, and of righteousness, I can no

---

[65] *Life of Archibald Alexander*, 518, 519.

[66] *Live of Samuel Miller*, II, 318, 319.

[67] George Junkin, Isaac Brown, James Blythe, C.C. Cuyler, and W.W. Philips represented the conservatives; the Princeton men present were the three professors (Alexander, Miller, Hodge) and J.W. Alexander.

[68] Isaac V. Brown, *A Historical Vindication of the Abrogation of the Plan of Union by the Presbyterian Church in the United States of America* (Philadelphia: William and Alfred Martien, 1855), 175,176; Baird, *History of the New School*, 509-512.

more doubt than I can doubt that the Gospel is from heaven."[69] Alexander attended the 1837 Assembly and voted for many of the Old School reforms. Hodge eventually admitted that the "moral blame" rested on the New School men who "threw their shield around the clearest forms of error, to protect it from the slightest censure," and were therefore the "real dividers" that had driven the conservatives to "this extremity."[70]

Catastrophe of 1837

When the 1837 Old School pre-Assembly convention met, there were 52 presbyteries represented, including significant participation by the Southern churches who had decided to support the Old School. Dr. Baxter of Union Seminary in Virginia was chosen to preside over the convention and it was determined that something must be done about slavery. A paper was read by Plumer of Virginia urging that no action on slavery be taken. Breckinridge, an abolitionist, suggested a compromise as he was determined that the subject not deter the Old School from its course. He argued that the Presbyterian heritage had already settled the question and no further mention on the subject should be had in either the convention or the Assembly. The Southern men accepted the compromise, even though some of them had hoped for a declaration that the church would never act on slavery. Baxter and Plumer fully supported the convention position.[71] The decisive moves contemplated by the Old School convention had significant input from Southern delegates who now advocated separation from the New School. Later at the Assembly itself, Baxter and Plumer would play important roles in leading the Assembly to annul the Plan of Union and to eject four Synods. After the 1837 Assembly, Baxter assured the South: "If the separation begun should be carried out, the Presbyterian Church by getting clear of the New School, will at the same time get clear of abolition."[72]

The convention gave most of its attention to the doctrinal questions. Reports were heard from throughout the church corroborating that "contempt and hostility to the doctrines of the Confession were freely avowed, and the heresies of Taylor and

---

[69] *Life of Samuel Miller*, II, 234.

[70] Charles Hodge, "A Plea for Voluntary Societies," *Biblical Repertory* IX (January 1837): 145.

[71] Smith, "The Role of the South in the Presbyterian Schism," 55-58. Smith asserted: "The conclusion is unavoidable; whatever form it may have taken, there was an explicit understanding and a binding agreement that the Old School abolitionists would, for conviction and conscience, oppose any church declaration on slavery. Their safety thus assured, the South voted solidly for the excision of the Synods of Western Reserve, Genesee, Geneva, and Utica." For more detail on the slavery aspect of the 1837 Pre-Assembly Convention, see Edmund A. Moore, "Robt. J. Breckinridge and the Slavery Aspect of the Presbyterian Schism," *Church History* IV (December, 1935): 282-294.

[72] Staiger, "Abolition and the Presbyterian Schism," 408-412.

policy of Finney were openly cherished."[73] A committee drafted the "Testimony and Memorial" for the Assembly that described 16 doctrinal errors[74] which the memorialists claimed to "have conclusive proof, are widely disseminated in the Presbyterian Church." These errors "strike at the foundation of the system of Gospel grace; ... from the days of Pelagius and Cassian to the present hour, their reception has uniformly marked the character of a Church apostatizing from 'the faith once delivered to the saints,' and sinking into deplorable corruption." The memorialists decried the errors as "dishonoring to Jesus Christ, contrary to his revealed truth, and utterly at variance with our standards ... preached and written by persons who profess to receive and adopt our scriptural standards." The errors are "promoted by societies operating widely through our churches" and they are "openly embraced by almost entire Presbyteries and Synods." The convention's memorial emphasized the 1836 Assembly where these errors were "at last virtually sanctioned, to an alarming extent...."[75]

In addition to the doctrinal errors, the "Testimony and Memorial" presented a list of departures from Presbyterian order and discipline along with recommended measures to reform the church. These reforms included abrogating the Plan of Union, disassociation with the American Home Missionary and Education Societies, requiring explicit adoption of the standards in presbyteries, enforcing discipline against heretical ministers, and adopting appropriate measures to separate unsound bodies and members from the church. The Old School convention was determined to act in the 1837 Assembly whether or not she had the majority votes.[76]

When the Assembly convened, the Old School nominee, Dr. David Elliot, was elected moderator over the New School candidate, Baxter Dickinson, by a vote of 137 to 106. With an Old School majority firmly established, the proposed reform measures were methodically implemented. The Plan of Union was abrogated with 143 yeas and 110 nays.[77] A second resolution called for inferior judicatories that were charged with disorder to appear before the next Assembly, for a committee to be appointed to come up with a plan of procedure, and for these judicatories to be denied their seats in the next Assembly until their cases were decided. These proposals elicited sharp protests[78] from New School men who claimed the Assembly had no right to try inferior courts or to exclude them from seats in the Assembly. After heated discussion, the question was called and the resolutions passed by a vote of 128 to 122.[79]

---

[73] Baird, *History of the New School*, 517.

[74] The Assembly adopted the memorialists' list of 16 errors as its testimony on doctrine. *Minutes of the General Assembly*, 1837, 468, 469.

[75] Ibid., 518-521. Baird said the memorial document was carefully revised by Dr. Miller at the request of the committee. The revised version was adopted by the 1837 Assembly.

[76] Ibid., 521, 522.

[77] *Minutes of the General Assembly*, 1837, 421, 422.

[78] Ibid., 441, 442, 473, 474.

[79] Ibid., 421-426; Baird, *History of the New School*, 522-525.

The Assembly attempted to resolve the procedural chaos by appointing a committee, with equal representation from the two parties, to pursue a plan for the voluntary division of the church. The two groups agreed on a number of practical issues but could not arrive at consensus on the process to implement the division.[80] This attempt having failed, the Old School returned to the business of dismantling the church. With the New School protesting at each point, the Old School continued its purging. The dilemma over which judicatories to cite for heresy and disorder was resolved in part by interpreting the abrogation of the Plan of Union as thereby exscinding the Synods of Western Reserve, Utica, Geneva and Genesee which the Old School considered offspring of the Plan of Union. Additional Synods (Albany, New Jersey, Michigan, Cincinnati and Illinois) were directed to investigate alleged errors in some of their presbyteries and report back to the General Assembly. The elective affinity Presbytery of Philadelphia was dissolved. A General Assembly Board of Foreign Missions was appointed and the American Education and Home Missionary Societies were requested to cease operations within the ecclesiastical boundaries of the church.[81]

As the Assembly finally adjourned, the New School called a meeting at Albert Barnes's church the next day. The New School men adopted a number of resolutions which controverted the Assembly's pronouncements of rampant heresy in the Presbyterian Church. The ejection of Synods and abrogation of the Plan of Union were condemned as unconstitutional measures that blatantly violated Presbyterian polity. It was recommended that all New School presbyteries send commissioners to the 1838 Assembly as their constitutional right. If the next Assembly denied seats to any of the illegally exscinded Synods, then New School commissioners would immediately take actions to organize a "constitutional" General Assembly of the Presbyterian Church in the United States of America.[82]

The schism, that not many years past had been unthinkable, was here and both parties had to accept it as an unalterable reality. The Old School would entertain no thoughts of retracting any of the reform measures of 1837; New School attempts to challenge the unconstitutional acts of 1837 were short-lived. The impasse, that had in recent years hindered the fruitful labors of the church, had finally been resolved by formal separation. An ecclesiastical armistice would now allow each church body to pursue its vision of Presbyterianism unhindered by the distractions of party strife. By 1838 there would be two Presbyterian Churches in America with each claiming to be the faithful heir of the Presbyterian heritage.

Most historians of this period agree that the great divide between the Old School and New School was dissension over doctrine. Notwithstanding the essential validity of that assertion, it is also necessary to appraise the broader issues of the

---

[80] For Old School and New School committee reports on amicable separation see *Minutes of the General Assembly*, 1836, 430-437.

[81] Ibid., 442, 449, 450, 452, 472,473, 496, 497; Baird, *History of the New School*, 529-532.

[82] Baird, *History of the New School*, 537-538.

time which also contributed to the great Presbyterian schism. Abolition, missions, church polity, and revivalism each played a significant role in the journey toward final dissolution of the Presbyterian Church. The complex rivalry produced by the compounding of these issues was more than well-intentioned Presbyterians could tolerate in one another. Each of the issues was exacerbated by doctrinal undercurrents which hardened each side to the conviction that they alone were on the side of righteousness. As the 1830s unfolded, trust eroded, charity dissipated, and the exercise of raw ecclesiastical power for party advantage created a chasm that was impassable.

At the foundation of the Presbyterian crisis was ardent debate over what it meant to be Presbyterian. Every doctrinal discussion during this era ultimately was directed back to the doctrinal standards. And this brought the inevitable question about the exact meaning of the Presbyterian subscription vow. Conservative Old School men believed the vitality of the church either stood or fell according to the degree of strict adherence to the Confession and Catechisms. Liberal New School men, on the other hand, believed that as long as one embraced the essential doctrines of the gospel, ministerial integrity was sufficiently safeguarded. Between these polarities stood a large number of moderate Presbyterians, both Old and New School, who believed that while a certain degree of doctrinal latitude was always to be expected, the essential doctrines of Calvinism must always be safeguarded if confessional subscription is to have integrity.

Extremists in both parties naively thought that they could demand their own private right of interpreting subscription without regard for the greater sense of the whole church. There was actually more consensus on subscription than is often acknowledged but much of the consensus got lost in the heat of battle. Confusion between the two parties intensified as accusations flew and each group increasingly viewed the other in the most extreme light. The Princeton professors and astute clergymen of both parties, in their more sober moments, knew that most Presbyterians warmly held the fundamental Calvinism of the Confession even though they had diverse convictions about a number of ecclesiastical issues. This was the common understanding of Presbyterians who had charitably lived with one another in the early decades of the nineteenth century. The turbulent 1830s destroyed that peaceable spirit and pitted men against one another who in years past had stood shoulder to shoulder in the American Calvinist ranks.

As the crisis approached, the two parties frequently misunderstood one another and became more resolved to vindicate their own convictions. In this context of suspicion, it was popularly believed that the two parties were absolutely opposed on the subscription question. Extremists in each camp caricatured the other side unfairly and condemned their opponents wholesale. In the midst of the chaos, Princeton tried to offer conscientious analysis that both critiqued New School aberrations as well as reproving Old School fanaticism. The Princeton professors believed the greater parts of the New School were orthodox Calvinists who appropriately honored the Confession of Faith. Reconciliation became impossible, however, as the controversial issues of revivalism, missions, polity, and abolition spiraled out of control, ultimately pushing the church to the precipice of division.

The great schism was finally consummated in 1838, but this was only the beginning of nineteenth-century separations. Sectional differences which had been conveniently buried in the 1830s would again rise to plague the Presbyterian Church. The New School Presbyterians divided in 1858 and the Old School would follow in 1861. The year 1838 was a time for new beginnings as the Old School and New School now stood as independent ecclesiastical bodies.

CHAPTER 7

New School Presbyterians

New School Presbyterians were very bitter towards the Old School for its Exscinding Acts which stand as "one of the most fearful tyrannies in the history of all time" from the New School perspective. In hindsight the New School men felt that the Plan of Union was a convenient pretext for their exclusion; if there had been no Plan of Union, it would have been something else for the grievances had become intolerable from the Old School side. It just so happened that many whom they had already determined to exclude had more or less to do with the Plan. The moderates of the two parties had been unable to meet each other and thus the ultras had triumphed in producing a schism.[1]

New School beginnings as a distinct church were a time of great challenge for the new ecclesiastical body. The organizing years were beset by enormous obstacles both within and without. The new church was not of its own design but had become a historical necessity due to the process of exclusion from the other Presbyterian body. New School historian Edward Morris describes the situation: "Indeed, the exscinded party was at first little more than a confused collection of ministers, churches, organizations, swept away together as by some resistless flood, – an aggregation but dimly conscious of any unity in purpose or prospect, and wholly unprepared to take any immediate steps toward consolidating themselves in one unified, compact, effective organization."[2]

In this complex situation, there was significant diversity of opinion about whether or not independent ecclesiastical existence was desirable. Some wanted to explore reunification with the Old School; others wanted to seek some sort of compromise and those who wanted to pursue a new church structure disagreed about the best process of forming a new organization. The New School churches had lost property and endowments and were "resourceless and impoverished almost to the point of despair." To further confuse the situation, the 1837 Old School Assembly had invited the exscinded brethren back to the church if they would

---

[1] "Spirit of American Presbyterianism, Division, No. II," *Presbyterian Quarterly Review* III (March 1855):659, 683.

[2] Edward D. Morris, *The Presbyterian Church New School, 1837-1869: An Historical Review* (Columbus, Ohio: The Chaplin Press, 1905), 74. Morris was ordained by the New School in 1852 and served several pastorates. In 1867 he became professor of Church History at Lane Theological Seminary and later was appointed as professor of Systematic Theology, teaching at Lane until 1897. He was elected moderator of the reunited Northern Presbyterian Church in 1875.

accept the decisions and jurisdiction of the Old School party. Another source of potential dissipation was the action of the Congregational Association of New York in August of 1837 which advised all churches organized under the Plan of Union to withdraw from the Presbyterian Church, i.e., leave the excluded synods. The New School was put to the test between two fires, both the Old School and the Congregationalists trying to dismember it.[3] Morris said of this difficult situation: "bitter debates, and strife, suits respecting church property, unseemly rivalries between churches, and other disastrous events followed, and it was soon manifest to all that the career of the new denomination, should one be organized, must be attended by widespread rupture, struggle, sacrifice, and the keenest sorrow."[4]

A New Church

The first step toward organizing the New School Presbyterian Church was a gathering of delegates from the excluded synods along with representatives of other sympathizing parts of the Presbyterian Church at Auburn, New York in August of 1837. These 169 persons met to consider what course to pursue in this emergency situation. Under a strong moderator, Dr. James Richards, professor of Systematic Theology at Auburn Seminary, the convention declared that the cutting away of the four synods by the late Assembly was unconstitutional and based upon unsupported charges, therefore, the synods should send commissioners to the next General Assembly as usual. In addition to these ecclesiastical pronouncements, the Auburn Convention made specific declarations on the doctrinal issues at the heart of the controversy.[5]

In response to the 1837 list of sixteen New School errors presented to the General Assembly, the New School men had asserted their own commitment to Calvinism in the counter document "Errors and True Doctrines." The Assembly had rejected their explanation, therefore, leaving New School heterodoxy as a foregone conclusion. This imputation of unsoundness in the faith did not stand without further response from the New School. At the Auburn convention in the summer of 1837, the delegates articulated their own definitive declaration of Calvinistic orthodoxy. Building upon the earlier explanation that had been presented to the Assembly, the New School carefully crafted a document explaining its understanding of what the Westminster Confession of Faith intended to teach.[6]

---

[3] "Spirit of American Presbyterianism" (March 1855): 681.

[4] Morris, *The Presbyterian Church New School*, 74-76.

[5] Some material in this chapter and chapter eleven has appeared earlier in *The Journal of Presbyterian History* 82:4 (2004): 221- 243. Used by permission.

[6] Professor Edward Morris said that Baxter Dickinson drafted the Auburn Declaration. See *The Presbyterian Church New School*, 87,88; see also article on Dickinson in *Encyclopedia of the Presbyterian Church in the United States of America*, ed. Alfred Nevin (Philadelphia: Presbyterian Publishing Company, 1884). Dickinson served as a Professor of Sacred Rhetoric and Pastoral Theology at Lane (1835-39) and Auburn Seminary (1839-47). He was moderator of the New School General Assembly in 1839.

The so-called "Auburn Declaration" offered a commentary on each theological point at issue by indicating how New School expositions of the doctrine were indeed orthodox Calvinism. On each point of the Declaration, under the heading of "true doctrine," the New School indicated where it believed Old School interpretation had been "defective and possibly erroneous." Under each heading the New School authors framed their declarations in such a way to answer Old School charges of Pelagian and Arminian errors. This document, intended as a commentary on the Confession, was their own protest against the narrow confessional exposition of the conservative party and an affirmation of what they cherished as essential doctrinal truth.[7]

In the preface to the Auburn Declaration, the New School leaders admitted that in the midst of revivals, indiscretions took place and "human obligation is sometimes urged in a manner that favors Arminian errors." But, these errors have never been sanctioned by the presbyteries or synods that have been excluded by the Old School and "... all such departures from the sound doctrine or order of the Presbyterian Church we solemnly disapprove."[8]

At the Auburn Convention, the New School highlighted the fact that they "cordially embrace the Confession of Faith of the Presbyterian Church." They affirmed acceptance of the Confession as containing the system of doctrine taught in Holy Scripture "as understood by the Church ever since the Adopting Act of 1729." Explicit reference is made to the 1729 principle of stating one's "scruples" before the presbytery as an essential element of Presbyterian subscription. A portion of the 1729 morning minute is quoted verbatim in the New School platform adopted at the convention.[9]

---

[7] Ibid., 83.

[8] See "Report of the Committee on Doctrine" in Maurice W. Armstrong, Lefferts A. Loetscher, Charles A. Anderson, eds. *The Presbyterian Enterprise: Sources of American Presbyterianism*, (Philadelphia: The Westminster Press, 1956): 167; the Auburn Declaration in its entirety is found in this work.

[9] Ibid., 167. The Auburn Convention declared: "And in case any minister of the Synod, or any candidate for the ministry, shall have any scruple with respect to any article or articles of said confession, he shall in time of making said declaration, declare his scruples to the Synod or Presbytery; who shall, notwithstanding, admit him to the exercise of the ministry within our bounds, and to ministerial communion if the Synod or Presbytery shall judge his scruple *not essential or necessary* in *Doctrine, Worship, or Government*." (italics theirs) The New School considered the morning and afternoon minute of 1729 as the "Adoption of the Westminster Standards;" see Wm. E. Moore, *A New Digest of the Acts and Deliverances of the General Assembly of the Presbyterian Church in the United States Compiled by the Order and Authority of the General Assembly* (Philadelphia: Presbyterian Publication Committee, 1861), 18,19. The 1850 Old School Assembly Digest also listed the morning and afternoon minute together as "The Adopting Act;" see *A Digest of the Acts of the Supreme Judicatory of the Presbyterian Church in the United States of America. Arranged to Illustrate the Constitutional Rules of the Church. By Order of the General Assembly* (Philadelphia: Presbyterian Board of Publication, 1850), 181,182. By contrast Baird's 1856 Digest described the morning minute as the "Act Preliminary to the Adopting Act;" see Samuel J.

It was hoped that the moderate spirit of the Auburn Convention would convince the Old School party to take a more tolerant stance and avoid the scandal of schism. The exscinded synods did send commissioners to the Assembly of 1838, nevertheless, when the Assembly convened these delegates were not recognized as members of the Presbyterian Church. At this point, commissioners from 29 presbyteries outside the excluded synods, believing that the Constitution was being nullified by this exclusion of commissioners, proceeded to elect their own Assembly officers and then adjourned to another location in order to transact the business of the "true" Presbyterian General Assembly. By this act, those who withdrew had in effect constituted a new denomination.

The first formal act of the New School Assembly was the adoption of a resolution that condemned the excision of the four synods and declared the right of these synods to full standing in the Presbyterian Church. Next, the new body elected trustees and directors for all church properties including the seminaries. A number of additional actions were taken by the new Assembly. Among the most important steps: the value of both the American Home Missionary Society and American Education Society was affirmed; the rule of the Assembly that required examining ministers transferring from one presbytery to another was rescinded; the Confession of Faith and Form of Government was recommended for greater circulation among the presbyteries.

A committee appointed by the Assembly drafted a "Narrative of the State of Religion" which was subsequently adopted by the Assembly and distributed to the churches. Much emphasis in the essay was upon the revivals of religion that had blessed 234 of their churches over the past year. The General Assembly rejoiced in the "rich effusions" the Holy Spirit visited among so many of their churches. And the *Narrative* commended the three seminaries, Union, Auburn and Lane, which shared the doctrinal convictions of the New School Assembly.[10] The New School

---

Baird, *A Collection of the Acts, Deliverances, and Testimonies of the Supreme Judicatory of the Presbyterian Church from its Origin in America to the Present Time. With Notes and Documents Explanatory and Historical: Constituting a Complete Illustration of Her Polity, Faith, and History* (Philadelphia: Presbyterian Board of Publication, 1856), 4, 5.

[10] Union Seminary, started by New York Presbyterians in 1836, was predominately New School in its orientation. All four of the original clerical founders had been active in the voluntary societies. The preamble in the founding documents stated that Union's purpose was to advocate moderate views and "to live free from party strife, and to stand aloof from all the extremes of doctrinal speculation...." Robert Handy comments: "...the New School stamp was clearly evident as the founders protested what they regarded as the over-rigid subscription to the Westminster Confession on the part of the Old." See Robert T. Handy, "Union Theological Seminary in New York and American Presbyterianism, 1836-1904," *American Presbyterians* 66 (Summer 1988):115-122; see also George Lewis Prentiss. *The Union Theological Seminary in the City of New York: Historical and Biographical Sketches of its First Fifty Years* (New York: Anson D. F. Randolph and Co., 1889). On Auburn Seminary see John Quincy Adams, *A History of Auburn Theological Seminary 1818-1918* (Auburn, New York: Auburn Seminary Press, 1918). For a review of the New School

Assembly firmly asserted the orthodoxy of the churches comprising the new denomination and repudiated charges of doctrinal looseness. The *Narrative* stated: "And from nearly every Presbytery here reported, the answer has come up distinct and full, that there is a careful vigilance in regard to doctrinal correctness and a good degree of energy in maintenance of scriptural order among our churches ... the imputations which have been cast upon many Presbyteries and churches are unfounded and calumnious. It is not denied that there have been individuals among us by whom erroneous views have been promulg[at]ed, and injudicious measures for the salvation of men resorted to: but it is denied that the Presbyteries have sanctioned such instructions or tolerated such measures."[11]

The 1838 New School Assembly also issued a "Pastoral Letter" to her churches in which an account of the Presbyterian controversies leading up to the rupture was discussed and a justification for the actions taken. Included in the letter was a statement wherein devotion to the Westminster Standards was made explicit: "We love and honor the Confession of Faith of the Presbyterian Church as containing more well-defined, fundamental truth, with less defect, than appertains to any other human formula of doctrine, and as calculated to hold in intelligent concord a greater number of sanctified minds than any which could now be framed; and we disclaim all design past, present or future to change it."[12]

One of the objections raised by the Old School had been the proliferation of Abbreviated Creeds that were being utilized in large numbers of Presbyterian Churches. Some asserted that this undermined the Presbyterian commitment to the Confession of Faith. The New School men appointed a special "Committee on Abbreviated Creeds" which reported to both the 1838 and 1839 General Assemblies. In 1838 the committee only had access to a few short statements of faith and made a brief report on the ones it had reviewed: "...these summaries or abbreviated creeds, as far as they go in the statement of doctrines, notwithstanding slight and unessential discrepancies are none of them at variance with the system of doctrine taught in the Confession of Faith of the Presbyterian Church... and like the Confession of Faith itself, to be more fully explained and enlarged upon in the whole course of scriptural instruction in doctrine and practice."[13]

By the 1839 General Assembly meeting the Committee on Abbreviated Creeds had examined creeds from 25 presbyteries and offered a more detailed report. Again the essential orthodoxy of the abbreviated creeds was asserted: "...we have found the creeds adopted by these Presbyteries, and recommended to their churches, with very few exceptions, full and sound to a gratifying extent." The committee noted that the Stated Clerk had informed the committee of two churches in Oswego

---

Calvinistic theology taught at Lane Theological Seminary see Edward D. Morris, "The Theologians of Lane" in *Thirty Years at Lane and other Lane Papers*, n.p., 1897.

[11] *Minutes of the General Assembly of the Presbyterian Church in the United States of America*. (New School) New York: Published by Stated Clerks, 1838-1858. Reprint. Philadelphia: Presbyterian Board of Publication and Sabbath-School Work. 1894, 35-42.

[12] Ibid., 34.

[13] Ibid, 25.

Presbytery that had "endeavored to remove every thing from their creeds that is objectionable to an Arminian." These churches were asked to examine their creeds and if they were found defective, correct them. The report concluded, "We believe that the Presbyteries are the proper bodies to correct these evils; and we rejoice to know that many are actively and vigilantly engaged in the work."[14]

The 1839 General Assembly again issued a "Pastoral Letter" to the churches which stressed that the New School held in common with the other body "the great essential truths of the gospel, not deviating in matters of faith, from the system of our Confession." Further, the letter asserted unique New School perspectives and offered an apologetic for them. One of those distinctives was the cooperative spirit which both rejoiced with and participated in the promotion of the gospel with those outside the Presbyterian denomination. They acknowledged that this has subjected them to suspicions and censures. The attitude of cooperation, they believed, decreased the attitude of rivalry, enhanced missions, exhibited to the world a "catholic spirit" and rather than "spreading the Shibboleths of sect" was intent on "saving the souls of men." The letter acknowledged the painful contest for principle in the legal battle over contested property and why, for conscience sake, the New School had resisted the "exercise of such high and dangerous ecclesiastical power."[15]

That same year, the New School Assembly also issued "A Declaration of the General Assembly, Setting Forth the Present Position of Our Beloved Zion, and the Causes Which have Brought us into our Peculiar Position." Behind this address was an expressed desire "to free ourselves and our churches from the imputation of the sin of causing division." In order to do this, the Assembly document rehearsed a retrospective on Presbyterianism in America from the beginnings up until the present division. The New School men argued that history demonstrated that the mother Presbytery of 1706 was formed upon "liberal Christian principles." The 1729 Adopting Act was quoted in full as evidence of these liberal principles. Presbyterian history provided evidence that the Presbyterian Church could not "legally or righteously legislate 60,000 of their brethren out of the church." The Declaration concluded: "In view of these facts, we, the General Assembly convened in the First Presbyterian Church, at Philadelphia, on the 16th day of May, 1839, appealing to Almighty God, for the purity of our motives, and the rectitude of our measure, and professing a deep regret for this grievous breach in the professed body of Christ, and solemnly protesting that the sin of this schism does not lie at our door, throw ourselves upon the candour and wisdom of the Christian world for the rectitude of our proceedings in the painful circumstances in which we have been placed."[16]

In 1840 the General Assembly adopted a "Declaration of Principles." One of the highlighted issues was the constitutional protection that is the "birth-right of every

---

[14] Ibid., 57, 58.
[15] Ibid., 70-76.
[16] Ibid., 77-82.

Presbyterian." Having been treated unjustly by the Old School brethren, the new church was determined to treat one another fairly under the constitution of the church. They stated, "... no man may be impeached, discredited, or disfranchised by private judgment, the spirit of calumny, or any other anti-constitutional process, in our whole connection; that a charitable construction of the motives and the characters of all our fellow-servants as brethren in Christ, so long especially as they remain in our communion, in good standing, as members of his body, or officers of his kingdom, may be every where cultivated, as devoutly obligatory as well as courteous and proper."[17]

The history of the New School Presbyterian Church in the decade of the 1840s was a time of developing organizational structure and administration. Separation from the other body came to be viewed as an accepted fact with no expectation of a quick reunion. Eventually the claims to property in the Old School Church were abandoned because litigation would be too long and too painful. New School churches continued to experience the encouraging signs of the visitation of the Spirit through numerous revivals and increasing numbers of new church members through profession of faith. On the other hand, tensions with the other Presbyterian body were not abated as conservative voices in the Old School relentlessly attacked the New School. One vexing problem that preoccupied the New School was the regular submission of memorials on domestic slavery during each Assembly.[18] These discussions were contentious and would finally produce a schism in the New School church by 1857. Morris described the decade of the 1840s as a time of survival for the New School as she "was sailing each year between the deep sea of Congregationalism and the rugged cliffs of a conservative Presbyterianism." The surprising factor was that the new church actually grew during this period.[19]

---

[17] Ibid., 103.

[18] The New School sought a median position as antislavery moderates between the extremes of the radical immediatist abolitionists and conservatives. Their position has been characterized as "cautious, centrist and contradictory." There is debate among historians of the New School concerning the degree to which abolitionists in the New School body pushed the General Assemblies to become increasingly critical of slavery. There seemed to be a delicate balancing act going on in the New School - attacking slavery as evil, yet, not wanting to alienate the Southerners and preserve union in the New School. See Hugh Davis, "The New York Evangelist, New School Presbyterians and Slavery," *American Presbyterians* 68 (Spring 1990):14-23; Andrew E. Murray, *Presbyterians and the Negro – A History* (Philadelphia: Presbyterian Historical Society, 1966); Victor B. Howard, "The Anti-Slavery Movement in the Presbyterian Church, 1835-1861" Ph.D. diss., Ohio State University, 1961; George M. Marsden, "The New School Presbyterian Mind: A Study of Theology in Mid-Nineteenth Century America" Ph.D. diss., Yale University, 1966; Irving S. Kull, "Presbyterian Attitudes toward Slavery," *Church History* 7 (June 1938): 101-114. For perspective on the abolition movement in the Northern Churches see John R. McKivigan, *The War Against Proslavery Religion: Abolitionism and the Northern Churches, 1830-1865* (Ithaca, New York: Cornell University Press, 1984).

[19] Morris, *History of the Presbyterian Church New School*, 113.

New School Calvinism

By the 1850s the New School had embraced a fuller sense of self-identity as a vibrant distinct body of Presbyterians. Gone was any hope of early reunion with the Old School and a new spirit of strength filled the New School Church as she began to stretch her own muscles and establish herself as a denomination. It was with a sense of pride that the New School men, who had been ejected from the Presbyterian Church, now began to prove themselves worthy as an independent denomination.[20] Despite Old School efforts to destroy them, they had risen from the dust. One New School writer exclaimed: "... we the true successors in name and fact, in spirit and in truth of the Presbyterian Church in the United States, were to be driven forth dispirited, broken, a scattered remnant, never again to lift up our front in the presence of those who had rent our Church, reviled our orthodoxy, poured contempt upon our learning, doubted our piety, sneered at our revivals of religion, and persuaded themselves that it was utterly beyond our power ever again to rally or to make a stand for ourselves, our children or our altars. Verily they have been disappointed."[21]

In 1852 the New School Presbyterian Church established its own journal, *The Presbyterian Quarterly Review.*[22] Examining the pages of its ten years of existence, it is abundantly clear that a chief goal of the periodical was to both justify the New School Church's existence and to defend her distinctives. For the New School men, who viewed themselves as the "true" constitutional Presbyterian Church, it was simply a matter of demonstrating how their branch continued to exhibit the characteristics of "American Presbyterianism" that had emerged in the eighteenth century. They believed the historical records were on their side and went to great lengths in the *Review* to substantiate those claims.

In the very first issue of the new journal, the editors took two articles to review the background of their new denomination and rehearsed the unjust impugning of her character by the other branch of the church. The *Review* editors reminded readers that those who had rent the Presbyterian Church believed, "the exscinded portion was radically unsound in theology, and without any fixed attachment to church order." But now after fifteen years of existence as a denomination, "... in the body with which we are connected, no man has moved to alter a tittle of the Confession of faith, or an essential principle of Presbyterian church government." The charge of unsoundness is unsubstantiated; in fact, the brief history of the New

---

[20] Ibid., See chapter 4, "Organization and Advance, 1850-1859" for an overview of this decade in the life of the New School Presbyterian Church.

[21] "The Spirit of American Presbyterianism" *Presbyterian Quarterly Review* I (December 1852): 519.

[22] The editor of *The Presbyterian Quarterly Review* was Ben J. Wallace; the associate editors were Albert Barnes, Thomas Brainerd, John Jenkins and Joel Parker. Also, assisting with editing the new journal were the professors in New York Union, Auburn and Lane Theological Seminaries.

School as a separate body has demonstrated her commitment to biblical Calvinism. The editors stated: "So far as we are informed, there is not a minister of our body who does not love and cherish the Westminster Confession of Faith as the best human delineation of biblical theology; while all are prepared to bow implicitly and finally and fearlessly, before the only infallible standard, the word of God. '*Our church standards as symbols for union, but the Bible for authority*,' is the motto of our denomination."[23]

The *Review* believed that Calvinism had been distorted and deemed it their responsibility to defend "old fashioned, Catholic, American Presbyterianism." The editors go on the offensive and state the specific distortions against which they will take a stand:

> This Review is 'set for the defense of the gospel' against all assailants, especially those who professing to abjure philosophy, yet philosophize the Almighty into a tyrant, and man into a victim; who represent a holy God as creating sin in a human soul, anterior to all moral acts, and then punishing that soul for being as he made it; who teach that man has no ability to do his duty whatever, but is worthy of eternal punishment for not enacting natural impossibilities; who limit the atonement offered for a race to the elect alone, and then consign to a deeper damnation, souls for rejecting an atonement, which in no sense was ever provided for them. These excrescences on sound Calvinism, these parasites which antinomian metaphysics have engrafted on the glorious doctrines of grace, we shall deem it our duty to lop off.... As we love the Westminster Confession of Faith and the Catechisms, we shall stand ready to vindicate them from Arminian, Socinian, and infidel assaults on the one side, as well as Antinomian glosses on the other.[24]

The New School mission was described in the *Review* by four principles each of which was contrasted with an opposite tendency. These four principles, are "...our characteristic peculiarities, the life and genius of our body, and their defense and maintenance, our special mission." The four principles:

> I. Religious Liberty, in contrast with ecclesiastical power, by the antagonisms of which American Presbyterianism was severed into two bodies.
> II. A living Calvinism, in contrast with a rigid dogmatic system, enforced in the *ipsissima verba* of the formularies.
> III. A co-operative Christianity, in contrast with an exclusive ecclesiasticism.
> IV. The aggressive, in contrast with the exclusively conservative type, of Christianity.[25]

In explaining the meaning of the second principle the editors explored the relationship of theology and piety. It is "living Calvinism" as expressed in the

---

[23] "Our Church and Our Review," *Presbyterian Quarterly Review* I (June 1852): 3-5.

[24] Ibid., 9, 10.

[25] "The Mission of the Presbyterian Church," *Presbyterian Quarterly Review* I (June 1852): 15.

Adopting Act and the 1758 Basis of Reunion that has been the vital element in American Presbyterianism. The New Side and the Log College are the "true line of succession" of the living Calvinism as described in "The Log College" by Dr. Alexander. The New Side believed "that while they held the great vitals of the system intact and sacred, they were to be allowed to give it power and influence and life, in practical personal application, especially amidst the outpourings of God's Spirit, without incurring suspicion of heresy, or being condemned by the cold-hearted and formal, for disloyalty to truth, or disorderly measures for doing good and saving souls."[26]

Without the element of piety, Calvinism was a "sepulchre of departed glory." Calvinism likewise was necessary for piety as that great system of truth that provides the "moral vertebrae" of piety. The editors explained:

> But this strongly vertebrated system, probably more than any other, needs for its perfection to be clothed all over, made living, true, beautiful and influential, by the infusion of inward life, the harmonious and free working of genial piety.... Since the settlement of the Augustinian controversy, and the re-establishment of the same fundamental truths, by the Herculean labours of Calvin, this has been the *desideratum* – to have a living Calvinism. Without piety, it tends to formalism and a freezing orthodoxy or Antinomianism, as Arminianism degenerates into more nervous sentimentalism, or ungovernable enthusiasm, for lack of substance.[27]

There must be a protest when "mere accuracy of system, and swearing in the *ipsissima verba* of formularies, is the sole recommendation of excellence." Since 1821 the Presbyterian Church has had a "strong gravitation towards dry orthodoxy." The struggle was not for "latitudinarian forms of expression, capricious opposition to hallowed phraseology, or license for fanatical measures, though there is always liability to these extremes, but for the life and soul of a chosen system of faith and order." It is the old controversy of dogma and life and in such a case the higher law of doing good and saving souls must govern "if the choice is forced on us by circumstances or the exercise of power." Orthodoxy and piety are necessary and should be blended into harmony. Orthodoxy protects the church from licentiousness and disorder, piety preserves the church from formalism and inaction.[28]

Between the years 1852 and 1855, the *Review* carried a series of five articles entitled, "The Spirit of American Presbyterianism." These articles expounded in detail the great themes of the New School mind. An essential framework throughout the articles was the idea that there had always been two great elements in the Presbyterian Church of America from its beginning. One group exhibited a "rigid" spirit which primarily was made up of the Scottish whose plan was to transplant the Presbyterian Church of Scotland in America. The New School men labeled this party a "foreign Presbyterianism." The other party, "liberal" in spirit, was comprised

---

[26] Ibid., 21, 22.
[27] Ibid., 19-21.
[28] Ibid., 22, 23.

of more diverse Reformed elements from England, Ireland, Wales, France, Germany and Holland. This party had its affinity with the Puritans of New England and was more distinctly "American" in "a new and unparalleled age and country." The great question was: which of these branches contains the "genuine Spirit of American Presbyterianism."[29] The editors of the review framed the question thus: "In a word, was it a foreign Church, rigid in view, stereotyped in plans, planted here to remain forever the same, or was it intended from the first and so carried out along the whole stream of our history, that this Church should be something freer, more liberal, more catholic, more biblical and more progressive than any Reformed Church of the old world?"[30]

The two elements had maintained different perspectives on subscribing the Confession. One party has demanded *ipsissima verba* and the other thought "systematic subscription better."[31] American Presbyterianism has always attempted to embrace both the conservative and the progressive element. This tension can be a healthy one for the church at its best, yet, it can be a destructive factor if either party is in the extreme. The New School men stated: "... whenever one or the other has been too prominent, there has been a one-sided tendency; ... wherever both elements have been in full activity and cordial compromise, we have had the greatest and noblest Church on earth, just because both elements are needed...."[32] And, "... we have always considered the union of both the elements of our Church the true ideal of American Presbyterianism, both being defective when alone."[33]

Colonial Heritage

New School historians argued that the make-up of the original body of Presbyterians in America was quite diverse. The early Presbyterians were not solely of the pure Scottish heritage which tended to more rigidity in temperament. There were also Irish Presbyterians, English, Dutch, Welsh as well as Congregationalists from New England that made up more than half of the 29 ministers that comprised the first Synod in 1717. Presbyterianism in America was a mixed body from the beginning and exhibited a compromise spirit in bringing these diverse elements together into one church. There was not a purely Scottish model of Presbyterianism established in America.[34] The New School editors stated: "... while Makemie and

---

[29] "The Spirit of American Presbyterianism," December 1852, 475-477.

[30] Ibid., 477.

[31] The New School liked to caricature the Old School as maintaining subscription to every word of the confession, when in fact, this was true only of a small but vocal segment of the Old School Church.

[32] "The Spirit of American Presbyterianism," *Presbyterian Quarterly Review* II (December, 1854): 477, 478.

[33] "The Spirit of American Presbyterianism," *Presbyterian Quarterly Review* II (September, 1853): 231.

[34] See "The Spirit of American Presbyterianism," in *Presbyterian Quarterly Review* III (March 1855): 648-653 and "The Spirit of American Presbyterianism" in *Presbyterian*

Andrews agreed on a real Presbyterianism as the basis, they yet modified it from the Scottish form so far as to make it – like everything else that has grown large and powerful in America – a compromise of national habit and peculiarity upon one idea, but that idea harmonizing all views by being enlarged and liberalized. We can readily grant that the New Englandism of that day was nearer to Presbyterianism than the present; but the idea that New England was Presbyterian after the Scottish fashion, can be shown to be an entire mistake."[35]

The New School believed their body more truly represented the foundations of the Presbyterian Church in America. The 1729 Adopting Act, the "Corner Stone and Magna Carta" of American Presbyterianism, is now most faithfully upheld according to its original intent by the New School Presbyterian Church. The New School maintained that the Adopting Act emphasized the principle of subscribing to the Westminster Confession in all its essential and necessary articles, allowing for the declaration of acceptable scruples, provided that these extra-essential points of doctrine did not compromise the integrity of the system of doctrine contained in the Confession. Their view asserted that the Adopting Act "... formally adopts the Westminster Confession and Form of government, as a system, for the substance of them; or in other words, establishes as the basis of the Church, the necessary and essential articles only, of Calvinism and Presbyterianism."[36]

The *Review* rejected Old School accusations that the New School had interpreted the Adopting Act as subscription to the fundamental doctrines of Christianity only. These charges brought great offense to New School men who resented the implications of sanctioning fraud "of a kind most odious – touching their ordination vows at God's altar."[37] There are not even a few "no-creed men" among the sixteen hundred New School clergy. The New School vehemently rejected Old School assertions of looseness on subscription. "The two branches of our Church have been separated these sixteen years, and if there had been any seed of heresy, any tendency to 'looseness' it would have shown itself. Yet, though possessing the most perfect freedom, we have spent our time, not in destroying, but in placing buttresses around Calvinism and Presbyterianism."[38] The New School men affirmed the historic view of American Presbyterian subscription. The editors of the *Review* stated:

> We do not know a minister in our Church who believes, or asserts, that the Presbyterian Church ever intended to ordain ministers or ruling elders, or to admit them to exercise

---

Quarterly Review II (September 1853): 215-218. In the September 1853 article, the editors listed the nationality of all 29 clergy in the 1717 Synod and pointed out that their list and the one in Hodge's *Constitutional History of the Presbyterian Church* are almost identical. See Charles Hodge, *Constitutional History of the Presbyterian Church in the United States of America*, Part I (Philadelphia: Presbyterian Board of Publication, 1851), 80-84.

[35] "Spirit of American Presbyterianism," September 1853, 215, 216.

[36] Ibid., 245.

[37] Ibid., 220.

[38] "Spirit of American Presbyterianism," December 1854, 474.

their ministry, on their adopting the Confession of Faith and Form of Government, as containing the necessary and essential principles of Christianity. The universal opinion, so far as we know, in our Church, and certainly the opinion of the Editors of this Review is, that the Presbyterian Church as a body, since 1729, has required her officers to adopt the Confession of Faith as containing the Calvinistic system; that she still requires the same thing, and that the meaning of the requirement is, that she does not allow her officers to hold any other system than the Calvinistic, for example, the Arminian, the Pelagian, the Socinian systems; but, that in minor points lying within the scope of the Calvinistic system, she allows liberty of opinion and speech, in accordance with the idiosyncrasies of varying minds amongst her officers. And the same thing is true as to the Form of Government; she requires Presbyterianism, but allows minor differences. And after this plain statement, we shall consider it disingenuous in any man to hold up our Church to odium, as maintaining the loose idea that she demands in her officers a mere general adherence to evangelical Christianity, such as she requires of her catechumens and church members.[39]

The language of the Adopting Act was unequivocal. The New School editors boasted, "If we had employed a 'Philadelphia lawyer' to write out our principles – subscribing to the Calvinistic system and the Presbyterian Form of Government, with liberty in all minor points in both – he could not have accomplished it more entirely than the Synod did in the Adopting Act."[40]

To support their understanding of the 1729 "scruples," the New School point to the Old School's Ashbel Green. Dr. Green understood the Adopting Act to include both the morning minute and the afternoon declaration as equal parts of the subscription commitment. The editors quoted Green from the *Christian Advocate*:

Why, it is reasonable to ask, was the long preamble of 'expressions or distinctions' ever made, if it was to have no effect – if it was to be regarded as so much waste paper! Why, especially have an order made, as was done in 1735, 'that each Presbytery have the WHOLE Adopting Act inserted in their Presbytery book?' We confess we have been surprised and grieved at what to us appears an inexplicable inconsistency between the averments in these two deliberately prepared papers of our ancient Synod – the more so *because we think there are pretty strong indications that, even after this, the whole of the Adopting Act – the former part as well as the latter – was kept in view in the matter of subscription* (italics theirs).[41]

The editors declared that the Adopting Act was "eminently wise" and could be the "only basis upon which the true American Presbyterian Church can properly rest."[42] According to New School historian E.H. Gillett, American Presbyterianism has practiced a "liberal spirit" concerning the adoption of the Standards. The original latitude envisioned by the Adopting Act has been maintained throughout

---

[39] "Spirit of American Presbyterianism," December, 1852, 486.

[40] Ibid., 493.

[41] Ashbel Green, *Christian Advocate*, Vol. xi, pp. 412-13 quoted in "The Spirit of American Presbyterianism" *Presbyterian Quarterly Review* (September 1853): 227.

[42] "Spirit of American Presbyterianism," Sept. 1853, 231.

Presbyterian history in America. Gillett asserted that historically the manner of adopting the Confession has been guided by the original spirit of the Adopting Act as understood to include both the Preliminary Act and the Afternoon Minute. The records show that the Adopting Act was a compromise.[43]

Gillett supplied evidence of how the Adopting Act was perceived by contemporaries with several historical illustrations. He quoted Archibald Alexander's comment about a seceder from the Presbyterian Church who "left our church on account of the 'Adopting Act' which permitted candidates to make some exceptions when they received the Confession." The withdrawal of Alexander Craighead from the synod on account of the Adopting Act was another example since Craighead declared that the "principle inducement" to his departure was that neither the synod nor presbytery had genuinely adopted the Westminster Confession. Additional evidences were the charges of laxness which prompted the synod's action in 1736.[44]

Gillett cited the case of New Castle Presbytery and its dealings with the withdrawal of John Cuthbertson. In the controversy, New Castle Presbytery had stated:

... all religious truths and duties are not equally important.... Some ... are but circumstantial and some fundamental. It is the duty of the strong to bear the infirmities of the weak ... but if there ought to be forbearance, then it will follow that some religious truths and duties ought not to be terms of communion in the church. The pretense of keeping the church pure is plausible at first sight, and seems mighty friendly to strict holiness, but they involve themselves by the above principle in an unhappy contradiction; for if they are for holding fast every truth and duty, let them hold these among the rest, viz., that every truth and duty is not equally great, and may not be made equal terms of communion; that brotherly love and the communion of saints are more excellent than many other duties in religion; that we ought to bear with some mistakes and weaknesses in our brethren, and not unchurch them for some different sentiments and practices. Now if such things as these are cast out of religion for the sake of purity, what kind of purity is it? It is a kind of strictness beyond what our Lord and his apostles taught, there let it be *Anathema.*[45]

There was also testimony outside the bounds of the Synod of Philadelphia. Gillett presented data from other contemporary Presbyterian bodies in America to demonstrate how the Adopting Act "has given occasion for the charge of latitudinarianism against the Presbyterian Church." American Presbyterians from the time of the Adopting Act have allowed a certain degree of diversity. He

---

[43] E.H. Gillett, "The True Character of the Adopting Act," *American Presbyterian and Theological Review* VII (January 1869): 54. Gillett claimed to agree with Hodge that the Adopting Act must be understood as a compromise that drew the support of divergent parties in the church. See also E.H. Gillett, *History of the Presbyterian Church in the United States of America*, Vol. I (Philadelphia: Presbyterian Publication Committee, 1864), 1-58.

[44] Ibid., 44, 45.

[45] Ibid., 50.

contended that the term "essential" had a well established historical meaning, coming out of the subscription controversies that had agitated English and Irish dissenters in the time since 1716.[46]

The history following the original Adopting Act evidenced efforts by the Scottish and Irish elements, that were coming over in great numbers every year, to urge their more rigid view of subscription on the Presbyterians in America. This came to a head in the 1736 declaration of the Synod that adopting the Confession of Faith was "without the least variation or alteration, and without any regard to said distinctions." The New School editors of the *Review* contended, "This is the *ipsissima verba* theory, full-fledged." They added, "The action of the Synod was directly contrary to the spirit of the Adopting Act." As far as the New School men were concerned, the declaration of 1736 was a revision that changed the meaning of subscription from its original intent in 1729. Hodge and the New School men agreed that the 1736 position advocated strict subscription to the standards. The New School men accused Hodge of wanting it both ways – he admits 1729 was a compromise, yet, implies that the rigid stance of 1736 is consistent with 1729. For the New School, the 1736 declaration was a departure from the original compromise commitment of 1729. From their vantage point, this new strict statement on subscription was the genesis of the schism of 1741.[47]

Gillett argued that the strict interpretation of the Adopting Act, which was offered by the Synod of Philadelphia in 1736, was caused in part by a reaction to the case of Samuel Hemphill. Since Hemphill had appealed to the Adopting Act itself to justify his position, this caused "alarm," and propelled the Synod "to give the Adopting Act the most rigorous interpretation possible" in order to assure their flocks of ministerial orthodoxy. The Synod of 1736 declared that they have and still do adopt the Westminster Confession and Catechisms "without the least variation, or alteration, and without any regard to such distinctions." Gillett offered this analysis of the statement: "It may well have been understood to imply more than it asserted, which was in substance the entire acceptance of the standards by the members then present ...The assertion therefore that the Synod 'have adopted' etc., 'without the least variation or alteration,' may be left to stand for what it is worth – an interpretation simply of a historical act, while it does not profess to prescribe any new terms of ministerial communion, but only sets forth the attitude which the Synod for the time being chose to assume."[48]

New School men viewed the colonial schism in the church as essentially a matter of different attitudes towards the church and ministry. At the heart of Old Side/New Side tension was more than different views on subscription, rather there was a "difference in their spirit." Looking carefully at the three key issues of revival,

---

[46] Ibid., 45-48.

[47] "Spirit of American Presbyterianism," December 1852, 494, 495. The New School writers were reacting to Charles Hodge's *Constitutional History of the Presbyterian Church in the United States of America* (1840) which had been republished in 1851.

[48] E.H. Gillett, "The Men and the Times of the Reunion of 1758," *American Presbyterian and Theological Review* (July 1868): 420-423.

education and subscription, the *Review* editors noted that there was essentially one tension in the 1741 schism- conservatism versus progress. Every person by nature is progressive or conservative. The cause of Presbyterian schism has been two varying organisms. One segment resisted change and sought to preserve the doctrine and practice of the church as she had been. Another segment was more concerned for the perishing souls of men. They suggested that George Whitefield did not cause the Presbyterian division but he was the occasion of bringing into strong relief the essential characteristics of the parties. [49]

The New School embraced the "revival spirit of our fathers" and viewed the New Side revivalists as their ecclesiastical forefathers. In the mid 1850s New School men lamented that there had been a "suspension of the influences of the Spirit" in their day. As a church, the New School longed for the former days. "Our earnest desire is to witness such scenes as those which clustered around Edwards and Whitefield, Blair and the Tennents, Davies and Dickinson. Our souls break for the longing which we have after the Holy Spirit, and we would plead as starving men for bread, that His mightiest influences might be poured out upon us. This is our characteristic faith and hope as a denomination."[50] Acknowledging that there were excesses during the eighteenth-century revivals, nevertheless, a vital work of God had occurred. The mission of the Presbyterian Church may be described as "*Calvinism in a revival*" (italics theirs).[51] The New School editors declared, "Our fathers loved and sought revivals of religion, and so do we, The evils are dust in the balance, the good is illimitable and everlasting!"[52]

Given this general perspective, nevertheless, the New School acknowledged that there were genuine differences over doctrinal issues and the matter of subscription. The doctrinal difference is explicitly indicated in the 1741 protest of the Old Side against the New Side being allowed to sit in the Synod. The Old Side asserted that a continued union was "absurd and inconsistent, when it is notorious that our doctrine and principles of church government, in many points, are not only diverse, but directly opposite." In addition to this proclamation, there was indication that the Old Side regarded the action of 1736 as differing from the 1729 Adopting Act. The New School editors quoted from the Old Side Protest: "We protest that no person, minister or elder, should be allowed to sit and vote in this Synod, who hath not received, adopted or subscribed, the said Confession, Catechism and Directory, as our Presbyteries respectively do, ACCORDING TO OUR LAST EXPLICATION OF THE ADOPTING ACT" (capitalization theirs).[53] The editors of the *Review* interpreted this last phrase as a reference to the 1736 action which, according to their reading, had changed the meaning of subscription. The Old Side in effect had altered the compact: "And on this declaration, inter alia, *the New Side formed the*

---

[49] "Spirit of American Presbyterianism," December 1854, 468, 469.

[50] "Spirit of American Presbyterianism," June 1854, 125.

[51] "The Presbyterian Church Intelligently Preferred," *Presbyterian Quarterly Review* IV (March 1856): 656.

[52] "Spirit of American Presbyterianism," June 1854, 130.

[53] "Spirit of American Presbyterianism," Dec. 1852, 502.

Synod of New York, because the compromise was violated, the Adopting Act repudiated, and another Presbyterianism introduced" (italics theirs).[54]

Additional evidence for the intolerant stance of the Old Side, was indicated in the first act of the Synod of Philadelphia after the New Side had departed. Ashbel Green recorded: "The first thing done by the Synod was to make a new act relative to the subscription of the Westminster Confession and Catechism, *without any qualification whatever*" (italics theirs).[55]

Gillett suggested that the event which gave "permanent shaping to the policy and spirit of the American Presbyterian Church, and entitled it, at the same time, to the epithets Calvinistic and liberal" was the reunion of 1758. The reunion basis "planted itself on the ground of the Adopting Act of 1729" without any reference to either the 1730 or the 1736 interpretation. He claimed this was significant and intentional on the part of the New Side men who desired to maintain the allowance for scruples which the Adopting Act clearly provided.[56]

According to the editors of the New School *Review,* the all-important question, for tracing the true character of Presbyterianism in America, is: when the Old Side and New Side came together in 1758, was it based on the understanding of 1729 or 1736? The language of the Plan of Union clearly refers back to the original Adopting Act. The editors pointed out that the articles of the plan refer to the Confession and Catechisms as "an orthodox and excellent system of Christian Doctrine" and made distinctions concerning things "indispensable in doctrine or Presbyterian government." This language, suggested the editors, corresponded to the language of the Adopting Act which spoke of "necessary and essential articles." In the negotiations between the Synods of Philadelphia and New York, the New Side men had emphasized that the "paragraph about essentials" was an important article that cannot be dispensed. The 1758 reunion agreement was characterized by the New School in this way: "In a word, it rejected the *ipsissima verba* theory, and placed the Church again on the Adopting Act, or Compromise-Foundation."[57]

Gillett offered this evaluation of the 1758 reunion: "Thus the New Side had secured the *thing,* while less scrupulous about the form. They had acted in consistency with themselves throughout. They made the Adopting Act, *as received in* 1729, the fundamental position which they resolved to occupy. They allowed a latitude in what they accounted non-essentials" (italics his).[58] Both the Synod of New York in 1745 and the reunited Synod of 1758 had taken their stand on the original Adopting Act. Neither Synod had made mention of the modification of 1730 or the explication of 1736. Gillett believed this is implicit evidence that the original latitude of 1729 was embraced as it was before it had been tampered with.[59]

---

[54] Ibid., 495-497.

[55] Ashbel Green, *Christian Advocate,* xi, 413 quoted in "Spirit of American Presbyterianism," September 1853, 238.

[56] Ibid., 443.

[57] "Spirit of American Presbyterianism," December 1852, 498.

[58] Ibid., 430.

[59] Gillett, "The True Character of the Adopting Act," 55.

As the eighteenth-century American Presbyterian churches grew a national organized denomination emerged. Building upon her earlier history, the Presbyterians endorsed the original 1729 principles. Documentary evidence for a "system" view of subscription was witnessed in the explicit language of the terms of subscription adopted by the first Presbyterian General Assembly in 1789. The phrase "system of doctrine" was utilized as the specific terminology of subscription and this official articulation has been in place ever since in American Presbyterianism. Attempts at union with the Dutch Reformed and the Associate Reformed Synods in the 1780s were rebuffed. The New School men believed this was providential as it spared the new national church from "suicidal rigidity." There was a broadness and liberality in 1789 that is similar to that of 1729 and 1758.[60] The *Review* editors offered this summary of the period up to the first General Assembly:

> Is the reader satisfied? We have traced this stream to its parent fountains, and is anything more needed to show that a standard-principle of the American Presbyterian Church was and is, that allowing minor differences of opinion, our officers adopt the Confession, as a system; that is, the Calvinistic system as distinguished from all others, and not the *ipsissima verba* of the Confession, 'without variation or alteration, and without regard to the distinctions' of the Adopting Act? The phraseology, it will be seen, is uniformly (except in 1736, which issued in schism) the same, and it is preserved and carried into our present form of subscription.[61]

The nineteenth-century New School practice of a moderate Calvinist[62] spirit was the same attitude that had been evidenced in eighteenth-century constitutional discussions on Presbyterian confessional subscription. The principle of liberty of conscience and allowance for diversity in expressing the Reformed system of the Confession was embedded in the constitutional documents of American Presbyterianism. Given this perspective, the New School historians believed their church had every right to the title, "The Presbyterian Church in the United States of America." From 1729 onward Presbyterians had practiced confessional subscription in the spirit of the original Adopting Act. Gillett stated: "Our church has afforded shelter too long and too extensively to varied interpretations of the doctrines of our standards, to allow us to set its history over against a liberal interpretation of the Adopting Act, and the attempt to do so can result only in its own defeat. We have been as a church, for the most part, consistent in tolerating diversities of belief,

---

[60] "The Spirit of American Presbyterianism," June 1854, 135.

[61] "The Spirit of American Presbyterianism," December 1852, 497, 498.

[62] New Schoolers used the phrase "Moderate Calvinism" to portray themselves as holding the middle ground between conservatives and radicals. Robert W. Patterson, Moderator of the 1860 General Assembly, described this as a "distinctive feature of our body" in his sermon to the Assembly delivered on May 17. Due to the request from a large number of commissioners, the sermon was published. See "The Position and Mission of Our Church," *Presbyterian Quarterly Review* IX (July 1860): 119,120. Patterson characterized "Moderate Calvinism" as a "toleration of a generous and liberal construction of the Westminster Confession of Faith."

substantially sound and Scriptural, however varied among themselves. The Adopting Act, as we claim to understand it, has been no false symbol of our subsequent history."[63]

Understanding the Schism

New School writers in the mid-nineteenth century were very concerned for accuracy in understanding the heritage of Presbyterianism. They believed that some Old School historical interpretations had unfairly caricatured both eighteenth-century Presbyterian practice and the early nineteenth-century factors leading up to the Old School/New School ecclesiastical separation. The factors behind the schism of 1837-38 were indeed very complex. The editors of the *Presbyterian Quarterly Review* suggested that part of the demise of a united Presbyterian body in America was the introduction of "foreign elements" into the Presbyterian Church. The 1801 Plan of Union with New England Congregationalists had been in keeping with the spirit of Presbyterianism; this spirit had always encouraged charity and union. In fact, very little opposition was registered against the plan in 1801. Since 1758 Presbyterians had attempted union with Scottish, Dutch and German Reformed Churches to form a Reformed body in America. The editors described the Presbyterian ecumenical mood at the opening of the nineteenth century: "It was in entire accordance with the spirit of the Church, from the beginning, as to its general character, and was only part of a vast system of union, charity and enlarged Christianity.... The spirit of the time was that of the conscript fathers of the Republic and of the primitive Christians, the spirit which binds a continent into one affectionate nation, and a world into one loving Church."[64] Notwithstanding the charitable beginnings, this union would cause grave difficulties for Presbyterianism in the coming decades.

In 1817, the General Assembly review of the Records of the Synod of Philadelphia noted that the Assembly did not approve of a pastoral letter and resolution from the Synod to its Presbyteries urging them to call to account all ministers who might be suspected of embracing Hopkinsian doctrines. The Assembly conveyed this sentiment: "... the Assembly regret that zeal on this subject should be manifested in such a manner as to be offensive to other denominations, and especially to introduce a spirit of jealousy and suspicion against ministers in good standing, which is calculated to disturb the peace and harmony of our ecclesiastical judicatories." The Assembly pointed out that a section of the Pastoral Letter from the Synod of Philadelphia "appears capable of being construed as expressing an opinion unfavorable to revivals of religion, the Assembly would only observe that they cannot believe that venerable Synod could have intended to express such an opinion." Two protests were entered against this statement of the Assembly. In view of these circumstances, the Assembly appointed a committee to

---

[63] Gillett, "The True Character of the Adopting Act," 52, 53.
[64] "The Spirit of American Presbyterianism," June 1854, 145.

prepare a Pastoral Letter from the Assembly to the Presbyterian Churches. The Assembly Letter affirmed the prayer and efforts for revivals as well as encouraging the cultivation of affection for all Christians.[65]

The New School editors highlighted certain "admirable remarks" of the 1817 Assembly Letter which addressed the issue of tolerating doctrinal differences in the Presbyterian Church. They cited this portion:

> That differences of opinion, acknowledged on all hands to be of the minor class, may and ought to be tolerated among those who are agreed in great and leading views of divine truth, is a principle on which the godly have so long and so generally acted, that it seems unnecessary, at the present day, to seek arguments for its support. Our fathers, in early periods of the history of our Church, had their peculiarities and diversities of opinion; which yet, however, did not prevent them from loving one another, from cordially acting together; and by their united prayers and exertions transmitting to us a goodly inheritance. Let us emulate their moderation and forbearance, and we may hope to be favored with more than their success. Surely those who can come together on the great principles of our public standards, however they may differ on non-essential points, ought not to separate, or to indulge bitterness or prejudice against each other.[66]

The Old School *Presbyterian Magazine* had published several articles in reaction to the *Presbyterian Quarterly Review* series on the spirit of American Presbyterianism. Citing the above portion of the Pastoral Letter of 1817, the New School editors declared: "The Presbyterian Magazine had better give it up. If he wishes the Exscinding Branch of the Church to be rigid, be it so, but he has no right to involve our fathers in the same narrow defiles."[67]

In 1822 a second foreign element entered the Presbyterian Church – the rigid Associate Reformed Seceders. The Seceders were strict men that insisted on: the *ipsissima verba* adoption of the doctrinal standards,[68] the right of each Presbytery to examine every minister regardless of how long he had been in the Church, and implementing strict Presbyterianism in all the new settlements. The Seceder "lives on law and dotes on hair splitting." New Schoolers pointed out that the crisis in the Presbyterian Church soon followed once the Seceders were "admitted into our

---

[65] "The Spirit of American Presbyterianism," June 1854, 146, 147. Drs. Hoge, Herron, Spring and Miller were appointed to prepare the letter.

[66] Quoted in "Sprit of American Presbyterianism," June 1854, 147 and September 1853, 228, 229.

[67] "Spirit of American Presbyterianism," September 1853, 229.

[68] Seceder views of subscription were characterized thus: "insisting upon subscription to the *ipsissima verba*, not of God's Book, but of four hundred and fifty pages of uninspired matter, elaborated by certain wise and good men, fallible like ourselves, two hundred years ago, by order of the British Parliament! ... when a cordial offer is made of subscription to this Symbol in all its great features and outlines, they still insist on its being taken word for word, or rending the Church in twain!" "Spirit of American Presbyterianism," December 1854, 479, 480.

citadel." The Act and Testimony was clearly Seceder in its spirit and tendency.[69] The ingrafting of both Congregationalists and Seceders into the Presbyterian body was an explosion waiting to happen. The New School editors observed:

> It was in this year [1821] that the action was commenced for the union of the Associate Reformed Church with ours; action, we fear, that was one of the most influential causes of all our troubles. It introduced a second foreign element into our body. The motive, in the large introduction of both Congregationalist and Seceders, was no doubt pure and catholic, but it ought to have been a serious question then, one now unhappily solved with untold sorrow, whether materials so widely diverse could exist together.... Was it reasonable to ask a man accustomed to the gossamer government of a Massachusetts Association, to stand side by side in a Presbytery with an *ipsissima verba* Seceder? Was it not expecting too much of human nature, was it not a somewhat romantic magnanimity to suppose, that our American Presbyterianism possessed the magic power to bring into harmonious co-operation that man who could only realize spirit at all through rigid form, and him who could only realize form at all as a disagreeable necessity of spirit? ... and the men brought into our body from the Associate Reformed, were but so many wedges to drive asunder the grand old Presbyterian oak ... strangers came in upon our fair heritage from the right hand and the left.[70]

On the question of voluntary associations versus ecclesiastical boards, the prime tension was not the methodology of church expansion but a different concept of the church. The issue was more a question of what kind of Christianity shall be planted in the new regions – a rigid and exclusive Presbyterianism or the evangelical faith generally? The New School, which abhorred sectarianism, took a more liberal view and was willing to give up on many minor points in the interest of a more ecumenical Christianity.[71]

There were genuine doctrinal distinctions between the two branches of the Presbyterian Church, but, the New School asserted that these differences had to do more with articulating and explaining the Reformed tradition rather than core doctrines of Calvinism. This diversity was "in regard to certain minor and unessential points." New School men believed that particular methods or theories used to explain Calvinism might be improved upon. Some of these old theories may need to be laid aside "for the purpose of making the doctrines in question more fresh and powerful." The problem was that some of the Old School "could not distinguish between ideas which differ, and those which, apparently differing, are really the same." If a "bookish" New School man used a word more common in New England than in Pennsylvania or Virginia, the Old School would shout "New Haven!"[72]

The New School editors asserted that the "self-styled orthodox" never truly sought a friendly explanation from their New School brethren nor was an attempt made to discern their real opinions. Many misunderstandings occurred as the rigid

---

[69] "The Spirit of American Presbyterianism," June 1854, 152-154.

[70] Ibid., 147-149.

[71] "The Spirit of American Presbyterianism," December 1854, 469-472.

[72] Ibid., 472-475.

party stood aloof from their brothers and "brooded over imaginary heresy." Some of the Old School leaders had already made up their minds apart from thorough investigation. "Heresy and disorder were foregone conclusions and their reputation as confessors and prophets depended upon making it out." The editors added: "We are afraid that beyond a certain point of time, even charity, which 'thinketh not evil' cannot accord to these leaders a strong desire to find their brethren innocent, or the Church pure." While both parties of the Presbyterian Church "had the preservation of the palladium at heart," nonetheless, Old School leaders "preached a crusade against fancied heresy." The editors concluded: "The whole thing was a gigantic blunder."[73]

The driving force behind the party tensions was the impetus given by Ashbel Green and Robert Breckinridge. Under their leadership the conservative party strove to maintain the status quo. As a new generation of ministers entered the Presbyterian Church they brought with them a new style of ministry. The older men who had a "respectable and ponderous style" became out of date. The whole church had been "tending in the direction of revivals of religion and practical piety" ever since the time that Dr. Green attacked Mr. Barnes. Yet, some in the quieter parts of the country had not caught this spirit. Green gathered around him a group of like-minded men in Philadelphia who appealed to the old ways.[74] Resistance to change was also a part of the ethos of the Seceders, "... if a psalm-book contained such poetry as would have horrified David, and was sung to such music as would have caused Solomon to stop his ears, they insisted upon its being perpetuated to the millennium as sacred. They were suspicious of all change as though it were error."[75] Sadly, sentiments degenerated into a contest for influence in the Presbyterian Church. "As the matter went on and the parties were more clearly defined and the breach widened, the state of mind that hoped or sought a settlement and arrangement passed away, and the controversy then became much more nearly a naked struggle for power."[76]

The New School editors admitted that their forefathers had advanced the tensions within Presbyterianism. New England men contributed much to the cause of the division. They critique the New England mind: "The mind of New England is often more acute than comprehensive, often sharp rather than wise. It maneuvers too much. It is not sufficiently straight-forward. Too much doubling and winding both loses time and lessen confidence ... Its reforms are often superficial, its agitations fanatical, its theology not well considered." The New Englanders disregarded the prejudices of their brethren and this "was misunderstood to mean much more than was really intended." Emmons and Hopkins carried out the ideas of Edwards and Bellamy to "extreme consequences" which excited alarm. But, protested the editors, the views of Hopkins and Emmons "do not prevail in our church and our young

---

[73] Ibid., 474, 475.
[74] Ibid., 476, 477.
[75] Ibid., 480.
[76] Ibid., 474, 475.

clergymen especially have, in most cases, very little sympathy with them." They also point out that historically, some of the Old Schoolers were Hopkinsian and certain New Schoolers such as Drs. Ely and Cox were anti-Hopkinsian.[77]

In the 1820s and 1830s new problems emerged as the revival preachers used more creative approaches to reaching people with the gospel. Certain "metaphysical explanations" that were common in the schools and pulpits were jettisoned by the revival preachers who viewed this "scholastic philosophy" as an impediment to people "feeling the power of the truth." The revivalists preached that men would go to perdition for their own sin, the atonement was for all persons and that man had the ability to accept Christ as his Savior. When criticized for not using the precise phraseology and the stereotyped phrases of the orthodox, the revival preachers response was plain: "This phraseology had been abused to the ruin of souls. Men have been rocked to sleep in the cradle of orthodoxy. Men have had apologies framed for their impenitence by doctors of divinity.... We cannot consent to be co-workers with Satan in the ruin of souls."[78]

The New School men acknowledged that recklessness had attended the success of the revivals in those days just as there had been envy from those who experienced no such power. The editors believed that, "a sincere desire to make the truth of God most efficient for its purpose, was the primary motive in the theological inquiries of these times.... And we fearlessly assert that, in the great mass of the Presbyterian ministry, there was no essential departure from Calvinism."[79]

In addition to some New School excesses, there had also been a lack of sensitivity to Old School concerns in the years immediately preceding the schism. New School majorities in the Presbyterian General Assemblies had shown a "failure of consideration for the prejudices and scruples" of the Old School brethren. This was their great fault, "not heresy of doctrine or impropriety of measures."[80]

The New School men were convinced that the history of Presbyterianism up until the schism of 1837/1838 demonstrated the veracity of their assertion that the New School as a church had exhibited the spirit and ethos of what historically it had meant to be Presbyterian in America. The New School parts of the Presbyterian Church, while maintaining a seemingly broader perspective on subscription than some of their Old School brethren, had consistently maintained a substantive attachment to essential Calvinism throughout the first half of the nineteenth century. The New School editors wrote in 1852: "If the entire exscinding body should become Arminian tomorrow, and all New England should go with them, our Church would remain Calvinistic from deeply rooted principle.... Our churches never were more thoroughly attached to the Confession of Faith, the Form of Government and the traditions of their fathers."[81]

---

[77] Ibid., 485-488.
[78] Ibid., 490.
[79] Ibid., 490.
[80] Ibid., 497.
[81] Ibid., 474.

One implication of New School Calvinistic orthodoxy was that the two bodies of Presbyterians ought to be part of one unified Presbyterian Church. The New School editors asserted: "The result of a careful examination by any solid and competent mind would be that both parties are thorough Calvinists, one as much as the other, the difference being only one of temperament, culture and acumen, and that there is no reason, but only prejudice, in the way of their working kindly in the same church."[82] The theme of reunification was an ideal for which the New School consistently maintained an open mind. The factors that led to separation were real but there had been serious mistakes on both sides. On the whole, New School men believed that there were no good reasons for the two bodies to remain separate permanently.

---

[82] Ibid., 490.

CHAPTER 8

Old School Charles Hodge

One of the chief spokesmen for the Old School was Professor Charles Hodge of Princeton Seminary. His years at Princeton (1820-1878) spanned the entire era of Old School/New School debates. Hodge was a very vocal participant in all the ecclesiastical matters of this period and wrote extensively on the topic of confessional subscription both before and after the schism. For Hodge and his fellow Old School brethren, debates between the two parties of the Presbyterian family always came back to the question concerning the extent to which ministers should be expected to hold the doctrines of the Presbyterian Standards. In the midst of this on-going debate among Presbyterians, Charles Hodge consistently articulated the "old moderate plan"[1] of the Princeton men.

When reunion discussions surfaced in the 1860s, one banner of Old School resistance to reunite with the New School was the voice of the *Biblical Repertory and Princeton Review* of which Hodge was an editor.[2] Yet, even here, there was an increasing realization of more common commitment to the Confession in the two branches than previous perceptions had indicated. In the process, Presbyterians of both parties seemed to realize in a deeper way the broad unanimity that existed in the church on the subject of subscription to the Standards.

The *Constitutional History*

Hodge's major work that addressed the subscription issue was *The Constitutional History of the Presbyterian Church in the United States of America* written between 1838-1840. Hodge described his goal in writing this history: "as I hope may be the case, it will tend to increase the respect and affection of Presbyterians for the church of their fathers."[3] As an Old School man, Hodge believed his church was the

---

[1] James W. Alexander, *Life of Archibald Alexander* (New York: Charles Scribner's, 1854), 474.

[2] This was the perspective of the New School men. See J. F. Stearns, "Historical Sketch of Reunion," *American Presbyterian Review* New Series, I (July 1869): 583.

[3] A.A. Hodge, *Life of Charles Hodge* (New York: Charles Scribner's sons, 1880), 317. Hodge clearly favored the Old Side party as he describes the early history of eighteenth-century American Presbyterians. Not all of Hodge's Princeton colleagues agreed with his interpretation of this period. Hodge's critique of Great Awakening emotionalism and the New Side preachers deeply troubled Archibald Alexander who believed the New Side was right to support the revivals. Alexander wrote a history of the Log College preachers and the

legitimate heir of the colonial Presbyterian heritage. One of his key points was the documentary evidence for historic confessional subscription.

The catalyst for the *Constitutional History* was the recent Presbyterian schism (1837-38) and the questions it raised about the origin and constitution of the Presbyterian Church. Which branch followed in the train of their Presbyterian forefathers? What is the historic understanding among Presbyterians of the terms of ministerial communion? Was the traditional condition of ministerial communion "assent to the essential doctrines of the Gospel" as some in the New School had suggested? The *Constitutional History* was written in part to demonstrate that the historical evidence disavowed this assertion. The core of the matter was interpreting the true intent of the original Adopting Act of 1729.[4]

Hodge dismissed criticism leveled at the Westminster Standards as a divisive statement of faith. Referring to eighteenth-century adoption of the Standards, he stated:

> It is strange that this measure, after the lapse of a century, should still be held up to reprobation by members of our own communion. Every other church has a creed, why should not the Presbyterians be allowed to have one? ... If it was so sectarian in 1729, to adopt the Confession of Faith, why, in the course of more than a hundred years, has the adopting act never been repealed?[5]

For Hodge it was unjust to ascribe either "sectarian bigotry" or "heartless orthodoxy" to the 1729 Synod. It was grossly unfair to suggest that the original supporters of the Confession were "less zealous in their religion" than those opposed to creeds. In the case of the revival, some of the Presbyterians most adverse to the Confession were the most critical of the revival. Hodge countered that commitment to doctrinal orthodoxy indeed had produced significant fruit in Christian history. "The strictest churches have been the most pious, laborious, and

---

Awakening in 1845 which was much more favorable to the Tennents and the New Side. See Archibald Alexander, *Biographical Sketches of the Founder and Principal Alumni of the Log College. Together with an Account of the Revivals of Religion Under Their Ministry* (Princeton: J.T. Robinson, 1845; reprint, Philadelphia: Presbyterian Board of Publication, 1851).

[4] Charles Hodge, *Constitutional History of the Presbyterian Church in the United States of America* (Philadelphia: Presbyterian Board of Publication, 1851), Part I, 10. Hodge's dominant objective in the *Constitutional History* was to demonstrate that confessional subscription had never meant assent to the "essential doctrines of the gospel" only. He reiterated this point repeatedly throughout his *History* and appeared to believe this was the common view of the New School. In the Introduction, Hodge cited several examples from New School authors which he believed indicated this position.

[5] Ibid., 129,130. Note Hodge stated that the Adopting Act is still in force in the Presbyterian Church. This was an important admission and explains his determination to interpret the act correctly.

useful churches. And the strictest age of any particular church has almost always been its best age."[6]

The *Constitutional History* was an attempt to establish by documentary evidence that the first generations of American Presbyterians practiced full subscription to the Confession of Faith. Repeatedly, Hodge highlighted this issue. His contention was that the original Adopting Act affirmed a strict subscriptionist stance and subsequent synodical statements in 1730 and 1736 unequivocally strengthen this position.[7]

No man who was not a Calvinist should be admitted to the ministry according to the intent of the original 1729 Synod. The Adopting Act was introduced out of concern to protect the Presbyterians from Arminianism and Socinianism. Since this was its design, it should be clear that the ideal was to affirm not only the "essentials" of Christianity but the Reformed expression of Christianity in particular. Therefore, it was self evident that the phrase "essential and necessary articles" in the ordination vow referred to "any essential feature of Presbyterianism."[8]

Hodge admitted that there are several possible motives behind the Adopting Act. Some argued that the wording of the 1729 Act was a compromise, each giving a little, in order to avoid schism. Others suggested that the working outcome was language that each one could fully support as his own position. Hodge favored the latter perspective, yet, he indicated that whatever may have been the case, it was never the purpose of the framers to make ministerial communion solely rely on the "necessary doctrines of Christianity." The historical record of the acts of the 1729 Synod indicate that after working through their scruples together, the Synod unanimously agreed to adopt the whole Confession with the allowed exceptions in chapters twenty and twenty-three. "Such was the latitudinarianism of those days," concluded Hodge.[9]

According to Hodge, while the original Synod's aim must be carefully considered, it was certainly the right of later Synods to modify that position. There was a distinction to be made between the meaning of the Adopting Act and what had been the actual practice of the church. He observed:

> Those who are enamored with what they take to be the meaning of that act, forgetful of their low opinion of the power of Synods, seem to regard it as unalterable. They speak as though the Synod of 1729 had authority not only over inferior judicatories, but over all succeeding Synods. This is certainly a strange assumption. Had the Synod of 1729 made the reception of the apostles' creed the condition of ministerial communion, that

---

[6] Ibid., 133,134.
[7] Ibid., 142.
[8] Ibid., 150, 151.
[9] Ibid., 154.

of 1730 had as good a right to require assent to every proposition in Calvin's Institutes and Commentaries.[10]

Hodge suggested that even if one were to grant that the original act was "latitudinarian" (which he does not believe is the case), it was repealed by the act of 1730. Furthermore, the acts of 1730 and later 1736 never have been altered by any Synod until the General Assembly of 1788. He asserted that "the very ambiguity of the adopting act was the occasion of that doctrine ['essential and necessary doctrines of the gospel'] being repudiated, and a strict adherence to the Confession enjoined with a frequency and clearness which otherwise would not have been called for."[11]

In addition to the reaffirmations of 1730 and 1736, Hodge surveyed the actions of Presbyteries and Synods in the following decades to ascertain if there was any additional light on the issue. He concluded that all the records of the courts of the church indicate consistent reaffirmations of the very strict positions taken in 1730 and 1736. The language was unequivocal and the intended meaning was clear to all Presbyterians of that time.

In his overview of the period up until the first General Assembly, Hodge dealt with the issues related to the separation and reunion of the Synods of New York and Philadelphia (1741-1758). Article one of the 1758 Plan of Union reiterated the American Presbyterian commitment to the Westminster Standards with these words:

> Both Synods having always approved and received the Westminster Confession of Faith, and Larger and Shorter Catechisms, as an orthodox and excellent system of Christian doctrine, founded on the word of God, we do still receive the same as the confession of our faith and also adhere to the plan of worship, government and discipline, contained in the Westminster Directory, strictly enjoining it on all our members and probationers for the ministry, that they preach and teach according to the form of sound words in said Confession and Catechism, and avoid and oppose all errors contrary thereto.[12]

Hodge argued that this was nothing less than the wholesale adoption of the Standards. And subscription was certainly understood in the Calvinistic sense. He explained:

> Both bodies declare that they always have received, and do still receive the Westminster Confession as the confession of their faith ... Every minister and probationer is strictly enjoined to avoid all errors contrary to the standards thus assumed. There must be an end of all confidence among men if such language can be used by those who make assent to the essential and necessary doctrines of the gospel, the term of ministerial communion; if an Arminian, Pelagian, Roman Catholic, or

---

[10] Ibid., 171.

[11] Ibid., 185, 186.

[12] *Digest of the Supreme Judicatory of the Presbyterian Church* (Philadelphia: Presbyterian Board of Publication, 1850), 184. (Old School).

Quaker, can say that he receives a strictly Calvinistic creed as the confession of his faith![13]

One of the primary elements in eighteenth-century reunion discussions had to do with the matter of personal conscience. This had been at the heart of the schism of 1741 when the Presbytery of Brunswick had been unwilling to submit to an act of Synod. In the 1758 Plan of Union between the Synods of New York and Philadelphia, article two declared:

> That when any matter is determined by a major vote, every member shall either actively concur with, or passively submit to such determination; or, if his conscience permit him to do neither, he shall, after sufficient liberty modestly to reason and remonstrate, peaceably withdraw from our communion, without attempting to make any schism. Provided always, that this shall be understood to extend only to such determinations as the body shall judge indispensable in doctrine or Presbyterian government.[14]

Some New School advocates of loose subscription (in mid-nineteenth century) had related this reunion article to the concept that candidates for the ministry should be required to assent to no more than the "essential doctrines of the gospel." Hodge countered,

> This article does not relate to the adoption of the Confession, or to the admission of new members, but to submission to the decisions of ecclesiastical judicatories. All their acts and determinations were to be concurred in or submitted to, unless conscience forbade it. In that case the dissentients should not be disowned, unless the Synod should think the matter essential to their doctrines or discipline.... It simply says, what it is presumed no one ever has denied, that deposition, the highest ecclesiastical censure, ought not to be inflicted for slight aberrations from our standards ... it would be equally preposterous to depose a minister who should deny that the Pope was antichrist, when you could inflict no higher penalty upon him for the avowal of complete infidelity.[15]

Allowance for differences was made explicit in the 1758 Plan of Union. This has been a fundamental premise for the functioning of church courts in relation to any potential discipline of a minister. Commenting on the paragraph about "essentials," Hodge stated:

> Neither Synod was disposed to make 'every truth or duty' a term of communion; and each had made the adoption of the Westminster Confession of Faith a condition of admission into the sacred office. The article in question indeed did not relate to the admission of members, but to their exclusion; ... this Synod did not make adherence to the mere essential doctrines of the gospel the condition of ministerial communion. This

---

[13] Hodge, *Constitutional History*, I, 178.

[14] *Digest of the Presbyterian Church*, 1850 (Old School), 184.

[15] Hodge, *Constitutional History*, Part I, 176, 177.

is indeed evident from the form of expression adopted in the article itself, which speaks of what is essential 'in doctrine or discipline.' The discipline intended is the discipline adopted by the Synod, and the doctrine intended is the system of doctrine which they had adopted.[16]

An enlightening incident that bears on the subscription question, according to Hodge, was the case of Samuel Harker, a member of the Presbytery of New Brunswick. Harker was eventually suspended for Arminian opinions by the Synod in 1763. Rev. Harker complained that the action of the Synod of New York and Philadelphia against him violated his rights to private judgment and scruples over articles non-essential. Harker appealed to the Adopting Act of 1729 as proof of his stance. In 1764 John Blair offered a written rebuttal on behalf of the Synod. Blair attempted to clarify the meaning of "essential and necessary" as understood by the Synod. Blair replied to Harker: "But the Synod say essential in doctrine, worship, or government, *i.e.* essential to the system of doctrine contained in the Westminster Confession of Faith, considered as a system ... That, therefore, is an essential error in the Synod's sense, which is of such malignity as to subvert or greatly injure the system of doctrine...."[17]

Several things are worthy of note here. First, Blair appeared to be offering a different understanding of subscription with his emphasis on the phrase "system of doctrine." The implication was that "system of doctrine" may not necessarily be inclusive of every article (with the exceptions of chapters 20 and 23, of course). This suggested a broader interpretation of the Adopting Act than was implied in the declarations of 1730 and 1736. Secondly, Hodge's commentary on Blair's statement is noteworthy for its admission that Blair's perspective was a legitimate position on adherence to the standards. Hodge observed: "This interpretation of the act is of course not official, and is below that given by the Synod itself in 1730, which allowed of no dissent except from the clauses so often referred to. Mr. Blair's interpretation is the most liberal for which there is any sanction in the declarations or practice of the church."[18]

Blair's interpretation was supported by the Synod's basis for excluding Harker: "The Synod judged that these principles are of a hurtful dangerous tendency, giving a false view of the covenant of grace, perverting it into a new-modeled covenant of

---

[16] Ibid., Part II, 273.

[17] *The Synod of New York and Philadelphia Vindicated*, 10,11; quoted in Hodge, *Constitutional History*, Part I, 170; Part II, 274.

[18] Hodge, *Constitutional History*, Part I, 170. According to Hodge, the Harker incident indicated that there were three perspectives represented in the Presbyterian Church by the 1760s - the Synod's official strict subscriptionist stance, Harker's loose subscriptionist interpretation and Blair's median position which interpreted subscription as the affirmation of the Calvinist 'system of doctrine' found in the Confession. The action of Synod to remove Harker clearly refuted the extreme loose position. Full subscription or system subscription was tolerated as a valid interpretation of the Synod's commitment to the Standards at this point in time.

works, and misrepresenting the doctrine of the divine decrees as held by the best reformed churches; and, in fine, contrary to the word of God, and our approved standards of doctrine."[19] Harker's teaching, in the Synod's judgment, subverted the Reformed system of the Confession. The highlighted doctrines contested by the Synod (covenant of grace, divine decrees) were deemed to be "essentials" of that system.

Hodge claimed that the Harker affair was the only case of discipline for doctrinal error on the minutes of the reunited Synod up until the first General Assembly in 1789. In fact, the unanimity of the church at this time was quite amazing considering the fact that there were 177 American Presbyterian clergy by 1788. Hodge said, "It is probable there never was a period of equal length in the history of our church, in which there was such a general and cordial agreement among our ministers on all doctrinal subjects."[20] As evidence of this unity of convictions, He cited a letter written by a minister in 1775. A Rev. Dr. King wrote to a friend:

> I think that our Synod will be very cautious, as they have hitherto been, with respect to the admission of ministers from Europe, and especially from such places as are suspected of encouraging Arminianism, &c., and where they are so lax as to the admission of candidates. It is a particular happiness for us as yet, that we have been cautious, and Divine Providence has favored our endeavors; for I do not know that any minister belonging to our Synod can be reasonably suspected of leaning to any but the Calvinistic scheme.[21]

In 1786 there were ecumenical discussions with the Synods of the Dutch and Associate Reformed Churches. Committees from each body were asked to state both their formulas of doctrine and their mode of adherence to those doctrines. The committee from the Synod of New York and Philadelphia wrote a report which was accepted by the Synod. The report stated:

> The Synod of New York and Philadelphia adopt, according to the known and established meaning of the terms, the Westminster Confession of Faith as the confession of their faith; save that every candidate for the gospel ministry is permitted to except against so much of the twenty-third chapter as gives authority to the civil magistrate in matters of religion.... The Synod also receives the Directory of public worship, and form of Church government recommended by the Westminster Assembly, as in substance agreeable to the institutions of the New Testament. This mode of adoption we use because we believe the general platform of our government to be agreeable to the sacred Scriptures; but we do not believe that God has been pleased so to reveal and enjoin every minute circumstance of ecclesiastical government and

---

[19] Ibid., Part II, 309.

[20] Ibid., 309, 310. This point helps explain Hodge's perspective on the practice of strict subscription during this era. Early Presbyterians, who shared unanimity in doctrinal views, found that their personal convictions lined up exactly with the totality of the Confession. Hodge also implied here that this had not been the case since the colonial era.

[21] Ibid., 417.

discipline as not to leave room for orthodox churches of Christ in these *minutiae*, to differ with charity from each other.[22]

Hodge commented:

> As to the document itself, it is impossible for language to be more explicit as to all the points to which it relates. The Confession of Faith is said to be the confession of the faith of the Synod, save that new members were allowed to object to certain clauses in the twenty-third chapter. The very exception greatly strengthens the case. That the new members were required to adopt the Confession, except those clauses, shows that nothing else was allowed to be rejected. This is precisely what the old Synod twice, unanimously and authoritatively, in 1730 and 1736, declare was the mode in which the Confession was to be adopted. This was the condition of ministerial communion then established, and which the Synod in 1786 declared they still adhered to. The evidence as to this point is the stronger from what is said of the manner in which the Directory was adopted. The Confession of Faith was received entirely with the single exception specified, according to the known and established meaning of the words; but the Directory was received only for substance, and reason is given for this mode of adoption.[23]

In 1787 the Synod adopted changes in chapters 20 and 23 of the Westminster Confession and ordered that the altered Confession be printed along with the Form of Government and Discipline; these together making up the constitution of the church. When the General Assembly was formed in 1789 this revised version of the Confession was adopted as the constitution of the Presbyterian Church. Hodge argued:

> If then the Westminster Confession is a part of our constitution, we are bound to abide by it, or rightfully to get it altered. Ever since the solemn enactment under consideration, every new member or candidate for the ministry had been required to give his assent to this confession, as containing the system of doctrines taught in the word of God. He assents not merely to absolutely essential and necessary articles of the gospel, but to the whole concatenated statement of doctrines contained in the Confession. This, whether right or wrong, liberal or illiberal, is the constitutional and fundamental principle of our ecclesiastical compact.[24]

For Hodge, the early documents from American Presbyterianism displayed consensus on the meaning of subscription. Some of the broad New School interpretations were in error, for there 'is not a line upon our records' which suggested that ministers were only required to assent to the "essential and necessary doctrines of the gospel." On the contrary, ministers were expected to embrace the Reformed system of doctrine contained in the standards. Hodge concluded: "If then,

---

[22] *Minutes of the Synod of New York and Philadelphia*, 1786; quoted in Hodge, *Constitutional History*, Part I, 179, 180.

[23] Ibid., 180, 181.

[24] Ibid., 183.

explicit official declarations and the actual administration of discipline can decide the question, it is clear that our Church has always required adherence to the system of doctrine contained in the Westminster Confession of Faith as a condition of ministerial communion."[25]

Reply to Dr. Cox

Hodge's earliest essay on subscription came in connection with an 1831 article he had written on regeneration.[26] Dr. Samuel Cox had responded to Hodge's essay and Hodge printed this communication from Cox in the *Review*. In his reply to Dr. Cox's letter, Hodge expressed his views on the meaning of the subscription formula. The question was, "... with what degree of strictness is the phrase 'system of doctrine' as it occurs in the ordination service, to be explained?" Hodge said two extreme answers "equally to be lamented" argued for either a too loose or too strict of an interpretation of the phrase. After explaining how the two extremes fall short, he offered what he considered the historic view of the Presbyterian Church.[27]

He first reproached the overly strict stance which made the ordination vow, "... not only involve the adoption of all the doctrines contained in the Confession, but to preclude all diversity in the manner of conceiving and explaining them." Several factors demonstrated the danger of this extreme. First, this position "is making the terms of subscription imply more than they literally import." There are different modes of understanding or explaining a doctrine.

Secondly, a strict viewpoint implied a "degree of uniformity" that never has existed in the church. The Westminster Divines produced a Confession that was a compromise. "When adopted by the Presbyterian Church in this country, it was with the distinct understanding that the mode of subscription did not imply strict uniformity of views. And from that time to this, there has been an open and avowed diversity of opinion on many points..."[28]

---

[25] Ibid., 185.

[26] See *supra*, 79-81.

[27] Charles Hodge, "Remarks on Dr. Cox's Communication" in *Biblical Repertory and Theological Review* III (1831): 520.

[28] Ibid., 520, 521. This comment appears to contradict what he says in the *Constitutional History* which is written 7 years later. This liberal interpretation of 1729 is consistent, however, with what Hodge would write in the 1850s and 1860s. In the later years, when Hodge is attacked by his conservative Old School colleagues for his lax views on subscription, he pointed out that he had said the same things 30 years previously; see *infra* n. 37. The polemic atmosphere surrounding the *Constitutional History*, written immediately after the schism, may account for Hodge's stress on eighteenth-century uniformity in his *Constitutional History*. Hodge believed some New School men had interpreted 1729 as not requiring assent to the Calvinism of the Confession; his objective in the *Constitutional History* was to destroy that argument by emphasizing the strict interpretation of 1736. It should be noted, however, that even in the *Constitutional History*, Hodge acknowledged that the actual practice of church discipline has been based upon the broader "Calvinistic system"

The third problem with strict subscription was the practical difficulty of such a tenet. This "unauthorized strictness would ruin any church on earth" and be impossible to enforce "in the present state of human nature."[29] Hodge said, "It is clearly impossible, that any considerable number of men can be brought to conform so exactly in their views, as to be able to adopt such an extended formula of doctrine precisely in the same sense."[30] He also objected to latitudinarian views which will produce "disastrous results." The words "system of doctrine" clearly meant the Calvinistic system and any other construction of these words was dishonest. Those who would interpret "system of doctrine" to mean "the great fundamental doctrines of the gospel" distort the meaning of the words. It would be better to modify the church's creed and remain honorable men than to endorse lax subscription that violates integrity. "There seems to be no more obvious principle, than that while a body professes to hold certain doctrines, it should really hold them." Hodge believed the lax view, "opens the door to all manner of heresies, and takes from the Church the power of discipline for matters of opinion."[31]

Hodge was dismayed by the abuse countenanced in both extremist camps. "While some may be disposed to resort to the discipline of the Church to correct mere diversity of explanation; others seem disposed to wink at the rejection of acknowledged constituent doctrines of the Calvinistic system."[32] Hodge was convinced that the majority of nineteenth-century Presbyterians held neither position, rather they were disposed to understanding the ordination vow as a commitment to the Calvinist system of the Confession, albeit, allowing for diversity in the expression of the Reformed system of the Standards.

Ninety percent of Presbyterian clergy would acknowledge that diversity was permissible, yet, the difficulty remains as to where the line should be drawn. This was a "delicate and difficult question." The phrase, "system of doctrine" entails a definite idea of "a regular series of connected opinions, having a mutual relation and constituting one whole." Adopting the system of the Confession involved belief in the series of doctrines that make up that system. And it was that system in

---

interpretation. Hodge admitted: "And by system of doctrine, according to the lowest standard of interpretation, has been understood the Calvinistic system as distinguished from all others. There are indeed many, whose views of subscription are such, that they could not adopt the Confession of Faith, unless they were able to receive every distinct proposition which it contains. This may be right; but it is believed that no attempt has ever been made to enforce the discipline of the church against any individual who was not believed to reject some of the distinctive features of the Calvinistic system as contained in our Confession." *Constitutional History*, 11,12.

[29] Ibid., 523.

[30] Ibid., 521. The large number of Presbyterian clergy by 1831 could not be expected to have unanimity of views as was the case one hundred years before; see *supra* n. 20. Hodge was making a very practical observation as he now argued Blair's position as the answer to the subscription dilemma of his own day.

[31] Ibid., 523, 524.

[32] Ibid., 525.

opposition to other systems of belief. Hodge offered several illustrations of diversity in explaining certain doctrines in the system. For instance, he pointed to the various explanations given to the "vicarious atonement of Jesus Christ." Hodge observed that, "... some may adopt the strict *quid pro quo* system; others the infinite value theory; others that of its universal applicability; and yet all hold the doctrine itself."[33]

Given the appropriate diversity in expression, the central question remained as to the extent of that latitude. Hodge answered that the "essentials" of a doctrine must remain intact. How then can it be determined whether or not one's explanation exceeded the allowable boundary? This must be determined by both the individual in his conscience before God and the Presbytery that must judge these matters. This was the purpose of Presbytery examinations. "It is their business to decide this very point, whether the candidate believes or not the doctrines of our standards, and they are under the solemn engagements to God and their brethren, to do this honestly." Hodge added, "And, here the matter must be left." As long as Presbyteries are conscientious about "admitting no one who rejects or explains away any of the doctrines constituting the system contained in the Confession" there should be no serious problem.[34]

"Adoption of the Confession"

Hodge offered his most extensive essay on the Presbyterian subscription issue in the pages of the *Biblical Repertory and Princeton Review* in 1858. Here he reiterated some of his points made vs. Dr. Cox and incorporated much of his research from the *Constitutional History*. One of the reasons for the essay was an outcry from a few Old School men over a comment by Hodge in an issue of the *Biblical Repertory and Princeton Review*. Hodge was giving his annual review of the General Assembly and he offered his perspective on Dr. Breckinridge's proposal that the General Assembly authorize the writing of a biblical commentary that "shall be in accordance with the Westminster doctrines of this church." Hodge opposed this concept and indicated the inherent difficulty of achieving agreement on such a commentary. He wondered: "If it is not only difficult but impossible to frame a creed as extended as the Westminster Confession, which can be adopted in all its details by the ministry of any large body of Christians, what shall we say to giving the sanction of the church to a given interpretation of every passage of Scripture?"[35] It would be impossible to require Presbyterian ministers to profess full subscription to the Confession: "We could not hold together a week, if we made the adoption of all its propositions a condition of ministerial communion."[36]

---

[33] Ibid., 522.

[34] Ibid., 523.

[35] Charles Hodge, "The General Assembly," *Biblical Repertory and Princeton Review* XXX (July 1858): 561.

[36] Ibid.

Based upon the negative reaction to these statements, Hodge concluded that apparently there was still confusion in the Old School camp about the meaning of adopting the doctrinal standards. He was astonished at the uproar in the "Old-school press" over his advocacy of what he considered the historic understanding of subscription. Indeed, what he had stated in the review article on the General Assembly was the identical position he had held for 30 years. What were these new objections to the Old School view? Why have these voices been silent for 30 years if his views were deemed to be in error?[37]

Hodge responded to these criticisms in no uncertain terms. He began his rebuttal by suggesting two principles by which one may interpret the meaning of oaths and professions of faith: "the plain historical meaning of the words" and "the intention of the party imposing the oath or requiring the profession." Hodge asked the question: "What is the true sense of the phrase, 'system of doctrine,' in our ordination service?" There are three answers that have been offered to this question. Hodge took up each one in turn and offers a forceful defense for his viewpoint.[38]

Some said the ordination vow asked the candidate to adopt the Confession for "substance of doctrine." Hodge's first objection to this position was that the definition is vague and equivocal. Two potential meanings may be attached to this understanding:

> By substance of doctrine may be meant the substantial doctrines of the Confession; that is, those doctrines which give character to it as a distinctive confession of faith, and which therefore constitute the system of belief therein contained. Or it may mean the substance of the several doctrines taught in the Confession, as distinguished from the form in which they are therein presented.[39]

If one referred to the substance or essence of a *system of doctrines* [italics mine] then the substance of that system is the system. If however, one spoke of the substance of a particular doctrine then it must have a particular form to have meaning. The substance or general truth of a doctrine is not the doctrine itself. One cannot separate the substance from the form of a doctrine. Hodge illustrated his point with the doctrine of original sin: "The different forms in which this general truth is presented, make all the difference, as to this point, between Pelagianism, Augustinianism, Romanism, and Arminianism."[40]

---

[37] Hodge, "Adoption of the Confession of Faith," *Biblical Repertory and Princeton Review* XXX (October 1858): 669.

[38] Ibid., 671.

[39] Ibid., 673. The phrase "substance of doctrine" was a major source of confusion between Old School and New School. Different persons attached different ideas to this terminology as Hodge indicated. Some who used the phrase agreed with Hodge's views on subscription, others, used these words to justify significant departures from traditional Calvinism.

[40] Ibid.

The second objection Hodge raised to the "substance of doctrine" position was its being "contrary to the mind of the church." He argued that the constitutional acts of the church prove beyond the shadow of a doubt the intended meaning of the ordination vow. He quoted in full the Adopting Act of 1729, including both the morning "preliminary act" and the afternoon minute. He cited them both as a record of the "fundamental act" which the church has "never repealed or altered."[41]

As far as Christian communion is concerned, the 1729 Synod declared that all whom Christ welcomes into his kingdom are welcome in the Presbyterian Church. Ministerial communion is established on a higher condition requiring adoption of "the system of doctrine" contained in the Westminster Confession of Faith and Catechisms. Hodge understood adopting the "system of doctrine" to be the meaning of the 1729 phrases: "adopt the said Confession and Catechisms as the confession of our faith" and "agreement in opinion with all the essential and necessary articles of said Confession;" and the two phrases are "an equivalent form of expression." Concerning exceptions to the confession, Hodge commented, "the only exceptions allowed to be taken were such as related to matters outside that system of doctrine, and the rejection of which left the system in its integrity."[42]

Hodge further objected that the phrase "substance of doctrine" has "no definite assignable meaning." He stated: "No one knows what a man professes who professes to receive only the substance of a doctrine, and, therefore, this mode of subscription vitiates the whole intent and value of a confession." The concept of doctrine is a truth in specific form. One who does not hold the doctrines of the Confession in the form in which they are presented, cannot be said to hold the said doctrines. If one professed this mode of adopting the Confession of Faith, it would be dishonest for it is no real adoption of the doctrines at all.[43]

The final objection to the "substance of doctrine" view was that this concept does nothing but produce "the greatest disorder and contention." It was this viewpoint, "more than all other causes," that produced the 1837 division in the Presbyterian Church. There were ministers who professed to adopt the Confession under this understanding of subscription that "rejected almost every doctrine which gives that system its distinctive character." Hodge listed as illustrations of distinctive doctrines of the system – original sin, inability, efficacious grace and definite atonement. These are essential tenets of the Augustinian/Calvinist system that distinguish it

---

[41] Ibid., 673-674.

[42] Ibid. This was a broader perspective on allowable exceptions than what Hodge had suggested in the *Constitutional History*. The old Synod of Philadelphia, according to Hodge, had only permitted scruples to chapters 20 and 23 of the Confession. In order to free Dr. Hodge from the charge of inconsistency, it might be possible to argue that the *Constitutional History* simply tells the eighteen-century story as it was; later, Hodge gave a fuller explanation of his own views on 1729 and how it could validly be interpreted by nineteenth-century Presbyterians. In 1858, Hodge seemed to be interpreting the Adopting Act through the lens of actual ecclesiastical practice during his lifetime. Compare his views as expressed to Dr. Cox *supra* n. 27.

[43] Ibid., 678, 679.

from Pelagian or Arminian schemes of explaining these doctrines. If the latitudinarian principle of adopting the confession were to be embraced again, it will "produce like disasters" as the schism of 1837.[44]

Just as Hodge protested that the substance of doctrine position would destroy Presbyterian unity, he likewise believed that an "every proposition" understanding "cannot be carried out without working the certain and immediate ruin of the church." This new scheme of *ipsissima verba*, Hodge called an "impracticable theory." He candidly remarked that he could not name more than a dozen ministers who would affirm all the propositions in the Confession. If this "new rule of subscription" were enforced there would be a mass exodus from the Old School Assembly.[45] Hodge included in the number that would leave the church, the editors of the *Presbyterian* and the "venerable 'G' of Richmond, Virginia." He added: "As we have no desire to sit thus solitary on the ruins of our noble church, we enter a solemn protest against a principle which would work such desolation." He continued, "To adopt every proposition contained in the Westminster Confession and Catechism, is more than the vast majority of our ministers either do, or can do."[46]

Hodge believed strict subscription, at this juncture of the church's history (late 1850s), was the self-righteous "mingled spirit of the Pharisee and Dominican." He added, "God forbid that such a spirit should ever gain the ascendency in our church." Mandating all-inclusive adoption of the Standards would be asking the majority to abandon their Christian conscience and commit sin.[47] This stance would put persons in the position of "overwhelming temptations" to profess what they do not believe.[48] Hodge observed:

> It is a perfectly notorious fact, that there are hundreds of ministers in our church, and that there always have been such ministers, who do not receive all the propositions contained in the Confession of Faith and Catechisms. To start now, at this late day, a new rule of subscription, which would either brand these men with infamy, or exclude them from the church, is simply absurd and intolerable.[49]

In addition to the pragmatic problem of tearing the church asunder, Hodge pointed to a number of other objections to the "every proposition" interpretation. The criticisms of the every proposition view parallel his attacks on the substance of

---

[44] Ibid.

[45] Hodge apparently did not identify *ipsissima verba* with the eighteenth-century understanding of subscription since he refers to this as a "new rule." The New School unfairly caricatured the Old School view as *ipsissima verba* which was here vehemently repudiated by the Old School master. There were a few Old School voices that seemed to advocate this ultra-strict interpretation but it was rejected by Hodge and the Old School majority as well as the entire New School.

[46] Ibid., 685-688.

[47] Ibid., 688.

[48] Ibid.

[49] Ibid., 685.

doctrine principle. His first point was that this new definition was contrary to the "plain, historical meaning" of the words. To adopt the system of doctrine in the Standards and to adopt every proposition were "two very different things." The words "system of doctrine" were definite and "serve to define and limit the extent to which the Confession is adopted." A candidate for the ministry professed to adopt the Reformed system of doctrine contained in the Confession and "no one can rightfully demand of him either more or less." Hodge believed there were many propositions in the Confession "which lie entirely outside the system, and which may be omitted, and yet leave the system in its integrity."[50]

Secondly, Hodge insisted that the "every proposition" perspective was contrary to "the mind of the church." There are a number of ways that the mind of the church has been made manifest. Hodge made an obvious observation:

> If the church intended that the candidate should adopt every proposition contained in the Confession of Faith, why did she not say so? It was very easy to express that idea. The words actually used do not, in their plain, established meaning, express it. The simple fact that no such demand is made, is evidence enough that none such was intended.[51]

Again, Hodge argued his median position utilizing the official explanations given by the original Synod of 1729. The Synod of Philadelphia had explicitly excluded certain clauses relating to the civil magistrate in chapters 20 and 23. Yet, the ministers received the Confession as "the confession of their faith." The formula of adoption does not include the exception of clauses in the two chapters. "It was not considered necessary to make that exception, because the language was not intended to extend to every proposition, but only to 'the system of doctrine.' This was the church's own official explanation of the sense of the words in question."[52]

Testimony from the men of that first Synod offered an important glimpse of the mind of the church. Among the original ministers in the Synod there were three groups. The first group, represented by Dickinson, was opposed to all creeds as a test of one's orthodoxy. A second group, represented by Creaghead, wished for

---

[50] Ibid., 680, 681. Nine years later, during Old School negotiations with the New School, Hodge reiterated this notion that certain statements in the Confession lie outside the Reformed "system." For example, he wrote: "A man may be a true Augustinian or Calvinist, and not believe that the Pope is the Antichrist predicted by St. Paul or that the 18th chapter of Leviticus is still binding." See "The General Assembly," *Biblical Repertory and Princeton Review* XXXIX (July 1867): 506.

[51] Hodge, "Adoption of the Confession of Faith," 681.

[52] Ibid., 682. This was Hodge's clearest intimation of how he harmonized the *Constitutional History* with his other writings. In essence, he was stating that the permissible exceptions in 1729, 1736 (chapters 20, 23) demonstrated the principle that exceptions to the Confession are indeed allowed and considered consistent with adopting the Confession as a whole at ordination. These exceptions were understood as non-essential to the "system of doctrine." Because of this constitutional principle handed-down from colonial Presbyterians, Hodge could justify his arguments against the two extreme positions.

unqualified adherence to all that the Confession contained. A third group, "containing the great body of the Synod" urged that the sense of adoption be to "the system of doctrine" in the Confession. In the words of the preamble to the Adopting Act, the Synod decided to receive the Confession "in all the essential and necessary articles" which, said Hodge, was synonymous with "system of doctrine" as elsewhere expressed.

Differences soon arose as to the exact meaning of the formula. The phrase "in all essential and necessary articles" was interpreted by Samuel Harker to mean the essential doctrines of the gospel. On the other side, Mr. Creaghead seceded from the Synod because he believed the Synod never truly adopted the Confession in all its articles. These difficulties called for further explanation. In the later clarifications, we have the true mind of the framers of the formula. As definitive evidence, Hodge cited both the reply of Samuel Blair to Mr. Creaghead and the reply of John Blair to Mr. Harker. Samuel Blair told Creaghead that the Synod did indeed adopt all the articles of the Confession excepting only certain clauses. John Blair replied to Harker that what the Synod meant by "essential in doctrine," was the "system of doctrine" taught in the Westminster Confession of Faith. Hodge declared: "Such is the explanation of the adoption of the Confession of Faith, given by the original framers of the act, and by their contemporaries. They did not merely receive it for 'substance of doctrine,' nor did they adopt all the propositions which it contains, but they received 'the system of doctrine' therein taught in its integrity."[53]

The final indicator of the mind of the church on this subject was the uniform action of church courts. Hodge argued that the records of the church indicated that no one has ever been denied entrance into the Presbyterian ministry "simply because there are propositions in the book to which he could not assent." Neither are there records of one being suspended or deposed on such grounds. As long as one could honestly affirm the Calvinist system of the Standards he was not expected to affirm every detail of the Confession.[54]

Practicing Discipline

A significant tension with his Old School brethren had been disagreement over the proper grounds of ecclesiastical discipline. Hodge believed that there was room for honest doctrinal diversity in the Presbyterian Church which did not impair the integrity of the system of doctrine in the Confession. Hodge declared, "It is not enough that a doctrine be erroneous, or that it be dangerous in its tendency; if it be not subversive of one or more of the constituent elements of the Reformed faith, it is not incompatible with the honest adoption of our Confession."[55]

---

[53] Ibid., 683-685.

[54] Ibid., 685.

[55] Charles Hodge, "Retrospect of the History of the Princeton Review," in *Biblical Repertory and Princeton Review*, Index Volume (Philadelphia: Peter Walker, 1871), 22.

Hodge described two classes of doctrines which illustrate the discord over allowable diversity among Old School men. There was one class of doctrines which though not unimportant have been tolerated in the "purest Calvinistic churches." This class of doctrines involved the permitted breadth in explaining the Reformed faith. Hodge cited differences in defining the imputation of Adam's sin, the atonement and regeneration. The key element was that one affirms the essentials of the doctrines integral to the system. On Christ's work of atonement, the critical question concerned a real substitutionary atonement and one should not be brought under discipline who can affirm this, though he may differ on the extent of that atonement. "If he taught that the work of Christ was a real satisfaction to the justice of God, it was not made a breaking point, whether he said it was designed exclusively for the elect, or for all mankind."[56]

A second class of doctrines, however, were "entirely inconsistent with the 'system of doctrine' taught in our Confession of Faith." Hodge enumerated several doctrines he placed in this category:

> Men came to teach that mankind are not born in a state of sin and condemnation; that no man is chargeable with either guilt or sin until he deliberately violates the known law of God; that sinners have plenary ability to do all that God requires of them; that regeneration is the sinner's own act; that God cannot certainly control the acts of free agents so as to prevent all sin, or the present amount of sin in a moral system; that the work of Christ is no proper satisfaction to Divine justice, but simply symbolical or didactic, designed to produce a moral impression on intelligent agents; that justification is not judicial, but involves a setting aside of the law, as when the Executive remits the penalty incurred by a criminal.[57]

The strain between Old School men arose because some in the strict Old School party desired to invoke discipline against not only men holding the second class of doctrines that subvert the Reformed system but also against those who merely differed in expressions of the same Calvinist faith. This censoriousness was divisive according to Hodge. He described Princeton's resistance to follow the extremists: "It was considered unreasonable and unfair to condemn one man for errors which had been, and continued to be, tolerated in others ... It was impossible that they could be brought with unanimity to concur in sustaining charges so heterogeneous, embracing doctrinal statements with which only a small minority of the church could agree."[58]

Before any formal reunion discussions between the two Presbyterian branches in the North began, Hodge publicly asked the question: "is it the present duty of these bodies to unite and become one church, as they were before the division?" He believed that this union was desirable if it could occur without the "sacrifice of principle" and if it could be a "real and harmonious" union. Do the original grounds

---

[56] Ibid., 23.
[57] Ibid., 23, 24.
[58] Ibid., 25.

that separated Presbyterians continue? Two issues, from his perspective, were the root of the split – the presence of Congregationalists in the Presbyterian body who never adopted the Presbyterian standards (for faith or order) and discord over doctrine. The major problem with the Congregationalists was not polity but that they were "almost without exception found among either the abettors or protectors of false doctrine."[59] For Hodge, the causes of the Presbyterian division culminated in a disagreement over the rightful exercise of discipline. He explained:

> As to doctrine, the difference was not that all the Old-school were orthodox and all the New-school heterodox; not that errors which a large part of the New-school party rejected did in fact more or less prevail among our ministers and churches; but the great and vital difference was, whether these errors should be a bar to ministerial communion.[60]

This diversity over discipline in doctrinal matters stemmed from distinct perspectives on the sense in which subscription to the Confession was to be understood. Discipline and admission to ministerial office in the New School (at least in some quarters) was governed by a perspective that viewed subscription as only binding one to the "essential and necessary doctrines" of Christianity not Calvinism *per se*. This interpretation, the Old School had implicitly disavowed by its condemnation of errors in 1837.[61]

Hodge's conviction was that the New School separated from the Old School, therefore, it was a question of whether or not the New School wanted to return to the Presbyterian Church and "whether they are willing to endeavor to secure, by the proper exercise of discipline, that the candidates for ordination and ordained ministers shall embrace the Calvinistic system of doctrine, as presented in the Westminster Confession and Catechisms, in its integrity. If they are willing to do this, we can see no conscientious objection to their return."[62] When reunion discussions officially commenced in 1866, Hodge fully immersed himself in these issues and in several instances found himself in the eye of the storm. In his annual reports on the General Assembly during the reunion negotiation years (1866-1870), he consistently questioned New School authenticity of commitment to the Confession because of what he considered the New School historic practice of "broad church" principles.

Opposed to reunion with the New School, Hodge insisted that the "preliminary act" of 1729 was not in actuality a part of the Adopting Act but "an act preliminary to the actual adoption of the Westminster Confession." It was the afternoon session

---

[59] Charles Hodge, "Principles of Church Union, and the Reunion of the Old and New School Presbyterians," *Biblical Repertory and Princeton Review* XXXVII (April 1865): 288, 296.

[60] Ibid., 296.

[61] Ibid., 289.

[62] Ibid., 299, 300.

which was understood by the Synod to be the adopting act itself.[63] Hodge was arguing against the position of New School historian E.H. Gillett whose *History of the Presbyterian Church*, suggested that the preliminary act should take precedence.[64] According to Gillett, the later statements of the Synod in 1730 and 1736 cannot fairly be taken to supersede the original intent of the Synod. Since the New School had published Gillett's work, Hodge took this as endorsement of Gillett's position which "advocates the lax principle as the fundamental and constitutional basis of the church."[65]

Hodge asserted that the original doctrinal points condemned by the Old School were the critical elements that distinguished the two parties. These points defined what the Old School considered to be doctrines that were outside the boundaries of acceptable confessional integrity. If the New School would but officially declare that they likewise condemned these doctrines then "a common understanding be attained as to what doctrines are, and what are not to be tolerated in the Presbyterian churches."[66] If reunion was to be upon the basis of adopting the standards of doctrine then there must be tacit commitment to the actual statements of the Confession itself. Hodge cited several examples where confessions of faith were adopted, yet, denied in practice. "Rationalists in Germany adopted the Augsburg Confession; Socinians in Geneva adopted Calvin's Catechism; men of all shades of doctrine, from Romanism to Pelagianism, subscribe the Thirty-nine Articles. This was against the conscience of Old-school Presbyterians, and they were determined never to sanction such modes of subscription."[67]

For Hodge, the safeguard was to require that "the doctrines constituting that system should be adopted in the form in which they are stated in the standards of the church." This was not asking for *ipsissima verba* for the whole Confession but a use of the confessional language itself to affirm adoption of the essentials of the system that make up the Confession. A practical solution that Hodge offered was to view the Shorter Catechism as containing the essentials of the Calvinist system of the Confession. "Let the basis of doctrine be the Confession and Catechisms without note or comment; and require that the doctrines should be adopted in the form therein stated. For ourselves we should be willing to license, or ordain any candidate for the ministry, (so far as his orthodoxy is concerned), who would intelligently and cordially answer in the affirmative the several questions in the Shorter Catechism.

---

[63] Charles Hodge, "General Assembly," *Biblical Repertory and Princeton Review* XXXIX (July 1867): 513.

[64] See E. H. Gillett, *History of the Presbyterian Church in the United States of America* (Philadelphia: Presbyterian Publication Committee, 1864), Vol. I, 47-58.

[65] Hodge, "General Assembly," (July 1867): 516. At this juncture, Hodge emphasized the afternoon minute as the "Adopting Act" to counter Gillett's argument. Previously, in his 1858 article, he had utilized the morning minute to make his arguments against the "every proposition" view; see *supra* n. 37.

[66] Hodge, "Principles of Church Union," 310.

[67] Hodge, "Protest and Answer," *Biblical Repertory and Princeton Review* XL (July 1868): 471, 472.

As much as this we believe the Church is bound in conscience and good faith to demand. More than this it were unreasonable to require."[68]

Hodge's thorough study of the historical sources and his own ecclesiastical experience had taught him that there was but one conclusion to the nineteenth-century question of subscription to the Westminster Confession. For American Presbyterians, confessional subscription had meant neither adherence to every jot and title of the Confession nor a minimalist "essentials of the gospel" position. Hodge emphatically stated:

> There never was a period in our history in which all our ministers agreed in adopting every proposition contained in the Confession and Catechisms. It is notorious that such agreement does not now exist. On the other hand, to demand less than the adoption of the Calvinistic system in its integrity, would destroy the purity and harmony of the church.[69]

Presbyterians in the eighteenth century, according to Hodge's analysis, had practiced a strict subscription imbedded in the original Adopting Act itself. This conservatism was promoted by an amazing unanimity of views among ministers of this era. By the early nineteenth century, however, Hodge observed more diversity of views among the clergy which was both expressed publicly and openly tolerated in a much larger Presbyterian Church. Nonetheless, these differences among orthodox Calvinists were considered allowable within the historic Presbyterian mode of adopting the Confession. According to Hodge, the criterion for acceptable diversity was the consideration of whether or not one's exception to the standards undermined the Reformed "system of doctrine" in the Confession. This was understood as the original intent of the Adopting Act which had allowed exceptions to certain portions of the Confession.

While Hodge advocated that the examination of ministers must be left in the hands of presbyteries, he was skeptical about some of the New School presbyteries carrying out this responsibility prudently. His objections to reunion would always return ultimately to his doubts about New School resolve to exercise discipline. Hodge believed that some of the New School men, who had habitually practiced extreme toleration, would continue to countenance a degree of laxity beyond that demanded by an honest use of the ordination vow.

---

[68] Ibid., 476. This is an intriguing suggestion. What makes it interesting is the number of doctrinal points (in the Confession of Faith) which the Shorter Catechism does not include. This was certainly the most far-reaching proposal Hodge ever made on the subject of confessional subscription.

[69] Hodge, "Principles of Church Union," 304.

CHAPTER 9

Presbyterians in the South

Any retelling of the nineteenth-century Southern Presbyterian[1] story must highlight the long controversy over domestic slavery and the journey to emancipation. The African question seemed to lie just below the surface of every major crisis Presbyterians faced before, during and after the War Between the States. Whether it was *ante-bellum* abolition frenzy, self-righteous Yankee emancipation or the oppressive Reconstruction era, Southerners could not escape the all-encompassing ramifications of slavery. Solidarity against these forces was one of the factors driving Presbyterians in the South toward one another.

Agitation over the slavery question was the constant irritant of Southern Presbyterians during the first half of the nineteenth century. Even after the schism of 1837/38, neither party could fully escape the all-consuming question. The New School would become stridently anti-slavery while the Old School attempted to avoid the controversy. For both branches of the Presbyterian Church, it was a festering sore that would eventually poison the unity of the church. The second half of the nineteenth century would witness American Presbyterians divided North and South rather than Old School and New School.

The New School General Assembly of 1839 had declared that the slavery question should be handled by the lower judicatories acknowledging that the church was comprised of those "who honestly differ in opinion" on the subject of slavery.[2] Nevertheless, by 1846 the New School pronounced outright denunciation of slavery as "an unrighteous and oppressive system, and is opposed to the prescriptions of the law of God, to the spirit and precepts of the Gospel." At the same time, the New School declared its opposition to "all divisive and schismatical measures, tending to destroy the unity and disturb the peace of our churches" indicating its desire to avoid schism over the issue. Twenty-nine delegates voted against the 1846 anti-slavery resolutions and of these twenty-one were from Southern states.[3]

---

[1] The terms "Southern Presbyterian" or "Southern Church" will be used broadly to refer to antebellum Presbyterians located in the Southern states (both Old School and New School) as well as the later separate denomination, The Presbyterian Church in the Confederate States of America (PCCSA), 1861-1865 and The Presbyterian Church in the United States (PCUS), 1865-1983.

[2] *Minutes of the General Assembly of the Presbyterian Church in the United States of America.* (New School) 1839 (New York: Published by Stated Clerks, 1838-1858. Reprint; Philadelphia: Presbyterian Board of Publication and Sabbath-School Work, 1894), 22.

[3] Ibid., 28, 29.

By 1850 the New School pressed the issue again and began to raise the controversial specter of church discipline for slaveholding. In 1853 the New School General Assembly asked presbyteries to report on their progress in cleansing the church of the evil. Southern presbyteries ignored this directive. Three years later, in the wake of the debate in Kansas and the Dred Scott case, New School abolitionists pushed for disciplinary action against Southerners. Reaction in the South was predictable. Presbyterians in the South had historically urged the Northern brethren to be patient and let the South rid herself of slavery in her own way. With threats of church discipline at the threshold, Southern New School men responded by defending their peculiar institution. New School minister Dr. Fred A. Ross of Alabama wrote, "Let the Northern philanthropist learn from the Bible that the relation of master and slave is not sin per se. Let him know that slavery is simply an evil in certain circumstances ... Let him learn that slavery like all evils has its corresponding and greater good; that the Southern slave, though degraded compared with his master, is elevated and ennobled compared with his brethren in Africa." And to the South, Ross said: "Let him believe that slavery, although not a sin, is a degraded condition, – the evil, the curse of the South, – yet having blessings in its time to the South and to the Union. Let him know that slavery is to pass away in the fullness of Providence. Let the South believe this, and prepare to obey the hand that moves their destiny."[4]

Ross and his fellow Southern brethren had united with the New School out of conviction. They were committed to the theological principles upon which the New School had stood for twenty years. One of those foundational principles had been freedom of conscience on slave holding. This liberty had been steadily eroding over the two decades of New School existence as a separate body. The original compact was being severed by New School abolitionists who mocked the Southern conscience and pushed through the Assembly ecclesiastical pronouncements condemning slavery. Southerners felt themselves more and more excluded from the New School body as Northern agitation became intolerable.

United Synod of the South

Having endured the relentless "abolition spirit" in the New School body for many years, the Southern New School men finally abandoned the New School Assembly to form their own denomination.[5] Southern delegates to the 1857 New School General Assembly at Cleveland called for a new Assembly to be formed in an "Address of Protest" against the New School body. The address protested the "political agitation" and "ultra abolitionist sentiments" in the New School that were advocating discipline for slaveholding. Southern New School men countered: "there is not the most remote allusion to slave-holding in our standards," therefore, this is a

---

[4] Fred A. Ross, Slavery *Ordained of God*. (Philadelphia: J.B. Lippincott & Co.,1857),1.

[5] Some material in this chapter and chapter ten has appeared earlier in *The Westminster Theological Journal* 66:1 (Spring 2004): 203-226. Used by permission.

"palpable violation of the spirit and letter of the Constitution of the Church." If the church disciplines slave holders, this will be "an ecclesiastical despotism as tyrannical as that which has distinguished the Church of Rome.... we consider that the Assembly has so far departed from the Constitution of the Church as to render our adherence to it undesirable and impossible."[6]

The stated goal of these protesters was to form a new ecclesiastical body "in which the agitation of the Slavery question will be unknown." An invitation was issued to "all Constitutional Presbyterians" throughout the land to unite with them in a new organization. The unifying principles of this new denomination would be commitment to "a common basis as to doctrine and government — and an understanding that, however, we may differ in our views respecting Slavery, the subject is never to be introduced into the Assembly either by Northern or Southern men....."[7]

Having declared their intent to depart the New School, then came the challenging task of determining the next course of action. Some opposed an independent course and favored returning to the New School, others desired that a new church be constituted; still others expressed hope that perhaps a reunion with the Old School body should be pursued. The Southern New School churches called for a Washington convention to be held in August 1857 in order to decide the future of their congregations.[8]

The Washington (Richmond) convention of 1857 adopted five resolutions: 1) Presbyteries in connection with the New School are urged to withdraw. 2) No ecclesiastical discipline may be exercised apart from the Constitution of the church. 3) The General Assembly may not judge lower judicatories without constitutional process. 4) Presbyteries opposed to the agitation of slavery are urged to appoint delegates to an Assembly to meet in April 1858 in Knoxville for the purpose of organizing "The United Synod of the Presbyterian Church in the United States of America." 5) The Convention delegates resolved to "adhere to and abide by the Confession of Faith of the Presbyterian Church, as containing the system of doctrine taught in the Holy Scripture; and that we adhere to the Form of Government and Book of Discipline of said Church."[9]

An additional resolution was adopted at Richmond which expressed a desire for the new United Synod to pursue union discussions "with our Old School brethren, could it be effected on terms acceptable on both sides." This had been a sentiment of some Southern New School men as early as the 1840s. Now, many of the churches had a strong penchant to unite with the Old School rather than form a new

---

[6] "The United Synod of the South" in *Presbyterian Historical Almanac and Annual Remembrancer of the Church for 1858-1859* (Philadelphia: Joseph M. Wilson, 1859), 135, 136.

[7] Ibid.

[8] Harold M. Parker, *The United Synod of the South* (Presbyterian Historical Society, 1988), 158-162.

[9] *Presbyterian Historical Almanac (1858-1859)*, 138. See also Parker, *United Synod of the South*, 173.

ecclesiastical body. Those favoring the pursuit of union with the Old School believed the divisive issues of 1837-38 had subsided.[10] When the resolution on potential union came to the floor of the convention there was no little debate upon the subject. Four primary concerns were raised against reunion with the Old School: the Excision Acts that must be repudiated, questions about subscription and the reexamination of ministers, doctrinal differences and the slavery issue. Dr. Charles Read of Richmond stated that union with the Old School would be a mistake for it was only a matter of time before Southern men in the Old School Assembly would be condemned for slavery just as the Southern New School had experienced in their body. A chief antagonist to union was A.H.H. Boyd[11] of Winchester, Virginia who told the Richmond Convention that with his theological views, it would be impossible to unite with the Old School Church.[12] Despite this strong opposition, the resolution for reunion discussions was adopted.[13]

The Old School press responded to reports of this resolution in very negative terms.[14] There was little interest in pursuing reunion with New School brethren. The *Central Presbyterian* had an observer at the Richmond Convention and reported how "incomprehensible" it was to see such doctrinal diversity among the Southern New School men. Dr. Boyd tried to answer this "incomprehensible mystery" in the *Presbyterian Witness* by explaining the contrasting Old School/New School methods of subscribing to the Confession of Faith. Boyd explained:

> The Old School insist that the Confession of Faith must be received, not merely as a whole, but as in every part the infallible truth. It is to them the Bible transcribed. They embrace it, as one of the editors has said. 'cover and all' – not only so, they insist that it must be understood in a certain prescribed way – they give no latitude of interpretation – Hence, then ministers are usually very careful to adopt the forms of expression common among the leaders of their sect. However wide the difference may in reality be among them in their theological views, by using nearly the same phrases, they avoid the appearance of difference. The New School on the other hand, subscribe to the Confession of Faith as their fathers before them subscribed to it. They receive it 'as the system of doctrines contained in the Holy Scriptures' – 'for substance of doctrine' if you please. They allow a latitude of interpretation. They have no

---

[10] Parker, *United Synod of the South*, 164-167. For a detailed account of the debate at the Richmond Convention see *Central Presbyterian*, September 5, 1857.

[11] Andrew Hunter Holmes Boyd, D.D., a Princeton Seminary graduate, was licensed to preach by the Presbytery of Winchester in 1837. From 1842 to 1865 he served as pastor of the New School Presbyterian Church in Winchester, Virginia.

[12] Thomas Cary Johnson, *A Brief Sketch of the United Synod of the Presbyterian Church in the United States of America*. Reprint, Vol. VIII (American Society of Church History), 16,17.

[13] The final vote was 10 in favor and 9 against the resolution according to Dr. Breckinridge of the Old School. He was opposed to any discussions with the New School and told the Old School Assembly that he agreed with the nine New School men! See George Howe "The General Assembly of 1858," *Southern Presbyterian Review* XI (1859): 326.

[14] See Parker, *United Synod of the South*, 169-170.

'Procrustean bed.' They do not insist that every minister in the connection shall use the same forms of expression, especially in matters not essential. – It is part of their creed, that while the bones and sinews of Calvinism are preserved, each minister may use whatever drapery best suits his taste, in making them presentable to the world. True, our Old School brethren cannot always see the Calvinism in the new clothes it sometimes wears; it looks suspicious to them, because it appears without the 'blue stockings;' but that is their fault, not ours.[15]

New School papers were also skeptical about reunion with the Old School and listed multiple reasons why reunion with the Old School would be impossible including differences in both doctrine and the manner of receiving the Confession of Faith. Dr. Boyd wrote that the "same differences exist now" as they did in 1837. The Old School and New School preach and teach differently on the atonement, original sin and human ability. Boyd continued, "... their General Assemblies continue to publish on these subjects, the same errors against which the New School have always protested." He further objected to the Old School method of subscription. "The Old School insist on all their ministers adopting the Confession, in its very letter – 'cover and all' – the doctrine of non-elect infants included. The New School only receive it as a general system of doctrines, acknowledging that there are some things in it, which if rigidly interpreted, they do not believe. And this, it should be remembered, was the manner of subscription among the fathers of Presbyterianism in the earliest times." In addition to these two key issues, Boyd listed several other reasons why he believed reunion with the Old School would be a mistake. He concluded: "Love them as followers of Christ we will, but unite with them until they repent of their treatment of us, and evince a better spirit, and return to the basis of the Constitution and the teachings of the Bible, we neither can nor will, while our present views of truth, and duty, remain."[16]

In April of 1858 The United Synod was officially organized in Knoxville. One of its first actions was the formal adoption of the Westminster Standards, Form of Government and Book of Discipline of the Presbyterian Church. The Southern New School declared: "... the United Synod do adhere to and abide by the Confession of Faith of the Presbyterian Church, as containing the system of doctrine taught in the Holy Scriptures;"[17] In order to stake out her ground, the new church also adopted a "Declaration of Principles" which articulated the foundations undergirding their new organization. Nine principles were enumerated, the first of which dealt with

---

[15] A.B. *Presbyterian Witness*, November 24, 1857. Boyd confessed, "To us, it is no matter of surprise that members of the Richmond Convention did not use the same expressions in explaining their theological views. They would hardly have been New School if they had."

[16] A.B. *Presbyterian Witness*, March 16, 1858. Boyd's additional objections included: difference in constitutional principles, wide dissimilarity of temper, the required reexamination of ministers, unsoundness of the Old School on slavery.

[17] *Presbyterian Historical Almanac* 1858-1859, 143-145; *Minutes of the United Synod of the Presbyterian Church in the United States, 1858*, (MS, Montreat, NC, Presbyterian Historical Foundation), 7-11.

how the United Synod understood subscription to the Westminster Confession and Catechisms. The statement read:

> In thus adopting the Westminster Confession of Faith as containing the system of doctrine taught in the Holy Scriptures, we adopt it in the sense in which we believe the fathers of the American Presbyterian Church received it, to wit: not as requiring an agreement in sentiment with every opinion expressed in said Confession, but a belief in the fundamental doctrines of Christianity, and in the doctrines which distinguish the Calvinistic system from the Pelagian, Socinian, Arminian, and other systems of Theology. This system we understand to include the following doctrines, viz: the Trinity; the Incarnation and Supreme Deity of Christ; the Fall and Original Sin; Atonement; Justification by Faith; Personal Election; Effectual Calling; Perseverance of the Saints; Eternal happiness of the righteous, and Eternal Punishment of the wicked. Whilst various modes of stating and explaining these truths may be adopted, yet when they are received according to the usual way of interpreting language, and as they have been understood by the great body of the Presbyterian Church in this country, from the period of the adoption of the Westminster Confession, in 1729, to the present day, the requisitions of the Confession of Faith are complied with, and all such persons are to be regarded as having received as their doctrinal creed this system of doctrines taught in the Holy Scriptures.[18]

It is noteworthy that each of the so-called "five points" of Calvinism would be covered under these heads of doctrine as well as the "essential truths of Christianity," i.e., orthodox views on the Trinity and Christology. The distinctive Reformed "doctrines of grace" are implied in the specific declaration that it is the "Calvinistic system" as opposed to the Arminian system that is in view.

Reunion Proposal and Old School Response

The Bills and Overtures Committee of the 1858 United Synod Assembly presented a paper on a proposed basis for reunion with the Old School. The report recommended that the United Synod appoint a Committee to confer with a committee from the Old School Assembly. Again, many of the New School men were reluctant to pursue union discussions with the Old School; nevertheless, they had a mandate from the Richmond Convention to follow through with a proposal for union. Some of the Southern New School churches were expecting this move as part of their consideration for joining the United Synod.

Dr. Boyd voiced his views that neither body was ready for a reunion. Initial reactions to the reunion idea among Old School men had been very negative and Boyd believed New School self respect would be compromised by overtures for union. The principles adopted by the United Synod had been his convictions for 20

---

[18] For the full text see *Minutes of the United Synod of the South*, 1858, 7-11; *Presbyterian Historical Almanac 1858-59*, 146-7; Parker, *United Synod of the South*, Appendix B, 312-317. The remainder of the "Declaration of Principles" dealt with the constitutional authority of the church and slavery.

years and he would not compromise them. One minister stated that if New School men were to find a home in the Old School, they must let us say that "Jesus Christ tasted death for every man." Dr. J.D. Mitchell told the Assembly that if the other branch would accept these principles there ought to be a jubilee proclaimed throughout the land. "If they will agree to receive the Confession of Faith on the plan of the Adopting Act of 1729, they will have yielded the point, the great point which had divided us so long, and we can cheerfully unite with them."[19] Several other delegates expressed their skepticism about the venture, suggesting that only a letter be sent rather than a committee. Despite these concerns, the United Synod proceeded to adopt the report and appointed a Committee to approach the Old School with terms for reuniting the two bodies.

The "Proposed Terms of Union" in the report noted that these terms are "indispensable to an honourable union on our part." Article one of the proposed plan stated: "We agree to unite as ecclesiastical bodies by declaring, as this Synod now does, our approval of the Westminster Confession of Faith, and Larger and Shorter Catechisms, as an orthodox and excellent system of [C]hristian doctrine – and also our adherence to the plan of Worship, Government, and the Discipline contained in the Westminster Directory."[20]

The proposed doctrinal terms reiterated the stance taken in the "Declaration of Principles." The third article read:

> Both parties agree that it is consistent with the requirements of the Westminster Confession of Faith, to receive said Confession according to the Adopting Act of 1729, to wit: as containing all the essential truths of Christianity, and also the doctrines that distinguish the Calvinistic from the Pelagian, Socinian, and Arminian systems of Theology. We agree, likewise, in believing that this system of doctrine includes the following truths, viz: the Trinity; the Incarnation and Deity of Christ; the Fall and Original Sin; Atonement; Justification by Faith; Personal Election; Effectual Calling; Perseverance of the Saints; the Eternal Happiness of the righteous, and Eternal Punishment of the wicked.[21]

Other terms in the plan addressed: prohibiting ecclesiastical judicatories from condemning or excluding other judicatories without trial; slaveholding cannot be a bar to church membership; and "in effecting this union, the Presbyteries connected with this Synod shall be united as Presbyteries, and without an examination of their ministers...."[22] The final article (8) of the plan, stipulated that should the Old School not favor reunion, the United Synod delegation propose "the establishment of a mutual correspondence in the future between us as ecclesiastical bodies." The

---

[19] "Meeting of the United Synod of the Presbyterian Church in the United States." *The Presbyterian Magazine* VIII (May, 1858): 213-216.

[20] For the full text of the reunion proposal see *Minutes of the United Synod* 1858, 14-15; *Presbyterian Historical Almanac* (1858-9) 146-147.

[21] Ibid.

[22] Ibid.

concluding term no doubt exposed the suspicion among many New School men that this blatantly partisan plan would indeed fail. The proposal as a whole was almost exclusively New School in orientation and, as might be suspected, was met with swift rejection by the Old School press and the Old School Assembly.[23]

C. Van Rensselaer, editor of the Old School *Presbyterian Magazine*, gave his readers a typical Old School response when he wrote that the New School terms would be "a virtual surrender by the Old School of principles and measures, several of which are regarded by a large portion of our body, as having been the salvation of the Presbyterian Church." He listed several items which are "unreasonable and absurd," one of which is "that the Adopting Act of 1729, required no more explicit reception of the Confession of Faith, than a general assent, i.e., for substance of doctrine."[24]

A desire for reunion with the New School had been expressed by some in the Southern Old School Synods of Virginia and Kentucky as early as the 1840s. The subject of reunion had reemerged in 1856 when the Old School Synod of Nashville expressed its wishes to reunite with the New School Presbytery of West Tennessee upon the basis of the reunion of the Synods of New York and Philadelphia in 1758.[25] On the whole, however, Southern Old Schoolers were not yet disposed to join hands with their New School brethren. The United Synod's overture for reunion was spurned by Southern stalwarts such as Robert J. Breckinridge, Moses Hoge, Benjamin M. Palmer and James H. Thornwell.[26] Breckinridge, at the 1858 Old School Assembly, protested the United Synod's assertion that the Old School should retract her action against the exscinded Synods, "a thing we did considerately, and prayerfully, and which has been approved by the Church, and approved by God." Hoge objected to appointing a Committee of Conference to meet with United Synod representatives because "they propose to us to change our views" which is "indelicate and improper."[27]

---

[23] See *Minutes of the General Assembly of the Presbyterian Church in the United States of America* (Old School) 1858 (Philadelphia: Presbyterian Board of Publication, 1837-1869), 289, 290.

[24] *Presbyterian Magazine* (May 1858): 216. Van Rensselaer, along with Dr. B.M. Palmer and a third presbyter were appointed as representatives of the Old School to meet with the New School committee and officially receive their reunion proposal.

[25] *Minutes of the Presbyterian Church in the United States*, 1857 (Old School), 39. When the Synod of Nashville's Minutes came up for review by the General Assembly, the Assembly noted that this proposed union was an exception because it was imperative that presbyteries "examine all who make application for admission into their bodies...."

[26] Dr. Thornwell died in 1862, therefore, he did not participate in the later debates in the Southern Presbyterian Church over reunion with the United Synod. With his high view of subscription to the Westminster Standards, one surmises that he would have stood with the other South Carolinians in opposing reunion with the New School. For an overview of Thornwell's thought on the Westminster Confession see W. Duncan Rankin, *James Henley Thornwell and the Westminster Confession of Faith* (Greenville, SC: Apress, 1986).

[27] George Howe, "The General Assembly of 1858" *Southern Presbyterian Review* XI (1859): 326.

Despite these and other objections, the Committee of Conference was appointed and met with the corresponding committee of the Southern New School. Having heard the United Synod's terms of union and reporting these back to the Old School Assembly, the Assembly then officially replied that both the "terms of union" and the "declaration of principles" adopted by the United Synod "do not form a basis for Conference." The Old School minute further stated,

> ... it can hardly be unexpected that we decline any official conference based on terms which appear to us to involve a condemnation of ourselves.... The subjects upon which the whole New School body differed from us, at the period of their secession from us, and the subjects upon which the two very unequal portions of that body have recently separated from each other, are questions upon which we, as a denomination, are at peace, and with regard to the whole of which we see no occasion to revise the understood and unalterable faith of our Church, or to enter upon fruitless conferences.[28]

The minute was unanimously adopted. The Old School had no desire to become entangled with the complex issues a reunion with the United Synod would entail.[29]

The New School proposal had seemed rather disingenuous – could the Old School be expected to yield every principle for which she had stood? It appears the United Synod's "Terms of Union" were more about her own self-identity and political necessity rather than a genuine overture for union. Undoubtedly, many sincerely desired to join with the Old School, however, a unilateral pronouncement of principles before negotiations began was sure to fail. Most of the New School men knew this was a futile attempt from the beginning. Despite this inauspicious beginning, just six years later the Old School and New School in the South would consummate union. By 1861 the "peaceful" Old School ranks would be abruptly divided and reunion with fellow Southern Calvinists would become more attractive.

Old School Schism of 1861

The Old School Presbyterian Church managed to maintain ecclesiastical oneness by taking a more conservative stance on slavery than that pursued by the New School. Typical of the Old School attitude were two resolutions adopted by the 1845

---

[28] *Minutes of the General Assembly*, 1858 (Old School), 230. Howe said that this Assembly minute with amendments was authored by Breckinridge. See Howe, "General Assembly of 1858," 329, 330.

[29] Thomas Cary Johnson reported an underlying unspoken reason for Old School resistance to union discussions. He described the Old School attitude: "She was not only tenacious of reputation for strict construction in theology, she had in the main kept clear of partisan and Un-Biblical discussion of the relation of slavery. She did not propose to excite such discussions at once by taking into her own communion a body with such a history as the United Synod had." This obstacle would be removed by 1861 with Southern secession from the Old School body, thus helping pave the way for reinvigorated reunion discussions. See Thomas Cary Johnson, *A Brief Sketch of the United Synod of the Presbyterian Church in the United States of America*, 27.

General Assembly: "Resolved, 1st That the General Assembly of the Presbyterian Church in the United States was originally organized, and has since continued the bond of union in the Church upon the conceded principle that the existence of domestic slavery, under the circumstances in which it is found in the southern portion of this country is no bar to Christian communion." The second resolution declared that to raise the question of church discipline for the holding of slaves was to be deplored "as tending to the dissolution of the union of our beloved country, and which every enlightened Christian will oppose as bringing about a ruinous and unnecessary schism between brethren who maintain a common faith."[30]

The Old School approach to this very sensitive issue met with the approbation of the South. Southern churches in the Old School were respected by their Northern counterparts and not persecuted for maintaining the slave system of the South. Alongside this ecclesiastical detente, however, was a crusade by Northern abolitionist agitators to rid the South of her peculiar evil. Presbyterians in the South deeply resented this radical abolition spirit. Southern resolve hardened as abolitionist rhetoric became more vicious. In 1840 Robert L. Dabney appraised Southern resistance in a letter to a friend: "I do believe that if these mad fanatics had let us alone, in twenty years we should have made Virginia a Free State. As it is, their unauthorized attempts to strike off the fetter of our slaves has but riveted them on the faster. Does this fact arise from the perversity of our natures? I believe that it does in part. We are less inclined to that which we know to be our duty because persons, who have no right to interfere, demand it of us."[31]

One of the chief arguments for keeping the abolitionist cause out of ecclesiastical deliberations was the doctrine of the spirituality of the church. Slavery was a civil relation and therefore belongs to the political sphere. The Church can only say what the Bible says, no more and no less; and the Holy Scriptures do not declare slavery sinful. Dr. James Henley Thornwell of South Carolina forcefully articulated these ideas in a 1851 essay, "The Relation of the Church to Slavery," which was widely

---

[30] *Minutes of the General Assembly*, 1845 (Old School), 16-18. E.T. Thompson underscored the importance of the Old School position of 1845: "The Old School Presbyterian cord did not snap until secession and war had come, and it was the action of the 1845 Assembly, sustained by subsequent Assemblies, which enabled it to remain intact." Ernest Trice Thompson, *Presbyterians in the South*, vol. 1 (Richmond: John Knox Press, 1963), 532.

[31] Quoted by Frank Bell Lewis in "Robert Lewis Dabney, Southern Presbyterian Apologist." Unpublished thesis (Duke University, 1946), 40; cited by Thompson, *Presbyterians in the South*, vol.1, 535. The hardened Southern perspective on slavery was still evident many years later in Dabney; see Robert L. Dabney, *A Defense of Virginia [And through Her of the South] in Recent and Pending Contests Against the Sectional Party* (1867; reprint, Harrison, Virginia: Sprinkle Publications, 1991).

distributed among Southern Presbyterians.[32] Thornwell passionately desired to preserve both the union and the Old School Church.

As hard as the peacemakers tried, they could not stem the rising tide of sectional animosity that was engulfing America. The political and social bitterness that had been smoldering for many years began breaking forth into flames by the late 1850s. In October of 1859 John Brown's raid at Harper's Ferry sent a wave of terror throughout the South. With Abraham Lincoln's election in 1860, whom the South considered a radical on the slavery question, the dissolution of the union appeared imminent. Amidst it all, the Old School still hoped to preserve ecclesiastical unity, nonetheless, with South Carolina's secession in December 1860 and the prospects of further armed conflict, the popular pressure was too great even for the resolve of the Old School.

The Old School Assembly convened in May 1861 in Philadelphia with very few Southern commissioners in attendance. An amiable spirit prevailed among the brethren, yet, the inevitable question had to emerge. After twelve days and much debate the moment of truth finally arrived when Dr. Gardiner Spring's resolution, which asserted the Assembly's loyalty to the Federal Government, was approved 156 to 66.[33] Immediately a protest was entered by Dr. Charles Hodge and 57 other commissioners. The protest stated: "The General Assembly in thus deciding a political question, and in making that decision practically a condition of membership to the Church, has, in our judgment, violated the Constitution of the Church, and usurped the prerogative of its Divine Master."[34] The protest was rebuffed and Southern Presbyterians, believing they had been unconstitutionally exscinded by the Assembly, began to withdraw in order to form a new and independent church. Southern indignation was expressed by each Synod as it formally withdrew from the Old School Assembly over the next few months.[35] To

---

[32] James H. Thornwell, "The Relation of the Church to Slavery," *Southern Presbyterian Review*, January 1852, in The Collected Writings of James Henley Thornwell, Vol. IV (Richmond: Presbyterian Committee of Publication, 1886), 381-397.

[33] See *Minutes of the General Assembly*,1861 (Old School, North). E.T. Thompson described the volatile atmosphere surrounding the Gardner Spring resolution: "To pass the resolution, it was recognized, would force the withdrawal of the Southern presbyteries; to refuse to do so, it was argued, might provoke secessions in the North. Heavy pressure was brought to bear from outside - by visitors in the balcony, by letters and telegrams from 'back home.' One morning a clerical-looking effigy was found hanging upon a tree opposite the church where the sessions of the Assembly were held, with a shingle attached to its feet upon which was inscribed, 'Death thus to clerical traitors.' " E.T. Thompson, *Presbyterians in the South*, vol. I, 564.

[34] Ibid., 339-341.

[35] For example, the Synod of North Carolina stated: "... whereas, by the tyranny and usurpation of the Government at Washington, the safeguards of the constitution have been broken down, threatening all that is dear in civil liberty and all that is precious in the inheritance received from our fathers; and whereas the several Presbyteries composing this Synod have in view of these deeds, as well as in view of the extraordinary endorsement of them by the General Assembly of the Presbyterian Church in the United States, requiring us

have remained a part of the Northern Assembly would have been tantamount to treason.[36]

All presbyteries that withdrew from the Old School North were invited to Augusta, Georgia to participate in the organization of a new Assembly. One of the early acts of the new organization was to seek the unity of all Presbyterian and Reformed bodies in the South. At the Augusta Assembly, the Committee on Foreign Correspondence offered a report which recommended that the Southern Church "earnestly endeavor to draw closer the bonds of Christian intercourse and communion between all Churches of like faith and order in the Confederate States of America." Citing Christ's words, "that they all may be one," the committee professed that they were "... impelled by a sincere desire to meet the full measure of responsibility which devolves upon us, as a branch of Christ's visible Church, in the accomplishment of this vastly important petition...." The report was adopted and to accomplish its end, the Assembly commissioned delegates to the Associate Reformed Synod of the South, the United Synod of the Presbyterian Church, the General Assembly of the Cumberland Presbyterian Church, the Independent Presbyterian Church and the German Reformed Synod. The delegates were given "full power and authority to arrange and adopt articles of permanent intercourse and correspondence, which, however, shall be submitted to the Assembly for its ratification or rejection."[37] A new spirit of fraternity overcame these Southerners who had formerly disavowed associations with Arminian Cumberland Presbyterians, unorthodox Independent Presbyterians and the New School United Synod. Undoubtedly the war had altered perspectives on the meaning of Christian unity. The action of the Assembly to seek closer relations with these bodies would be the first step in several Presbyterian unions in the Southern states during the 1860s.

Union with the Independent Presbyterian Church

The General Convention of the Independent Presbyterian Church was a very small denomination with churches in both Carolinas. By the time of the reunion with the Southern Presbyterian Church in 1863, the Independent Presbyterians only brought 11 churches, 4 ministers and about 900 members into the union.[38] The genesis of the Independent Presbyterian Church lay in the doctrinal aberrations of a Presbyterian

---

and our Churches to approve and pray for the success of measures so tyrannical and iniquitous, have formally and solemnly dissolved all connection with said General Assembly...." *Minutes of the Synod of North Carolina*, 1861, 18, 19. (Presbyterian Historical Society, Montreat, NC).

[36] Thompson, *Presbyterians in South*, II, 14.

[37] *Minutes of the General Assembly of the Presbyterian Church in the Confederates States of America*, 1861, 13.

[38] See Harold M. Parker, Jr., "Southern Presbyterian Ecumenism: Six Successful Unions," *Journal of Presbyterian History* 56 (1978): 93-95. Parker includes two tables which show the numerical statistics related to each of the six unions during the years 1863-1874.

clergyman, the Reverend William Cummins Davis. Davis withdrew from the Presbyterian Church in 1811 and was tried and deposed *in absentia*. The two South Carolina congregations that Davis served also withdrew from the Presbyterian Church and along with three other congregations adopted their own constitution in October of 1813.

Davis' peculiar theology was essentially contained in his treatise, *The Gospel Plan*.[39] In 1810 the Presbyterian General Assembly had condemned the book. The committee reviewing the book reported to the Assembly a list of errors that were "calculated to produce useless or mischievous speculations" and was of a "very dangerous tendency." The errors were placed in several different categories: doctrines "contrary to the Confession of our Church," modes of expression that are "unhappy," and unguarded expressions that are "contrary to the letter and spirit of the Confession." The erroneous doctrines were:

> 1) 'the active obedience of Christ constitutes no part of the righteousness by which a sinner is justified'; 2) 'obedience to the moral law was not required as the condition of the covenant of works'; 3) 'God himself is as bound in duty, (not obedience) to his creatures, as his creatures are bound in obedience or duty to him.... God's will is not the standard of right and wrong'; 4) 'God could not make Adam, or any other creature, holy or unholy'; 5) 'regeneration must be a consequence of faith; faith precedes regeneration'; 6) 'faith in the first act of it is not a holy act'; 7) 'Christians may sin willfully and habitually'; 8) 'if God has to plant all the principal parts of salvation in a sinner's heart to enable him to believe, the gospel plan is quite out of his reach, and consequently does not suit his case; and it must be impossible for God to condemn a man for unbelief, for no law condemns a man for not doing what he cannot do.'[40]

These doctrinal points were unmistakably Arminian and condemned by the General Assembly as "contrary to the Confession of Faith of our Church, and the word of God."[41]

Most of the Independent congregations were in upstate South Carolina and had close interaction with Presbyterian ministers in Bethel Presbytery; there were also a few churches within the bounds of Concord Presbytery of North Carolina. After Davis's death in 1831, Bethel Presbytery overtured the 1833 General Assembly to allow communion with the Independents. The General Assembly forbade this, questioning the Independent ministers' ordination, therefore, the proposal for shared communion "cannot be in the order of the gospel, and ought to be discouraged and discountenanced by every friend of the Redeemer's Kingdom."[42] Notwithstanding this ardent opposition from "Regular Presbyterians," the Independent Church

---

[39] William C. Davis, *The Gospel Plan, or Systematical Treatise on the Leading Doctrines of Salvation* (Philadelphia: Hopkins and Earle; Boston: Farrand, Mallory and Co., 1809). See *supra* chp.3, "Revivals in the South."

[40] *Minutes of the General Assembly of the Presbyterian Church in the United States of America* (Philadelphia, 1789-1837) 1810, 452, 453.

[41] Ibid.

[42] *Minutes of the General Assembly*, 1833, 493.

appeared to move back toward a more Calvinistic position on election, the decrees and perseverance of the saints by 1837.[43]

In 1857 Bethel Presbytery again approached the General Assembly concerning the Independent Presbyterian Church. This time it was a question of full ecclesiastical union with the Independents. The previous year, the Independent's General Convention had presented to Bethel Presbytery a proposed plan of union. The Independents believed the time for union had come. Article three of the plan dealt with the doctrinal question. The ministers, officers and churches consented to receive the Confession of Faith of the Presbyterian Church and the Book of Discipline. In addition to this confessional commitment, the Independents also asserted "the right to hold and teach these peculiar views of doctrine which have distinguished us as a denomination, without subjecting ourselves to censure or discipline, on the part of the Presbyterian Church; promising, however, that whilst we hold these doctrines to be true, and claim the right to teach them, yet in view of the 'peace and unity' of the church, we will not make them prominent points in our ministrations ..."[44]

Bethel Presbytery was convinced that the teaching of Davis's *Gospel Plan* had been abandoned by the Independents and they had confidence in the soundness of these brethren. Bethel Presbytery almost unanimously desired the union; Bethel's vote was 27 in favor and 3 opposed. It should be noted, however, that Bethel Presbytery revised portions of article three, no doubt to make the plan less objectionable to the Old School Assembly.[45] When the question about the Independent's desire to keep their doctrines surfaced at the 1857 Assembly, representatives of Bethel Presbytery answered that the Independents explain their views in a way that is satisfactory and they have committed not to make their peculiar doctrines prominent in their preaching.[46]

Even with these assurances, the Assembly declared it "cannot sanction the precise terms of the covenant that has actually been made." Thornwell is reported to have said on the floor of the Assembly: "We cannot receive into our ministry any who claim the right to teach doctrines not in our standards. This, those ministers do claim, although Bethel Presbytery says they are sound. These churches in the main are sound, but some parties in them retain their attachment to Mr. Davis's tenets. Our proposed action is just to say, we cannot receive you unless in good faith you

---

[43] See *The Constitution and Form of Government of the Independent Presbyterian Church in the United States of America*, 95,96; also, Harold M. Parker, Jr. "The Independent Presbyterian Church and the Reunion in the South, 1813-1863," *The Journal of Presbyterian History* 50 (Summer 1972): 92.

[44] *Minutes of the General Convention of the Independent Presbyterian Church*, 1856, 4-6; quoted in Parker "Independent Presbyterian Church,"102.

[45] Ibid.

[46] *Minutes of the General Assembly*, 1857 (Old School),13. It is also noteworthy that the Independent Churches had been involved with the emotional revivalism of the era, practiced "lay ordination," and embraced a hybrid ecclesiology that granted the General Convention no jurisdiction over local churches. These innovations were not the practices of the Old School.

adopt our standards. This is as much as we can do, or as ought to be asked."[47] The report of the committee of bills and overtures concerning this matter was unanimously adopted; the report described the issue in this way:

> The privilege claimed by the Independent ministers of holding and teaching doctrines not in harmony with the confession of faith, is a privilege, which even if harmless in this particular case, might be abused as a precedent and lead in other quarters and relations to serious mischief. The Assembly expresses the desire that these ministers may soon be able to embrace our standards without reservation, and in that case, the Presbytery of Bethel is hereby authorized to ratify the union without further application to this body, but in the event that the Independent ministers and churches cannot relinquish their peculiarities with a good conscience, this Assembly will cherish them in the bonds of Christian love, but cannot see its way clear to embrace them in the same denomination.[48]

Six years later, in 1863, Bethel Presbytery again approached the Presbyterian Church about union with the Independents. By this time the Old School Presbyterians in the South had formed their own body and had expressed their avowed intention to join with other Reformed bodies within the bounds of the Confederacy.[49] Delegates from the Independent Presbyterian Church were warmly welcomed and addressed the 1863 Southern Presbyterian Assembly which directed the Synod of South Carolina to consider a plan of union. A joint committee of the two churches met and produced a proposal for union. Again, the issue of Independent insistence on the right to teach their doctrines was included in negotiations. The proposed plan was very similar to the plan of 1857 but the statement about doctrinal reservations was excluded. There was an understanding, however, among the men on the joint committee that the Independents would be allowed to hold their views "without a challenge or interference on the part of the Presbyterian Church."[50]

---

[47] J.B. Adger, "The General Assembly of 1857," *Southern Presbyterian Review* X (July 1857): 317.

[48] *Minutes of the General Assembly*, 1857 (Old School), 42. While the intent of the General Assembly to require subscription to the standards is clear, it is interesting to observe the spirit of the response - acknowledging Independent views as "harmless" and the attitude of Christian brotherhood which was certainly absent in the 1833 response to the request for shared communion.

[49] *Supra*, n. 37.

[50] This quotation comes from the manuscript journal of Independent minister Robert Young Russell, vol. V, 41. Russell's papers and journal are located in the Historical Foundation, Montreat, NC. Russell was ordained by the Independent Presbyterian Church in 1826. He was moderator of the Convention at the time of reunion. Parker describes the new attitude toward the Independents in 1863: "Geographical proximity, political sentiment and ecclesiastical expediency overcame doctrinal differences." Parker, "The Independent Presbyterian Church," 105.

The Synod of South Carolina directed Bethel Presbytery to receive the Independent churches into organic union with themselves when they "receive and adopt the Confession of Faith of the Presbyterian Church in the Confederate States, as containing the system of doctrine taught in the Holy Scriptures." In December of 1863, Bethel Presbytery and the Independent Convention met in Yorkville, South Carolina in order to consummate the union. The Independent congregations had by that time individually voted for the merger. Some residual tensions surfaced during an interlocutory meeting of the two bodies. Certain members of Bethel Presbytery voiced objections to the use of the term "general" qualifying the word "system" in the Articles of Union.[51] They insisted the General Assembly required adopting the system of the Confession without qualification. Several Independent members responded that if it was expected that they were to "recant our peculiar doctrinal views" then they were unwilling to proceed with union.

As the final discussions unfolded, Independent minister Robert Y. Russell addressed the two bodies on the doctrinal question, making it clear that the Independents understood "from the representatives of the Assembly's delegates, that the distinctive peculiarities of our doctrinal tenets, though dissented to by your church would nevertheless be suffered, without subjecting us to unpleasant liabilities." Russell added: "These peculiarities I have imbibed from what I understand to be the teachings of the Bible, and until convinced of their being errors can never consent to renounce or abandon them. Should this right be denied me, I, for one, am unwilling to advance a step further forward in the path of this union, how desirable soever it may be to us both." Members of Bethel Presbytery replied that their business was not with the peculiar doctrines of the Independents but to inquire if the Independents were prepared to adopt the Confession sincerely. The Independents gave their assent in writing to the Westminster Confession of Faith and thus were welcomed as new members of Bethel Presbytery and the Old School Southern Presbyterian Church.[52]

Old School Pursues the New School

A more auspicious ecclesiastical and political context in the early 1860s set the stage for the eventual union of the Old School and New School in the Confederate States of America. The beginning of the War Between the States in April 1861 and the Old School schism a month later fostered a new reunion spirit. In several areas

---

[51] For details of the negotiations between the Southern Church and the Independent Presbyterian Church see W.A. Alexander and G.F. Nicolassen, *A Digest of the Acts and Proceedings of the General Assembly of the Presbyterian Church in the United States* (Richmond: Presbyterian Committee of Publication, 1911), 410-421.

[52] Russell, *Journal*, V, 61,62. The Independents adopted the Confession and it was understood that their subscription made allowances for the unique theological expressions that had characterized their denomination's 53 year history. Parker commented: "This interesting information from Russell's journal throws new light on the thesis that the southern Church kept her doctrine pure." See Parker, "The Independent Presbyterian Church," 107.

there had always been comradery between these Southern men as far back as the original division of 1837-38.[53] Official movement toward reunion in the South would originate with the Old School body in 1863.

A fraternal spirit had been fostered toward the New School in the Old School Synod of Virginia as early as the mid-1850s. Out of this synod would come some of the strongest support for reuniting with the New School men. From the beginning of the 1857 New School South exodus from the Northern New School, Professor Dabney, of Union Seminary in Virginia, had urged the New School men to unite with the Old School rather that pursue an Independent course. Dabney asserted, "We do, however, believe that among Southern New School Presbyterians there are thousands who are sound in doctrinal views and steadfast in attachment to the standards of our church ... we have no hesitation in avowing our conviction that a reunion with us, on the proper basis, will *for them* be the wisest, safest, and happiest solution of the difficulty into which our New School Brethren have been driven by the unrighteous action of their late Northern associates."[54]

Dabney had appealed to the New School men to consider their small numbers and the dearth of ministers they would face without joining with their fellow Southern Presbyterians. The Southern Presbyterian Church would not ask the New School men to "endorse the policy, the rightfulness, not even the constitutionality, of those measures of 1837." You have fulfilled your "duty of sympathizing testimony for the Northern brethren." Many of the Old School men agreed with you but chose to remain in the Old School body and overlook this error. The main objection to union in 1857, from the New School side, was that the Old School is "tainted with abolitionism." Dabney responded that the Old School position had satisfied Southerners, yet, he acknowledged that the day may come when the Old School too will split over "slavery agitation." If this occurs, you may come with us. Dabney queried: "Will not one, grand, mighty secession of Southern Presbyterians be better ...." The final question was that of examining ministers coming into new

---

[53] Parker cited three "bases for union" in which the Old School and New School men in the South had broad consensus even in 1837: the protest against the Exscinding Acts, the position on slavery and the fact that no Southern New School minister had signed the Auburn Declaration. "Thus was preserved their doctrinal integrity intact." From Parker's perspective, the 1864 reunion had its roots in these issues from the 1830s. See Parker, *United Synod of the South*, 250-251. Likewise, T.C. Johnson pointed out how the New School Southerners had been essentially conservative. "Indeed the New School people in the South seem never to have been generally charged with a prevalent leaning toward New School doctrines. They went with the New School party at the split of 1838 because of their friendship for New School men; because of the peculiar ecclesiastical moves of the Old School men, 1837-1838; and because of the extreme and unjustifiable representations made of the New School party by such men as Drs. Plummer and Breckinridge." T.C. Johnson, *A Brief Sketch of the United Synod*, 29.

[54] Robert F. Dabney, "Our Position," *Central Presbyterian*, July 11, 1857; in Robert L. Dabney, *Discussions: Evangelical and Theological*, vol. II (1890; reprint, London: Banner of Truth, 1967), 177.

presbyteries. "How can we be suspected of anything invidious when we do just the same with our own brethren."[55]

Dabney assured the New School men in 1857 that they would be welcomed and accepted as equals in a united Presbyterian Church in the Southern States. He claimed: "Should this union be formed, we have no humiliations to impose on our brethren commonly known as New School, no concessions to demand of them, but expect to meet them as equals."[56] The majority of the Old School Assembly disagreed with Dabney and the 1858 bid for union had disintegrated.

By 1863 the political and ecclesiastical situation had changed dramatically. Presbyterians in the South were in the mood for union. Old School/New School tensions had dissipated as both groups had joined the common cause of the Confederacy. John N. Waddell, a participant at the first meeting of representatives from both churches, described the atmosphere in the South:

> Time is a wonderful softener of asperities in all things, and whatever may have been the state of feelings on the part of some on both sides of this unhappy controversy which has been in existence for more than a quarter of a century, there is now left a very small amount of bitterness on the subject in any true Southern heart. I am persuaded that the spirit of party and strife in which it originated, has sunk into the grave with some of the disputants; and has been left on the northern side of Mason and Dixon's line with others, and that the great mass of the ministers and the people of both Churches cry out now for union.[57]

Lynchburg Conference

Dabney, who had favored union in 1858, reemerged as a key advocate for reunion when the 1863 General Assembly named him to the Committee of Conference (five clergy, two laymen) to confer with their counterpart in the United Synod.[58] A joint meeting was held in Lynchburg, Virginia in July of 1863. The central concern of the two committees was to produce a plan that would satisfy both groups. In order to do this, the joint committee eventually produced a six-point plan of reunion. As the two groups gathered, Dabney was the first to break the silence. He proceeded to give an

---

[55] Ibid., 178-182.

[56] Ibid., 182.

[57] John Waddell, "Meeting of the Committees of the Conference of the General Assembly and of the United Synod of the South," *Southern Presbyterian*, August 13, 1863.

[58] Thomas Cary Johnson claimed that Dabney "had reasons for desiring the union of the two bodies which he did not like to use publicly." Johnson said that Dabney did not want a New School seminary established in the South and union would be surety that this would not happen. Johnson also indicated that Dabney was aware that several "men of unsound views would soon pass away." Perhaps Dabney did hope for total absorption of the New School, nevertheless, throughout the reunion discussions he publicly defended New School orthodoxy. Thomas Cary Johnson, *The Life and Letters of Robert Lewis Dabney*, reprint, (Edinburgh: The Banner of Truth Trust, 1977), 287, 289.

impressive speech, to which Dr. Joseph Stiles of the New School responded: "Dr. Dabney's views are marked by entire fairness, and if the spirit of magnificent equity which breathes through them prevails in this joint committee, the breach between us is healed...."[59] The two committees proceeded to discuss at length, with "full, frank and fraternal expression," the points that had to be adjusted in order for union to occur. Waddell reported that a "spirit of harmony and brotherly love, of confiding candor and all absence of distrust or suspicion" permeated the meetings. Dr. Stiles and Dr. Dabney were appointed as a subcommittee to prepare a "declaration of principles and plan of union."[60]

The proposed plan was communicated to the joint committee the next day and "every article calmly, maturely, and candidly considered, and amended in word and form, until it was fully and satisfactorily understood and heartily adopted by all." The joint committee adopted, with a few modifications, the doctrinal articles which Dabney and Stiles presented. There were five additional articles dealing with ecclesiastical issues. Together with the doctrinal article, these comprised the complete Plan of Union which was presented to the 1864 Assemblies of the United Synod and the Presbyterian Church (C.S.A.).[61]

The doctrinal statements constituted Article I of the Plan of Union. There were six points in this article, each of which dealt with one of the "former grounds of debate" between the Old and New Schools. The opening paragraph acknowledged the doctrinal statements were necessary because "some have been supposed to hold the system of doctrines and church order in different senses."[62] The stated purpose of the clarifications was to "manifest our hearty agreement, to remove suspicions and offences, to restore full confidence between brethren, and to honor God's saving truth."[63]

Under each doctrinal point there was a counterbalancing of statements which affirmed both traditional Old School understanding as well as appreciating New School concerns. Several examples make this plain. Under the heading, "Fall of

---

[59] Ibid., 286; Johnson cited these words from Dr. McGuffey of the University of Virginia. Dr. Stiles had been elected as the Professor of Systematic and Pastoral Theology at the United Synod's new seminary which never materialized. Dr. Boyd was also to have been a professor according to Johnson. T.C. Johnson, *A Brief Sketch of the United Synod*, 36.

[60] Waddell, *Southern Presbyterian*, Aug.13,1863.

[61] Ibid. T.C. Johnson commented on the integrity of the doctrinal articles: "This doctrinal statement passed easily through the Committee's hands. It teaches clearly the kind of Calvinism taught in the Westminster standards and tacitly repudiates that false Calvinism which offends by extreme statement." Johnson said Dabney already had doctrinal articles written out when he came to the meeting. *Brief Sketch of the United Synod*, 31.

[62] The "different senses" in which some were believed to "hold the system of doctrine" was the crucial question for union as stated here in the preamble to the doctrinal articles. The joint committee's succinct statements provided common ground for understanding the Calvinistic sense of the Confession.

[63] *Presbyterian Historical Almanac and Annual Remembrancer of the Church for 1865*, vol. 7 (Philadelphia: Joseph M. Wilson, 1865), 316.

Man and Original Sin," the document stated that due to Adam's fall his "posterity are judicially condemned of God on account of that sin." The moral corruption of Adam's posterity is entire. Then it added: "But we equally reject the error of those who assert that the sinner has no power of any kind for the performance of duty. This error strips the sinner of his moral agency and accountableness, and introduces the heresy of either Antinomianism or Fatalism. The true doctrine of the Scriptures, as stated in our Confession, keeps constantly in view the moral agency of man, the contingency of second causes, the use of means, the voluntariness of all the creature's sin, and his utter inexcusableness therein." On the question of imputation, the joint committee explained: "And we mean that the guilt of their sin, which is imputed, is, according to the constant usage of theology, 'obligation to punishment,' and not the sinfulness of the act itself, which latter cannot, by imputation, be the quality of any other than the personal agents."[64]

A similar juxtaposition of Old School/New School perspectives was evidenced in the statement on Christ's atonement. The joint committee proclaimed:

> This atonement we believe, though by temporary sufferings, was, by reason of the infinite glory of Christ's person, full and sufficient for the guilt of the whole world, and is to be freely and sincerely offered to every creature, inasmuch as it leaveth no other obstacle to the pardon of all men under the gospel, save the enmity and unbelief of those who voluntarily reject it. Wherefore, on the one hand, we reject the opinion of those who teach that the atonement was so limited and equal to the guilt of the elect only, that if God had designed to redeem more, Christ must have suffered more or differently. And, on the other hand, we hold that God the Father doth efficaciously apply this redemption, through Christ's purchase, to all those to whom it was his eternal purpose to apply it, and to no others.[65]

Concerning the practical issue of promoting revivals, again, there was a carefully crafted tension. The article warned against imbalance:

> ... on the one hand, we testify, from our observation and the word of God, that it is dangerous to ply the disordered heart of the sinner with a disproportionate address to the imagination and passions, to withhold from his awakened mind scriptural instruction, and to employ with him such novel and startling measures as must tend to impart to his religious excitement a character rather noisy, shallow, and transient, than

---

[64] Ibid. Dabney concluded that the Westminster Divines did not commit themselves on the debated question of mediate or immediate imputation. He said, "The race sinned in Adam, and fell with him. But the Assembly [Westminster] will give no metaphysics, nominalistic or realistic, to explain the awful fact, because Scripture gives none." Robert L. Dabney, "The Doctrinal Contents of the Confession: Its Fundamental and Regulative Ideas, and the Necessity and Value of Creeds" in *Memorial Volume of the Westminster Assembly*, edited by Francis R. Beattie, et.al. (Richmond: The Presbyterian Committee of Publication, 1897); reprint, *The Westminster Confession and Creeds* (Dallas: Presbyterian Heritage Publications, 1983), 13.

[65] Ibid., 317.

deep, solid, and scriptural. But, on the other hand, we value, cherish, and pray for true revivals of religion, and wherever they bring forth the permanent fruits of holiness in men's hearts, rejoice in them as God's work, notwithstanding the mixture of human imperfection. And we consider it the solemn duty of ministers to exercise a scriptural warmth, affection, and directness in appealing to the understanding, hearts, and consciences of men.[66]

On the old controversy of voluntary societies, the joint committee agreed to a position of Christian liberty.

Whence it follows that the associated and organized acts of the people of God for the conversion of the world unto Christ, are the proper functions of these officers, or of church-courts constituted of them. Those who seek the world's conversion by societies of voluntary and human origin distinct from the branches of Christ's visible Church, therefore ought not to ask the officers and courts of the Church to relinquish these labors to them. Yet we can bid them God-speed in all their sincere efforts to diffuse the true work of God, and we concede to the members of our churches full liberty to extend to them such personal aid as their Christian consciences approve.[67]

Churches in each denomination could approve such positions which provided for a charitable spirit on issues that had been divisive in the past. A peaceable spirit pervaded the entire document and would eventually satisfy the majorities of both parties.

The carefully crafted doctrinal affirmations in the Plan of Union were interpreted by the joint committee as entirely consistent with adopting the Confession of Faith: "The General Assembly and the United Synod declare that they continue to sincerely receive and adopt the Confession and the Catechisms of the Presbyterian Church, as containing the system of doctrines taught in the Holy Scriptures, and approve of its government and discipline."[68] Both committees had understood one another on these points; the "Doctrinal Basis of Union" rejected the extreme positions of both Old and New School that would hinder full communion. The basis was adopted by the Lynchburg joint committee unanimously.[69] John N. Waddell, who had represented the Southern Church, described the attitude of committee

---

[66] Ibid.

[67] Ibid.

[68] Ibid., 316.

[69] One of the representatives from the Southern Presbyterian Church, E.T. Baird, had been unable to attend the Joint Committee on Union due to the War. He sent a communication to the General Assembly stating that "the doctrinal articles are Calvinistic and true," nevertheless, he had reservations that "in probably three places, the language is liable to misapprehension and might become the cause of trouble among ourselves." He further said that he did not "believe that any series of doctrinal articles could be framed which would not be obnoxious to the same objection." His main concern was not making anything but the constitution itself the basis of union. For the full text of the letter see *Presbyterian Remembrancer*, 1865, 319, 320.

members: "I would remark that the committee felt the necessity of guarding against too great laxity of terms on the one hand, and a needless stringency on the other hand."[70] If the spirit of the joint committee prevailed, a reunited church would exhibit the strengths of both Old and New School.

[70] *Southern Presbyterian,* Aug.13,1863.

CHAPTER 10

Southern Churches Unite

The committee members representing the Old School and New School churches at Lynchburg believed they had come up with a grand compromise. Not everyone in their constituent bodies concurred with that judgment. Participants at Lynchburg would have to convince the rival churches that reunion was in the best interest of everyone. Vocal elements in the Old School Southern church would put up stiff resistance to any perceived compromise with the New School.

Immediately following the publication of the "Basis of Union" from the Lynchburg conference, questions about the plan began to emerge. Requests were made not to discuss the plan in the newspapers of the church until it could be brought to the 1864 Assembly, however, the report was presented to several of the largest and most influential synods and the controversy began. The Plan of Union was endorsed by both the *Central Presbyterian* and the *Christian Observer* but the influential *Southern Presbyterian* came out against the plan.

Old School Resistance

The *Southern Presbyterian* editor, A.A. Porter, wrote a series of editorials opposing the plan and specifically attacked the doctrinal terms as "equivocal, lame, incomplete." Dr. John N. Waddell, a member of the joint committee, responded with several letters to the editor.[1] Porter expressed concern that the plan of union would "become an integral part of our standards, and to be placed on the same footing as our confession of faith...." Waddell replied that the intention of the committee was to use the doctrinal points in lieu of the "examination rule" for the United Synod men and "if they adopt it, as a basis of union, then the parties coming to us are understood to embrace it only as the interpretation of the Confession of Faith, received by the church, and no man can accept that confession simply for 'substance of doctrine,' but it must be done 'ex animo.'" Porter was willing to waive the required examination of ministers and receive United Synod brothers if they made a "simple declaration that they adopt our Confession of Faith, sincerely, in its plain sense."[2]

Porter was convinced that the proposed doctrinal statement "settles no point controverted between Old and New School, while it opens the door for continual

---

[1] *Southern Presbyterian*, Aug.20, 1863; Oct. 1, 1863.
[2] Ibid.; *Southern Presbyterian*, Sept. 10, 1863.

debate and strife." He criticized an indefinite statement on the atonement "which both the general and limited atonement men can adopt." He was distressed about the plan's statement on human ability which "yields to the New School theologians all they can desire." He added: "It does not matter much what kind of power it is the sinner has to perform his duty. If he has it, of any sort, that is enough, and the Old School doctrine is abandoned." Waddell defended the committee's statement on ability as a "true Calvinistic statement on this subject." He explained that the object of affirming human ability was "simply to vindicate our Calvinism from the charge of Antinomianism, or Fatalism, so often brought against it, to how that man was not a machine, but a rational free agent."[3]

Porter protested that the committee report was an attempt to "reconcile all differences and harmonize all parties... that is not after the manner of true, old fashioned Presbyterians...." This view was confirmed by "the fact that men are endorsing their report, who it is unquestionable are wide as the poles apart from our Old School theology." As an example, he pointed to the unanimous endorsement of the report by Winchester Presbytery of the United Synod and the infamous Dr. Boyd, well known for his New School views.[4]

Waddell's explanations had been of no avail to ebb increasing condemnation of the Plan of Union in the *Southern Presbyterian*. Professor Dabney of Union Seminary in Virginia, chair of the committee of conference for the Old School, wrote a long essay for the *Southern Presbyterian* published over four issues of the paper. Dabney resented the "temper of suspicion" that accused both committees of "uncandid concealments" with a design to cover up differences in the parties.[5]

Dabney rejected the notion that the new doctrinal declaration is unnecessary. The old formulas are accepted by both parties but a new formula is necessary "to test the existence of present differences of opinion." This was the very method used by the Old School in the "Western Memorial" and the "Act and Testimony" at the time of the schism. "Now it is strange that the necessity and utility of such a declaration should be denied by those who have constantly rejected the assertion by the New School that they hold the same Confession with ourselves, as a sufficient proof of their doctrinal soundness." The Confession was not going to be replaced; the doctrinal declaration was "the same old creed on some points" restated in new words.[6]

Dabney was unapologetic about acknowledging the "dishonor" done to religion by the Presbyterian schism. "A right cause can be advocated in a wrong spirit; ... we should be willing to confess that part of the guilt is ours." Love and harmony

---

[3] *Southern Presbyterian*, Aug. 13, 1863, Oct.1, 1863.

[4] Ibid.

[5] Robert L. Dabney, "Dr. Dabney on the Plan of Union" *Southern Presbyterian*, Dec.10, 1863; the four issues: Nov. 19, 1863; Nov. 27, 1863; Dec. 3, 1863; Dec. 10, 1863. At the conclusion of Dabney's articles were "remarks" by Porter that attempted to refute Dabney.

[6] *Southern Presbyterian*, Nov. 19, 1863.

prevailed in the meeting of the two committees and none of "these gracious emotions were indulged at the expense of fidelity to truth."[7]

The New School had historically assaulted the Old School for teaching man's inability, therefore, removing his responsibility. In light of this, the two committees had declared: "But we equally reject the error of those who assert that the sinner has no power of any kind for the performance of duty." Porter decried this statement. Dabney replied that, of course, the sinner has some kind of power to perform his duty. "If he had not he would not be a religious, nor a responsible being, but only an animal." He quoted Old School theologians as well as the Confession and Catechisms to demonstrate the common consent among Calvinists that a distinction is always to be made between fallen man's inability to "will any spiritual good" and "some sort of natural power for good" as a responsible creature. The only people who discard this distinction in any sense are Pelagians who give to the sinner "ability, both of will and faculties." Dabney added: "Every preacher of the Gospel who teaches that man is totally depraved, and yet responsible, illustrates it successfully."[8]

The "most serious objection" was to the statement on the atonement which Porter characterized as Pelagian error. Dabney justified the distinctions made in the statements on the atonement and admitted that "the United Synod had just cause of complaint against a few Old School men" whose "ultra" views had distorted Calvinist teaching. "And all intelligent Calvinists are accustomed to teach that the limitation which attaches to the atonement, is not in its nature, but only in its design; while their enemies, Arminian and Pelagian, industriously charge upon them what they as industriously repudiate, that they teach it is limited by its nature." It was proper for the committees to use "general terms" when referring to the nature of the atonement. "So does the Bible."[9]

No doubt the strong opinions for and against the Plan of Union in the pages of the *Southern Presbyterian* reflected the serious tensions throughout the church. Porter concluded his long series of articles by acknowledging that his "suggestions for amending the Plan of Union" have gone unheeded, nevertheless, "we are gratified by the assurance that what we have said and done has met the approval of many of the best and most judicious men in the Church." He admitted that the Plan of Union will probably be approved but his efforts "at least absolve us of all responsibility for the mischief that will follow."[10]

B.M. Palmer of New Orleans, a former South Carolinian, was one of the most outspoken opponents. He vehemently objected to the doctrinal portion of the proposed union and responded to Dabney's *Southern Presbyterian* articles in the pages of the *Southern Presbyterian Review*. Dr. Palmer's first objection was to the preamble which stated that the proposed union "will glorify God by promoting

---

[7] Ibid.

[8] *Southern Presbyterian*, Nov. 26, 1863.

[9] *Southern Presbyterian*, Dec. 3, 1863.

[10] *Southern Presbyterian*, Dec. 10, 1863.

peace, removing the *dishonor done to religion by former separations*"(italics mine). He believed that this statement implied a repudiation of the "Reform Measures of 1837." Dabney had defended the clause in question by interpreting this simply as an acknowledgment of the "unseemly heats" of the Old School in the excision and the fact that ecclesiastical separations do in fact dishonor religion. Both sides bear some guilt for the schism according to Dabney. In response, Palmer asserted that whatever may have been the intent of the committee, "the language is a virtual abjuration of all the principles so earnestly contended for in 1837.... As for ourselves, so far from regarding that separation a dishonor to religion, we account it one of the most beneficent and glorious reforms which grace the annals of the church."[11]

Palmer pointed out that the Southern New School men had joined hands with Northern brethren in a denomination that affirmed doctrinal distinctions at odds with Old School theology. The United Synod separated from the Northern New School without doctrinal protest, therefore, implicitly being in sympathy with New School theology. He stated: "There are good reasons why the doctrinal soundness of the United Synod should be called in question.... It is notorious that doctrinal differences lay at the bottom of the separation in 1837.... It is notorious, too, that the body now known as the United Synod voluntarily went out from us, and affiliated through twenty years with these errorists; separating at last from them, not upon doctrinal grounds, but upon a political question, and not until the fanatical fury of Northern radicals no longer permitted them a seat in their ecclesiastical councils."[12] Palmer accused the United Synod of tolerating serious error. He queried: "what are we to think of the doctrinal purity of men who, in their incomparable zeal for a mere constitutional safeguard or ecclesiastical right, are willing to see the truth of God turned into a lie, and the whole Gospel made of none effect through human traditions?"[13]

The United Synod had embraced a latitudinarian view of subscription according to Dr. Palmer. "It is moreover a suspicious fact, that the United Synod has never repudiated the partial and unsatisfactory subscription to the standards of the Church, which was one of the original grounds of offence against the New School party, with whom they have chosen to be identified. On the contrary, at their first meeting in 1858, they append to the declaration of their adherence to the Confession of Faith, a supplementary explanation which seems to us to recognize and to embody the fatal reservation of a subscription for 'substance of doctrine.'"[14] The United Synod's 1858 explanation of adopting the Confession is "couched in language far too indefinite." Palmer claimed: "There is the same equivocation with the words 'system of doctrine' which vitiated the subscription of New School men in 1837, and created such trouble in determining what was accepted and what was

---

[11] B.M. Palmer, "The Proposed Plan of Union," *Southern Presbyterian Review* XV (April 1864): 264-272.

[12] Ibid., 272, 273.

[13] Ibid.

[14] Ibid., 274.

renounced. It is a subscription which does not bind to an agreement in all that the Confession contains, but only in certain fundamental doctrines, the reception of which is all that is meant by the phrase 'system of doctrine taught in Holy Scriptures.'"[15]

Palmer characterized the New School perspective on subscription: "... the Confession is not to be interpreted according to the literal and obvious import of its own terms, but according to a certain sense in which these parties *believe* it to be received by the body of the church; so that the appeal evermore lies from the Confession to this general sense of the church in whatever way it may be collected, instead of ascertaining the sense of the church by reference at once to its acknowledged symbols" (italic his).[16] Opposed to this view, Palmer argued for full subscription to the standards: "What we desire of these brethren is a plain, straightforward adoption of the Church standards, in their simple and obvious import, without equivocation or reservation of any sort. This is the way in which we have subscribed them, and which we require of all intrants into the sacred office. This will go further to remove our suspicions than the most elaborate attempts to fence around and to define their assent, or the best balanced basis of union which can be drawn up by joint committees of conference."[17]

For Palmer, the plan of union as a whole appeared to be a "compromise between the parties." The theological statements yielded too much to New School sensitivities. He objected in principle to these doctrinal explanations, which would become the "authorized interpretation" and in effect become a "symbol superseding practically the Confession itself." Dabney had argued that the doctrinal points were merely declarations touching the former grounds of debate. Palmer countered that the proposed doctrinal basis was unnecessary because the Confession is the "arbiter of all differences which may emerge amongst them ...."[18] Palmer asserted:

---

[15] Ibid., 275. Palmer appeared to associate the "substance of doctrine" view with an "essentials of Christianity" subscription, rather than a more explicit "system of doctrine" view which the United Synod had articulated in the 1857 "Declaration of Principles." The system of doctrine in the Confession, as understood by the United Synod, is Calvinism as over against a Pelagian or Arminian system and not merely "certain fundamental doctrines" as Palmer seemed to suggest. Palmer was also concerned about what is not said in the United Synod's statement. He observed that while the United Synod spoke of the errors of Pelagians, Socinians and Arminians, there was a "studied silence" about the errors of Hopkinsians and Taylorites.

[16] Ibid.

[17] Ibid., 276.

[18] Ibid., 278-282. Palmer claimed that the Confession was the "arbiter of all differences," but, the Westminster Confession states: "The Holy Spirit speaking in the Bible is the supreme judge of all religious controversies, all decisions of religious councils, all opinions of ancient writers, all human teachings, and every private opinion." *Westminster Confession and Catechisms in Modern English*, Evangelical Presbyterian Church (Summertown Company, 2004) I. 10. The other factor not mentioned by Palmer is the role of presbyteries to interpret the Confession.

But we are satisfied with the creed we already have – a creed drawn out over the whole circle of divine truth, closely articulated and held together by the strictest logic – a creed prepared by the wisest men the Church of God has ever known, and at a period peculiarly favorable to the accomplishment of such a task – a creed wrought in the forge of abundant prayer and deliberation through a succession of months and years – and above all, a creed which has withstood the storms of more than two centuries, and which is bound up in the most precious associations of the people of God. Such a creed is not to be lightly added to, or taken from, and, least of all, to be superseded by a rival, surreptitiously introduced and covertly palmed upon the church. If there are parties whom our existing Confession does not satisfy, let the proposition be openly made to modify and improve it, and the church will then, at least, know what she has taken in hand; but we trust the Assembly will watch with jealous care, lest this modest declaration of agreement should be found to usurp the functions which belong only to an acknowledged and authoritative symbol.[19]

Beyond his conceptual concern with the doctrinal basis, Palmer was convinced that the proposed doctrinal affirmations subvert the Confession's understanding of the imputation of Adam's sin, the sinner's inability and the nature and extent of the atonement. He took exception to both what is said and what is left unsaid in the theological propositions. These brief affirmations were in some cases ambiguous and do not give the "whole doctrine." In the section addressing human inability, Palmer objected: "The feature of this paper, which makes it so fatal to the purity, and therefore to the peace, of the Church, is, that whilst it allows apparently the most innocent disclaimers on the part of our New School brethren, it does it in language so incautious as to open the door for the importation of the worst heresies that can afflict the Church of God."[20]

Palmer was not impressed with Dabney's defense, which, "our brother will live to regret that it was ever written." Dabney had cited Dr. Baxter and the Synod of Virginia in 1836 as authorities for his particular language about human ability. To this Palmer replied: "If so, it is only another illustration how unsafe are the doctrinal statements of the best men, which are drawn up for the purposes of concession and compromise. But this matter is not to be decided upon any other authority except that of our acknowledged standards."[21] He challenged Dabney's integrity with these words: "Is not this the identical language in which the hereditary enemies of Calvinism have always endeavored to excite the prejudices of unthinking and uncritical men? [A]nd are not these the arguments by which the old theology of the church has ever been assailed? We venture to say that this painful embarrassment would not have been felt by our excellent brother in his theological chair at Prince Edward: but as a committee man at Lynchburg, he has a new and strange role to

---

[19] Ibid., 282, 283.
[20] Ibid., 290-292.
[21] Ibid.

play, as the special advocate of New School opinions, and he works awkwardly in the harness."[22]

The committee's section on the atonement was woefully insufficient. Palmer candidly commented, "Upon this fundamental doctrine of atonement, the utterance of the committee should have been the most full and explicit, instead of being the most exceptionable in their whole paper." To support his objection, Palmer quoted from an article in the *Christian Observer* by Dr. A.H.H. Boyd, "an acknowledged leader in the United Synod," accusing him of equivocation and evasion on the nature of the atonement. Further, he accused Boyd of an Arminian view of the atonement's design. In the strongest terms, he condemned Boyd's understanding of the atonement of Christ "in behalf of the whole family of man." Palmer decried, "Our very flesh creeps as we transcribe these dreadful words, which do not fall short of positive blasphemy.... Christ's death confessed to be inefficacious, and failing of its design with reference to a part of those for whom He died! ... Is this, or any thing like this, the doctrine of our standards?"[23]

According to Palmer, the doctrinal statement was silent on whether the atonement was definite or indefinite in its intention. Since there was "a most painful and ominous silence – a silence, too, which is unquestionably intentional; ... there can be no doubt of the interpretation that will be put upon it as favoring the general atonement theory." Palmer asserted that, "this section of the committee's report by its very form and structure carries the Assembly over, and, so far as this utterance of the General Assembly can do it, the whole church over to the assertion of an indefinite atonement."[24]

Palmer summarized his review of the proposed plan of union by claiming that he had not "assailed the orthodoxy of the report, nor of those by whom it has been framed.... We do not impugn the doctrinal purity of any one of them, when we assert the ambiguities of the report." He was willing to have union with the United Synod if they were "really at one with us upon the great doctrines of grace." Palmer offered this recommendation:

And if they are with us in faith and order, let it be ascertained by a square and unreserved adoption of our acknowledged standards, in their obvious and literal import.

---

[22] Ibid., 293. Palmer correctly observed that the joint doctrinal statements affirmed New School theology. The New School men on the committee had unanimously endorsed them and they received widespread approval throughout the United Synod. Indeed the doctrinal statements were an attempt to acknowledge New School perspectives as orthodox Calvinism.

[23] Ibid., 297-303.

[24] Ibid., 304, 305. Palmer admitted Presbyterian diversity in this matter when he stated: "If it should be said, the Old School body has always tolerated a diversity of opinion upon the extent of the atonement, we answer, that is altogether a different affair from the Assembly affirming a general atonement, and construing it as the doctrine of the church, contrary, as we believe, both to the spirit and letter of our existing symbols." Palmer's specific concern was making general atonement the official confession of the church and not the fact that the Old School had tolerated this position.

All these attempts, by conventions and conferences, to construct platforms of union, only prejudice and retard the movement. Let us have no more of this nibbling at the Confession of Faith, and of this paring down its statements to the very minimum of orthodoxy. Let us have no more declarations of adherence to these sacred instruments, with an appendix of reservation and explanations like a codicil annulling a will. A plain, straightforward honest subscription to the Confession and other symbols, will place the parties on ground which both understand; and there will be union, when alone union can be found, *through the truth* (italics his).[25]

Additional opposition to the plan was voiced in several presbyteries of the Southern Church.[26] Professor J.B. Adger of Columbia Seminary presented a paper to the Presbytery of South Carolina denouncing the plan of union. Adger's paper demanded that the United Synod acknowledge New School doctrinal errors; the paper was unanimously adopted. The minutes of the presbytery recorded: "... this Presbytery looks upon it as inexplicable mystery how they should never have discovered and repudiated the errors of their former associates.... This Presbytery does not hesitate to declare that it is finally and unalterably opposed to any union with the United Synod except upon a formal and distinct repudiation by them of every one of the new school errors which have been entertained by those with whom they so long continued to maintain the closest fellowship."[27] Despite all the antagonism, the movement toward reunion was not curtailed.

Reunion of 1864

The General Assembly of the Southern Presbyterian Church convened in May 1864 in Charlotte, North Carolina. Debate on the proposal for reunion spread over four days; Palmer and Adger, unconvinced by the plan's supporters, continued their resistance. Adger raised constitutional questions about the process for ecclesiastical union and voiced his skepticism about the orthodoxy of the United Synod which had recently elected A.H.H. Boyd to be a professor in its proposed seminary. Palmer said the reputation of the United Synod was mixed; some say they are sound in the faith, others declare they are not. And these New School men have never made an unreserved subscription to the standards.[28]

Support for reunion was widespread and many spoke out in favor of union on the Assembly floor. Several presbyters commented that Presbyterians in their entire state were supporting union with the New School. In Virginia there were already New School men supplying Old School pulpits in anticipation of the union. Dr.

---

[25] Ibid., 306, 307.

[26] See Harold M. Parker, *The United Synod of the South* (Presbyterian Historical Society, 1988), 255-257 and Ernest Trice Thompson, *Presbyterians in the South*, vol. II (Richmond: John Knox Press, 1963), 120.

[27] *Minutes of the Presbytery of South Carolina*, (Spring 1864), 483-487. Quoted in Thompson. *Presbyterians in the South*, II, 120, 121.

[28] Parker, *United Synod of the South*, 258, 259.

Moses Hoge[29] of Virginia pointed to the recent reception of the Independent Presbyterian Church. The Independent Church had been received with minor differences, yet there was "union in essentials."[30]

Dabney's able defense of the plan "drew forth for him the most enthusiastic admiration of the body."[31] For two hours, he addressed the concerns raised about the doctrinal article. Dabney specifically countered three objections to union in a memorial to the Assembly from the Presbytery of South Carolina. First, was the charge that the General Assembly was being asked to deny the Old School principles of 1837. To this, Dabney replied: "... I assert that, meeting our New School brethren for the purpose you sent us to them, a generous language of concession was the proper one to use. We met, not to apportion the several measures of guilt upon the culprits, and to avenge it, but to reconcile, to heal, to place that old guilt and its bitter consequences in the road to a happy oblivion. Men who meet for such a purpose, if they are sincere, will think it much more appropriate to assume a generous share of the blame of former divisions, than enviously to seek to seal it upon former opponents, who they now profess to forgive."[32]

Secondly, the South Carolinians had challenged the statement on Original Sin as New School theology. The opposition believed the language of the article suggested the old New School distinction between natural and moral ability. The joint committee purposefully avoided using this nomenclature due to potential ambiguity, however, Dabney countered that "sound Calvinists" have used the distinction in an "orthodox sense." The plan's critics misunderstood the distinction of "power" and "ability." Dabney stated: "In the language of Calvinistic theology, the word *inability* has ever had a most sharply defined and specific meaning, as expressive of the lack only of one peculiar kind of power...." In fact, both parties made mistakes in the Old School/New School debates surrounding this issue. "When, therefore, Pelagians and Arminians charged, and weak, incautious Calvinists admitted, that our doctrine of inability denied to man *all power of any kind* – a phrase very common in controversy thirty years ago – both were in error"(italics his). This was the heart of

---

[29] Dr. Moses Hoge was pastor of the Old School Second Presbyterian Church in Richmond for 50 years.

[30] Parker, *United Synod of the South*, 256-259. The debate was covered by the *Christian Observer*, May 26 and June 2, 1864. See also Morton H. Smith, *Studies in Southern Presbyterian Theology* (Amsterdam, Drukkerij en Uitgeverij Jocob van Campen, 1962), 196-201.

[31] Thomas Cary Johnson, *A Brief Sketch of the United Synod of the Presbyterian Church in the United States of America* (reprint, vol. VIII American Society of Church History, 1894), 35.

[32] Robert F. Dabney, "Speech on Fusion With the United Synod" in *Discussions: Evangelical and Theological* vol. II (reprint, London: Banner of Truth, 1967), 300.

the theological debate of those days and the reason why the joint committee carefully considered its articulation of this doctrine.[33]

The joint committee had come to a mutual understanding on this question and the misperceptions on both sides have been dealt with in the published statement. "Now, we believe that if we and the United Synod are at one in belief, we have come to understand each other about this old 'bone of contention.' The task the committee had to do, then was to express that agreement in terms sufficiently perspicuous to make it appear whether there was substantial *harmony*, and at the same time *soundness*" (italics his). Dabney described the consensus on inability:

All intelligent Calvinists understand very well that it consists, not in the extinction of any of the powers which constituted man the creature he was before Adam's fall, and which make up his essence as a religious being, but in the thorough moral perversion of them all. The soul's essence is not destroyed by the fall; if it were, in any part, man's responsibility would be to that extent modified... His inability is 'inability of will.' This is the doctrine of Calvinists; and if it be pushed farther than this, so as to deny to man as fallen any of those natural powers, either active or passive, which constituted him a proper subject of religious responsibility, the effect is only disastrous.[34]

The third element in the South Carolina memorial was the statement on the atonement. Again, the charge of advocating New School views was the central concern. First, Dabney indicated how the criticisms were unfounded because there was an acceptable diversity on this doctrine. He stated, "... there is among Calvinists, among ourselves, a slight difference in the arrangement of some details concerning the atonement and its application; yet both classes have always recognized each other as holding the essentials of the doctrine of particular redemption." The critics raised the issue of the order of the decrees which Dabney said, "contain refinements that go beyond the word of God." It would be "preposterous and positively unjust" of the Southern Church to demand "admission of refined details" of the United Synod about which we are "not agreed among ourselves." The purpose of the committee was to state "those features of the doctrine which distinguish Calvinists hereupon from Arminians and the New England school, and to introduce sentences which should clearly and beyond a peradventure cut up by the root all the notions which reduce the atonement to a

---

[33] Ibid., 301-303. The doctrine of inability had been the chief concern of the New School in the 1830s. Dabney said: "The former party revived the charge, as old as Pelagianism, that our doctrine of *total inability* contravened the rational and moral intuitions of man; because where there is absolutely no power for duty, there can be no responsibility.... it was the uniform lever with which they endeavored to turn the Calvinistic theology into an absolute monstrosity. Why, sir, was not this cavil the *staple* of every one of the four propositions which the leaders of that party demanded of us to insert into the doctrinal teachings of the Assembly of 1837" (italics his)?

[34] Ibid., 303, 304.

didactic display, a moral drama, an exemplary incident, or a governmental expedient."[35]

The common Calvinist distinction between the nature and design of the atonement was significant. The nature of Christ's atonement "has no limits" and why should the report "be charged with error for using the same sort of language which the Bible itself does...." On the design of the atonement, the committee has also been clear. "But when the report proceeds to speak of the application of redemption, it declares, as I assert, in exact accordance with the spirit of our standards, that God applies it to all the elect, and to no others; and that this application is itself through the purchase of Jesus Christ." Dabney summarized the joint committee's perspective: "In a word, the committee intended to express summarily that sound, but not ultra, view of the atonement held by Calvinists, and expressed in the ancient formula, 'Christ died sufficiently for the race, efficaciously for the elect' ... I am led to believe that our effort to make a brief statement of the substance of this doctrine is rather happy...." Dabney admitted that the committee's statements may not be "absolutely the best" because language is always flexible and "an indefinite improvement may be made in the verbal dress of any thoughts by continued care and criticism. Notwithstanding, argued Dabney, the language used "would do."[36]

After prolonged debate, with multiple participants, the Assembly sought solution to the impasse by appointing a committee to recommend a course of action on the proposed plan of union. Each Synod was represented on the committee with one elder and one minister – Adger and Dabney were both on the committee. The group deliberated and then returned to the floor of the Assembly with a recommendation which included four resolutions. The first resolution expressed appreciation to the joint committee for their labors and great satisfaction with the "brotherly love and spirit of harmony" in which the work was carried out. The second resolution asserted that "the most satisfactory terms of union" would be "the cordial adherence of the two bodies to their existing symbols of faith and order."[37]

The third resolution involved four points where the plan should be amended to meet some of the concerns raised by opponents. Two amendments had to do with ecclesiastical process. Another amendment was the deletion of the phrase, "removing the dishonor done to religion by former separations." The most significant recommendation had to do with the doctrinal basis. The first paragraph of Article One was to remain; it stated that both bodies "continue sincerely to receive and adopt the Confession of Faith and Catechisms of the Presbyterian Church, as containing the system of doctrine taught in the Holy Scriptures and

---

[35] Ibid., 304-307.

[36] Ibid., 307-310. Dabney also indicated that the Reformed Tradition had made even broader statements on the atonement that "go farther than our report." He quoted the Heidelberg Catechism, answer to question 37, which said that Christ "bore in his body and soul the wrath of God against *the sin of the universal human race.*"(italics his), 310.

[37] *Minutes of the General Assembly of the Presbyterian Church in the Confederate States of America,* 1861-1865 (Augusta, Columbia),1864, 271.

approve of its government and discipline." But, the rest of the article, which described a common understanding on the controversial issues, was to be disregarded. This met the concern to unite on the basis of the standards not an additional creed.[38]

The fourth resolution, however, explained the rationale behind the recommended exclusion of the doctrinal section. "That the Assembly proposes the omission of the doctrinal proposition of article I on the following ground solely, viz: That, believing the *approval of those propositions* by the Committees of Conference, and *extensively among both bodies,* has served a valuable purpose, by presenting *satisfactory evidence* of such harmony and *soundness of doctrinal views* as may ground an honorable union, the Assembly does yet judge that it is most prudent to unite on the basis of our existing standards only, inasmuch as no actual necessity of other declarations of belief in order to a happy union now exist (italics mine)."[39]

The compromise plan met with the hearty approval of the Assembly. Both sides had a degree of victory – the joint committee had accomplished its task by bringing the Old School and New School men together in a moderate statement of Calvinism; the opponents of union had gained their prize of preserving the Westminster Standards, without interpretation, as the sole standard of doctrine in the Presbyterian Church.[40] The final vote on reunion in the Southern Church was 53 yeas and 7 nays. The opposition entered their reasons upon the record of the Assembly. Adger said that reunion is "a total letting-down of the Church's testimony in 1837; and on the ground of its tendency to give rise to future troubles and divisions in our Church." Palmer stated that he voted against the report "on account of the 4th resolution;" four others also listed the 4th resolution as the reason for their dissent. Commissioner Angus Johnson wrote: "I voted against the reception of the United Synod on the following grounds: 1st. For want of confidence in the doctrinal soundness of the entire body. 2d. Because the doctrinal basis agreed upon by the committees in

---

[38] Ibid.

[39] Ibid., 273. This statement was essential for candidly explaining the deletion as not discountenancing the common doctrinal understanding of the two parties. The paragraph admitted that the doctrinal points had met with the approval of the vast majority of both churches. The Old School and New School in the South had achieved an understanding and recognized one other as orthodox Calvinists according to the public explanations that were given by the joint committee. There was widespread support for the original plan in both Old School as well as New School presbyteries. T.C. Johnson related: "Prior to the meeting of the General Assembly in 1864, Synods and Presbyteries in both the Churches had adopted the proposed plan of union sent forth by the Committees of Conference." T.C. Johnson, *A Brief Sketch of the United Synod*, 37.

[40] Parker said: "That a compromise had been worked out in the committee is without question. Both Dabney and Palmer had won their points. Palmer had raised sufficient questions about the possibility of looser interpretation of the doctrinal statement, and had objected to adding it as an additional doctrinal standard of the Church. He was thus responsible for its defeat as a part of the basis for reunion. Dabney won his point in having the total revised Plan approved." *The United Synod of the South*, 260.

conference is not sufficiently explicit."[41] It is clear from these explanations that the Assembly implicitly was endorsing the doctrinal explanations of the original plan as sound.

In addition to the doctrinal issue there were a few minor modifications to the plan by the Southern Church. These changes were acceptable to the United Synod which unanimously adopted the amended plan of union in August of 1864.[42] Despite the overwhelming support for reunion, the Presbytery of South Carolina took one parting shot. At the 1864 Fall meeting of the presbytery, a "Testimony and Memorial" was adopted. This statement was chiefly directed at two issues, the constitutionality of the union and New School errors. The South Carolinians were still convinced that the General Assembly had no right in the Constitution to ratify a union with another denomination. On the doctrinal question, the presbytery gave this testimony:

> Against the effect of this union, forcing us as it does, into the endorsement of the Theology of men, whose unsoundness has not been denied by their associates in the United Synod ... that avowedly maintained the errors, condemned by the Assembly in 1837, and that severed their connection with these latter, not because they repudiated their errors and had borne testimony against them, but, merely, because they had been by them condemned as guilty of the sin of slavery. Again, we cannot but regard this measure, as almost tantamount to a reversal of the glorious testimony borne by our

---

[41] *Minutes of the General Assembly, PCCSA*, 1864, 277. It was known that the New School body contained several men appearing to have somewhat Arminian tendencies. T.C. Johnson gave this characterization of those under suspicion by the Old School: "Dr. J.D. Mitchell preached Arminianism and now Calvinism. He was very inconsistent; but without doubt believed that his theology differed from the Old School. In a letter to Dr. A.H.H. Boyd of Winchester, Va., he referred to his Church's having for its doctrinal basis an *unlimited atonement*. Dr. A.H. H. Boyd held a view of the atonement akin to that taught by Dr. John Brown of the Secession Church in Scotland – a view that the atonement was for all in such a sense as that *all may have life* (italics his). He was, says Dr. Dabney, 'frankly a semi-Pelagian'.... When Dr. Frederick A. Ross taught Arminianism it was probably from lack of accurate knowledge. He did not know what he was doing; he seems to have regarded himself as a Calvinist. The few other men who in its early years had been known for teaching New Theology were Northerners destined in the early years of the war to betake themselves North." *A Brief Sketch of the United Synod*, 28,29. Johnson's picture may be accurate, nevertheless, it should be noted that these men were considered among the key leaders of the United Synod. Mitchell and Ross were both appointed to the reunion committee; Boyd was the author of the "Declaration of Principles," unanimously adopted when the United Synod was established. It would be inaccurate to suggest these men did not represent their church's theology.

[42] Due to the exigencies of the war only 7 of the 14 presbyteries of the United Synod were represented at the 1864 Lynchburg General Assembly. The presbyteries in Tennessee, which had been unable to attend, were still divided on union with the Southern Church. See E.T. Thompson, *Presbyterians in the South*, Vol. II, 121.

beloved Church in 1837, and, as opening the door for controversies in the future, which may cause to be re-enacted the struggles of '34, 5, 6, 7 and 8.[43]

South Carolina had no spirit for compromise. The doctrinal discussions between the two denominations had acknowledged a mutual recognition of one another as orthodox Calvinists. The fourth resolution, to which Adger, Palmer, et. al., had objected, explicitly stated this fact. There was some persistent resistance, but, most Presbyterians in the South, Old and New School, had a broader vision of Presbyterianism and had moved beyond the old divisions of the 1830s. Thomas Cary Johnson, described the 1864 reunion: "This union was honorable to both parties, and has been a source of great blessing to Southern Presbyterianism."[44]

Cumberland Presbyterians

In 1861 the newly constituted Southern Presbyterian Church had expressed a desire to seek closer communion with the Cumberland Presbyterian Church.[45] By the conclusion of the War, efforts were underway to discuss organic union with the Cumberland Presbyterians. The 1867 meetings between the joint Committees of Organic Union shed further light on how the Southern Presbyterian Church viewed subscription to the Confession of Faith. While the union ultimately did not come to pass, the negotiations signaled a willingness to include broader perspectives in the Presbyterian family.

The Cumberland Presbyterian Church had its roots in the frontier revivals at the turn of the century in Kentucky and Tennessee. A separate denomination was initiated when a group of ministers in Cumberland Presbytery were ejected in 1805 by the Synod of Kentucky for teaching doctrines contrary to the Confession of Faith. By 1829 a Cumberland Presbyterian General Assembly had been established. The new denomination produced its own version of the Westminster Confession which modified the traditional language about predestination and human ability toward a more Arminian viewpoint. The Cumberland Church had grown significantly in the South and the West by the 1860s.[46]

---

[43] *Minutes of Presbytery of South Carolina*, Fall Session, Oct.3, 1864, 21-29. The South Carolinians were correct about the reunion being a reversal of 1837. The New School had not changed its views; the reversal was on the Old School side which now openly tolerated the New School version of Calvinism.

[44] Thomas Cary Johnson, *A History of the Southern Presbyterian Church* (New York: The Christian Literature Co., 1894), 438; *A Brief Sketch of the United Synod*, 38.

[45] See *supra* chp. 9, n. 37.

[46] See W.B. Evans, "The Cumberland Presbyterian Church" in *Dictionary of the Presbyterian & Reformed Tradition in America*. ed. D.G. Hart and Mark A. Noll. (Downers Grove, Illinois: InterVarsity Press, 1999); Thompson, *Presbyterians in the South*, I, 144-165; Thomas H. Campbell, *Good News on the Frontier: A History of the Cumberland Presbyterian Church* (Memphis: Frontier Press, 1965); E.K. Regin, *We Believe and So We*

The two committees met in August of 1867. The Southern Presbyterian committee was chaired by Dr. J.O. Stedman and included Dr. John N. Waddell who had also served in the successful negotiations with the United Synod of the South. The Cumberland committee was chaired by Dr. Stanford G. Burney. The Southern Church committee presented a paper which suggested that the two historic issues upon which the churches had been divided (the necessity of an educated ministry and the doctrine of fatalism) should no longer be a hindrance to union. The paper asserted that the Cumberland Church "is now unanimous as to the necessity of an educated ministry, in the sense in which our standards make it obligatory."[47]

Concerning the supposed doctrine of fatalism in the Confession, the Southern Presbyterian committee pointed out that the Confession's teaching had been misconstrued in former days. In fact, the Westminster Standards do not teach fatalism even in the disputed passages and "in many other passages both the free agency of the creature and the contingency of second causes are distinctly asserted;" given these facts, the two churches should seek union. The paper concluded: "we would, as the representatives of the mother Church, from which our brethren withdrew, most cordially invite them to form a union with us upon the basis of the old standards as they were held by their fathers and ours previous to the separation, *the same liberty in the construction of those standards to be given as was then allowed and has since been given in the union of the Old School and New School bodies in the South*" (italics mine).[48]

The Cumberland committee also produced a paper outlining its conditions upon which a union could be consummated. The paper acknowledged a willingness to yield on the question of ministerial educational requirements; however, they respectfully request that the Cumberland modified version of the Confession be substituted for the Confession of the Presbyterian Church. If the Cumberland Confession is not acceptable then the existing Presbyterian Confession of Faith should be "modified substantially." The paper proceeded to list recommended changes in chapters 3, 5, 8, 10 and 17 of the Confession of Faith and corresponding parts of the Catechisms.[49]

The Southern Presbyterian committee replied that while some of the proposed changes would be acceptable, other changes are "so fundamental in their character" that they would have to receive further instruction from the General Assembly. The

---

Speak: a Statement of the Faith of Cumberland Presbyterians (Memphis: Cumberland Presbyterian Church, 1960). See *supra* chp. 3, "Revivals in the South."

[47] *Minutes of the General Assembly of the Presbyterian Church in the United States* 1865-1872 (Richmond), 1867, Appendix, 174.

[48] Ibid.

[49] Ibid., 174-176. The proposed changes primarily related to the decrees of God, the doctrine of providence and the nature of the atonement. These were significant alterations, however, as it was observed: "the Cumberland Committee in the changes they proposed in our received symbols of doctrine, showed that they at least were free from the charge so often made against the Church, of Arminianism in any gross sense of the descriptive term." "The General Assembly," *Southern Presbyterian Review* XIX (January, 1868): 102.

Cumberland representatives then requested that their papers be referred to the Southern Assembly. At this juncture the joint meetings were dissolved with mutual expressions that closer communion might be achieved. The 1868 Southern Assembly declared that the present time was very unfavorable to making changes which would be "so materially modifying the system of doctrine which has for centuries been the distinguishing peculiarity and eminent glory of the Presbyterian churches both of Europe and the United States." This was the end of formal negotiations with the Cumberland Presbyterian Church.[50]

There were additional underlying concerns that caused many Southern Presbyterians to be cautious about joining with the Cumberland Church. Dr. James A. Lyon, a member of the committee representing the Southern Presbyterian body, raised questions about the size of the Cumberland Church and being swallowed up by them; most of the Cumberland ministers were uneducated and power in the church would shift into their hands. The numbers issue also related to the doctrinal questions. Lyon made this observation: "In some instances we have received men of large experience, or eminent gifts, without requiring strict and literal compliance with the requisitions of the Confession of Faith. This however, is the *exception* to the rule. But in the event we merge ourselves into a Church where the majority of the united body will fall short of the requirements of our standards, then the exception will become the *rule*."(italics his)[51]

Another barrier to union was the ever present subject of slavery and the war. The Cumberland committee had also requested that "the amicable adjustment of the political and sectional issues touching slavery and rebellion" of the Cumberland Presbyterian Church be accepted. This was understood by Southern Presbyterians as implying that slaveholding and the rebellion were sinful. This opinion "our Church could never consent to endorse." While the doctrinal issues got primary attention, the sectional question was still painful. The editor of the *Southern Presbyterian Review* declared: "A large portion of the ministry and members of the Cumberland Presbyterian Church were abolitionists."[52]

Southern Moderation

The reunion of 1864 demonstrated the moderate spirit of the Southern Old School majority that warmly embraced the New School. While Southern New School men were generally of a more conservative stripe, they were New School men nonetheless. The 1858 "Declaration and Principles" clearly espoused both the New School view of subscription and the traditional doctrinal positions associated with the New School. The reunion of 1864, just 6 years later, was not a repudiation of

---

[50] Ibid. In 1906, the Northern Church would reunite with the Cumberlands.

[51] Letter from Dr. James A. Lyon to Dr. James O. Stedman, chair of committee, July 16, 1867. See *Minutes of the General Assembly*, PCUS, Appendix (1867), 177, 178. Note Lyon's acknowledgment that Southern Presbyteries have always received men into the ministry who do not hold strictly to the Confession of Faith.

[52] "The General Assembly," *Sothern Presbyterian Review* XIX (January 1868): 103.

New School doctrine but rather a clear affirmation of a broader Calvinism. The doctrinal statement issued by the two committees acknowledged the validity of New School interpretations as orthodox Calvinism. The strict Calvinist party recognized this and resisted the reunion to the end.

The proposed reunion plan had reached out in fraternal charity to New School sensitivities. Voluntary societies were declared worthy of the church's support and persons should have liberty of Christian conscience on the matter. Revivals are to be supported notwithstanding their emotional excesses on occasion. Distinctive New School beliefs on the doctrines of inability and atonement were affirmed. The New School could ask no more concessions than these. These broader perspectives were implicitly acknowledged to be consistent with the Calvinistic "system of doctrine" in the Westminster Standards.

Some argue that the Old School/New School reunion in the South was made purely on the basis of the strict Old School position.[53] This clearly is not the case. The New School gave hearty approval to the plans because the doctrinal statements had satisfied them fully. To suggest that the United Synod had entirely compromised its conscience, so unabashedly proclaimed in the 1858 "Declaration of Principles," is inconceivable for human nature and contrary to the historical record of the doctrinal discussions. New School men considered themselves free to preach their distinctive New School Calvinism within the cordial bonds of the Presbyterian Church in the South. And many of the Old School men freely acknowledged as much.

The amended plan of 1864 simply asked for adoption of the Standards without explanation. The history of the negotiations in Southern reunion discussions made it abundantly clear that there had been a meeting of the minds on the nature of subscription. The fourth resolution of the amended plan explicitly stated this fact notwithstanding the protest of the "ultra" party. Within this context of charitable balancing of viewpoints, the 1864 reunion was desirable and honorable for both branches of the Presbyterian Church in the South.

In the end it was deemed safest to append no doctrinal explanations to the Westminster Standards lest a new creed be in force *de facto*. Both parties agreed to this as the best method for reunion. The old creed of Presbyterians would alone be sufficient for they had understood one another on the issues that had divided them for almost thirty years. Neither party was asked to compromise its conscience on deeply held convictions; all embraced the Westminster Standards and they agreed that in that common Calvinism was room for diversity of expression.

Union with the Independent Presbyterians and the attempted merger with the Cumberland Presbyterians also point to the moderate Calvinism of the Southern

---

[53] Morton H. Smith has claimed that the New School "united with the Old School Southern Assembly on the latter's terms and without any hesitancy regarding subscription to the Standards in the strict sense." Smith, *Studies in Southern Presbyterian Theology*, 35; see also Smith, "Presbyterians of the South," *Westminster Theological Journal*, part 2 (April 1964/65):155.

Church. In both instances there was openness to fellowship with Presbyterian brothers that did not strictly embrace every part of the Confession of Faith. In the case of the Independents and the New School South a diversity of theological persuasion was openly embraced as consistent with the adoption of the Westminster Standards. This was a Calvinism that appreciated the breadth of the Reformed Tradition.

The Southern Church in the last decades of the nineteenth century continued to build upon the broad reunion spirit of 1864. Subscription to the standards was consistently understood as being commitment to the "system of doctrine" of the Confession, i.e., essential Calvinism and not wooden attachment to every article, some of which are not fundamental to that system. This was the general practice of Southern presbyteries which were now comprised of New School as well as Old School presbyters.

A definitive statement of Southern Presbyterian practice is evidenced in the Assembly's commentary on subscription in 1898. Brazos Presbytery overtured the General Assembly to comment on the meaning of the words "system of doctrine" as found in the Book of Church Order, Paragraph 119, Section 2. The 1898 Assembly responded:

> *First,* The words 'system of doctrine' as applied to the whole body of truth contained in the Confession of Faith, being not ambiguous, but sufficiently, definite and plain, the Assembly considers it unnecessary, and therefore declines to give any further definition. *Second,* The use of the words 'system of doctrine' in the terms of subscription preclude the idea of the necessary acceptance of every statement in the standards by the subscribers, but involves the acceptance of so much as is vital to the system as a whole. Difference of opinion as to whether any divergences are or are not vital to the system, when of sufficient importance, should be determined judicially by the proper ecclesiastical courts.[54]

---

[54] *Minutes of the General Assembly*, PCUS, 1898, 223. The Assembly replied in a matter of fact way which indicated that this was the common understanding of the church and not some new interpretation. This statement of the Southern Assembly was cited by a very popular Presbyterian book of the era, *The Creed of Presbyterians*, as the proper understanding of the 1729 Adopting Act. See Egbert Watson Smith, *The Creed of Presbyterians* (New York: The Baker and Taylor Company, 1901), 14,15. George W. Knight, III has interpreted the 1898 statement emphasizing the phrase, "the whole body of truth." He stated: "The 1898 Assembly required all officers to adopt the whole body of truth contained in the Confession of Faith and statements vital to that system but not necessarily every statement if a statement is not vital to that system." George W. Knight, III, "Subscription to the Westminster Confession of Faith and Catechisms," in *The Practice of Confessional Subscription*, ed. David W. Hall (Lanham, Maryland: University Press of America, 1995), 131. Knight appears to be missing the main point of the 1898 declaration which addresses the inquiry about the phrase, "system of doctrine." The Assembly demurred defining the boundaries of the "system of doctrine" because that was the purview of presbytery. The other likely reason that an explanation was deemed unnecessary was that the

Apparently, even in the closing years of the nineteenth century, there were still some individuals within the Southern Church that believed presbyters should subscribe to the Confession *in toto*. This is not surprising as there had always been a few vocal advocates of strict subscription who vehemently opposed any compromise with the "latitudinarian" New School party. Nevertheless, the overwhelming majority of Southern Old School Presbyterians had been in favor of joining with the New School. The 1898 Assembly statement was in the clearest possible language and underscored the Southern Church's commitment to the historic practice of subscription as understood in the reunion consensus.[55] Consistent with Presbyterian polity, church courts determine what does and does not constitute an essential ("vital") of the Calvinistic system of the Confession.

Due to the moderate spirit of mainstream Southern Presbyterianism, the Old School/New School schism was healed in Dixie. The times underscored the importance of unity in essential elements and a willingness to tolerate theological differences. A common foe made Southern Presbyterians rethink the substantive value of those things that formerly had been the basis of bitter division since the 1830s. Ecclesiastical unity among Presbyterians in the South was restored; unfortunately, the sectional divide would run much deeper.

---

phrase had a definite historical meaning - the "system of doctrine" refers to the distinctive Calvinistic system of the standards. The Assembly emphasis is upon the admissibility of exceptions which was implied in the phrase "system of doctrine." Scruples were permitted as long as they were not "vital to the system" which reflected the principles of the Adopting Act. The 1898 statement was a succinct restatement of the morning minute of 1729.

[55] The Northern Church would likewise maintain its commitment to confessional subscription late into the nineteenth century. In 1890 as the General Assembly considered revising the Westminster Standards; the Northern Assembly instructed the Committee on Revision that "they shall not propose any alterations or amendments that will in any way impair the integrity of the Reformed or Calvinistic system of doctrine taught in the Confession of Faith." *Minutes of the General Assembly*, PCUSA, 1890, 86.

CHAPTER 11

Northern Reunion and Sectional Division

Within a few years of reunion in the South, the northern church would begin similar negotiations on reunion. A number of events paved the way for the beginning of reunion discussions in the North. One major factor was the Southern departure from the New School Assembly in 1857. Abolition had become a preoccupation of New School Assemblies for many years. Southerners in effect were forced out by the firm New School anti-slavery stance and left with no option but to seek a new ecclesiastical organization. One New School historian wondered if this had been a mistake:

> It will always be a question whether it was wise for the young Church, with so many practical problems at hand calling for early solution, with so many other difficulties besetting it, to carry on for twenty years in every Assembly from first to last so distracting and divisive a discussion as that which slavery elicited, – whether the successive judgments and measures were all constitutional, equitable, considerate enough in view of all the difficulties developed, – whether the assumption of authority by the later Assemblies did not resemble too closely the course and action of 1837, – whether it would not have been better to refrain at least from disciplinary proceedings which could have no possible issue but division and separation.[1]

Other factors contributing to the emerging openness to northern reunion was the removal of New School ecclesiastical entanglements with non-Presbyterians which the Old School believed had diluted the ecclesiastical and theological integrity of Presbyterianism. The 1801 Plan of Union and New School association with voluntary societies had been key points of contention between the two parties for a long time. The 1801 Plan of Union had been set aside by 1852 and the New School partnership with the American Home Missionary Society was dissolved in 1860. These changes removed serious obstacles to potential reunion discussions from an Old School perspective.

Another pivotal landmark was the beginning of the War Between the States. In the Old School this produced a schism with the Southerners who resisted Old School attempts to declare absolute loyalty to the Federal Union. The Southern Old School Church (Presbyterian Church in the Confederate States of America) held its first separate General Assembly in 1861. This Old School schism in turn made

---

[1] Edward D. Morris, *The Presbyterian Church New School, 1837-1869: An Historical Review* (Columbus, Ohio: The Chaplain Press, 1905), 145.

Northern New School abolitionists much more open to pursuing reunion with fellow Northern Presbyterians. From the beginning of the war, the Northern New School church was intensely loyal to the Federal Government.[2] The New School abhorred slavery and the Southern rebellion that supported this evil institution. Northern Old School commitment to the union, and its increasingly open condemnation of slavery was very attractive to the Northern New School that perceived this as positive movement toward their own position.

After the War Between the States had been concluded, the national spirit of binding up the old wounds made its way into the churches of America, many of whom had split over sectional issues. There was an earnest desire expressed by some for a "Federal Union" of evangelical denominations. Initial meetings to explore this union took place in the spring of 1865 in New York, Philadelphia and Boston. And there were new advocates for a specific confederation of the Presbyterian bodies in America. Among Northern Presbyterians, the union spirit had begun to be voiced even before the war's conclusion. The 1863 Old School Assembly had received a memorial favoring reunion with the New School and by 1864 both Assemblies had received such overtures from their presbyteries.

Henry B. Smith and New School Subscription

When reunion negotiations were initiated in 1866, a primary goal was to arrive at a consensus on the question of subscription to the standards. Both parties were suspicious and hesitant to fully trust the other party's intentions. Each perceived the other to hold a rigid position and both branches believed the other had compromised Presbyterian principles. Nevertheless, candid interaction began to reveal more of a consensus on this divisive issue than either side had anticipated. Meetings of the Joint Committee produced declarations attempting to define the intended meaning of subscription. The spirit of distrust, however, still prevailed in much of the church. Given the historical doctrinal tensions between the two schools, some suspected that the reunion deliberations were disingenuous. Had confessional integrity been compromised and reunion become an end in itself no matter what the cost?

It was inconceivable to some Old School men that the New School could seriously and honestly affirm the standards as the confession of their faith. It was equally incredulous to New School men that the Old School would actually endorse liberty by allowing exceptions to parts of the doctrinal standards. Despite this underlying skepticism, progress was made in understanding one another. New School clarification of its position was most ably articulated by Professor Henry Boyton Smith of Union Seminary in New York.[3]

---

[2] See Lewis G. Vander Velde, The *Presbyterian Churches and the Federal Union 1861-1869* (Cambridge: Harvard University Press, 1932), 337-378.

[3] Henry B. Smith (1815-1877) was the leading theologian of the New School during the period of reunion negotiations. Ordained as a Congregational pastor in 1847, he transferred his ministerial credentials to the New School Presbyterian Church. He was editor of the *American Theological Review*, later renamed the *American Presbyterian Theological Review*,

At the New School Assembly of 1864, Dr. Henry B. Smith, the retiring moderator, had preached the opening sermon entitled, "Christian Union and Ecclesiastical Reunion" based on Ephesians 4:13. Smith urged his New School brethren to earnestly pursue union with their Old School counterparts. There are three prime conditions for reunion – a spirit of mutual concession, acceptance of the integrity of the Presbyterian system of church order and an affirmation of the Presbyterian doctrinal standards. On the third point, Smith suggested that, "the reunion be simply on the basis of the Standards, which we equally accept without private interpretation – interpreted in their legitimate grammatical and historic sense in the spirit of the Adopting Act, and as containing the system of doctrine taught in the Holy Scriptures. My liberty here is not to be judge of another man's conscience. Any other view not only puts the Confession above the Scriptures, but also puts somebody's theological system above the Confession."[4]

Smith would play a vital role in the reunion negotiations because of the respect for him in both parties and his consistent voice for maintaining historic Presbyterianism as the bedrock for reunion. When Charles Hodge attacked the reunion plan in 1867, it was Smith that ably defended the New School position. Hodge indicted the New School for holding to a latitudinarian principle of subscription.[5] Professor Smith countered that this was an unjust accusation against New School Presbyterians. The New School had been accused of embracing heresy, false doctrine and "evasive subscription;" and all of these charges were unproven.[6] On the contrary, the New School had "uniformly repudiated the principle" with which she was being charged. The whole plan of reunion was staked on this vital point of uniformity in interpreting the form of assent to the Standards. According to Smith, there is no ground of difference between the two schools on the question of subscription.[7]

Smith concurred with Hodge's perspective that the form of assent was properly understood as including adoption of the "system of doctrine" in the Confession. The Calvinistic or Reformed system was adopted and this meant more than mere affirmation of the "essential doctrines of Christianity." Likewise, an "every proposition" position was an improper interpretation of the form of assent to the Confession. Smith cited favorably Hodge's article of 1831 which opposed the two extremes of either latitude or strictness in interpreting the form of subscription. As

---

from 1859-1874. See Lewis F. Stearns, *Henry Boynton Smith* (Boston: Houghton, Mifflin and Company, 1892); Henry Boynton Smith (Mrs.), ed., *Henry Boynton Smith: His Life and Work* (New York: A.C. Armstrong & Son, 1881).

[4] Henry B. Smith quoted in J.F. Stearns, "Historical Sketch of the Reunion," *American Presbyterian Review* New Series, I (July 1869): 576.

[5] Henry B. Smith, "Presbyterian Reunion" in *American Presbyterian and Theological Review* V (October 1867): 624-665. Smith was responding to an essay on "Reunion" by Charles Hodge in the July 1867 issue of the *Princeton Review*. Hodge's article had been reprinted and circulated in pamphlet form.

[6] Ibid., 658.

[7] Ibid., 640, 641.

one example of New School concurrence with Hodge's position, Smith pointed out that Albert Barnes, in his defense before the Second Presbytery of Philadelphia in 1835, directly referred to Hodge's 1831 article as expressing his own views.[8]

Hodge's claim that the New School held an indefinite "substance of doctrine" view of subscription was unjust. Smith countered: "We disallow the phrase 'substance of doctrine' because it is indefinite, easily misunderstood, and does not suggest the right theory." There is no evidence that the New School as a body has ever supported such a viewpoint. Smith added, "by many New School men it was publicly and definitely denied." The New School also rejected the *ipsissima verba* theory as "inconsistent with the plain terms of the Adopting Act, and with the uniform practice of the Presbyterian church." According to Smith the median position was the correct one. He stated:

> The right theory is found in a simple and honest interpretation of the ordination formula, 'that we receive the Confession of Faith as containing the system of doctrine taught in the Holy Scriptures.' This declares that the system of the Confession is the system taught in the Bible. The system of the Confession, as everybody knows, is the Reformed or Calvinistic system, in distinction from the Lutheran, the Arminian, the Antinomian, the Pelagian, and the Roman Catholic. No one can honestly and fairly subscribe the Confession who does not accept the Reformed or Calvinistic system.[9]

Smith believed there was a tension between the Adopting Act of 1729 and the Synod's declaration of 1736. While the Adopting Act clearly allowed for scruples to be stated, as long as the scruple was not about an "essential and necessary article," the 1736 statement mandated a stricter interpretation which forbade making "distinctions." Smith was skeptical about the 1736 pronouncement which implied that no scruples may be admitted. He stated, "we do not see how they could say this, seeing that, as a matter of fact, those distinctions are referred to in the Adopting Act itself, where it says that 'scruples' were proposed and a 'solution of them' agreed upon." Smith argued that unless one acknowledged the principle of allowing scruples, there could be no substantial objection to the "every proposition" stance.[10]

Smith agreed with E. H. Gillett's perspective that the 1736 Synod adopted a "too unqualified" interpretation of the form of assent. The later synod had no right to undo what the Adopting Act had unmistakably affirmed, i.e., allowing a minister to state his scruples. The 1736 pronouncement seemed to imply a denial of all distinctions. Smith observed: "But they seem to deny that any 'distinctions' whatever were made by the Synod of 1729, or could be made; and this is plainly incorrect."[11]

---

[8] Ibid., 641, 642. See Charles Hodge, "Remarks on Dr. Cox's Communication," *Biblical Repertory and Theological Review* III (October 1831): 520-525.

[9] Ibid., 643.

[10] Ibid., 643, 644.

[11] Ibid., 645.

According to Smith, Hodge's perspective that the 1736 Synod was addressing Dickinson's position, distinguishing essentials and non-essentials of Christianity, was not at all certain from the records. Smith defended Gillett as an historian for simply telling the facts as the documents record them. It does not follow that Gillett was endorsing Dickinson's view. Gillett does not say, according to Smith, that the New School adopted the theory of "essentials of Christianity" as their theory of subscription.[12] Smith repudiated Hodge's suggestion that the New School understanding of subscription implied that the Confession be received "as containing the essential doctrines of Christianity and nothing more." Smith exclaimed: "This we directly and unanimously deny."[13]

Smith argued that the first article of the Plan of Union was perfectly clear to everyone. That article affirmed that the Westminster Confession shall continue to be sincerely received and adopted as containing "the system of doctrine" taught in Holy Scripture. He commented, "What theory of assent is here implied? Manifestly, and that only, of accepting 'the system' as Calvinistic. There is not a hint about 'substance of doctrine;' there is not a sidelong allusion to 'essentials of Christianity only.' Everybody knows that the 'fair historical' sense of the Confession is plainly and resolutely Calvinistic.... No candid mind can give any other sense to this article, than that it endorses the view, that the Confession is to be received in its integrity as containing the Reformed system of faith."[14]Smith asserted that this historical understanding of the Confession was uniformly acknowledged by the New School. He added: "Among honest and candid men, there is really no doubt or question as to what subscription implies. Any candidate, before any of our presbyteries, who should say that he received the Confession 'as containing the essential principles of Christianity and no more,' would be unhesitatingly rejected by them."[15]

Within the boundaries of accepting the Confession in its "fair historical sense" there has always been in the Presbyterian Church allowable difference in explaining individual doctrines. Smith continued: "These allowable differences must, of course, be such as do not impair the integrity of the system, as distinguished from Lutheranism, Arminianism, Pelagianism, etc., nor vitiate any one of the doctrines that make up the system. But within these limits, there have been, and still are, very considerable diversities." These differences have always been present throughout the history of the Reformed Tradition.[16]

---

[12] Ibid. Hodge had criticized Gillett's *History of the Presbyterian Church* for its interpretation of the Adopting Act; E.H. Gillett, *History of the Presbyterian Church in the United States of America* 2 vols. (Philadelphia: Presbyterian Publication Committee, 1864). For Hodge's reaction to Gillett see Charles Hodge, "Reunion," *Princeton Theological Review* XXXIX (July 1867): 515, 516. See *supra* chp. 7 "Colonial Heritage."

[13] Ibid., 665.

[14] Ibid., 646, 647.

[15] Ibid., 648.

[16] Ibid. Smith cited the following as examples of this diversity: "In Switzerland there was a Stapfer as well as a Turrettine; in France, there was the school of Saumur as well as that of

Smith highlighted three points about which there had been differences between the Old School and New School – imputation, ability and the extent of the atonement. Some of the New School men have denied the immediate imputation of Adam's sin; man's inability has been defined by certain New School men as "moral;" and some, while denying a universal application of the atonement, have none the less affirmed a general provision of the atonement. The differences in explaining these doctrines are not inconsistent with an "honest" acceptance of the Confession of Faith and thus should not be a bar to ministerial communion in the Presbyterian Church. He recalled that Hodge himself has admitted that ministers have never been excised from the church for *explanations* of particular doctrines but for the *rejection* of said doctrine.[17]

Professor Edward Morris of Lane Seminary concurred that a distinction has always existed between the essence of a doctrine and its "accidents or accessories; between the fact incorporated in a dogmatic statement and the theory or theories employed to account for that fact; between the essential truth affirmed in an article of belief and the explanations or illustrations introduced in exposition of the truth." Morris used the doctrine of original sin as an illustration. The Calvinist theologians and confessions all affirmed the fact of Adam's sin affecting posterity, yet, "no man pretends to be able to comprehend or explain the doctrine of the fall of Adam, and its bearing upon the present character and condition of men; ... it involves mysteries which human reason, enlightened by divine revelation, can not fathom." Likewise, divine sovereignty and human freedom, both of which are incorporated into our Calvinistic system, are mysteries that defy explanation. Morris admitted: "All the cardinal truths of our religion, and especially those which are essential parts of our Calvinistic belief, are like mountains, whose gilded summits we clearly see, and whose main outlines we more or less vaguely discern, but whose deep foundations lie concealed in the comprehending wisdom of him by whom the facts themselves were graciously revealed for our salvation."[18]

Montauban; the Heidelberg Catechism and the Decrees of Dordt are both Reformed Confessions, yet different in tone; Supralapsarianism, Sublapsarianism, and the Theology of the Covenants were varying forms of the one Calvinism; the Confession of Westminster itself was a compromise between theological parties; our own Adopting Act recognizes differences upon points 'not essential or necessary.' The Calvinism of Edwards was of a different type from that even of Dickinson and Davies; Alexander and Woods, Ashbel Green and Richards, did not agree on all points. The Erskines and Glas, Dick and Hill, John Brown and Chalmers, were all Calvinists with variations. Every theological system and every Confession, is to a certain extent an adjustment of antagonisms."

[17] Ibid., 649, 650.

[18] Edward D. Morris, "The Reformed or Calvinistic Sense," *American Presbyterian Review* New Series, I (April 1869): 256, 257. Morris suggested that Charles Hodge agreed with him on this point. He quoted from a July 1867 article in the *Princeton Review* where Hodge stated: "Original Sin is one thing, the way in which it is accounted for is another."

The different doctrinal explanations typically associated with the New School have in fact been tolerated in both branches of the Presbyterian Church according to Henry Smith. He pointed out:

> We have some pretty thorough Old School men on almost all the points in the New School; we know many Old School ministers who can only be classified as New School in point of doctrine. The Old School is divided on the question of immediate and mediate imputation; the distinction between natural and moral inability and ability, is recognized by many of their divines; and they very generally preach that the atonement is sufficient for all, while we agree with them that it is applied only to the elect.... Both parties already have the same Confession of Faith and Catechism, the best extant. All that we can do is to accept them in their essential and necessary articles, with a recognition of possible, though guarded, diversities of explanation, the system and doctrines remaining in their integrity.[19]

Smith countered the accusation that the New School tolerated men who embraced New Haven Theology. The New School has "virtually condemned this system" and does not ordain men that hold it. He admitted that the doctrines associated with New Haven theology indeed deny some of the cardinal doctrines of the Reformed system. But, the New School's position on these matters was made manifest in the "Explication of Doctrine" drawn up at the Auburn Convention in 1837. Many of the accusations leveled against the New School are not substantiated but rely merely on "hearsay and rumor" and the "exaggerations and eccentricities of individuals." In contrast, the Auburn Declaration was "authentic and documentary evidence."[20]

Smith acknowledged the reality of diversity:

> There are differences among ourselves; there are differences in the Old School also; there have always been, and may always be, differences in the church. For there is the mysterious region where the infinite and the finite, divine and human agency, come together; and what moral vision has penetrated that mystery? Here is where moral obligation, moral agency, and personal responsibility are at stake. Divine sovereignty and human freedom here come to their closest contact, and the problem of theology is to save both. There is a fair and broad distinction between natural and moral ability and inability. The differences here, as they actually exist, are of more or less, rather than of Yes and No. We do not all agree in our philosophy and metaphysics; and do we need to do so, in order to ministerial fellowship? If anyone so holds the fact of man's freedom and ability as to deny the doctrines of God's omnipotence, and of original sin, he of

---

[19] Smith, "Presbyterian Reunion," 650. Smith did not believe the Old School as a body expected strict compliance on these issues. Smith asked: "Does it mean, that we must repeat its shibboleths of immediate imputation, unqualified inability, and a partial atonement? If this is what it means, both the Old School and the New School ought to understand it; and then we shall see, whether even the Old School is prepared to make this an imperative condition. If it is, reunion is undesirable and impossible. We will concede all we can, but concessions have their limits." "Presbyterian Reunion," 660.

[20] Ibid., 652, 654.

course could not accept our Confession of Faith, and would be rejected by our presbyteries.[21]

Some men are inconsistent; persons may not agree on the inferences that others draw from a particular position. Toleration must be allowed and it is unfair to suggest that Presbyterians should "tie ourselves down to any single extreme." Smith continued:

> Some may hold and continue to teach immediate imputation, an unqualified inability, and an exclusive limitation in the very design of the atonement. But no one has the right to say that such views are essential to the integrity of the Reformed system, or to an honest adhesion to all its doctrines. Any school that does this, assumes what it has no right to assume; it creates a narrow and partial standard of orthodoxy, to which we owe no allegiance. Even if we held the same doctrines, we would deny the dictation. No man and no school can say, that historical Calvinism is necessarily identified with such partial views; other men, the best, wisest and most learned in both schools, know that this is not the case.[22]

Smith insisted that the "bulk of our ministry" has never gone with either the extreme explanations of the older Calvinism or the theories of the New Divinity. The New School occupies the middle ground. "In this middle and temperate zone lies the solid faith of our churches, making them strong for solid work." And this *via media* is orthodox Calvinism. The New School does in fact affirm the essential tenets of the Reformed Tradition that have distinguished her among the other Protestant churches.[23]

---

[21] Ibid., 654, 655.

[22] Ibid., 655.

[23] Ibid., 656, 657. Smith characterized New School theology: "We believe that God created all things from nothing, by the word of his power; that in his all-wise providence He sustains and governs all his creatures and all their actions; that by his decree all things stand, that in his wise, holy and eternal purpose all our destiny, for time and for eternity, is embraced – yet so that violence is not done to the will of [the] creature, nor is the liberty and contingency of second causes taken away, but rather established. We also confess the essential doctrines, which make the distinguishing and vital substance of the Reformed system, – original sin, as derived from Adam, since we sinned in him and fell with him in his first transgression; total depravity, which makes us averse to all good, and unable, of ourselves, to repent and believe – yet so that this inability is moral, rooted also in our personal responsibility, and stricken with our own and not merely a foreign guilt, the atoning work of our Lord, not symbolical and governmental only, but also a proper sacrifice for sin, and thus a satisfaction to the divine justice as well as a revelation of the divine love; the covenant of redemption, wherein this atonement was made so general as to be sufficient for all and to be offered unto all, and so particular as to be effectually applied in the salvation of believers; personal election unto everlasting life, and the final perseverance of those who are effectually called. Justification only by the righteousness of Christ, regeneration only by the power of the Holy Ghost, sanctification, progressive here and completed hereafter, and endless life in Christ, we equally confess and believe. With all the diversities of the imperfect

It was Smith's conviction that Old School and New School "substantially agree" in doctrinal belief. Where there are differences, these may in honesty be affirmed as consistent with the constitution of the church. Smith wrote:

There are no differences which do not fairly come under historical Calvinism. We can both receive the Reformed system of faith, and its individual doctrines, in their integrity, while differing in explanations and proportions. If we did not believe this, we would not, and could not, favor reunion. Apart from theological technicalities and philosophical explanations, we are one in accepting that grand old system of faith, Pauline, Augustinian and Reformed, which has been the vital substance and stay of the church in its main conflicts with error and unbelief.[24]

Smith believed that the "groundless imputations" of doctrinal unsoundness, latitudinarianism and dishonest subscription attack the faith and honor of New School men. These accusations have been met with the "unanimous denial of all our journals." He resented the tone of Hodge's article, which he said, attempts "to claim a monopoly, not only on Presbyterian orthodoxy, but also of the Presbyterian conscience."[25]

The suggestion that New School men on the Joint Committee have "hoodwinked" the Old School men, by misrepresenting the "real views" of the church, was not credible. "Nobody can believe that the Joint Committee was so blind, weak and silly." Hodge had asserted that the present Plan for Union "abandons the principles" on which the Presbyterian Church was founded. This was a gross exaggeration and a cruel accusation. Smith retorted that, as a matter of fact, the very concessions on doctrine and subscription that Hodge supported in his article are "all for which we really contend." Smith added: "We say that we adopt the principle of subscription which he advocates."[26]

Smith was convinced that reunion would strengthen the mission of the church and remove the reproach brought upon "our common Christianity" by continued strife and separation. He embraced a vision of a unique American Presbyterianism that while building on her Old World roots, yet, charted her own course. Smith asked the question:

---

and jarring speech of earth, there is amongst us a substantial accord in that which makes the unison and melody of the one language of heaven." For an overview of distinctive New School doctrines see series of articles in *Presbyterian Quarterly Review* (1854-56, nos. IX, XI, XII, XIV, XVI) on "Old and New Theology." Article topics include: original sin and depravity, justification, atonement, regeneration and ability; "'Old and New School' Theology," *Presbyterian Quarterly Review* VIII (January 1860):353-399; George F. Duffield, "Doctrines of the New School Presbyterian Church," *American Presbyterian and Theological Review* New Series, I (July 1863): 561-635.

[24] Ibid., 656.

[25] Ibid., 658, 659. See Hodge, "Reunion." *Princeton Theological Review*, July 1867.

[26] Ibid., 658-660; See also n., 665.

Why may we not forget or tolerate our non-essential differences, and rise to the full stature of our work? The strength of Presbyterianism is in its doctrine and polity; its weakness is, in its tenacity for non essentials – here is the main cause of its divisions. This is not in harmony with the spirit of the nineteenth century, with the true spirit of American Presbyterianism, or with the spirit of Christianity. We need a broader basis for our work. Ours must be an American, and not an imported, still less a merely Scotch, Presbyterianism. Much as we love and honor Scotland, we can not there find the perfect type for our free and growing church.[27]

No one could question Smith's Reformed orthodoxy, but, a question remained in some Old School minds concerning the extent to which Smith's views reflected the New School perspective as a body. In November of 1867, the overwhelming New School support of the ecumenical Presbyterian National Union Convention[28] and its strong affirmation of the Westminster Standards seemed to answer most remaining concerns about New School convictions. At the Convention, it had been Smith who put forward the phrase that the Confession should be "received in its proper historical sense, that is the Calvinistic or Reformed sense." Writing about the convention in 1869, J.F. Stearns said: "And from that time to this we have never heard from any quarter in our branch of the church a single voice dissenting from the position there taken by their delegates. The result proved, as might have been expected, eminently acceptable to all candid men in both parties. Even Dr. Hodge had whispered to Dr. Musgrave that it met his approval. It had, no doubt, a most important influence in producing harmony and confidence between the two parties in all parts of the church."[29]

Road to Reunion

In March of 1868 the Joint Committee of Reunion met in Philadelphia to complete their recommendations to the General Assembly of both bodies. When it came to the doctrinal article, several phrases were added to the article to clarify what was meant by "the Confession of Faith shall continue to be sincerely received and adopted." The so-called "Smith amendment" from the Convention was included which declared that assent to the Confession was understood in "the Calvinistic or Reformed – sense." To meet New School concerns the "Gurley amendment" was also added to the first article. The Gurley amendment stated, "It is also understood that various methods of viewing, stating, explaining and illustrating the doctrines of

---

[27] Ibid., 662, 663.

[28] The Presbyterian National Union Convention originated in a proposal from the Synod of the Reformed Presbyterian Church "to inaugurate measures to heal Zion's breaches and to bring into one the divided portions of the Presbyterian family." Though it had no official ecclesiastical sanction, all the Presbyterian Churches in America sent delegates. See "The Philadelphia Presbyterian Union Convention," *American Presbyterian and Theological Review* VI (January 1868): 104-138.

[29] J. F. Stearns, "Historical Sketch of the Reunion," *American Presbyterian Review* New Series I (July, 1869): 584.

the Confession which do not impair the integrity of the Reformed or Calvinistic system, are to be freely allowed in the united church as they have hitherto been allowed in the separate churches." The New School men believed the Gurley amendment safeguarded "reasonable liberty within the limits of the Confession which our Presbyterian standards manifestly contemplate."[30] The joint committee added to the terms an explanation of why it believed the Smith and Gurley amendments were useful:

> The same confession is adopted by all. It is adopted in the same terms as containing the same system. To make this agreement the more determinate, the Committee have given this system its historic name. At the same time that we mutually interchange these guarantees for orthodoxy, we mutually interchange guarantees for Christian liberty. Differences always have existed and been allowed in the Presbyterian Churches in Europe and America, as to modes of explaining and theorizing within the metes and bounds of the one accepted system. What exists in fact, we have undertaken to express in words. To put into exact formulas what opinions should be allowed and what interdicted, would be to write a new Confession of Faith. This, neither Branch of the Church desires. Your Committee have assumed no such work of supererogation. Neither have they made compromises or concessions. They append no codicil to the old Symbols. They have asserted, as being essential to all true unity, the necessity of adopting the same Confession and the same System, with the recognition of liberty on either hand, for such differences as do not impair the integrity of the system itself; which is all the liberty that any branch of the great Calvinistic family of Churches has ever claimed or desired. Your Committee cannot see how it was possible for them to employ language more precise and guarded, unless they were prepared to substitute 'private interpretation' for the recognized standards of the Church. To go further in either direction than they have done, would certainly lead to useless and endless 'trifles of words.' Language somewhere must find a limit. It would be impossible so to frame expression on this subject, that those who are opposed to Reunion may not find occasion to cavil and object. But the Committee hope and trust that the Article now reported will commend itself to all fair-minded men, as containing what is precise, yet not exclusive; definite, yet not rigid; specific, yet not inflexible; liberal, without laxity; catholic, without latitudinarianism. If exact uniformity in all shades of opinion, in technical adjustments, in philosophic theories, be regarded as essential to union, we should earnestly recommend the indefinite adjournment of the present movement. Nor

---

[30] Ibid.," 585. A Special Committee was appointed by the 1868 New School Assembly to respond to the Committee on Reunion's report. The Committee addressed the concern within the New School that Presbyteries in the reunited church might oppress New School men. They answered that the necessary safeguards were in place. The Special Committee replied: "The man whose sentiments do not violate the Calvinistic system cannot be hurt ... If the man is not out of the pale of his former church's orthodoxy, he cannot be in danger from any ecclesiastical court's rigidity or bigotry." *Minutes the General Assembly of the Presbyterian Church in the United States of America* (New School) vol. II 1859-1869 (New York: Presbyterian Publication Committee, reprint, Presbyterian Board of Publication and Sabbath School, 1894), 1868, 511.

would consistency allow us to rest here; our present organizations should be dissolved and exchanged for disintegration and individualism.[31]

The "Terms of Reunion" along with the committee's explanation was presented to the two Assemblies in May of 1868. In the Old School Assembly objection was primarily raised to the explanatory clauses of the doctrinal article. In the New School Assembly, there was concern about the tenth article which affirmed the right of presbyteries to examine ministers who are in good and regular standing. After no little debate, both Assemblies by very large majorities adopted the plan. In the Old School Assembly, a minority who had objected to the reunion plan entered a formal protest. The protest was answered by a committee appointed to the task and chaired by Professor William G.T. Shedd of Union Seminary.

The "Answer to the Protest" was approved and adopted by the Old School Assembly. The "Answer" declared that New School Calvinism was indeed orthodox and it affirmed that the 1837 New School pronouncement of "true doctrines" in the 1837 Auburn Declaration "embrace all the fundamentals of the Calvinistic creed."[32] The Old School Assembly said the allegation of New School tolerance of Pelagian and Arminian tenets was "without foundation." In no uncertain terms, the "Answer to the Protest" proclaimed:

> The Assembly is fully satisfied that any instances of laxity of doctrine among the New School which have been exhibited, are exceptional cases, and that the great body of the other Church sincerely and firmly stand upon the basis of our common standards ... this General Assembly holds and affirms that it not only commits, but binds any ecclesiastical body that should receive it to pure and genuine Calvinism.... And it must be distinctly observed, that if any doctrines had been hitherto allowed by the New School body which 'impair the integrity of the Calvinistic system,' they are not to be allowed in the united Church under the terms of union. Such doctrines are condemned, and any one who may teach them will be subject to discipline.[33]

Despite the Old School Assembly's rejection of the protest, it nevertheless wanted to appease the minority that had raised objections to the reunion plan. The Old School Assembly, while approving the Report of the Joint Committee on Reunion, expressed its preference that both the Smith and Gurley amendments be

---

[31] *Minutes of the General Assembly* (New School), 1868, II, 506. See William Adams, "The Reunion" in *Presbyterian Reunion Memorial Volume 1837-1871* (New York: DeWitt C. Lent and Company, 1870), 279, 280.

[32] A.A. Hodge pointed out how these 16 essential points of doctrine are "authoritatively interpreting the sense in which the Westminster Confession of Faith is accepted by large branches of the Presbyterian Church." He cited the action of the 1868 Old School Assembly that endorsed the Auburn Declaration as containing "all the fundamentals of the Calvinistic creed." A.A. Hodge, *Commentary on the Westminster Confession of Faith* (Philadelphia: Presbyterian Board of Publication and Sabbath School Work, 1885), Appendix II, 544.

[33] Adams, "The Reunion," 288. Adams was citing the 1868 Minutes of the Old School Assembly.

left out, believing that "by omitting these clauses the basis will be more simple and more expressive of mutual confidence." The New School Assembly meanwhile had adopted the report of the Joint Committee. Confusion ensued during the next months as New School presbyteries approved the original plan by a large majority while Old School presbyteries were much divided. Some Old School presbyteries approved the plan, others approved the amended proposal with the omissions and still others rejected the plan as the only overture before them to be considered.[34]

In order to address this confusion, the New School members of the reunion committee met in January of 1869 and produced a letter to New School presbyteries to inform them as to the current state of affairs and recommended that presbyteries at a regular meeting express their assent to the proposed Old School amendment omitting the two phrases in the first article. They also recommended the omission of the tenth article which read: "It is agreed, that the Presbyteries possess the right to examine ministers applying for admission from other Presbyteries; but each Presbytery shall be left free to decide for itself when it shall exercise the right."[35] The New School committee members felt the same principle was at stake, only applied to polity rather than doctrine. The hope was that if these actions were taken the next General Assemblies could move to formal reunion without delay of another year.

While the New School committee members were willing to concede the omission of the objectionable portions of article one, they were also careful to state that the underlying liberty affirmed in the Smith and Gurley amendments would not be sacrificed. In the address to the New School presbyteries, the committee men state, "It must, however, be well understood, that, by agreeing to the omissions in question, the Presbyteries do not relinquish nor deny the right to all reasonable liberty in the statement of views and the interpretations of the Standards, as generally expressed in the First Article as it now stands; and also that that interpretation of their own language by the Joint Committee in the preamble and conclusion of their May 1868 Report is to be accepted as the true interpretation."[36]

In May of 1869 both Assemblies met in New York City within walking distance of one another. With the confusing situation in the Old School presbyteries and the persistent resistance of an Old School minority, some of the New School men were losing their patience with the whole matter. Stearns reported that, "in the New School portion of the church a considerable degree of coldness had begun to manifest itself. Not a few of them began to feel that they had been trifled with." Nevertheless, a "spirit of love and concord" prevailed and a new committee of conference was appointed with five ministers and five ruling elders from each Assembly. On the seventh day, a report signed by all twenty of the committee members was presented. This revised 1869 Plan of Reunion succinctly stated the

---

[34] Stearns, "Historical Sketch of the Reunion," 587, 588.

[35] *Minutes of the General Assembly* (New School), 1868, 504.

[36] "Address of the Reunion Committee to the Presbyteries" quoted in Stearns, "Historical Sketch of the Reunion," 589.

doctrinal basis: "The reunion shall be effected on the doctrinal and ecclesiastical basis of our common Standards; The Scriptures of the Old and New Testaments shall be acknowledged to be the inspired word of God, and the only infallible rule of faith and practice; the Confession of Faith shall continue to be sincerely received and adopted as containing the system of doctrine taught in the Holy Scriptures."[37]

The new reunion basis excluded the Gurley amendment which had made explicit the principle of allowing diverse explanations of Calvinism "as they have hitherto been allowed in the separate Churches." The basis simply affirms the traditional subscription language to which both bodies already gave allegiance. One should note, wrote Stearns, that the intent of the excluded amendment was retained in the preamble of the 1869 plan which declared: "each recognizing the other as a sound and orthodox body according to the Confession." Stearns described this phrase as a "frank and full acknowledgment of equal standing of both churches in respect to their orthodoxy." The New School was very pleased with this mutual affirmation.[38]

When this line of the Report was read in the Old School Assembly there was spontaneous applause. Dr. Musgrave, the chairman of the committee, told the Old School Assembly: "in the preamble, each recognized the other as sound in the faith founded on the Confession. Hence the united body will never tolerate heresy. They had understood each other, also, on the question of liberty. The impression had been made that the Old School would tolerate no difference of opinion, but insist on the *ipsissima verba* doctrine. There always have been shades of opinion in the old church. May the day never come when one man shall think for all. There must be allowed reasonable liberty of opinion."[39] The Old School vote was 290 yeas and 9 nays.

In the New School Assembly, when the question was called, the whole Assembly rose in affirmation and the Moderator declared its unanimous adoption. After singing a hymn and a prayer, a committee was dispatched to announce the decision to the other Assembly. Even with both bodies overwhelmingly endorsing reunion, and the powerful reunion spirit in the air, it would take due diligence to make it work. Even with the refined plan of reunion agreed upon, the human element of working together would be paramount. Stearns, who had been a part of the reunion negotiations throughout, highlighted this truth:

And we shall need on both sides the greatest charity, forbearance and mutual conciliation. In particular those who think themselves the special guardians of

---

[37] Ibid., 592. J. G. Montfort observed: "It is a curious as well as an interesting part of the history of the reunion movement, that in yielding to the fears of the doubting, and to the importunities of opposers, by trying to add explanations to the standards for the sake of liberty or safety, almost all have become convinced that the most practicable and safe basis is the standards pure and simple." In the process of discussing the explanatory clauses it was made manifest that a substantial unity existed. J. G. Monfort, "Progress of the Reunion Movement" *American Presbyterian Review* New Series, I (April 1869): 314, 315.

[38] Ibid., 596.

[39] Ibid., 596, 597.

orthodoxy will have to be very considerate in their application of their principles, and those who are zealous for liberty of thought and language will have to be very wise and moderate in their use of it. We stand upon the Confession of Faith by the most solemnly renewed pledges to each other, and wherein our views differ from those of our brethren, we are bound to express our differences that they will not through any fault of ours be mistaken by them for departures from our common standards. Boldness of thought and expression may be a virtue. But it must not be allowed unnecessarily to hinder charity.[40]

New School Vindication

The New School had dreamed of reunion ever since the schism. Once shamed by her Old School brethren in the Exscinding Acts she could now lift her head in triumph. The schism had been a scandal and was resolved by a reaffirmation of mutual respect and brotherhood among the American Presbyterians. The reunion was a vindication of New School integrity that had suffered unjust prejudice at the hands of a reactionary Old School in 1837. There had been extremists in the New School body but they never had been as influential as the Old School had suspected. The New School had demonstrated her orthodoxy during the three decades of separation and the Old School eventually recognized the tragedy of a continuing schism among brethren who shared a common Calvinism.

At the heart of the New School ethos had been the priority of gospel witness. New Schoolers consistently viewed the proclamation of the good news as the core of their existence as Presbyterians. Even Presbyterian distinctives were to be subservient to the higher calling to spread the gospel. The New School had freely joined hands with other Christians in the voluntary associations. This "catholic spirit" was one of the legacies of the New School that served as a counterbalance to the Old School penchant to exalt precision in Reformed doctrine as the cardinal mark of the true church.

For New School men, piety was equally valued with theology. Doctrinal integrity must always issue in integrity of life and faithfulness in service. The life of the Spirit was yearned for as the church looked heavenward for divine visitation through revivals. Revival winds blew through the New School branch of the church and for this she rejoiced greatly.

In the 1869 Plan for Reunion, the New School understanding of subscription was now officially recognized by the Old School as an authentic understanding of allegiance to the doctrinal standards of the Presbyterian Church. The reunited church would practice confessional subscription henceforth after the New School pattern which had also been the majority perspective of the Old School. The two branches understood one another on this point and affirmed the original spirit of the 1729 Adopting Act. Now it was acknowledged publicly and without equivocation that Presbyterians received and adopted the Calvinistic system of the Westminster

---

[40] Ibid., 589.

Standards, nonetheless, admitting that there have always been a diversity of ways in which that system may be validly expressed. The New School had firmly upheld this conviction for the duration of the separation; she had never wavered on this point and had all along argued that this was the historic practice of American Presbyterians from the beginning. The New School version of American Calvinism was vindicated.

New School historian Edward Morris viewed the northern reunion as a grand illustration of the spirit of "American Calvinism." This was "Calvinism adjusted in both form and spirit to our country, our people, our time." It was less scholastic, less rigid and allowance for diversity of opinion was generously welcomed. In the reunion, this liberty was in the context of a shared Calvinism. Morris characterized the 1869 reunion:

> In that memorable compact, which made ours the largest Presbyterian body in the world, there was no compromise, no ignoring of any essential element in the common Calvinism. Doctrine still held the foremost place. Both parties having adhered to the same standards during their separation, adopted those standards anew, and made their common belief – the creed rather than sacrament, or order, or mode of worship – the primary basis of their combination. Neither confessed any doctrinal aberration or divergence; neither claimed or admitted any superior orthodoxy. Both were true in that compact to the spirit of historic Presbyterianism in holding forth essential unity of faith as the only basis on which a Presbyterian Church can safely stand.... And their unification, though incited largely by other considerations, was the result essentially of their mutual trust, their intelligent confidence in each other, as first of all, and always, Reformed and Calvinistic.[41]

Spirituality of the Church

With the end of the War Between the States and the departure of the Presbyterian Southerners, the road to Northern reunion had become much easier. Old and New School in the North had been firmly committed to the preservation of the Federal Union. Without the pressure of Southern sentiments, the Old School had become more openly in favor of abolition which pleased the New School. This shared social and political perspective had further bolstered the drive for reunion in the Northern

---

[41] Edward D. Morris, *Thirty Years in Lane and other Lane Papers*, n.p. III, 112. Morris further described American Calvinism as a particular "mode of Calvinistic thought and Calvinistic temper." He said, "It more easily subordinates the doctrinal to the practical, and holds the truth rather – as the Bible does – for what the truth accomplishes in life, than for what the truth is in abstract shape.... Freer and more flowing in its statements, and more catholic in its temper, it offers the gospel to all men more readily, and on scriptural grounds opens more widely the doors of grace. Under the pressure of its vast responsibility on this continent, it is suffused more largely with the missionary spirit, and demands to be stated not with technical completeness, but rather in such ways as will best commend it savingly to the unevangelized multitudes thronging to our shores."

Presbyterian branches. These Northern perspectives put the Southern Church in an uncomfortable position. Overtures for reunion would be initiated by the newly united Northern Assemblies but the Southern men were in no mood to forget the grievances of the last decade. Southern Old and New School men had keen memories of the strident prejudice repeatedly leveled against them by Northern Presbyterians over slavery and secession. Their sons had been slaughtered on the battlefields and they had been condemned as heretical slave holders by the Northern Assemblies.

A central element of the ongoing North/South Presbyterian division was the doctrine of the spirituality of the church. By 1861 each of the four branches of the Presbyterian family (Old School/New School, North and South) had committed themselves to support either the Federal Government or the Confederacy. Even the Southern Church, the most ardent advocate of the spirituality and independence of the church, had publicly declared the righteous cause of the Southern states. In 1862 the General Assembly of the Southern Church stated: "Deeply convinced that this struggle is not alone for civil rights and property and home, but also for religion, for the church, for the gospel.... The Assembly desires to record, with its solemn approval, this fact of the unanimity of our people in supporting a contest to which religion as well as patriotism now summons the citizens of this country...."[42]

In addition to backing opposing armies at war, there was Presbyterian sectional division on the slavery question. This tension would continue to grow as the Northern cause was increasingly identified with the emancipation of slaves. In 1864 a very forceful statement announced Southern Presbyterian opposition to abolition: "The long-continued agitations of our adversaries have wrought within us a deeper conviction of the divine appointment of domestic servitude, and have led to clearer comprehensions of the duties we owe to the African race. We hesitate not to affirm that it is the peculiar mission of the Southern Church to conserve the institution of slavery, and to make it a blessing both to master and slave."[43]

The Southern Church touted her formal adherence to the non-political character of the church as the key distinction between Presbyterians North and South. In 1870 the General Assembly authorized a tract which included all the public statements of the Assembly on this subject.[44] Southern Presbyterians would continue to justify

---

[42] "Narrative of the State of Religion," *Minutes of the General Assembly of the Presbyterian Church in the Confederate States of America* 1861-1865 (Augusta, Columbia), 1862. The Southern Church in 1876, responding to charges of inconsistency in this statement and others with the non-secular character of the church, admitted that the Assembly "transcends the limits of its authority" when it referred to a war as just or unjust. *Minutes of the General Assembly in the Presbyterian Church in the United States*, 1876, 294.

[43] *Minutes of the General Assembly*, PCCSA, 1864, 293. The 1876 Assembly clarified that the sense of slavery being a "divine appointment" had to do with the institution being "recognized and enforced by the Confederate States, and was an existing relation prevailing throughout its boundaries." *Minutes of the General Assembly*, PCUS, 1876, 233, 234.

[44] See *The Distinctive Principles of the Presbyterian Church in the United States; Commonly Called the Southern Presbyterian Church, as set forth in the Formal*

their separation from the Northern brethren based primarily upon this supposed commitment to the independence of the church from all political questions, the so-called "spirituality of the church."

One example of perpetual sectional tensions was highlighted in the steps leading to the 1869 union of the Old School Synod of Kentucky with the Southern Church. In 1861 the Old School Kentucky Presbyterians had decried the schism by the Southern Old School men to form a separate church. R.J. Breckinridge of Kentucky wrote a paper, adopted by the 1862 Northern Old School Assembly, condemning the Southern rebellion as "horrible treason ... plainly condemned by the revealed will of God."[45] This was offensive, however, to a large majority of the Kentucky Synod.[46] Further irritations came over the slavery question as the Old School North adopted increasingly strong abolitionist declarations during the war years. Finally, in 1865 the Northern Assembly condemned the Synod of Kentucky for taking exception to the Assembly's 1864 paper on slavery.[47]

Responding to this condemnation by the Assembly, Louisville Presbytery issued a "Declaration and Testimony against the Erroneous and Heretical Doctrines and Practices which have Obtained and been Propagated in the Presbyterian Church in the United States during the Last Five Years." The Presbytery testified "against that alliance which has been virtually formed by the church with the State; against the persecution which for five years past has been carried on with increasing malignity against those who had refused to sanction or acquiesce in these departures of the church from the foundations of truth and righteousness."[48] Breckinridge, in turn, offered a paper to the Synod of Kentucky charging those endorsing the "Declaration and Testimony" with contempt for the church and the Scripture. The paper was defeated by a vote of 107 against and 22 in favor; nevertheless, by a vote of 54 to 46 the Synod expressed its disapprobation of the spirit of the "Declaration and Testimony" which would bring further agitation to the church.[49]

Declarations, and Illustrated by Extracts from the Proceedings of the General Assembly, from 1861-1870. To which is added from the proceedings of the Old School Assembly from 1861-1866 (Richmond: The Presbyterian Committee on Publication, 1870).

[45] *Minutes of General Assembly of the Presbyterian Church in the United States of America* (Old School) 1837-1869 (Philadelphia: Presbyterian Board of Publication), 1862, 624-626.

[46] See Letter of the Synod of Kentucky to the Southern Assembly, *Minutes of General Assembly*, PCCSA, 1863, 181.

[47] *Minutes of the General Assembly*, PCUSA (Old School), 1865, 566. The paper was known as the "Stanley-Matthews paper."

[48] See "Declaration and Testimony" in *Concise Records of the most important proceedings, papers, speeches, etc., of the General Assembly of the Presbyterian Church in the United States of America, at its session held in St. Louis, A.D. 1866* (St. Louis: Missouri Presbyterian, 1866).

[49] For an overview of the Synod of Kentucky during this period see: Thomas Cary Johnson, *A History of the Southern Presbyterian Church* (New York: The Christian Literature Co., 1894), 439-452; Ernest Trice Thompson, *Presbyterians in the South*, vol. II (Richmond: John Knox Press, 1963), 156-172; Harold M. Parker, Jr., "The Synod of

The following Assembly of 1866 excluded the commissioners from Louisville Presbytery without a hearing, denounced the "Declaration and Testimony" as slanderous, forbade the seating of signers in presbyteries, and summoned the schismatics to the next Assembly for trial.[50] The Synod of Kentucky ignored these directives and seated all commissioners at its next meeting. Breckinridge and 31 other ministers who wished to follow the General Assembly's mandates, withdrew, with 108 ministers remaining in the Synod.[51] The 1867 General Assembly, in turn, declared that the seceders from the Kentucky Synod were the true synod. The Synod of Kentucky retaliated by pronouncing that the General Assembly had ceased to be a constitutional body and had by its acts separated from the Synod.[52]

At this point contact with the Southern Church was initiated to pursue the process of organic union with a body that has "preserved pure and unimpaired the constitutional Presbyterianism of the undivided church from 1837 to 1861." The Synod expressed its commitment to the Kingship of Christ and Presbyterian principles "against those who again may treacherously attempt to subvert the doctrine and order of Christ's house."[53] The Old School Synod of Kentucky officially united with the Southern Church in 1869. The doctrine of the spirituality of the church, pronouncements against slavery, and unjust ecclesiastical discipline had driven the Kentucky Synod into the arms of the Southern Church.[54]

Kentucky," *Journal of Presbyterian History*, 41 (1963):14-36; Louis B. Weeks, *Kentucky Presbyterians* (Richmond: John Knox Press, 1983).

[50] *Minutes of the General Assembly*, PCUSA (Old School), 1866. Known as the Gurley *ipso facto* order because it also declared the *ipso facto* dissolution of Presbyteries refusing to participate in the General Assembly orders.

[51] In the midst of all this ecclesiastical confusion, the Synod of Kentucky wrote a pastoral letter to the churches and people under its charge. The synod believed that the recent schism in her ranks was the "consummation of joint effects of the unscriptural deliverances and unconstitutional legislation of the General Assembly during six years past." The synod had hoped that the conclusion of the war would have brought "calmer times" to the Northern Assembly and a way would be opened for reunion with the Southern brethren. "But all these hopes have been disappointed.... They have enacted new terms of church-membership, and new conditions of ministerial qualification.... They have required us to punish our members with the censure and excommunication of the Church for political offenses from which the State released them." This is a "record of reckless violence and wrong," yet, throughout "we have kept in view the restoration of all our Churches on the basis of our standards, as it was held by the General Assembly before the late unhappy troubles in our country." *Minutes of the Synod of Kentucky*, October, 10, 1866 (Louisville: Harney, Hughs & Co., 1866), 27-29.

[52] The northern Assembly also adopted an Encyclopaedic Act known as the "Report of the Ten," which amassed the judicial cases of almost 200 men summoned to the Assembly.

[53] *Minutes of the General Assembly*, PCUS, 1867, 784.

[54] The Synod of Missouri joined the Southern Church in 1874. The Synod's history during this period was very similar to the Synod of Kentucky. The "Declaration and Testimony" as well as the Gurley *ipso facto* order also split the Presbyterians in Missouri. The Missouri Synod joined the Southern Church in order to maintain its witness for the "exclusiveness of the spiritual vocation of the church" against "any church stained with

Correspondence North and South

Having recently witnessed the shameful treatment of their Kentucky brethren by the Northern Old School body, the Southern Church was in no mood to discuss reunion when approached by the Northern Assembly in 1870. The New School North, which had just recently reunited with the Old School body in 1869-70, had been notorious for its vehement attacks on Southern secession and slaveholding. Presbyterians North and South had explicitly condemned one another over the issues of secession and slaveholding during the entire decade of the 1860s. Only five years had passed since hostilities ceased and memories of the war were still too vivid. When the newly united Northern Church sent delegates to the Southern Assembly in 1870, with overtures for correspondence and union, the Southern men found this incredible.

The Northern delegates brought greetings and presented their paper to the Southern Assembly which tried to listen politely. The Northern overture stated that the "terms of reunion between the two branches of the Presbyterian Church at the North, now happily consummated, present an auspicious opportunity for the adjustment of such relations." The Northern Church naively believed that the reunited church as a new entity automatically wiped away the abuse and vilification of the South by the two parent denominations.[55]

The Southern Assembly decided upon an interlocutory meeting at night to debate an appropriate response to the Northern proposals. A number of Southern delegates spoke in favor of establishing relations with the Northern Church and forgetting past grievances. Finally, late in the evening, Dabney boldly spoke out against the Northern body and reversed the tone of the meeting. An eyewitness recorded the gist of Dabney's diatribe against Northern aggressors: "I hear brethren saying it is time to forgive. Mr. Chairman, I do not forgive. I do not try to forgive. What! forgive these people, who have invaded our country, burned our cities, destroyed our land! No I do not forgive them." Dabney compared the Northern Church to a tiger, that having devoured its prey is now satisfied. These strong feelings resonated in the hearts of the Southern men and the meeting soon ended. Dr. Green, who was present, writes: "But all were agreed that the tiger was in those people. We wanted to have no more to do with them."[56]

---

political corruptions." *Minutes of Synod of Missouri*, 1874, 22. See E.T. Thompson, *Presbyterians in the South*, vol. II, 175-182, 191-194; T.C. Johnson, *History of the Southern Presbyterian Church*, 452-454.

[55] *Minutes of the General Assembly*, PCUS, 1870.

[56] Thomas Cary Johnson, *The Life and Letters of Robert L. Dabney* (reprint, Edinburgh: the Banner of Truth Trust, 1977), 352-354. Looking back several years later, Dabney described his speech at the 1870 Assembly: "I then argued that the deep, instinctive recoil of the best and holiest in our communion from the embrace of the misguided men who had murdered our sons and our country, was not unreasonable, not unchristian revenge, not malice, but a lawful and necessary moral sentiment.... The moment the Northern Assembly claimed the right to impose Lincolnism on our consciences by their spiritual authority, they made Lincolnism a constituent part of their ecclesiastical system.... The abolition majority

The Northern Church's paper was officially answered by the Assembly from the pen of Dr. B.M. Palmer, chairman of the Committee on Foreign Correspondence. The report pronounced a list of obstacles that prevented any correspondence between the two churches." Palmer listed four barriers: the spirituality of the church, the northern union of Old School/New School, the unconstitutional treatment of the Kentucky Synod, and the injurious accusations against the Southern Church.[57] That Church and State issues were foremost in the Southern mind is self evident in Palmer's report and the debate which ensued. The first resolution declared:

Both wings of the now united Assembly, during their separate existence before the fusion, did fatally complicate themselves with the state in the political utterances deliberately pronounced year after year, and which, in our judgment, were a sad betrayal of the cause and kingdom of our common Lord and Head. We believe it to be solemnly incumbent upon the Northern Presbyterian Church, not with reference to us, but before the Christian world and before our divine Master and King, to purge itself of this error, and, by public proclamation of the truth, to place the crown once more upon the head of Jesus Christ as the alone King of Zion; in default of which the Southern Presbyterian Church, which has already suffered much in maintaining the independence and spirituality of the Redeemer's kingdom upon earth, feels constrained to bear public testimony against this defection of our late associates from the truth.[58]

There was significant debate on Palmer's paper in the Assembly, with opponents arguing that hatred and a bitter spirit lay behind this attack on the Northern Church. Palmer's paper was "deemed unnecessarily harsh" by some and the Assembly conceded that courtesy at least required that they appoint a committee to confer with the delegates from the Northern Assembly. When the vote was taken on the committee report, it was 83 in favor and 17 opposed. Dr. Henry J. Van Dyke, a Northern delegate, upon hearing the resolutions read and adopted, is reported to have said: "They have stripped every leaf from the olive branch, and made a rod of it to beat us with."[59]

After the Southern Assembly formally adopted Palmer's resolutions, the document was communicated to the Presbyterian Church of the North. The committee of delegates reported back to the Northern Assembly that their attempt to open a "friendly correspondence" with the Southern Church had failed because of the "declarations and conditions which we cannot consistently accept, because they

---

took the freest scope to assert and argue that State secession was the sin of rebellion.... And a holy mob of Abolitionists would have dragged them right out of the church, and, for the greater glory of God, murdered their '*dear Southern brethren*' in the streets"(italics his). *Life and Letters*, 353-354.

[57] *Minutes of the General Assembly*, PCUS, 1870, 529; *Minutes of the General Assembly*, PCUSA, 1870, 57.

[58] Ibid.

[59] T.C. Johnson, *Life and Letters of Dabney*, 355; Thomas Cary Johnson, *The Life and Letters of Benjamin Morgan Palmer* (Richmond: Presbyterian Committee of Publication, 1907), 320.

involve a virtual pre-judgment of the very difficulties concerning which we invited the conference;" there was no basis for conference with the Southern Church who heralded demands before any conference had begun. Nevertheless, the report concluded: "We earnestly hope that the negotiation thus suspended may soon be resumed under happier auspices, and hereby declare our readiness to renew our proposals for a friendly correspondence whenever our Southern brethren shall signify their readiness to accept in the form and spirit in which it has been offered."[60]

One of the Southern objections, albeit a secondary one,[61] was the "broad church" union of Northern Old School and New School. Resolution two in Palmer's original paper had stated:

> The union now consummated between the Old and New School Assemblies, North, was accomplished by methods which, in our judgment, involve a total surrender of all the great testimonies of the Church for the fundamental doctrines of grace, at a time when the victory of truth over error hung long in the balance. The United Assembly stands of necessity upon an allowed latitude of interpretation of the Standards, and must come at length to embrace nearly all shades of doctrinal belief. Of those failing testimonies we are now the sole surviving heir, which must lift from the dust and bear to the generation after us.[62]

Opposition to this paragraph surfaced in the debate among the Southern delegates. The Southern Church had reunited with the New School in the South; therefore, this objection was an unjust ground of difference between the two reunited Presbyterian branches.

Dr. F.A. Ross from Alabama, formerly of the United Synod, raised the question of Southern hypocrisy during Assembly debate over the resolutions:

---

[60] "The General Assembly," *Princeton Review* (July 1870): 447,448. See also *Minutes of the General Assembly*, PCUSA, 1870. The Northern body approached the Southern Church again in 1873 and was again met with Southern resistance. *Minutes of the General Assembly*, PCUSA, 1873, 502,503. The Southern answer to the Northern overture, stated: "... having, in 1870, distinctly stated the barriers to official correspondence between us, and our brethren having failed to remove them unequivocally, we are constrained by fidelity to truth to decline official intercourse until the fundamental difficulties set forth in our declaration of 1870 are removed, or until we shall be enabled to see our error in this regard." *Minutes of the General Assembly*, PCUS, 1874, 499.

[61] New School errors were not the primary reason the Southern Church resisted correspondence with the North. Notwithstanding the outspoken feelings of some, e.g., a few men like Palmer who had consistently resisted reunion with the New School, the majority of the Old School in the South had warmly embraced New School Southerners as fellow Calvinists. The Southern Church was united however in its bitter resentment of incessant Northern condemnation of the war as rebellion and declarations that slave holders should be subject to church discipline.

[62] *Minutes of the General Assembly*, PCUS, 1870, 529,530; *Minutes of the General Assembly*, PCUSA, 1870, 57.

But the Old School South and the New School South have done the same thing. *Dr. Barnes is the front of New Schoolism; still I believe he would have agreed to the basis of union determined upon in Lynchburg in 1863.* That arrangement has not changed the preaching of any one. Every member of the United Synod has the right to preach just as he preached before; every member of the Old School has the right to preach just as he did before. Where is the difference between the union of the two branches in the North and those in the South? In both cases there was some preliminary discussion as to terms, but finally in both cases they united on the basis of the standards pure and simple. Why, then, should we object to corresponding with them on the ground that they have effected just such a union as we had done before (italics his)?[63]

New School men were not the only ones to take offense at Palmer's accusations of Northern compromise with New School error. Dr. Rice declared:

You know very well, Mr. Moderator [Dabney], that I am an Old School man; that I was one of the very last to consent to the union of our church in the Synod which was consummated in 1864. Now, having agreed to that union, and these New School brethren having come among us we are called upon to maintain the doctrines of God's house, and we are bound to stand by those brethren and regard them as integral portions of our church. And therefore it is not right for us to say we object to holding intercourse with the Northern Assembly because they received the New School. *It is true that there is a wide difference between the two positions*; *but we have accepted these brethren as a part of ourselves*, and I trust that you will do nothing that will make it appear that we are not one, for we are one (italics mine).[64]

After the vote, the Committee of Foreign Correspondence was asked to prepare a letter for the churches explaining the Assembly's position on the Northern Church.[65]

---

[63] *Christian Inquirer and Free Commonwealth* XLII, June 1870 quoted in "Delegation to the Southern General Assembly," *Princeton Review* (July 1870): 452. Note Ross's statement that the 1864 doctrinal basis was entirely satisfactory to New School men. Harold M. Parker Jr. has suggested that certain New School men rejected the original explanatory declarations which were agreed upon in Lynchburg, therefore, they were removed from the final plan of union. See Harold Parker, "Southern Presbyterian Ecumenism: Six Successful Unions," *Journal of Presbyterian History* 56 (1978): 101. Parker does not present evidence to support his assertion. It appears the New School almost unanimously approved of the joint doctrinal statements; it was only a small group of Old School men that rejected the statements as a compromise with New School "heresy." As the 1864 Old School South Assembly minute indicated, the final draft of the union plan excluded the doctrinal agreement because the two parties had understood one another. It was unnecessary to reunite upon anything but traditional subscription to the standards. See *supra*, chp. 10, "Reunion of 1864."

[64] Ibid. Rice acknowledged Old School/New School differences, yet, reminded the Assembly that they had determined to accept this diversity by virtue of the 1864 union with the United Synod. This was John Holt Rice, D.D. (1818-1878) a pastor who served churches throughout the Southern States; he is not be confused with his uncle Dr. John Holt Rice (1777-1831) who was President of the seminary at Hampton Sydney.

[65] The vote in the Southern Assembly was 83 ayes and 17 nays and the names were ordered to be recorded. *Minutes of the General Assembly*, PCUS, 1870, 530, 531.

The supposed differences between Old School/New School reunions South and North were described in the Pastoral Letter, which was authored by Palmer:

> The Synod of the South united with us upon the first interchange of doctrinal views, upon a square acceptance of the Standards, without any metaphysical hair-splitting to find a sense in which to receive them, and without any expunging of whole chapters from the history of the past, with the sacred testimonies with which these are filled. It is not, therefore, the amalgamation of these bodies at the North, simply considered, which embarrasses us; but it is the method by which it was achieved – the acceptance of the Standards in no comprehensible sense, by which the united Assembly becomes a sort of broad Church, giving shelter to every creed lying between the extremes of Arminianism and Pelagianism on the one hand, and of Antinomianism and Fatalism on the other.[66]

Northern reaction to Southern acrimony toward the reunion of 1869-70 was indignant. The *Princeton Review* observed:

> ... whoever else might venture such a charge, the Southern Church cannot, without tabling the like charge against itself, for it has done the same thing. Some years ago it coalesced with the New School Synod South upon the doctrinal basis of the standards pure and simple.... But we deny that 'more care has been taken to secure orthodoxy in the Southern church.' So far from this, plans of union were rejected twice by the Northern church, because they contained the slightest qualification of the standards; and it was thus proved that no union was possible except on the pure and simple standards. Not only so, but we boldly affirm ... that no latitude of doctrine can be found in the Northern, which has not been tolerated freely and without question in the Southern church.[67]

Van Dyck told the Northern Assembly:

> ... that these two Assemblies, by their re-union, have totally cast aside all their former testimonies for the doctrines of grace; that this reunited Assembly stands necessarily upon an allowed latitude in the interpretation of the standards of the church, such as must ultimately result in bringing in all forms of doctrinal error – this I strenuously deny. (Applause.) And I say frankly, affectionately, and sadly to you – and if it shall reach their ears, to our Southern brethren – if they wait for us to stultify ourselves by

---

[66] "Pastoral Letter," *Minutes of the General Assembly*, PCUS, 1870, 540. There is great irony in Palmer's characterization of the two reunions. The criticisms he directed against the Northern reunion are the very same reasons he gave for resisting union with the United Synod in 1864. Palmer here defended the Southern Old School reunion with the New School which he had both opposed throughout and voted against. His letter spoke of a unity in Southern views that was evidenced in the first joint meeting, yet, Palmer himself had denied that the 1863 joint doctrinal statement was theologically sound. The Southern Assembly endorsed the whole letter, but, the Assembly vote on Palmer's resolutions was not unanimous which was indicative of the perceived hypocrisy.

[67] "Delegation to the Southern General Assembly" *Princeton Review* XLII (July 1870): 451, 453.

admitting such things as these before we enter into negotiations, we shall all have to wait for the settlement of these difficulties until we get to the General Assembly of the first-born in heaven. (Applause)[68]

The Southern Church utilized the 1869-1870 reunion to construct another objection to the Northern Church, though it was hardly objective. Regardless of the rancor over whose reunion was more sanctified, the chief obstacle to communion in Southern eyes was ecclesiology. The Southern Presbyterian Church viewed itself as the last bastion of ecclesiastical orthodoxy. The Northern Church had sold her soul to "Lincolnism" and "Erastian doctrine." The lone testimony of the faithful Southern Church was a sacred trust from her Scottish ancestors. The Assembly's pastoral letter declared: "The pure white banner borne by the Melvilles, the Gillespies and the Hendersons, those noble witnesses of another age, for a pure spiritual Church has fallen into our hands to uphold.... we feel it a higher duty and a grander privilege to testify for our Master's kingship in his Church, than to enjoy all the ecclesiastical fellowship which is to be purchased at the expense of conscience and of truth."[69] The grand old Presbyterian polity had not perished but would live on in the Southern Presbyterian Church.

The Southern Assembly at Louisville spurned the Northern Presbyterian overtures for union. An outright apology was due to the Southern Church and she would never compromise her testimony for a true Presbyterian ecclesiology. Northern men must recant their error to "bind the Church of our divine Lord to the wheels of Caesar's chariot." Of course, this was an unreasonable expectation. Northern men could no more disavow their support for the Federal Government than Southern men could declare slaveholding a sin. The whole affair was an insurmountable impasse from the beginning. It is no surprise that the 1870 attempt at fraternal relations was a failure.

Dabney and Palmer had been on opposite sides in the reunion discussions with the United Synod, but, on fraternal correspondence with the North, they were of one mind. These two men dominated the 1870 Assembly and fully convinced the Southern brethren that fraternal relation, much less union, with Yankee Presbyterians was totally out of the question.[70] Dabney who had always advocated

---

[68] Ibid., 449.

[69] "Pastoral Letter," *Minutes of the General Assembly*, PCUS, 1870, 541.

[70] Old School stalwart, Samuel J. Baird, was still scolding both Palmer and Dabney in the late 1880s for their misrepresentation of the facts about Northern union. Southern charges that the reunion of 1869 "introduced Pelagian heresies and broad church principles into the united body" are unfounded. Baird retorted: "... when the two branches of the church reunited, there were very few remaining of the known teachers of error; and of the younger generation of preachers, graduates of Auburn and of Union, in New York, the standard of orthodoxy was probably to the full as high as those of the Old School seminaries. In fact, the opposition to Pelagian heresy is nowhere more pronounced than in the instructions of Drs. Smith and Shedd, successive professors of theology in Union." Samuel J. Baird, *The Discussion on Reunion: A Review* (Richmond, Virginia: Whittet & Shepperson, 1887), 6,7.

reunion with Southern New School men was fiercely set against any fellowship with the Northern Presbyterian Church, Old School or New School. The Southern mind was already made up – there would be no union with the North. In the decades to follow repeated attempts were made to heal the breach, all to no avail.[71]

It is painfully obvious, that what perpetually separated *post-bellum* American Presbyterian bodies North and South was not theological diversity but the residual pain from the war and reconstruction. For Southerners, the church was the last place of refuge and they had no interest in fellowship with self-righteous Northern churchmen. Nor were Northerners easily willing to forget the "evils" of slavery and armed rebellion against their government.

Southern Presbyterians were not open to any discussions that entertained the idea of potential union with the Northern Presbyterian Church. It was inconceivable that they could sit side by side in church courts with those who viewed them as perpetrators of heinous crimes. The yoke of reconstruction was the only burden their tired Southern shoulders could bear. Palmer told the 1870 Southern Assembly: "I am a disfranchised man ... the boy who waits on my table at twelve dollars a month dictates to me at the polls who shall be my master. I have no vote. I am an exile in the land of my birth. My only consolation is that I have a home in the church of God. I want peace, and do not, therefore, want to be involved in any of these complications. We have not approached them [the Northern Church] with any disturbing proposition. Why should they come and disturb us, and seek to divide brethren who are united?"[72] Palmer just wanted the Northern Church to go away. No doubt many of his Southern brethren felt the same way. It would be over one hundred years before the sectional bodies would reunite in 1983.

---

[71] For an overview of correspondence with the Northern Church see E.T. Thomson, *Presbyterians in the South*, vol.II, 223-264 and T.C. Johnson, *A History of the Southern Presbyterian Church*, 422-479. See also Benjamin Morgan Palmer, "Fraternal Relations" *Southern Presbyterian Review* (April 1883): 306-330. For Dabney's defense of the Southern Church's independence see "What is Christian Union" *Central Presbyterian* (May 11,18, 1870) and "Broad Churchism" the opening sermon to the 1871 Southern Assembly; both of these essays are in Robert F. Dabney, *Discussions: Evangelical and Theological*, vol.II, (reprint, London: Banner of Truth, 1967), 430-463.

[72] "Delegation to the Southern Assembly," *Princeton Review* XLII (July 1870): 453.

Conclusion

Despite the tragic sectional division, there are important lessons that emerged out of the reunions of the Old School and New School in the South and the North. It is a great irony that out of the War Between the States and its aftermath, a significant consensus emerged on some of the old issues. After decades of separation, Presbyterians returned to organic union *via* the old method of compromise. The reunification process, in the North and South, displayed an attitude of moderation that sought the greater good of the whole church above sectarian interests. The colonial spirit of compromise for the sake of union, which had produced the original Adopting Act of 1729, was alive and well in the nineteenth century.

Empirical data from the eighteenth century had offered a contradictory picture of colonial Presbyterianism. Old and New School historians found earlier sources to support their own particular views of confessional subscription. As the nineteenth-century parties continued to debate the meaning of the Adopting Act, it became increasingly evident that both Old and New School actually practiced confessional subscription in a similar manner. In the crucible of ecclesiastical conflict, schism and reunion negotiations, Presbyterians came to understand one another more fully and realized that all sides embraced a commitment to both the Calvinistic system of the Confession and to liberty of conscience as expressed in the compromise of 1729.

From the beginning, the subscription controversy in America had been about the constant struggle to maintain middle ground against excessive viewpoints. Whenever Presbyterians have veered from the compromise, it has been destructive of unity. The nineteenth century gives us a clear picture of this fact. Whether it be the ultra Old School clamoring for strict subscription or the extremist New School advocacy of minimalist subscription, the end result was the same. Immoderate voices produced disharmony and distrust among brethren. Old School men were suspicious about the degree of doctrinal latitude allowed in some New School presbyteries; the New School did not trust the Old School and believed their strict spirit inhibited the spread of the gospel. Some of the concerns had substance, most were misunderstandings.

The period of separation produced four distinct Presbyterian denominations, each with a unique ethos and at the same time a serious attachment to Presbyterianism. Their common commitment to the essential elements of Reformed theology and Presbyterian polity drew the parties back together. Throughout the time of division, each branch of the Presbyterian Church maintained subscription to the Westminster Standards as a term of ministerial communion. By the time of the reunions, the overwhelming majority of each group had found its way back into the old Presbyterian common ground on confessional subscription. Most of the earlier controversial issues between the two parties still existed in the 1860s; nevertheless, the church had decided it could live with those differences.

The New School ministers, while often perceived as enemies of confessional subscription, were in fact strong advocates of the principles of 1729. Throughout the nineteenth century, the majority of New School men had a solid attachment to the Confession of Faith. They allowed more theological diversity than their Old School counterparts but there were confessional boundaries to that latitude which they openly acknowledged. New School Presbyterians were moderate Calvinists who loved the Reformed Tradition, but, were unwilling to allow the Westminster Standards to become the only test of one's orthodoxy. They were generally conservative, but also embraced an openness to flesh out traditional Reformed theology in new ways.

The Southern New School was welcomed by their Old School brethren back into full ecclesiastical fellowship after candid and thorough discussion of their theological differences. Distinctive New School doctrines were freely allowed in the reunited church contrary to some accounts which inaccurately herald a monolithic Old School Southern Church after the reunion. The Southern Old School decided that New School explanations of Calvinism did not undermine the system of doctrine in the Westminster Standards. Union was consummated despite the few ultra conservative voices who decried this compromise with the Southern New School. There was no healing of the fracture between the Southern and the Northern Church. The pain and bitterness created by the outcome of the War Between the States was too all encompassing to make a reunited national Presbyterian Church a reality in the nineteenth century.

The Old School/New School reunions are the high-water mark of the subscription controversy in American Presbyterianism. As large national bodies by the late 1850s, the two main branches of Presbyterianism in America reaffirmed the foundational principles of the Adopting Act in the formal plans of union negotiated between Old School and New School. The compromise of 1729 again proved to be the prudent path for peace. The reunited Presbyterian Churches continued to receive and adopt the Westminster system of doctrine while allowing officers to declare scruples which did not transgress the "essential and necessary articles." The reunions of 1864 and 1869 endorsed the median position of confessional subscription which both championed Calvinism and provided for the reality of differing perspectives within that common Calvinism.

In the midst of the heated controversy of the Old School/New School era, Charles Hodge and his Princeton colleagues were the voice of reason. Hodge resisted the extremist camps within the New School and Old School alike. Though a staunch Old School advocate, he realized that the majority of the New School was conservative and the guilt by association foisted upon them by Old School radicals was unjust. Hodge consistently defended the 1729 principles of subscription, challenging strict subscription as impractical and lax subscription as dishonest. The old pattern of allowing exceptions, yet, affirming the essential Calvinism of the Confession, was the only fair way to handle confessional subscription. This method was the historic practice of the American Presbyterian Church and any other approach destroyed integrity.

Hodge towers above the Old School/New School era. Few churchmen wrote as much as he did about the spectrum of issues that emerged during this volatile period for church and nation. He ultimately concurred with the terms of confessional subscription in the 1869 Plan of Union; however, he remained skeptical about the reunion itself. Hodge's chief concern was that the New School would not have the will to exercise discipline against doctrinal aberrations. Here Hodge anticipated the great challenge that Presbyterians would face in the twentieth century. Hodge's suspicions were correct – solving the subscription dilemma would not safeguard the church from theological error. Combating unacceptable doctrinal innovation is won and lost in the trenches of church courts.

Several insights surface from the Presbyterian reunions of the 1860s that may be profitable for the Church in the twenty-first century. Reunion in the nineteenth century was accomplished because, despite the party tensions, there was a shared allegiance to the historic Reformed theology of the Westminster Standards. Contemporary mainline Protestant churches often do not share a common theological system; therefore, the severe fracturing of those denominations is no surprise. The history of Presbyterianism in America accentuates the fact that without the bond of shared theological convictions, the Church will shatter. The increasing mainline Protestant abandonment of historic Christian orthodoxy may be the handwriting on the wall.

The lesson for Evangelicals is the necessity of vigilant care for the sacred middle ground of historic orthodoxy which holds the Church together in truth and love. The key to maintaining that *via media* is a charitable spirit between brethren who fellowship with integrity around the "essential and necessary articles" and mutually respect each other in "extra-essential and not-necessary points of doctrine." Christian unity is found in the central truths we share together as followers of Christ.

The historic strength of Presbyterianism has been her simultaneous commitment to both a robust Reformed theology and the Great Commission. The New School legacy reminds the Church that the spread of the gospel must be her primary task; and the priority of that mission requires that Christians maintain a catholic spirit toward brethren in traditions outside their own. The Old School heritage, on the other hand, reminds the Church that adherence to the great doctrines of the Reformation provide a sure foundation for faithful and effective gospel witness; and departure from that tradition invites the demise of the Church. The Old School/New School reunions are a poignant reminder that subscription to the Presbyterian creed is inescapably a call to love one another.

IN NECESSARIIS UNITAS
IN NON NECESSARIIS LIBERTAS
IN OMNIBUS CARITAS

Bibliography

Adams, John Quincy. *A History of Auburn Theological Seminary.* Auburn, New York: Auburn Seminary Press, 1918.

Adams, William. "The Reunion." In *Presbyterian Reunion: A Memorial Volume, 1837-1871,* 246-315. New York: DeWitt C. Lent & Co., 1870.

Adger, J. B. "The General Assembly of 1857." *Southern Presbyterian Review* X (July 1857): 276-319.

Alexander, Archibald. *Biographical Sketches of the Founder and Principal Alumni of the Log College. Together with an Account of the Revivals of Religion Under Their Ministry.* Princeton: J.T. Robinson, 1845. Reprint. Philadelphia: Presbyterian Board of Publication, 1851.

— "The Early History of Pelagianism." *Biblical Repertory and Theological Review* II (January, 1830): 77-113.

— "An Inquiry Into That Inability Under Which the Sinner Labours, and Whether it Furnishes any Excuse for His Neglect of Duty." *Biblical Repertory and Theological Review* III (July 1831): 360-83.

— "Review of 'Nature of Atonement.'" *Christian Advocate* II (February 1824): 76-84; (March 1824):119-129.

— "The Present State and Prospects of the Presbyterian Church." *Biblical Repertory and Theological Review* VII (January 1835): 56-72.

— *Thoughts on Religious Experience.* Philadelphia: Presbyterian Board of Publication, 1841.

Alexander, James W. *Life of Archibald Alexander.* 1854. Reprint, Harrisonburg: Sprinkle Publications, 1991.

Alexander, W.A. *A Digest of the Acts and Proceedings of the General Assembly of the Presbyterian Church in the United States.* Richmond, Virginia: Presbyterian Committee of Publication, 1888.

Alexander, W.A. and G.F. Nicolassen. *A Digest of the Acts and Proceedings of the General Assembly of the Presbyterian Church in the United States.* Richmond: Presbyterian Committee of Publication, 1911.

Ahlstrom, Sydney E. "Scottish Philosophy and American Theology." *Church History* XXIV (September 1955):257-72.

The Alleged Doctrinal Differences of the Old and New School Examined. By an Old Disciple. Auburn, New York: Wm. J. Moses, 1855.

Armstrong, Maurice, Charles Anderson, and Lefferts Loetscher, eds. *The Presbyterian Enterprise: Sources of American Presbyterian History.* Philadelphia: Westminster Press, 1956.

Atwater, Lyman. "Dr. George Duffield on the Doctrines of New-School Presbyterians." *Biblical Repertory and Princeton Review* XXXIX (October 1867): 655-75.

— "The General Assembly." *Biblical Repertory and Princeton Review* XL (July 1868): 417-476.

— "Jonathan Edwards and the Successive Forms of New Divinity." *Biblical Repertory and Princeton Review* XXX (October 1858): 585-620.

— "Proceedings of the Late Assemblies on Re-union." *Biblical Repertory and Princeton Review* XLI (July 1869): 423-448.

Baird, Robert. *Religion in America: or, an Account of the Origin, Progress, Relation to the State, and Present Condition of the Evangelical Churches in the United States.* New York, 1844.

Baird, Samuel J. *A Collection of the Acts, Deliverances, and Testimonies of the Supreme Judicatory of the Presbyterian Church from its Origin in America to the Present Time.* Philadelphia: Presbyterian Board of Publication, 1856.

— *The Discussion on Reunion: A Review.* Richmond, Virginia: Whittet & Shepperson, 1887.

— *The First Adam and the Second.* Philadelphia: Lindsay & Blakiston, 1860.

— *A History of the New School.* Philadelphia: Claxton, Rensen & Haffelfinger, 1868.

— Review of "The Men and Times of the Reunion of 1758" by E.H. Gillett. *Biblical Repertory and Princeton Review* XL (October 1868): 608-632.

Balmer, Randall and John R. Fitzmier. *The Presbyterians.* Westport Connecticut: Greenwoodd Press, 1993.

Barker, William S. "The Hemphill Heresy Case and Subscription to the Westminster Confession." *American Presbyterians* (Winter 1991): 1-14.

— "The Samuel Hemphill Heresy Case (1735) and the Historic Methods of Subscribing to the Westminster Standards." In *The Practice of Confessional Subscription,* ed. David W. Hall, 149-170. Lanham, MD: University Press of America, 1995.

— "A Response to Professor George Knight's Article 'Subscription to the Westminster Confession of Faith and Catechisms.' " *Presbyterion* (Spring-Fall 1984): 64-71.

— "Subscription to the Westminster Confession of Faith and Catechisms." *Presbyterion* (Spring-Fall 1984):1-19.

— "System Subscription." *Westminster Theological Journal* 63 (2001): 1-14.

Barnes, Albert. *The Atonement in its Relation to Law and Moral Government.* Philadelphia: Parry & McMillan, 1859.

— *Church Manual for the Use of The First Presbyterian Church in the City of Philadelphia.* Philadelphia: Isaac Ashmead, 1841.

— *How Shall a Man be Just with God?* Philadelphia: Presbyterian Publication Committee, 1854.

— *An Inquiry into the Scriptural Views of Slavery.* Philadelphia: Perkins & Perves, 1846.

— *Notes, Explanatory and Practical on the Epistle to the Romans.* New York: Leavitt, Lord & Co., 1835.

— *Sermons on Revivals.* New York: J.S. Taylor and Co., 1841.

— *The Way of Salvation: A Sermon Delivered at Morristown, New Jersey, February 8, 1829 Together With Mr. Barnes's Defense of the Sermon, read Before the*

Synod of Philadelphia, at Lancaster, October 29, 1830; and His "Defense" before the Second Presbytery of Philadelphia, in Reply to the Charge of the Rev. George Junkin. New York: Leavitt, Lord, and Company, 1836.

Beattie, Francis R. *"The Nature and Use of Creeds."* In *The Presbyterian Standards: An Exposition of the Westminster Confession of Faith and Catechisms.* Richmond: The Presbyterian Committee of Publication, 1896.

Beecher, Lyman. *Autobiography, Correspondence etc., of Lyman Beecher.* Edited by Charles Beecher. 2 Vols. New York, 1864-65.

— *Works.* Vol. III: *Trial before the Presbytery of Cincinnati,* June 1835: Remarks on the Princeton Review. Boston: John P. Jewett & Company, 1852-1853.

Benedetto, Robert. *Guide to the Manuscript Collection of the Presbyterian Church, U.S.* Westport, Connecticut: Greenwood Press, 1990.

The Biblical Repertory and Princeton Review. Index Volume From 1825-1868. Philadelphia: Peter Walker, 1871.

Brackett, William O., Jr. "The Rise and the Development of the New School in the Presbyterian Church in the U.S.A. to the Reunion of 1869." *Journal of the Presbyterian Historical Society* XIII (September 1928): 117-140; (December 1928): 145-74.

Breitenbach, William. "The Consistent Calvinism of the New Divinity Movement." *William and Mary Quarterly* 41 (April 1984): 241-264.

"A Brief View of Presbyterian History and Doctrine." Philadelphia: Presbyterian Publication Committee, n.d.

Briggs, Charles A. *American Presbyterianism: Its Origin and Early History.* New York: Scribner's, 1885.

— *Theological Symbolics.* New York: Scribner's, 1914.

Brown, Isaac V. *A Historical Vindication of the Abrogation of the Plan of Union by the Presbyterian Church in the United States of America.* Philadelphia: William S. and Alfred Martien, 1855.

Bynum, William B. "Heresy, Slavery, and Prophecy: The World of William Cummins Davis." *Journal of Presbyterian History* 78 (Winter 2000): 263-284.

Calhoun, David B. *Princeton Seminary.* 2 Vols. Edinburgh: The Banner of Truth Trust, 1994.

Campbell, Thomas H. *Good News on the Frontier; a History of the Cumberland Presbyterian Church.* Memphis: Frontier Press, 1965.

Cheeseman, Lewis. *Differences Between the Old and New School* Presbyterians. Rochester, New York: Erastus Darrow, 1848.

Christian Observer. Philadelphia, 1864.

Coalter, Milton J., Jr. *Gilbert Tennent, Son of Thunder: A Case Study of Continental Pietism's Impact on the First Great Awakening in the Middle Colonies.* Westport Connecticut: Greenwood Press, 1986.

Coalter, Milton J., Jr., John Mulder, Louis Weeks, eds. *The Confessional Mosaic.* Louisville: Westminster/John Knox, 1990.

Concise Records of the most important proceedings, papers, speeches, etc., of the General Assembly of the Presbyterian Church in the United States of America, at its session held in St. Louis, A.D. 1866. St. Louis: Missouri Presbyterian, 1866.

Conforti, J. A. *Samuel Hopkins and the New Divinity Movement: Calvinism, the Congregational Ministry, and Reform in New England Between the Great Awakenings.* Grand Rapids: Christian University Press, 1981.

The Constitution of the Presbyterian Church in the United States of America. Philadelphia: Towar and Hogan, 1827.

The Constitution of the Presbyterian Church in the United States of America; Containing the Confession of Faith, the Catechisms, the Government and Discipline and the Directory for the Worship of God, Ratified and Adopted by the Synod of New York and Philadelphia held at Philadelphia May 16, 1788, and continued by Adjournment until 28th of same Month. Philadelphia: Thomas Bradford, 1792.

The Constitution and Form of Government of the Independent Presbyterian Church in the United States of America as Adopted by the Churches in Convention, Held at Salem Church, in Union District, South Carolina, A.D. 1833: Together with Mr. Davis's Solemn Appeal to an Impartial Public, Columbia, 1839.

Cox, Samuel. "Reply of Dr. Cox." *Biblical Repertory and Theological Review* III (October 1831): 482-514.

Cranfield, Sherman B. "Reunion of the Synods of New York and Philadelphia." *Presbyterian Quarterly Review* (January 1859): 353-380; (April 1859): 529-563.

Crocker, Zebulon. *The Catastrophe of the Presbyterian Church in 1837, Including a Full View of the Recent Theological Controversies in New England.* New Haven: B. & W. Noyes, 1838.

Cross. *Burned-over District: The Social and Intellectual History of Enthusiastic Religion in Western New York, 1800-1850.* Ithaca, NY: Cornell University Press, 1950.

Dabney, Robert F. *A Defense of Virginia [and Through Her of the South] in Recent and Pending Contests Against the Sectional Party.* 1867. Reprint, Harrisonburg, Virginia: Sprinkle Publications, 1991.

— "Broad Churchism." *The Central Presbyterian* May 18, 1871. In *Discussions: Evangelical and Theological,* Vol. II. 447-463. 1890. Reprint. London: Banner of Truth, 1967.

— *Discussions: Evangelical and Theological,* 4 Vols. Reprint. London: Banner of Truth, 1967.

— "Dr. Dabney on the Plan of Union." *Southern Presbyterian.* Nov. 19, 1863; Nov. 27, 1863; Dec. 3, 1863; Dec. 10, 1863.

— "The Doctrinal Contents of the Confession: Its Fundamental and Regulative Ideas, and the Necessity and Value of Creeds." In *Memorial Volume of the Westminster Assembly,* edited by Francis R. Beattie, et. al. Richmond: The Presbyterian Committee of Publication, 1897. Reprint, *The Westminster Confession and Creeds.* Dallas: Presbyterian Heritage Publications, 1983.

— "Fraternal Correspondence." *Southern Presbyterian*, May 1876. In *Discussions: Evangelical and Theological*. Vol. II. 464-471. 1890. Reprint. London: Banner of Truth, 1967.

— "Our Position." Central Presbyterian July 11, 1857. In *Discussions: Evangelical and Theological*. Vol. II. 176-183. 1890. Reprint, London: Banner of Truth Trust, 1967.

— "Speech on Fusion with the United Synod." In *Discussions: Evangelical and Theological*. Vol. II. 298-311. 1890. Reprint, London: Banner of Truth Trust, 1967.

Davis, Clair. "Creedal Changes and Subscription to the System of Doctrine." *The Presbyterian Guardian* 36 (March 1967): 45-47.

Davis, Hugh. "The New York Evangelist, New School Presbyterians and Slavery, 1837-1857. *American Presbyterians* 68 (Spring 1990): 14-23.

Davis, William C. *The Gospel Plan, or Systematical Treatise on the Leading Doctrines of Salvation*. Philadelphia: Hopkins and Earle; Boston: Farrand, Mallory and Co., 1809.

"Declaration and Testimony." In *Concise Records of the most important proceedings, papers, speeches, etc., of the General Assembly of the Presbyterian Church in the United States of America, at its session held in St. Louis, AD. 1866*. St. Louis: Missouri Presbyterian, 1866.

"Delegation to the Southern General Assembly." *The Biblical Repertory and Princeton Review* XLII (July 1870): 444-454.

Dickinson, Jonathan. *Remarks Upon a Discourse Intitled An Overture, Presented to The Reverend Synod of Dissenting Ministers sitting in Philadelphia, in the Month of September, 1728*. New York: John Peter Zenger, 1729.

— *Remarks Upon A Pamphlet, Intitled, A Letter to a Friend in the Country, containing the Substance of a Sermon preached at Philadelphia, in the Congregation of the Rev. Mr. Hemphill*. Philadelphia: Andrew Bradford, 1735.

— *A Sermon Preached at the opening of the Synod At Philadelphia, September 19, 1722. Wherein is Considered the Character of the Man of God, and his Furniture for the Exercise both of Doctrine and Discipline, with the true boundaries of the Churches Power*. Boston: Thomas Fleet, 1723.

— *A Vindication of the Reverend Commission of the Synod In Answer to Some Observations On their Proceedings against the Reverend Mr. Hemphill*. Philadelphia: Andrew Bradford, 1735.

Dictionary of Christianity in America. eds. Daniel G. Reid, Robert D. Linder, Bruce L. Shelley, Harry S. Stout. Downers Grove, Illinois: Intervarsity Press, 1990.

Dictionary of the Presbyterian & Reformed Tradition in America. eds. D.G. Hart and Mark A. Noll. Downers Grove, Illinois: Intervarsity Press, 1999.

Digest of the Acts and Proceedings of the General Assembly of the Presbyterian Church in the United States, 1861-1965. Atlanta: John Knox, 1967.

A Digest of the Supreme Judicatory of the Presbyterian Church in the United States of America. Philadelphia: Presbyterian Board of Publication, 1850.

The Distinctive Principles of the Presbyterian Church in the United States; *Commonly Called the Southern Presbyterian Church, as set forth in the Formal* *Declarations, and Illustrated by Extracts from the Proceedings of the General* *Assembly, form 1861-1870. To which is added from the proceedings of the Old* *School Assembly from 1861-1866.* Richmond: The Presbyterian Committee on Publication, 1870.

Douglass, Earl L. "The Westminster Assembly, Its History, Formularies and Abiding Values." Philadelphia: Presbyterian Historical Society, 1943.

Dow, Daniel. *New Haven Theology and Taylorism Alias Neology in its Own* *Language.* Thompson, Connecticut: George Roberts, 1834.

A Draught of the Form of Government and Discipline of the Presbyterian Church in *the United States of America.* New York: S. and J. Loudon, 1787.

Duffield, George. "American Presbyterianism." A Sermon Delivered Nov. 11, 1853. Philadelphia, 1854.

— "Doctrines of the New School Presbyterian Church," *American Presbyterian and* *Theological Review* New Series, I (July 1863): 561-635.

Duncan, J. Ligon. "Owning the Confession: Subscription in the Scottish Presbyterian Tradition." In *The Practice of Confessional Subscription,* ed. David W. Hall, 77-92. Lanham, Maryland: University Press of America, 1995.

Dwight, Timothy. *Theology: Explained and Defended, In a Series of Sermons,* 10th ed. New Haven: T. Dwight and Son, 1839.

Edwards, Jonathan. *The Works of President Edwards.* New York: Leavitt and Allen, 1843.

— *The Works of Edwards,* Vol I. *Freedom of the Will,* ed. Paul Ramsey. New Haven: Yale University Press, 1957.

Ellis, George Elwood. "National Creed and Unity: The Significance of the Subscription Controversy for the Development of Colonial Presbyterianism." Ph.D. diss., Temple University, 1983.

Ely, Ezra Stiles, *A Contrast Between Calvinism and Hopkinsianism.* New York: S. Whiting and Co., 1811.

Encyclopedia of the Presbyterian Church in the United States of America, ed. Alfred Nevin. Philadelphia: Presbyterian Publishing Company, 1884.

Evans, E. B. "The Cumberland Presbyterian Church." In *Dictionary of the* *Presbyterian & Reformed Tradition in America,* ed. D. G. Hart and Mark A. Noll. Downers Grove, IL: InterVarsity Press, 1999.

Ferm, Robert L. *A Colonial Pastor, Jonathan Edwards the Younger.* Grand Rapids: William B. Eerdmans Publishing Co., 1976.

Finney, Charles G. *The Memoirs of Charles G. Finney,* eds. Garth M. Rosell and Richard A. G. Dupuis. Grand Rapids: Zondervan, 1989.

Foote, William Henry. *Sketches of North Carolina, Historical and Biographical,* *Illustrative of the Principles of a Portion of her Early Settlers.* New York: Robert Carter, 1846.

— *Sketches of Virginia, Historical and Biographical.* First Series. 1850. Reprint. Richmond: John Knox Press, 1966.

— *Sketches of Virginia*, Second Series. Philadelphia: J. B. Lippincott & Co., 1855.

"The Formula for the Public Admission of Members to the Church." Proposed by the Third Presbytery of Philadelphia. 1860. Presbyterian Historical Society, Philadelphia.

Freundt, Albert. "Adopting Act" and "Jonathan Dickinson." In *Dictionary of the Presbyterian & Reformed Tradition in America*, ed. D. G. Hart and Mark A. Noll. Downers Grove, Illinois: InterVarsity Press, 1999.

Fule, Aurelia T. "The Book of Confessions and the "Confession of 1967." *American Presbyterians* 66 (Winter 1988): 326-334.

Gaustad, Edwin Scott. *The Great Awakening in New England*. New York: Harper and Row, 1957.

Gillett, E.H. *History of the Presbyterian Church in the United States of America*. 2 Vols. Philadelphia: Presbyterian Publication Committee, 1864.

— "The Men and the Times of the Reunion of 1758." *American Presbyterian and Theological Review* VI (July 1868): 414-443.

— "The True Character of the Adopting Act." *American Presbyterian and Theological Review* VII (January 1869): 29-58.

Goen, Clarence C. "Broken Churches, Broken Nation: Regional Religion and North-South Alienation in Antebellum America." *Church History* 52 (March 1983): 21-35.

Green, Ashbel. "The Present State of the Presbyterian Church," *Christian Advocate* IX (July 1831): 362-66.

— "Review of Review" *Christian Advocate* IX (December, 1831): 637-52; X (March 1832): 114-25.

Green, Henry W. "The Trial of the Reverend William Tennent." *Biblical Repertory and Princeton Review* XL (July 1868): 322-344.

Griffin, Edward, *An Appeal to the Presbyterian Church on the Subject of the New Test*. n.p., 1819.

Guelzo, Allen C. *Edwards on the Will: A Century of American Theological Debate*. Middletown, Connecticut: Wesleyan University Press, 1989.

— "An Heir and a Rebel: Charles Grandison Finney and the New England Theology." n.p., n.d.

— "Jonathan Edwards and New Divinity." In *Pressing Toward the Mark: Essays Commemorating Fifty Years of the Orthodox Presbyterian Church*, ed. Charles G. Dennison and Richard C. Gamble, 147-167. Philadelphia: The Committee for the Historian of the Orthodox Presbyterian Church, 1986.

Hall, David W. ed. *The Practice of Confessional Subscription*. Lanham, Maryland: University Press of America, 1995.

Hall, David W. and Joseph H. Hall. *Paradigms in Polity*. Grand Rapids: Wm. B. Eerdmans Publishing Co., 1994.

Hambrick-Stowe, Charles E. *Charles Finney and the Spirit of American Evangelicalism*. Grand Rapids: Wm. B. Eerdmans, 1996.

Handy, Robert T. *A History of Union Theological Seminary in New York*. New York: Columbia University Press, 1987.

— "Union Theological Seminary in New York and American Presbyterianism, 1836-1904." *American Presbyterians* 66 (Summer 1988): 115-122.

Handy, Robert T., Lefferts A. Loetscher, and H. Shelton Smith. *American Christianity: An Historical Interpretation with Representative Documents.* New York: Scribner's, 1960.

Hardman, Keith J. "Jonathan Dickinson and the Course of American Presbyterianism, 1717-1747." Ph.D. diss., University of Pennsylvania, 1971.

Hart, D.G. "The Critical Period for Protestant Thought in America." *Journal of Ecclesiastical History* 38 (1987): 254-70.

Harvey, Joseph. *An Examination of the Pelagian and Arminian Theory of Moral Agency As Recently Advocated by Dr. Beecher in His "Views in Theology."* New York: Ezra Collier, 1937.

Hatfield, Edwin F. "The Presbyterian System: Its Reasonableness and Excellency." Philadelphia: Presbyterian Publication Committee, n.d.

— Review of *History of the New School* by Samuel J. Baird. *American Presbyterian Review* VII (January 1869): 94-100.

Heimert, Alan and Perry Miller. eds. *The Great Awakening: Documents Illustrating the Crisis and Its Consequences.* Indianapolis: Bobbs-Merrill, 1967.

Hill, William. *A History of the Rise, Progress, Genius, and Character of American Presbyterianism: Together with a Review of the Constitutional History of the Presbyterian Church in the United States of America, by Chas. Hodge, D.D. Professor in the Theological Seminary at Princeton, N.J.* Washington City: J. Gideon Jr., 1839.

Hirrel, Leo Phillip. "The Ideology of Antebellum Reform Within the New School Calvinist Community." Ph.D. diss., University of Virginia, 1989.

A History of the Division of the Presbyterian Church in the United States of America. By a Committee of the Synod of New York: M.W. Dodd, 1852.

Review of *A History of the Division of the Presbyterian Church in the United States of America.* By a Committee of the Synod of New York. *Presbyterian Quarterly Review* I (March 1853): 655-675.

Hodge, Archibald Alexander. *A Commentary on the Confession of Faith.* 2nd ed. Presbyterian Board of Publication and Sabbath School Work, 1885.

— *The Life of Charles Hodge.* New York: Charles Scribner's Sons, 1880.

Hodge, Charles. "Act and Testimony." *Biblical Repertory and Theological Review* VI (October 1834): 505-22.

— "The Act and Testimony No. II." *Biblical Repertory and Theological Review.* Vol. VII (January 1835): 110-34.

— "Adoption of the Confession of Faith." *Biblical Repertory and Princeton Review* XXX (October 1858): 669-692.

— Review of "Barnes on the Epistle to the Romans." *Biblical Repertory and Princeton Review* VII (April 1835): 285-340.

— "A Brief History and Vindication of the Doctrines Received and Established in the Churches of New England, with a Specimen of the New Scheme of Religion

Beginning to Prevail. By Thomas Clap." *Biblical Repertory and Princeton Review* XI (July 1839): 369-404.

— *The Church and its Polity.* New York: Scribner's, 1878.

— *The Constitutional History of the Presbyterian Church in the United States of America.* Part I, II. Philadelphia: William S. Martien, 1840. Reprint. Philadelphia: Presbyterian Board of Publication, 1851.

— "The General Assembly of 1835." *Biblical Repertory and Theological Review* VII (July 1835): 440-82.

— "General Assembly of 1836." *Biblical Repertory and Theological Review* VIII (July 1836): 415-76.

— "General Assembly of 1837." *Biblical Repertory and Theological Review* IX (July 1837): 407-85.

— "General Assembly of 1838." *Biblical Repertory and Theological Review* X (July 1838): 457-503.

— "The General Assembly." *Biblical Repertory and Princeton Review* XXX (July 1858): 555-564.

— "The General Assembly." Biblical Repertory and Princeton Review XXXVIII (July 1866): 480-497.

— "The General Assembly." *Biblical Repertory and Princeton Review* XXXIX (July 1867): 440-522.

— "The General Assembly." *Biblical Repertory and Princeton Review* XLI (July 1869): 401-422.

— "General Assembly." *Biblical Repertory and Princeton Review* XLII (January 1870): 425-443.

— Review of *A History of the New School* by Samuel J. Baird. *Biblical Repertory and Princeton Review* XLII (January 1870): 105-138.

— Review of *A Plea for Voluntary Societies and a Defense of the Decisions of the General Assembly of 1836 Against the Strictures of the Princeton Reviewer and Others. By a Member of the General Assembly* by John S. Taylor *Biblical Repertory and Theological Review* IX (January 1837): 101-120.

— "Presbyterian Reunion." *Biblical Repertory and Princeton Review* XL (January 1868): 53-83.

— "Principles of Church Union, and the Reunion of Old and New-School Presbyterians." *Biblical Repertory and Princeton Review* XXXVII (April 1865): 271-313.

— "Protest and Answer." *Biblical Repertory and Princeton Review* XL (July 1868): 456-476.

— "Recent Developments Respecting Presbyterian Reunion." *The Biblical Repertory and Princeton Review* XLI (April 1869): 290-308.

— "Remarks on Dr. Cox's Communication." In *Biblical Repertory and Theological Review,* III (October, 1831): 514-43.

— "Retrospect of the History of the Princeton Review." In *Biblical Repertory and Princeton Review, Index Volume.* Philadelphia: Peter Walker, 1870, 1871.

— "Reunion." *Biblical Repertory and Princeton Review* XXXIX (July 1867).

— "Review of an Article in the June Number of *The Christian Spectator* Entitled 'Inquiries Respecting the Doctrine of Imputation,' " *The Biblical Repertory and Theological Review,* II (October, 1830): 425-72.

— "Review of Finney's *Lectures on Systematic Theology*." XIX (April 1847): 237-77.

— "Review of 'Regeneration and the Manner of Its Occurrence' " *Biblical Repertory and Theological Review* II (April 1830): 250-97.

— "Review on Barnes on Romans." *The Presbyterian,* June 4, May 21, May 28, 1835.

— "Slavery." *Biblical Repertory and Princeton Review* VIII (April 1836): 268-305.

— *Systematic Theology.* 3 Vols. Reprint. Grand Rapids: Wm. B. Eerdmans Publishing Company, 1979.

Hodgson, Francis. *An Examination of the System of New Divinity: Or, New School Theology.* New York, 1839.

Hopkins, Samuel. *The Works of Samuel Hopkins with a Memoir of His Life and Character,* ed. Edward A. Parks. 3 Vols. Boston: Doctrinal Tract and Book Society, 1854.

Hotchkin, James H. *A History of the Purchase and Settlement of Western New York and of the Rise, Progress, and Present State of the Presbyterian Church in that Section.* New York: M. W. Dodd, 1848.

"How Should Natural Ability Be Preached." *Presbyterian Quarterly Review.* VIII (October 1859): 177-191.

Howard, Victor B. "The Anti-Slavery Movement in the Presbyterian Church, 1835-1861," Ph.D. diss., Ohio State University, 1961.

Howe, George. "The General Assembly of 1858." *Southern Presbyterian Review* XI (July 1858): 264-343.

— *History of the Presbyterian Church in South Carolina.* 2 Vols. Columbia: Duffie and Chapman, 1870; Walker, Evans and Cogswell, 1883.

Hutchinson, George P. *The Problem of Original Sin in American Presbyterian Theology.* Presbyterian and Reformed Publishing Co., 1972.

Ingram, Paul R. "*Two Churches in Conflict: Differences of Theology and Mission under Presbyterian-Congregational Union.*" M.A. Thesis. St. Louis: Covenant Theological Seminary, 1987.

"Inquiries Respecting the Doctrine of Imputation." *Quarterly Christian Spectator* II (June 1830): 339-45.

Janeway, Jacob. *The Appeal Not Sustained or an Answer to a Pamphlet Entitled 'An Appeal to the Presbyterian Church on the Subject of the New Test.'"* n.p. , 1820.

Johnson, Thomas Cary. *A Brief Sketch of the United Synod of the Presbyterian Church in the United States of America.* Reprint. Vol. VIII American Society of Church History, 1894.

— *A History of the Southern Presbyterian Church.* New York: The Christian Literature Co., 1894.

— *The Life and Letters of Benjamin Morgan Palmer.* Richmond: Presbyterian Committee of Publication, 1907.

— *The Life and Letters of Robert Lewis Dabney*. Reprint. Edinburgh: The Banner of Truth Trust, 1977.

Junkin, George. *The Vindication, Containing a History of the Trial of the Rev. Albert Barnes by the Second Presbytery, and by the Synod of Pennsylvania*. Philadelphia: William S. Martien, 1836.

Kelly, Douglas. "New School-Old School Split in the Presbyterian Church U.S.A." December 1966. (photocopy).

Kennedy, William S. *The Plan of Union: or a History of the Presbyterian and Congregational Churches of the Western Reserve with Biographical Sketches of the Early Missionaries*. Hudson, Ohio: Pentagon Steam Press, 1856.

Knight, George W. III. "A Response to Dr. William Barker's Article 'Subscription to the Westminster Confession of Faith and Catechisms.' " *Presbyterion* (Spring-Fall 1984): 56-63.

— "Subscription to the Westminster Confession of Faith and Catechisms." *Presbyterion* (Spring-Fall 1984): 20-55.

— "Subscription to the Westminster Confession of Faith and Catechisms." In *The Practice of Confessional Subscription*. ed. David W. Hall, 119-148. Lanham, Maryland: University Press of America, 1995.

Kull, Irving S. "Presbyterian Attitudes toward Slavery," *Church History* 7 (June 1938): 101-114.

LeBeau, Brian F. "The Subscription Controversy and Jonathan Dickinson." *Journal of the Presbyterian Historical Society* 54 (Fall 1976): 317-335.

Leith, John. *Assembly at Westminster: Reformed Theology in the Making*. Richmond, Virginia: John Knox Press, 1973.

"Letter of the Synod of Kentucky to the Southern Assembly," *Minutes of General Assembly of Presbyterian Church in the Confederate States of America*. 1863.

Lingle, Walter and John Kuykendall. *Presbyterianism: Their History and Beliefs*. Richmond, Virginia: John Knox Press, 1978.

Loetscher, Frederick W. "The Adopting Act." *Journal of the Presbyterian Historical Society* XIII (December 1929): 337-355.

— "Early American Presbyterianism." *Journal of the Presbyterian Historical Society* 13 (March 1928): 337-355.

Loetscher, Lefferts. A *Brief History of Presbyterianism*. Philadelphia: Westminster Press, 1983.

— *The Broadening Church: A Study of Theological Issues in the Presbyterian Church Since 1869*. Philadelphia: University of Pennsylvania Press, 1954.

— *Facing the Enlightenment and Pietism: Archibald Alexander and the Founding of Princeton Theological Seminary*. Westport, Connecticut: Greenwood Press, 1983.

Logan, Samuel T. "Transition to the New World." In *Pressing Toward the Mark: Essays Commemorating Fifty Years of the Orthodox Presbyterian Church*, ed. Charles G. Dennison and Richard C. Gamble, 113-130. Philadelphia: The Committee for the Historian of the Orthodox Presbyterian Church, 1986.

Longfield, Bradley J. *The Presbyterian Controversy: Fundamentalists, Modernists, and Moderates*. New York: Oxford University Press, 1991.

Loveland, Anne C. *Southern Evangelicals and the Social Order 1800-1860.* Baton Rouge: Louisiana State University Press, 1980.

Lyon, James A. "The General Assembly at Augusta." *Southern Presbyterian Review* XIV (January 1862): 630-639.

Maffy-Kipp, Laurie F., Leigh E. Schmidt and Mark Valeri eds. *Practicing Protestants: Histories of Christian Life in America 1630-1965,* eds. (Baltimore: John Hopkins Press, 2006).

McClurkin, P.T. "Presbyterianism in New England Congregationalism." *Journal of Presbyterian History* 31 (1953): 245-56; (1954): 109-14.

McCormac, Earl R. "Missions and the Presbyterian Schism of 1837." *Church History* 32 (March 1963): 32-45.

— "The Development of Presbyterian Missionary Organizations: 1790-1870." *Journal of Presbyterian History.* 43 (1965): 149-173.

McKivigan, John R. *The War Against Proslavery Religion: Abolitionism and the Northern Churches, 1830-1865.* Ithaca, New York: Cornell University Press, 1984.

Marsden, George. *The Evangelical Mind and the New School Presbyterian Experience.* New Haven: Yale University Press, 1970.

— "The New School Heritage and Presbyterian Fundamentalism." *Westminster Theological Journal* 32 (May 1970): 129-47.

— *The New School Presbyterian Mind: A Study of Theology in Mid-Nineteenth Century America.* Ph.D. diss., Yale University, 1966.

— "Reformed and Presbyterian." In *Reformed Theology in America.* ed. David F. Wells. Grand Rapids: Wm. B. Eerdmans, 1985.

M'Calla, W. L. *A Correct Narrative of the Proceedings of the Presbytery of Philadelphia Relative to the Reception and Installation of Mr. Albert Barnes.* Philadelphia: Russell and Martien, 1830.

Mead, Sidney E. Review of *The Forming of An American Tradition,* by Leonard Trinterud. *Christian Century* 67 (1950): 430-433.

— "The Rise of the Evangelical Conception of the Ministry in America, 1607-1858." In *The Ministry in Historical Perspective.* eds. H. Richard Niebuhr and Daniel D. Williams, 207-249. New York: Harper, 1956.

"Meeting of the 'United Synod of the Presbyterian Church in the United States.' " *Presbyterian Magazine* VIII (May 1858): 208-217.

Melton, Julius. *Presbyterian Worship in America: Changing Patterns Since 1787.* Richmond: John Knox Press, 1967.

Millard, James. A *Digest of the Acts and Proceedings of the General Assembly of the Presbyterian Church in the United States.* Richmond, Virginia: Presbyterian Committee of Publications, 1945.

Miller, John. "Report of the Committees of Conference of the General Assembly and the United Synod of the Presbyterian Churches in the Confederate States of America, on the Subject of a Union Between the Two Bodies." *Southern Presbyterian Review* III (April 1864): 252-264.

Miller, Perry. *Jonathan Edwards.* New York: Meridian Books, Inc., 1959.

Miller, Samuel. "Church Attachment and Sectarianism." *The Presbyterian Magazine* IV (January 1854): 1-6.

— "Historical Review of the Church (Old School Branch) Since 1837." In *Presbyterian Reunion: A Memorial Volume, 1837-1871*, 1-49. New York: DeWitt C. Lent & Co., 1870.

— *"A Letter of the Rev. Samuel Miller D.D. Addressed to the Members of the Presbyterian Church in the United States on the Present Crisis in Their Religious and Theological Concerns."* Hartford: Printed by B. Gleason & Co., 1853.

— *Letters to Presbyterians on the Present Crisis in the Presbyterian Church in the United States.* Philadelphia: Anthony Finley, 1833.

— *Presbyterianism: The Truly Primitive and Apostolical Church of the Church of Christ.* Philadelphia: Presbyterian Board of Publication, 1835.

— *The Utility and Importance of Creeds and Confessions: Addressed Particularly to Candidates for the Ministry.* Philadelphia: Presbyterian Board of Publication, 1839.

Miller, Samuel, Jr. *The Life of Samuel Miller.* Philadelphia: Claxton, Remsen and Haffelfinger, 1869.

Minutes of the Presbyterian Church in America, 1706-1788. Edited by Guy S. Klett. Philadelphia: Presbyterian Historical Society, 1976.

Minutes of the General Assembly of the Presbyterian Church in the Confederate States of America. Augusta, Columbia, 1861-1865.

Minutes of the General Assembly of the Presbyterian Church in the United States of America. Philadelphia, 1789-1837.

Minutes of the General Assembly of the Presbyterian Church in the United States of America. (New School) Vol. I: 1838-1858, Vol. II: 1859-1869. New York: Presbyterian Publication Committee. Reprint. Presbyterian Board of Publication and Sabbath School, 1894.

Minutes of the General Assembly of the Presbyterian Church in the United States of America. (Old School) Philadelphia: Presbyterian Board of Publication, 1837-1869.

Minutes of the General Assembly of the Presbyterian Church in the United States, Richmond, 1865-1872, 1898.

Minutes of the General Assembly of the Presbyterian Church in the United States of America. Philadelphia: Presbyterian Board of Publication, 1870.

Minutes of the General Convention of the Independent Presbyterian Church, 1856.

Minutes of the Presbytery of South Carolina, Spring 1864; Fall 1864.

Minutes of the Synod of Kentucky, 1866.

Minutes of Synod of Missouri, 1874.

Minutes of the Synod of North Carolina, 1861.

Minutes of the United Synod of the Presbyterian Church in the United States of America, 1858-1861. Richmond, 1861.

Minutes of the United Synod of the Presbyterian Church in the Confederate States of America, 1862-1863. Richmond, 1863.

"The Mission of the Presbyterian Church." *Presbyterian Quarterly Review* I (June 1852): 12-32.

Monfort, J. G. "Progress of the Reunion Movement."*American Presbyterian Review* New Series, I (April 1869): 304-323.

Moore, Edmund A. "Robert J. Breckinridge and the Slavery Aspect of the Presbyterian Schism." *Church History* IV (December 1935): 282-294.

Moore, William E. *A New Digest of the Acts and Deliverances of the General Assembly of the Presbyterian Church in the United States of America.* Philadelphia: Presbyterian Publication Committee, 1861.

Moorhead, James H. "The Churches, Slavery, the Civil War, and Reconstruction: A Review Essay. *Journal of Presbyterian History* 78 (Winter 2000): 285-299.

— "The 'Restless Spirit of Radicalism': Old School Fears and the Schism of 1837." *Journal of Presbyterian History* 78 (Spring 2000): 19-33.

Morris, Edward D. *The Presbyterian Church New School, 1837-1869: An Historical Review.* Columbus, OH: The Chaplain Press, 1905.

— "The Reformed or Calvinistic Sense," *American Presbyterian Review* New Series, I (April 1869): 241-264.

— *Theology of the Westminster Symbols. A Commentary, Historical, Doctrinal, Practical, on the Confession of Faith and Catechisms of the Presbyterian Churches.* Columbus, OH, 1900.

— *Thirty Years in Lane and Other Lane Papers*, n.p., 1897.

Muether, John. "Contemporary Evangelicalism and the Triumph of the New School." *Westminster Theological Journal* 50 (1988): 339-347.

Murray, Andrew E. *Presbyterians and the Negro – A History.* Philadelphia: Presbyterian Historical Society, 1966.

Murray, John. *The Imputation of Adams Sin.* 1959. Reprint. Phillipsburg, New Jersey: Presbyterian and Reformed Publishing Co., 1979.

— "The Theology of the Westminster Confession of Faith." In *Collected Writings of John Murray*, Vol. 4, *Studies in Theology.* Edinburgh: Banner of Truth, 1982.

— "Creed Subscription in the Presbyterian Church." In *The Practice of Confessional Subscription*, ed. David W. Hall, 247-262. Lanham, MD: University Press of America, 1995.

Musgrave, George. "Exposition and Defense of the Basis of Reunion." *The Biblical Repertory and Princeton Review* XLI (July 1869): 449-62.

Nevin, Alfred. ed. "Adopting Act" and "Presbyterianism – 'True Blue.' " In *Encyclopedia of the Presbyterian Church in the United States of America: Including the Northern and Southern Assemblies.* Philadelphia: Presbyterian Encyclopedia Publishing Co., 1884.

Review of *A New Digest of the Acts and Deliverances of the General Assembly of the Presbyterian Church in United States of America* by William E. Moore. *Presbyterian Quarterly Review* IX (April 1861): 684-88.

Nichols, James H. "Colonial Presbyterianism Adopts Its Standards." *Journal of Presbyterian History* 34 (March 1956): 53-66.

Nichols, Robert Hastings. *Presbyterianism in New York.* ed. James Hastings Nichols. Philadelphia: Westminster Press, 1963.

— Review of *The Forming of an American Tradition*, by Leonard Trinterud. *Interpretation* 4, (July 1950): 366-370.

Noll, Mark A. "Introduction" in *Charles Hodge: The Way of Life.* ed. Mark A. Noll (Mahwah, NJ: Paulist Press, 1987.

— "The Contested Legacy of Jonathan Edwards in Antebellum Calvinism." *Canadian Review of American Studies* 19 (1988): 149-64.

— "The Irony of the Enlightenment for Presbyterians in the Early Republic." *Journal of the Early Republic* 5 (1985): 150-75.

— *The Princeton Theology 1812-1921: Scripture, Science, and the Theological Method from Archibald Alexander to Benjamin Warfield.* Phillipsburg, NJ: Presbyterian and Reformed, 1983.

— *Princeton and the Republic, 1768-1822.* Princeton: Princeton Univ. Press, 1989.

Nybakken, Elizabeth I. "New Light on the Old Side: Irish Influences on Colonial Presbyterianism." *Journal of American History* 68 (March 1982): 813-32.

"Old and New Theology." *Presbyterian Quarterly Review* III (June 1854): 89-121, (December 1854): 353-377; IV (March 1855): 630-647, (September 1855): 213-245, (March 1856): 578-619.

" 'Old and New School' Theology." *Presbyterian Quarterly Review* XXX (January 1860): 353-399.

"Our Church and Our Review." *Presbyterian Quarterly Review* I (June 1852): 1-12.

Palmer, Benjamin Morgan. "Fraternal Relations." *Southern Presbyterian Review* XXXIV (April 1883): 306-330.

— "The Proposed Plan of Union." *Southern Presbyterian Review* III (April 1864): 264-307.

Parker, Harold M. *Bibliography of Published Articles on American Presbyterianism, 1901-1980.* Westport, Connecticut: Greenwood, 1985.

— "The Independent Presbyterian Church and the Reunion in the South, 1813-1863." *Journal of Presbyterian History* 50 (Summer 1972): 89-110.

— "The New School Presbyterian Disruption in North Carolina." *The Iliff Review* XXXII (Spring 1975): 51-63.

— "Southern Presbyterian Ecumenism: Six Successful Unions." *Journal of Presbyterian History* 56 (1978): 91-106.

— "The Synod of Kentucky." *Journal of Presbyterian History* 41 (Fall 1963): 14-36.

— *The United Synod of the South.* Presbyterian Historical Society, 1988.

Payton, James R., Jr. "Background and Significance of the Adopting Act." In *Pressing Toward the Mark: Essays Commemorating Fifty Years of the Orthodox Presbyterian Church,* ed. Charles G. Dennison and Richard C. Gamble, 131-146. Philadelphia: The Committee for the Historian of the Orthodox Presbyterian Church, 1986.

Peters, Absalom. *A Plea for Voluntary Societies and a Defense of the Decisions of the General Assembly of 1836 Against the Strictures of the Princeton Reviewer and Others. By a Member of the General Assembly.* New York: John S. Taylor, 1837.

"The Philadelphia Presbyterian Union Convention." *American Presbyterian and Theological Review* (January, 1868): 104-138.

The Philadelphian. Philadelphia, 1830.

Pope, Earl A. "Albert Barnes, The Way of Salvation, and Theological Controversy." *Journal of Presbyterian History* 57 (Spring 1979): 20-34.

— *New England Calvinism and the Disruption of the Presbyterian Church.* New York: Garland, 1987.

— "New England Calvinism and the Disruption of the Presbyterian Church." Ph.D. diss., Brown University, 1962.

Posey, Walter Brownlow. *The Presbyterian Church in the Old Southwest 1788-1838.* Richmond: John Knox Press, 1952.

The Position, Relations and Prospects of the United Synod: In Reference to the Moral Issues Inbolded in the Present War. Adopted by Synod of Virginia, 25 October, 1862. Richmond: Charles H. Wynne, 1863.

"The Position and Mission of Our Church." *Presbyterian Quarterly Review* IX (July 1860): 105-127.

Prentiss, George Lewis. *The Union Theological Seminary in the City of New York: Historical and Biographical Sketches of Its First Fifty Years.* New York, 1889.

Presbyterian Historical Almanac and Annual Remembrancer. ed. Joseph M. Wilson. Philadelphia, 1859-1868.

The Presbyterian. Philadelphia, 1834-1836, 1838.

"The Presbyterian Church Intelligently Preferred" *Presbyterian Quarterly Review* V (March 1856): 640-58.

"The Presbyterian Church in the United States. Its Founders, Its Principles, and Its Acts." *The Presbyterian Magazine* III (February 1853): 90-96, (March 1853): 135-143, (April 1853): 184-192, (May 1853): 228-236, (August 1853): 382-428, (September 1853): 428-435.

"The Presbyterian Church – its Position and Work." *The Biblical Repertory and Princeton Review* XLII (January 1870): 132-147.

Presbyterian Reunion: A Memorial Volume, 1837-1871. New York: De Witt C. Lent & Co., 1870.

Presbyterian Witness. Richmond, 1857, 1858.

"Presbyterianism." *The Biblical Repertory and Princeton Review* XLIII (July 1871): 383-396.

"Presbyterianism Explained." Philadelphia: Presbyterian Publication Committee, n.d.

Princeton Versus The New Divinity. Articles From the Princeton Review. Edinburgh: The Banner of Truth Trust, 2001.

Rankin, Duncan W. *James Henley Thornwell and the Westminster Confession of Faith.* Greenville, SC: Apress, 1986.

Reed, R. C. *History of the Presbyterian Churches of the World.* Philadelphia, 1905.

Regin, E. K. *We Believe and So we Speak: A Statement of Faith of Cumberland Presbyterians*. Memphis: Cumberland Presbyterian Church, 1960.

Report of the Proceedings of the General Assembly of the Presbyterian Church in the United States of America. Philadelphia, 1868.

"The Reunion of the Synod of New York and Philadelphia." *Presbyterian Quarterly Review* VII (July 1858): 353-80; (April 1859): 529-63.

Rian, Edwin H. *The Presbyterian Conflict*. Grand Rapids: Wm. B. Eerdmans Co., 1940.

Rice, N.L. *The Old and New Schools*. Cincinnati: John D. Thorpe, 1853.

Richards, James. *Lectures on Mental Philosophy and Theology With a Sketch of His Life by Samuel H. Gridley*. New York: M.W. Dodd, 1846.

Riddle, David H. "The Scotch-Irish Element of Presbyterianism." *Presbyterian Quarterly Review* IV (September 1856): 200-227.

Riley, Henry A. *The Restoration: or the Hope of the Early Church Realized*. Philadelphia: Smith, English & Co., 1866.

Robinson, William Childs. *Columbia Theological Seminary and the Southern Presbyterian Church, 1831-1931*. Decatur, 1931.

Rogers, Jack. *Presbyterian Creeds*. Philadelphia: Westminster Press, 1985.

Ross, Fred A. *Slavery Ordained by God*. Philadelphia: J. B. Lippincott & Co., 1857.

Russell, Robert Young. *Journal*. Vol.V. 1861-1866. Manuscript. Presbyterian Historical Society. Montreat, NC.

Sandlund, Vivian. Robert Breckinridge. "Presbyterian Antislavery Conservative." *Journal of Presbyterian History* 78 (Summer 2000): 145-154.

Schafer, Thomas A. Review of *The Forming of an American Tradition*, by Leonard Trinterud. *American Presbyterians* 66 (Winter 1988): 213-218.

Schaff, Philip. *America: A Sketch of its Political, Social. and Religious Character*. Edited by Perry Miller. Cambridge, Mass.: The Belknap Press of the Harvard University Press, 1961.

— *The Creeds of Christendom*. 3 Vols. New York: Harper & Row, 1884.

— *The Harmony of Reformed Confessions, as Related to the Present State of Evangelical Theology*. New York: Dodd, Mead & Co.,1877.

Shedd, William G.T. *Calvinism: Pure and Mixed*. 1893. Reprint. Edinburgh: Banner of Truth, 1986.

Skilton, John, ed. *Scripture and Confession: A Book About Confessions Old and New*. Phillipsburg, NJ: Presbyterian & Reformed, 1973.

Smith, Egbert W. *The Creed of Presbyterians*. Philadelphia: Presbyterian Board of Publication, 1901.

Smith, Elwyn A. "The Doctrine of Imputation and the Presbyterian Schism of 1837-1838." *Journal of the Presbyterian Historical Society* 38 (September 1960): 129-151.

— *The Presbyterian Ministry in American Culture: A Study in Changing Concepts, 1700-1900*. Philadelphia: Westminster Press, 1962.

— "The Role of the South in the Presbyterian Schism of 1837-38." *Church History* 29 (March 1960): 44-63.

Smith, Henry B. "Christian Union and Ecclesiastical Reunion." In *Faith and Philosophy*. ed. George L. Prentiss. New York: Scribner, Armstrong & Co., 1877.

— "The Inspiration of Scripture." A *Sermon Delivered Before the Synod of New York and New Jersey in the First Presbyterian Church, Newark, New Jersey, October, 15, 1855*. New York: Published by the Direction of the Synod, 1855.

— "Presbyterian Reunion." *American Presbyterian and Theological Review* V (October 1867): 624-665.

— *System of Christian Theology*. Edited by William S. Karr. New York: A.C. Armstrong and Son, 1884.

Smith, Henry Boynton (Mrs.). *Henry Boynton Smith: His Life and Work*. New York: A.C. Armstrong & Son, 1884.

Smith, Morton H. *A Brief History of Subscription to the Creeds and Confessions with Particular Reference to Presbyterian Churches*. n.p. 2002.

— "The Case for Full Subscription." In *The Practice of Confessional Subscription*, ed. David W. Hall, 185-205. Lanham, MD: University Press of America, 1995.

— *The Case for Full Subscription to the Westminster Standards in the Presbyterian Church in America*. Greenville, SC: Greenville Presbyterian Theological Seminary Press, 1992.

— *How is the Gold Become Dim: The Decline of the Presbyterian Church, U.S., as Reflected in its Assembly Actions*. Jackson, Mississippi: The Steering Committee for a Continuing Presbyterian Church, Faithful to the Scriptures and the Reformed Faith, 1973.

— "The Presbyterians of the South, 1607-1861." *Westminster Theological Journal* XXVII (November 1964): 21-30; (May 1965): 140-160.

— *Studies in Southern Presbyterian Theology*. Jackson, Mississippi: Presbyterian Reformation Society, 1962.

Smylie, James H. *A Brief History of the Presbyterians*. Louisville, Kentucky: Geneva Press, 1996.

Southern Presbyterian. Columbia, 1863.

"The Spirit of American Presbyterianism." *Presbyterian Quarterly Review* I (December 1852): 473-493; I (September 1853): 207-246; II (June 1854): 123-154; II (December 1854): 467-503.

"Spirit of American Presbyterianism, Division, No. II." *Presbyterian Quarterly Review* (March 1855): 648-685.

Sprague, William Buel. *Annals of the American Pulpit*. 4 Vols. New York: Robert Carter and Bros., 1857-1858.

Staiger, Bruce. "Abolition and the Presbyterian Schism of 1837-38" in *Mississippi Valley Historical Review* XXXVI (December 1949): 391-414.

Stansbury, Arthur J. *Trial and Acquittal of Lyman Beecher before the Presbytery of Cincinnati, on the Charges Preferred by Joshua L. Wilson*. Cincinnati, OH, 1835.

— *Trial of the Rev. Albert Barnes before the Synod of Philadelphia, in the Session at New York, October, 1835*. New York, 1836.

"The State of the Country." *Presbyterian Quarterly Review* X (July 1861): 118-146.

Stearns, Jonathan F. *Henry Boynton Smith*. Boston: Houghton, Mifflin and Co., 1892.

— "Historical Sketch of the Reunion." *American Presbyterian Review* New Series, I (July, 1869): 569-600.

— "Historical Review of the Church (New School Branch)." In *Presbyterian Reunion: A Memorial Volume 1837-1871*, 50-102. New York: De Witt C. Lent & Co., 1870.

Stevenson, J. Ross. "The Adopting Act of 1729 and the Powers of the G.A." *Princeton Theological Review* 22 (1924): 96-106.

Stewart, John W. and James H. Moorhead, ed. *Charles Hodge Revisited: A Critical Appraisal of His Life and Work*. William B. Eerdmans Publishing Company, 2002.

Sweeney, Douglas A. *Nathaniel Taylor, New Haven Theology and the Legacy of Jonathan Edwards*. New York: Oxford University Press, 2002.

Sweet, William Warren. *Religion on the American Frontier*, Vol. II: *The Presbyterians* 1783-1840. New York: Harper & Brothers Publishers, 1936.

Taylor, Nathaniel W. "Application of the Principles of Common Sense to Certain Disputed Doctrines." *The Quarterly Christian Spectator* III (September, 1831): 453-76.

— *Concio ad Clerum*, A sermon delivered in the chapel of Yale College September 10, 1828. New Haven: Hezekiah Howe, 1828.

— *Essays, Lectures, Etc. Upon Select Topics in Revealed Theology*, New York: Clark, Austin and Smith, 1859.

— *Lectures on the Moral Government of God*, 2 Vols. New York: Clark, Austin, Smith, 1859.

— "On the Authority of Reason in Theology." *The Quarterly Christian Spectator* IX (March 1837): 151-61.

Thompson, Earl, Jr. "Lyman Beecher's Long Road to Conservative Abolitionism." *Church History* 42 (1973): 89-109.

Thompson, Ernest Trice. *Presbyterians in the South*, 3 Vols. Richmond: John Knox Press, 1963.

— "Presbyterians North and South – Efforts Toward Reunion." *Journal of Presbyterian History* 43 (1965): 1-15.

Thompson, John. *An Overture Presented to the Reverend Synod of Dissenting Ministers, Sitting in Philadelphia, in the Month of September, 1728*. Philadelphia. n.d.

Thompson, Robert Ellis. *A History of the Presbyterian Churches in the United States*. New York: The Christian Literature Co., 1895.

Thornwell, James Henley. "The Relation of the State to Slavery." *Southern Presbyterian Review*, January 1852. In *The Collected Writings of James Henley Thornwell*. Vol. IV. Richmond: Presbyterian Committee of Publication, 1886.

Trinterud, Leonard J. *A Bibliography of American Presbyterianism During the Colonial Period*. Presbyterian Historical Society, 1968.

— *The Forming of an American Tradition.* Philadelphia: The Westminster Press, 1949.

Vander Velde, Lewis G. *Presbyterian Churches and the Federal Union 1861-1869.* Cambridge: Harvard University Press, 1932.

Walker, Williston. *The Creeds and Platforms of Congregationalism.* New York: Charles Scribner's Sons, 1893.

— *A History of the Congregational Churches in the United States.* New York: The Christian Literature Co., 1894.

Volf, Miroslav and Dorthody C. Bass. Editors. *Practicing Theology: Beliefs and Practices in Christian Life.* Grand Rapids: William B. Eerdmans, 2002.

Warfield, Benjamin B. "The Confession of Faith as Revised in 1903." Richmond, 1904. In *Selected Shorter Writings of Benjamin B. Warfield* – II. ed. John E. Meeter. Nutley, New Jersey: Presbyterian and Reformed Publishing Co., 1973.

— "The Presbyterian Churches and the Westminster Confession." *Presbyterian Review* X (October 1889): 646-657.

— "The Significance of the Westminster Standards as a Creed." In S*elected Shorter Writings of Benjamin B. Warfield* – II. ed. John E. Meeter. Nutley, NJ: Presbyterian and Reformed Publishing Co., 1973.

Webster, Richard. *A History of the Presbyterian Church in America From its Origin Until the Year 1760 with Biographical Sketches of its Early Ministers.* Philadelphia: Joseph M. Wilson, 1857.

Weeks, Louis B. *Kentucky Presbyterians.* Richmond: John Knox Press, 1983.

Weirs, John R. "Henry B. Smith, Theologian of New School Presbyterianism." In *Pressing Toward the Mark: Essays Commemorating Fifty Years of the Orthodox Presbyterian Church,* ed. Charles G. Dennison and Richard C. Gamble, 183-199. Philadelphia: The Committee for the Historian of the Orthodox Presbyterian Church, 1986.

Wells, David, ed. *Reformed Theology in America.* Grand Rapids: Wm. B. Eerdmans Publishing Co., 1985.

Westercamp, Marilyn J. "Division, Dissension, and Compromise: The Presbyterian Church During the Great Awakening." *Journal of Presbyterian History* 78 (Spring 2000): 3-18.

— *Triumph of the Laity: Scots-Irish Piety and the Great Awakening, 1625-1760.* New York: Oxford University Press, 1988.

Weston, William J. *Presbyterian Pluralism: Competition in a Protestant House.* Knoxville: University of Tennessee Press, 1997.

Whelpley, Samuel. *The Triangle.* New York: O. Halsted, 1832.

Whitlock, Luder G., Jr. "The Context for the Adopting Act." In *The Practice of Confessional Subscription,* ed. David W. Hall, 93-104. Lanham, MD: University Press of America, 1995.

Woods, Henry. *The History of the Presbyterian Controversy with Early Sketches of Presbyterianism.* Louisville: N. H. White, 1843.

Wood, James. *Old and New Theology, or The Doctrinal Differences Which Have Agitated and Divided the Presbyterian Church,* 3rd ed. Philadelphia: Presbyterian Board of Publication, 1855.

Woods, Leonard. *History of Andover Theological Seminary.* Boston: James R. Osgood and Company, 1855.

— *Letters to Rev. Nathaniel W. Taylor.* Andover: Mark Newman, 1830.

Woolley, Paul. Review of *The Forming of an American Tradition,* by Leonard Trinterud. *Westminster Theological Journal* XII (May 1950): 166-171.

— Review of *The Broadening Church. A Study of Theological Issues in the Presbyterian Church Since 1869.* by Lefferts A. Loetscher. *Westminster Theological Journal* XVII (1955): 221-227.

Woodrow, James. "The General Assembly." *Southern Presbyterian Review* XIX (January 1868): 98-134.

— "The General Assembly of 1868." *Southern Presbyterian Review* XIX (July 1868): 430-448.

— "The General Assembly of 1870." *Southern Presbyterian Review* XXI (July 1870): 411-458.

Wright, Conrad. *The Beginnings of Unitarianism in America.* Boston: Starr King Press, 1955.

General Index

Studies in Christian History and Thought
(All titles uniform with this volume)
Dates in bold are of projected publication

David Bebbington
Holiness in Nineteenth-Century England
David Bebbington stresses the relationship of movements of spirituality to changes in their cultural setting, especially the legacies of the Enlightenment and Romanticism. He shows that these broad shifts in ideological mood had a profound effect on the ways in which piety was conceptualized and practised. Holiness was intimately bound up with the spirit of the age.
2000 / 0-85364-981-2 / viii + 98pp

J. William Black
Reformation Pastors
Richard Baxter and the Ideal of the Reformed Pastor
This work examines Richard Baxter's *Gildas Salvianus, The Reformed Pastor* (1656) and explores each aspect of his pastoral strategy in light of his own concern for 'reformation' and in the broader context of Edwardian, Elizabethan and early Stuart pastoral ideals and practice.
2003 / 1-84227-190-3 / xxii + 308pp

James Bruce
Prophecy, Miracles, Angels, *and* Heavenly Light?
The Eschatology, Pneumatology and Missiology of Adomnán's Life of Columba
This book surveys approaches to the marvellous in hagiography, providing the first critique of Plummer's hypothesis of Irish saga origin. It then analyses the uniquely systematized phenomena in the *Life of Columba* from Adomnán's seventh-century theological perspective, identifying the coming of the eschatological Kingdom as the key to understanding.
2004 / 1-84227-227-6 / xviii + 286pp

Colin J. Bulley
The Priesthood of Some Believers
Developments from the General to the Special Priesthood in the Christian Literature of the First Three Centuries
The first in-depth treatment of early Christian texts on the priesthood of all believers shows that the developing priesthood of the ordained related closely to the division between laity and clergy and had deleterious effects on the practice of the general priesthood.
2000 / 1-84227-034-6 / xii + 336pp

July 2005

Anthony R. Cross (ed.)
Ecumenism and History
Studies in Honour of John H.Y. Briggs
This collection of essays examines the inter-relationships between the two fields in which Professor Briggs has contributed so much: history—particularly Baptist and Nonconformist—and the ecumenical movement. With contributions from colleagues and former research students from Britain, Europe and North America, *Ecumenism and History* provides wide-ranging studies in important aspects of Christian history, theology and ecumenical studies.
2002 / 1-84227-135-0 / xx + 362pp

Maggi Dawn
Confessions of an Inquiring Spirit
Form as Constitutive of Meaning in S.T. Coleridge's Theological Writing
This study of Coleridge's *Confessions* focuses on its confessional, epistolary and fragmentary form, suggesting that attention to these features significantly affects its interpretation. Bringing a close study of these three literary forms, the author suggests ways in which they nuance the text with particular understandings of the Trinity, and of a kenotic christology. Some parallels are drawn between Romantic and postmodern dilemmas concerning the authority of the biblical text.
2006 / 1-84227-255-1 / approx. 224 pp

Ruth Gouldbourne
The Flesh and the Feminine
Gender and Theology in the Writings of Caspar Schwenckfeld
Caspar Schwenckfeld and his movement exemplify one of the radical communities of the sixteenth century. Challenging theological and liturgical norms, they also found themselves challenging social and particularly gender assumptions. In this book, the issues of the relationship between radical theology and the understanding of gender are considered.
2005 / 1-84227-048-6 / approx. 304pp

Crawford Gribben
Puritan Millennialism
Literature and Theology, 1550–1682
Puritan Millennialism surveys the growth, impact and eventual decline of puritan millennialism throughout England, Scotland and Ireland, arguing that it was much more diverse than has frequently been suggested. This Paternoster edition is revised and extended from the original 2000 text.
2007 / 1-84227-372-8 / approx. 320pp

July 2005

Galen K. Johnson
Prisoner of Conscience
John Bunyan on Self, Community and Christian Faith
This is an interdisciplinary study of John Bunyan's understanding of conscience across his autobiographical, theological and fictional writings, investigating whether conscience always deserves fidelity, and how Bunyan's view of conscience affects his relationship both to modern Western individualism and historic Christianity.
2003 / 1-84227-223-3 / xvi + 236pp

R.T. Kendall
Calvin and English Calvinism to 1649
The author's thesis is that those who formed the Westminster Confession of Faith, which is regarded as Calvinism, in fact departed from John Calvin on two points: (1) the extent of the atonement and (2) the ground of assurance of salvation.
1997 / 0-85364-827-1 / xii + 264pp

Timothy Larsen
Friends of Religious Equality
Nonconformist Politics in Mid-Victorian England
During the middle decades of the nineteenth century the English Nonconformist community developed a coherent political philosophy of its own, of which a central tenet was the principle of religious equality (in contrast to the stereotype of Evangelical Dissenters). The Dissenting community fought for the civil rights of Roman Catholics, non-Christians and even atheists on an issue of principle which had its flowering in the enthusiastic and undivided support which Nonconformity gave to the campaign for Jewish emancipation. This reissued study examines the political efforts and ideas of English Nonconformists during the period, covering the whole range of national issues raised, from state education to the Crimean War. It offers a case study of a theologically conservative group defending religious pluralism in the civic sphere, showing that the concept of religious equality was a grand vision at the centre of the political philosophy of the Dissenters.
2007 / 1-84227-402-3 / x + 300pp

Byung-Ho Moon
Christ the Mediator of the Law
Calvin's Christological Understanding of the Law as the Rule of Living and Life-Giving
This book explores the coherence between Christology and soteriology in Calvin's theology of the law, examining its intellectual origins and his position on the concept and extent of Christ's mediation of the law. A comparative study between Calvin and contemporary Reformers—Luther, Bucer, Melancthon and Bullinger—and his opponent Michael Servetus is made for the purpose of pointing out the unique feature of Calvin's Christological understanding of the law.

2005 / 1-84227-318-3 / approx. 370pp

John Eifion Morgan-Wynne
Holy Spirit and Religious Experience in Christian Writings, c.AD 90–200
This study examines how far Christians in the third to fifth generations (c.AD 90–200) attributed their sense of encounter with the divine presence, their sense of illumination in the truth or guidance in decision-making, and their sense of ethical empowerment to the activity of the Holy Spirit in their lives.

2005 / 1-84227-319-1 / approx. 350pp

James I. Packer
The Redemption and Restoration of Man in the Thought of Richard Baxter
James I. Packer provides a full and sympathetic exposition of Richard Baxter's doctrine of humanity, created and fallen; its redemption by Christ Jesus; and its restoration in the image of God through the obedience of faith by the power of the Holy Spirit.

2002 / 1-84227-147-4 / 432pp

Andrew Partington,
Church and State
*The Contribution of the Church of England Bishops to the House of Lords
during the Thatcher Years*
In *Church and State*, Andrew Partington argues that the contribution of the
Church of England bishops to the House of Lords during the Thatcher years was
overwhelmingly critical of the government; failed to have a significant influence
in the public realm; was inefficient, being undertaken by a minority of those
eligible to sit on the Bench of Bishops; and was insufficiently moral and
spiritual in its content to be distinctive. On the basis of this, and the likely
reduction of the number of places available for Church of England bishops in a
fully reformed Second Chamber, the author argues for an evolution in the
Church of England's approach to the service of its bishops in the House of
Lords. He proposes the Church of England works to overcome the genuine
obstacles which hinder busy diocesan bishops from contributing to the debates
of the House of Lords and to its life more informally.
2005 / 1-84227-334-5 / approx. 324pp

Michael Pasquarello III
God's Ploughman
Hugh Latimer: A 'Preaching Life' (1490–1555)
This construction of a 'preaching life' situates Hugh Latimer within the larger
religious, political and intellectual world of late medieval England. Neither
biography, intellectual history, nor analysis of discrete sermon texts, this book is
a work of homiletic history which draws from the details of Latimer's milieu to
construct an interpretive framework for the preaching performances that formed
the core of his identity as a religious reformer. Its goal is to illumine the
practical wisdom embodied in the content, form and style of Latimer's
preaching, and to recapture a sense of its overarching purpose, movement, and
transforming force during the reform of sixteenth-century England.
2006 / 1-84227-336-1 / approx. 250pp

Alan P.F. Sell
Enlightenment, Ecumenism, Evangel
Theological Themes and Thinkers 1550–2000
This book consists of papers in which such interlocking topics as the
Enlightenment, the problem of authority, the development of doctrine,
spirituality, ecumenism, theological method and the heart of the gospel are
discussed. Issues of significance to the church at large are explored with special
reference to writers from the Reformed and Dissenting traditions.
2005 / 1-84227-330-2 / xviii + 422pp

Alan P.F. Sell
Hinterland Theology
Some Reformed and Dissenting Adjustments

Many books have been written on theology's 'giants' and significant trends, but what of those lesser-known writers who adjusted to them? In this book some hinterland theologians of the British Reformed and Dissenting traditions, who followed in the wake of toleration, the Evangelical Revival, the rise of modern biblical criticism and Karl Barth, are allowed to have their say. They include Thomas Ridgley, Ralph Wardlaw, T.V. Tymms and N.H.G. Robinson.

2006 / 1-84227-331-0 / approx. 350pp

Alan P.F. Sell and Anthony R. Cross (eds)
Protestant Nonconformity in the Twentieth Century

In this collection of essays scholars representative of a number of Nonconformist traditions reflect thematically on Nonconformists' life and witness during the twentieth century. Among the subjects reviewed are biblical studies, theology, worship, evangelism and spirituality, and ecumenism. Over and above its immediate interest, this collection provides a marker to future scholars and others wishing to know how some of their forebears assessed Nonconformity's contribution to a variety of fields during the century leading up to Christianity's third millennium.

2003 / 1-84227-221-7 / x + 398pp

Mark Smith
Religion in Industrial Society
Oldham and Saddleworth 1740–1865

This book analyses the way British churches sought to meet the challenge of industrialization and urbanization during the period 1740–1865. Working from a case-study of Oldham and Saddleworth, Mark Smith challenges the received view that the Anglican Church in the eighteenth century was characterized by complacency and inertia, and reveals Anglicanism's vigorous and creative response to the new conditions. He reassesses the significance of the centrally directed church reforms of the mid-nineteenth century, and emphasizes the importance of local energy and enthusiasm. Charting the growth of denominational pluralism in Oldham and Saddleworth, Dr Smith compares the strengths and weaknesses of the various Anglican and Nonconformist approaches to promoting church growth. He also demonstrates the extent to which all the churches participated in a common culture shaped by the influence of evangelicalism, and shows that active co-operation between the churches rather than denominational conflict dominated. This revised and updated edition of Dr Smith's challenging and original study makes an important contribution both to the social history of religion and to urban studies.

2006 / 1-84227-335-3 / approx. 300pp

Martin Sutherland
Peace, Toleration and Decay
The Ecclesiology of Later Stuart Dissent
This fresh analysis brings to light the complexity and fragility of the later Stuart Nonconformist consensus. Recent findings on wider seventeenth-century thought are incorporated into a new picture of the dynamics of Dissent and the roots of evangelicalism.
2003 / 1-84227-152-0 / xxii + 216pp

G. Michael Thomas
The Extent of the Atonement
A Dilemma for Reformed Theology from Calvin to the Consensus
A study of the way Reformed theology addressed the question, 'Did Christ die for all, or for the elect only?', commencing with John Calvin, and including debates with Lutheranism, the Synod of Dort and the teaching of Moïse Amyraut.
1997 / 0-85364-828-X / x + 278pp

David M. Thompson
Baptism, Church and Society in Britain from the Evangelical Revival to
Baptism, Eucharist and Ministry
The theology and practice of baptism have not received the attention they deserve. How important is faith? What does baptismal regeneration mean? Is baptism a bond of unity between Christians? This book discusses the theology of baptism and popular belief and practice in England and Wales from the Evangelical Revival to the publication of the World Council of Churches' consensus statement on *Baptism, Eucharist and Ministry* (1982).
2005 / 1-84227-393-0 / approx. 224pp

Mark D. Thompson
A Sure Ground on Which to Stand
The Relation of Authority and Interpretive Method of Luther's Approach to Scripture
The best interpreter of Luther is Luther himself. Unfortunately many modern studies have superimposed contemporary agendas upon this sixteenth-century Reformer's writings. This fresh study examines Luther's own words to find an explanation for his robust confidence in the Scriptures, a confidence that generated the famous 'stand' at Worms in 1521.
2004 / 1-84227-145-8 / xvi + 322pp

Carl R. Trueman and R.S. Clark (eds)
Protestant Scholasticism
Essays in Reassessment
Traditionally Protestant theology, between Luther's early reforming career and
the dawn of the Enlightenment, has been seen in terms of decline and fall into
the wastelands of rationalism and scholastic speculation. In this volume a
number of scholars question such an interpretation. The editors argue that the
development of post-Reformation Protestantism can only be understood when a
proper historical model of doctrinal change is adopted. This historical concern
underlies the subsequent studies of theologians such as Calvin, Beza, Olevian,
Baxter, and the two Turrentini. The result is a significantly different reading of
the development of Protestant Orthodoxy, one which both challenges the older
scholarly interpretations and clichés about the relationship of Protestantism to,
among other things, scholasticism and rationalism, and which demonstrates the
fruitfulness of the new, historical approach.

1999 / 0-85364-853-0 / xx + 344pp

Shawn D. Wright
Our Sovereign Refuge
The Pastoral Theology of Theodore Beza
Our Sovereign Refuge is a study of the pastoral theology of the Protestant
reformer who inherited the mantle of leadership in the Reformed church from
John Calvin. Countering a common view of Beza as supremely a 'scholastic'
theologian who deviated from Calvin's biblical focus, Wright uncovers a new
portrait. He was not a cold and rigid academic theologian obsessed with probing
the eternal decrees of God. Rather, by placing him in his pastoral context and by
noting his concerns in his pastoral and biblical treatises, Wright shows that Beza
was fundamentally a committed Christian who was troubled by the vicissitudes
of life in the second half of the sixteenth century. He believed that the biblical
truth of the supreme sovereignty of God alone could support Christians on their
earthly pilgrimage to heaven. This pastoral and personal portrait forms the heart
of Wright's argument.

2004 / 1-84227-252-7 / xviii + 308pp